CAT
INTERACTIVE TEXT

Advanced
Paper 6

Drafting Financial Statements

BPP is the **official provider** of training materials for the ACCA's CAT qualification. This Interactive Text forms part of a suite of learning tools, which also includes CD-ROMs for tuition and computer based assessment, and the innovative, internet-based 'virtual campus'

This text has been specifically written to the **syllabus** and **Teaching Guide**.

- Clear language and presentation

- Plenty of activities, examples and quizzes to demonstrate and practise techniques

- Syllabus and teaching guide

- A new question and answer bank prepared by BPP authors

- Updated for FRS 21

FOR DECEMBER 2004 AND JUNE 2005 EXAMS

First edition 2003
Second edition June 2004

ISBN 0 7517 1652 9 (previous edition 0 7517 1172 1)

British Library Cataloguing-in-Publication Data
A catalogue record for this book
is available from the British Library

Published by

BPP Professional Education
Aldine House, Aldine Place
London W12 8AW

www.bpp.com

Printed in Great Britain by WM Print
Frederick Street
Walsall
West Midlands
WS2 9NE

All our rights reserved. No part of this publication may be reproduced, stored in a retrieval system or transmitted, in any form or by any means, electronic, mechanical, photocopying, recording or otherwise, without the prior written permission of BPP Professional Education.

We are grateful to the Association of Chartered Certified Accountants for permission to reproduce the syllabus, teaching guide and Pilot Paper Question Bank of which the Association holds the copyright. The Pilot Paper Answer Bank has been prepared by BPP Professional Education.

©
BPP Professional Education
2004

Page (v)

INTRODUCTION
How to use this Interactive Text – Syllabus – Study sessions –
Approach to examining the syllabus

PART A: INTRODUCTION TO FINANCIAL REPORTING

1	Introduction to financial statements	3
2	Fixed assets and stocks	19
3	Review of basic financial accounts	57
4	Accounting conventions	79

PART B: PREPARATION OF FINAL ACCOUNTS

5	Partnership accounts	97
6	Incomplete records	127
7	Limited companies	163

PART C: THE REGULATORY AND CONCEPTUAL FRAMEWORK

8	The regulatory framework	195
9	Reporting financial performance	207
10	Conceptual framework	225

PART D: ACCOUNTING STANDARDS

11	Contingencies and events after the balance sheet date	241
12	Intangibles and taxation	253

PART E: INTERPRETATION OF ACCOUNTS

13	Cash flow statements	275
14	Ratio analysis	295

PART F: SIMPLE CONSOLIDATED ACCOUNTS

15	Introduction to group accounts	329
16	The consolidated balance sheet	339
17	The consolidated profit and loss account	359

Contents

EXAM QUESTION BANK 371

EXAM ANSWER BANK 389

INDEX 409

REVIEW FORM & FREE PRIZE DRAW

ORDER FORM

HOW TO USE THIS INTERACTIVE TEXT

Aim of this Interactive Text

> To provide the knowledge and practice to help you succeed in the examination for Paper 6 *Drafting Financial Statements*.

To pass the examination you need a thorough understanding in all areas covered by the syllabus and teaching guide.

Recommended approach

- To pass you need to be able to answer questions on **everything** specified by the syllabus and teaching guide. Read the text very carefully and do not skip any of it.

- Learning is an **active** process. Do **all** the activities as you work through the text so you can be sure you really understand what you have read.

- After you have covered the material in the Interactive Text, work through the Pilot Paper Question Bank, checking your answers carefully against the Answer Bank.

- Before you take the exam, check that you still remember the material using the following quick revision plan.

    o Read through the chapter learning objectives. Are there any gaps in your knowledge? If so, study the section again.

    o Read and learn the key terms.

    o Look at the exam alerts. These show the sorts of thing that are likely to come up.

    o Read and learn the key learning points, which are a summary of each chapter.

    o Do the quick quizzes again. If you know what you're doing, they shouldn't take long.

This approach is only a suggestion. You or your college may well adapt it to suit your needs.

Remember this is a **practical** course.

- Try to relate the material to your experience in the workplace or any other work experience you may have had.

- Try to make as many links as you can to the other papers at this level.

Syllabus

SYLLABUS

Introduction

This booklet contains the Study Guide for Paper 6 (GBR): Drafting Financial Statements.

The Study Guide is designed to help you plan your studies and to provide more detailed interpretation of the syllabus for ACCA's Certified Accounting Technician examinations. It contains both the Syllabus and the Study Sessions for the paper, which you can follow when preparing for the examination.

The Syllabus outlines the content of the paper and how that content is examined. The Study Sessions take the syllabus and expand it into teaching or study sessions of similar length. These sessions indicate what the examiner expects of candidates for each part of the syllabus, and therefore gives you guidance in the skills you are expected to demonstrate in the examinations. The time to complete each session will vary according to your individual capabilities and the time you have available to study. Tuition providers offering face-to-face tuition are recommended to design courses with a minimum of two hours tuition per study session. However, repeated coverage of the material is vital to ensure your understanding and recall of the subject. Be sure to practice past examination questions to consolidate your knowledge and read your *student accountant* magazine regularly.

If you have any queries concerning the study guide, please direct them to:

Education Department
ACCA 29 Lincoln's Inn Fields London WC2A 3EE United Kingdom
tel: +44 (0)20 7396 5891/2 fax: +44 (0)20 7396 5968
e-mail: info@accaglobal.com

Additional information can be accessed on the ACCA website at:
www.accaglobal.com

© The Association of Chartered Certified Accountants
May 2003

ABOUT ACCA
ACCA is the largest and fastest-growing international accounting body, with over 300,000 students and members in 160 countries. ACCA has an extensive network of 70 staffed offices and other centres around the world.

Drafting Financial Statements (GBR)

AIMS

To understand and apply the techniques used to prepare year-end financial statements of partnerships and limited companies which comply with legislation and accounting standards, and to interpret financial statements and the relationships between their elements using ratio analysis.

OBJECTIVES

On completion of this paper, candidates should be able to:

- draft partnership and limited company financial statements from the appropriate information to comply with relevant legislation and accounting standards
- correctly identify and implement adjustments and identify unusual issues, referring such issues and any unresolved discrepancies to an appropriate person
- understand the importance of an organisation's procedures and policies, including confidentiality procedures
- prepare and interpret a limited company cash flow statement
- identify the general purpose of limited company financial statements
- identify the elements of limited company financial statements and the relationship between them
- interpret the relationship between the elements of financial statements using ratio analysis drawing valid conclusions and presenting interpretations and conclusions to the appropriate people.

POSITION OF THE PAPER IN THE OVERALL SYLLABUS

A thorough knowledge of Paper 1, *Recording Financial Transactions* and Paper 3, *Maintaining Financial Records*, is required for Paper 6.

SYLLABUS CONTENT

1 **General framework**
   (a) General purpose of financial statements, users and their needs
   (b) Financial statements and their relationship
       (i) profit and loss account
       (ii) balance sheet
       (iii) interaction of the profit and loss account and balance sheet
   (c) Elements of financial statements and their interaction
       (i) assets
       (ii) liabilities
       (iii) ownership interest
       (iv) gains
       (v) losses
       (vi) contributions from owners
       (vii) distributions to owners
   (d) Conceptual framework
       (i) Statement of Principles
       (ii) accounting concepts and policies
   (e) Regulatory framework
       (i) standard-setting process
       (ii) relevant accounting standards
       (iii) legal framework and obligations of directors
       (iv) statutory format of accounts and disclosure requirements
   (f) Notes to the financial statements.
       Only the following notes to the financial statements will be examinable:
       – statement of movements in reserves
       – fixed assets
       – disclosure of exceptional items
       – post balance sheet events
       – contingent liabilities and contingent assets
       – research and development expenditure
   (g) Business organisation
       (i) structure
       (ii) procedures and policies

2 **Preparing financial statements**
   (a) Preparation of partnership and limited company financial statements from a trial balance, including adjustments where appropriate for:
       (i) accruals and prepayments
       (ii) corporation tax
       (iii) dividends
       (iv) depreciation
       (v) bad and doubtful debts
       (vi) closing stocks
       (vii) issue of share capital

Syllabus

Drafting Financial Statements (GBR)

      (viii) revaluation of assets
      (ix) provisions
      (x) admission and retirement of partners
  (b) Taxation
      (i) presentation of corporation tax
  (c) Fixed assets
      (i) distinction between capital and revenue expenditure
      (ii) accounting for acquisition and disposal of assets
      (iii) depreciation – definition, reasons for and methods, including straight line, reducing balance and sum of digits
      (iv) research and development
      (v) elementary treatment of goodwill
  (d) Current assets
      (i) stock
      (ii) debtors, including accounting for bad and doubtful debts
      (iii) cash
  (e) Current liabilities and accruals
  (f) Shareholders' equity
  (g) Post balance sheet events
  (h) Contingencies
  (i) Reporting financial performance, including the statement of total recognised gains and losses

3 Cash flow statements
  (a) Preparation of a single company cash flow statement
  (b) Notes to the cash flow statement
  (c) Interpretation of a cash flow statement

4 Interpretation of financial statements
  (a) Ratio analysis
      (i) profitability
      (ii) liquidity
      (iii) efficient use of resources
      (iv) investor
      (v) financial position
  (b) Identification of unusual issues or trends
  (c) Presentation of reports targeted at the user and drawing appropriate conclusions

5 Consolidated accounts
  (a) Groups of companies – preparation of basic consolidated financial statements for a simple group
      (i) consolidated balance sheet
      (ii) consolidated profit and loss account
  (b) Overview of distinction between a subsidiary and an associate

EXCLUDED TOPICS
The following topics are specifically excluded from Paper 6:
- detailed or computational questions on deferred tax or discounting of provisions
- group cash flow statements
- joint ventures
- long-term contracts
- foreign currency, segmental reporting, impairment of assets, retirement benefits, derivatives and capital instruments
- merger accounting.

KEY AREAS OF THE SYLLABUS
The two main skills required for Paper 6, *Drafting Financial Statements* are:
- the ability to prepare basic financial statements and the underlying accounting records on which they are based
- an understanding of the principles on which accounting is based.

The key topic areas are as follows:
- preparation of financial statements for partnerships and limited companies
- basic group accounts – consolidated balance sheet and profit and loss account for a simple group
- elements of financial statements and the interaction between the elements
- accounting conventions and concepts
- interpretation of financial statements
- cash flow statements.

Study sessions

Drafting Financial Statements (GBR)

APPROACH TO EXAMINING THE SYLLABUS

The examination is a three-hour written paper. The paper consists of four compulsory questions.

Question 1	30 to 40 marks
Question 2	25 to 30 marks
Question 3	15 to 20 marks
Question 4	15 to 20 marks
Total	100 marks

ADDITIONAL INFORMATION

Accounting standards will not be examined until six months after they have been published. The cut off date for the June examination is 30 November preceding the June examination. The cut off date for the December examination is 31 May preceding the December examination.

STUDY SESSIONS

1. **Framework of financial reporting**
   (a) Explain the need for, and objectives of, financial statements
   (b) Identify the users of financial statements and their particular interests in the statements
   (c) Discuss how the accounting systems of an organisation are affected by its roles, organisational structure, its administrative systems and procedures and the nature of its business transactions
   (d) Describe and explain the following elements of the financial statements and their interaction:
      (i) assets
      (ii) liabilities
      (iii) ownership interest
      (iv) gains
      (v) losses
      (vi) contributions from owners
   (e) Identify the three stages of recognising elements for inclusion in financial statements

2. **Conceptual framework**
   (a) Discuss the nature and purpose of a conceptual framework
   (b) Explain the potential benefits and drawbacks of an agreed conceptual framework
   (c) Explain the role and general issues covered by the Statement of Principles
   (d) Identify and explain the qualitative characteristics of financial information
   (e) Discuss and apply accounting concepts and policies
   (f) Discuss the shortcomings of historical cost accounting and how they might be overcome

Drafting Financial Statements (GBR)

3 The UK regulatory framework
   (a) Explain the legal framework and obligations of directors
   (b) Explain the standard setting process and the role of the:
       (i) Financial Reporting Council
       (ii) Accounting Standards Board
       (iii) Urgent Issues Task Force
       (iv) Financial Reporting Review Panel

4 & 5 Fixed assets
   (a) Distinguish between capital and revenue expenditure
   (b) Explain, calculate and demonstrate the inclusion of the profit or loss on disposal in the profit and loss account
   (c) Account for the revaluation of fixed assets
   (d) Account for gains and losses on the disposal of revalued assets
   (e) Account for depreciation – definition, reasons and methods, including straight line, reducing balance and sum of digits
   (f) Account for changes in the useful economic life or residual value of assets
   (g) Explain how fixed asset balances and movements are disclosed in the financial statements

6, 7 & 8 Partnership accounts
   (a) Identify the key features of a partnership
   (b) Outline the advantages and disadvantages of operating as a partnership, compared with operating as a sole trader or limited company
   (c) Outline the conventional methods of dividing profit and maintaining equity between partners
   (d) Draft an appropriation account for a partnership
   (e) Distinguish between partners' capital and current accounts
   (f) Record the partners' share of profits and losses and their drawings in the ledger accounts
   (g) Record introductions and withdrawals in the ledger accounts
   (h) Draft the trading and profit and loss account and appropriation account and the balance sheet for a partnership from a trial balance incorporating period end adjustments including:
       (i) accruals and prepayments
       (ii) depreciation
       (iii) bad and doubtful debts
       (iv) closing stock
   (i) Explain why a revaluation is required after an admission, a change in the profit sharing ratio or a retirement
   (j) Revalue the partnership after such a change and calculate the goodwill
   (k) Make appropriate entries in the ledger accounts
   (l) Draft the partnership balance sheet after a change in the partnership
   (m) Draft the partnership balance sheet after a merger of two sole traders
   (n) Account for the dissolution of a partnership
   (o) Prepare final accounts from incomplete records

9, 10 & 11 Limited company financial statements
   (a) Prepare the financial statements for a limited company from a trial balance, including adjustments for items including:
       (i) corporation tax
       (ii) dividends
       (iii) depreciation
       (iv) bad and doubtful debts
       (v) closing stock
       (vi) share capital
       (vii) accruals and prepayments
       (viii) revaluation of assets
       (ix) provisions
   (b) Prepare a statement of total recognised gains and losses
   (c) Prepare the following notes to the financial statements:
       (i) statement of movements in reserves
       (ii) fixed assets
       (iii) exceptional items
       (iv) post balance sheet events
       (v) contingent liabilities and contingent assets
       (vi) research and development expenditure
   (d) Distinguish between extraordinary and exceptional items, including their accounting treatment and disclosure requirements
   (e) Derive missing figures from incomplete records

Drafting Financial Statements (GBR)

12 Statutory format of accounts and disclosure requirements
(a) State the requirements of the Companies Act regarding:
  (i) the duty to prepare annual accounts
  (ii) the form and content of prescribed formats
(b) Prepare the financial statements of limited companies in accordance with the prescribed formats and relevant accounting standards.
(c) Discuss relevant accounting standards and be able to apply them

13 Taxation
(a) Define current tax
(b) Account for current tax on the profits of companies (a detailed knowledge of deferred tax is not required)
(c) Draft appropriate disclosure in the published statements.

14 Goodwill and intangible assets
(a) Define and calculate goodwill
(b) Distinguish between purchased and internally generated goodwill
(c) Explain and apply the accounting treatment for both types of goodwill
(d) Explain and apply the requirements of Accounting Standards for Research and Development

15 & 16 Share and loan capital
(a) Distinguish between issued and authorised share capital and between called up and paid up share capital
(b) Distinguish between ordinary and preference shares
(c) Account for a share issue
(d) Explain the share premium account
(e) Define and account for a bonus issue
(f) Define and account for a rights issue
(g) Outline the advantages and disadvantages of a rights issue and a bonus issue
(h) Distinguish between the market value and nominal value of a share
(i) Explain why companies will be concerned with the value of their shares
(j) Define and account for debentures
(k) Explain the advantages and disadvantages of raising finance by issuing debentures rather than issuing ordinary or preference shares

17 & 18 Post balance sheet events, contingent liabilities and contingent assets
(a) Define a post balance sheet event
(b) Distinguish between adjusting and non-adjusting post balance sheet events
(c) Account for each category of post balance sheet event in the financial statements
(d) Define a provision, contingent liability and contingent asset
(e) Understand the general recognition principle
(f) Account for provisions, contingent liabilities and contingent assets

19, 20 & 21 Cash flow statements
(a) Explain the need for a cash flow statement
(b) Prepare a cash flow statement including relevant notes for a single company in accordance with accounting standards
(c) Appraise the usefulness of, and interpret the information in a cash flow statement

22, 23, 24 & 25 Consolidated accounts
(a) Describe and be able to identify the general characteristics of a parent company, investment, subsidiary and associated undertaking
(b) Describe the concept of a group and the objective of consolidated financial statements
(c) Describe the circumstances and reasoning for subsidiaries to be excluded from consolidated financial statements
(d) Prepare a consolidated profit and loss account and balance sheet for a simple group including adjustments for pre and post acquisition profits, minority interests and consolidated goodwill
(e) Explain why intra-group transactions should be eliminated on consolidation
(f) Account for the effects (in the profit and loss account and balance sheet) of intra-group trading and other transactions including:

Study sessions

Drafting Financial Statements (GBR)

    (i)   Unrealised profits in stock and fixed assets
    (ii) Intra-group loans and interest and other intra-group charges

26, 27, 28, 29 Interpretation of financial statements
(a) Calculate the following ratios:
    (i)   profitability
    (ii)   liquidity
    (iii) efficiency
    (iv) investor
    (v)   financial
(b) Analyse and interpret the ratios to give an assessment of a company's performance in comparison with:
    (i)   a company's previous period's financial statements
    (ii) another similar company for the same period
    (ii) industry average ratios
(c) Identify and discuss the limitations of ratio analysis
(d) Prepare a financial analysis report of a company in a suitable format

30, 31 & 32 Revision

APPROACH TO EXAMINING THE SYLLABUS

The examination is a three-hour written paper. The paper consists of four compulsory questions.

Question 1	30 – 40 marks
Question 2	25 – 30 marks
Question 3	15 – 20 marks
Question 4	15 – 20 marks
Total	100 marks

Additional information

Accounting standards will not be examined until six months after they have been published. The cut-off date for the June examination is 30 November preceding the June examination. The cut off for the December examination is 31 May preceding the December examination.

Prerequisite knowledge

Successful completion of Papers 1 and 3.

Analysis of past papers

The analysis below shows the topics which were examined in the first sitting of the current syllabus and in the CAT Pilot paper.

Marks

June 2004

1	Limited company accounts from trial balance	35
2	Cash flow statement	25
3	Partnership accounts	20
4	Ratio analysis	20

Pilot paper

1	Partnership accounts	40
2	Cash flow statement	25
3	Ratio analysis	20
4	Statement of Principles	15

Part A
Introduction to financial reporting

Part A
Introduction to financial reporting

Chapter 1   Introduction to financial statements

Chapter topic list

1   Introduction
2   The purpose of accounting information
3   The accounting equation
4   The main financial statements
5   Qualities of good accounting information
6   Organisational structure

The following study sessions are covered in this chapter.

		Syllabus reference
1(a)	Explain the need for and objectives of financial statements	1
1(b)	Identify the users of financial statements and their particular interests in the statements	1
1(c)	Discuss how the accounting systems of an organisation are affected by its roles, organisational structure, its administrative systems and procedures and the nature of its business transactions	1

Part A: Introduction to financial reporting

1 INTRODUCTION

1.1 CAT Paper 6 *Drafting Financial Statements* builds on the knowledge acquired in Papers 1 and 3, enabling you to draft year end financial statements and interpret financial statements for a range of organisations.

1.2 Remember as you work through this text that accounting is an interactive subject. You only get good at it through doing it. **Do not 'skip' any of the activities.**

2 THE PURPOSE OF ACCOUNTING INFORMATION

What is a business?

2.1 You should know by now what a business is. There are a number of different ways of looking at it. Some ideas are listed below.

(a) A business is a **commercial or industrial concern** which exists to deal in the manufacture, re-sale or supply of goods and services.

(b) It is an **organisation which uses economic resources** to create goods or services which customers will buy.

(c) It is an **organisation providing jobs** for people.

(d) It **invests money in resources** (for example it buys buildings, machinery and so on, it pays employees) in order to make even more money for its owners.

2.2 This last definition introduces the important idea of profit. Business enterprises vary in character, size and complexity. They range from very small businesses (the local shopkeeper or plumber) to very large ones (ICI). But the objective of earning profit is common to all of them.

KEY TERM

Profit is the excess of income over expenditure. When expenditure exceeds income, the business is running at a loss.

2.3 One of the jobs of an accountant is to measure income, expenditure and profit. It is not such a straightforward problem as it may seem and in later chapters we will look at some of the theoretical and practical difficulties involved.

Assets and liabilities

2.4 An asset is something valuable which a business owns or has the use of.

2.5 Examples of assets are factories, office buildings, warehouses, delivery vans, lorries, plant and machinery, computer equipment, office furniture, cash and also goods held in store awaiting sale to customers, and raw materials and components held in store by a manufacturing business for use in production.

2.6 Some assets are **held and used** in operations **for a long time**. An office building might be occupied by administrative staff for years. A machine might have a productive life of many years before it wears out. **Other assets** are held for only a **short time**. The owner of a newsagent shop, for example, will have to sell his newspapers on the same day that he gets

them, and weekly newspapers and monthly magazines also have a short shelf life. The more quickly a business can sell the goods it has in store, the more profit it is likely to make, provided, of course, that the goods are sold at a higher price than what it cost the business to acquire them.

2.7 You have come across assets in your earlier studies. Now consider a more formal definition, taken from an important document, the Accounting Standard Board's *Statement of Principles*.

KEY TERM

Assets are **rights** or other access to **future economic benefits** as a result of past transactions or events.

2.8 A machine is an asset because it gives:

Rights to future economic benefits	The machine will be used in the business to make products and earn revenue.
Because of past transactions	The machine was purchased at some time in the past.

2.9 A **liability** is something which is owed to somebody else. 'Liabilities' is the accounting term for the debts of a business.

2.10 **Examples of liabilities**

(a) A **bank loan** or bank *overdraft*. The liability is the amount which must eventually be repaid to the bank.

(b) **Amounts owed to suppliers** for goods purchased but not yet paid for. For example, a boatbuilder might buy some timber on credit from a timber merchant, which means that the boatbuilder does not have to pay for the timber until some time after it has been delivered. Until the boatbuilder pays what he owes, the timber merchant will be his creditor for the amount owed.

(c) **Taxation** owed to the government. A business pays tax on its profits but there is a gap in time between when a company declares its profits and becomes liable to pay tax and the time when the tax bill must eventually be paid.

(d) **Amounts invested in a business by its shareholders or owners**. This is explained in detail in paragraph 2.21 below.

2.11 The *Statement of Principles* also defines a liability.

KEY TERM

A **liability** is an obligation of an entity to transfer economic benefits as a result of past transactions or events.

Part A: Introduction to financial reporting

2.12 A bank loan is a liability because it gives:

| An obligation to transfer economic benefits | The loan must be repaid. |
| Because of a past transaction | The loan was taken out in the past. |

2.13 The *Statement of Principles* is covered in more detail in Chapter 10.

The business as a separate entity

2.14 So far we have spoken of assets and liabilities 'of a business'. But can an intangible entity such as a business can own assets in its own name, or have liabilities in its own name? There are two aspects to this question: the **strict legal position** and the **convention adopted by accountants**.

2.15 Many businesses are carried on in the form of **limited companies**. The owners of a limited company are its shareholders, who may be few in number (as with a small, family-owned company) or very numerous (for example in the case of a large public company whose shares are quoted on the Stock Exchange).

2.16 The law recognises a **company** as a **legal entity, quite separate from its owners**. A company may, in its own name, acquire assets, incur debts, and enter into contracts. If a company's assets became insufficient to meet its liabilities, the company as a separate entity might become 'bankrupt', but the owners of the company could not usually be required to pay the debts from their own private resources: the debts are not debts of the shareholders, but of the company.

2.17 **In law**, when a business is carried on not by a company, but by an **individual** (a sole trader) or by a **group of individuals** (a partnership), it is **not** regarded as a separate entity.

Case example

Suppose that Fiona Middleton sets herself up in business as a hairdresser trading under the business name 'Hair by Fiona'. The law now recognises no distinction between Fiona Middleton, the individual, and the business known as 'Hair by Fiona'. Any debts of the business which cannot be met from business assets must be met from Fiona's private resources.

2.18 However, **in accounting** a **business is** treated as a **separate entity from its owner(s)**. This applies whether or not the business is recognised in law as a separate entity, ie it applies **whether** the business is carried on by a **company or by a sole trader**. This is known as the **entity concept**.

> ### KEY TERM
> **Entity concept**: A business is a separate entity from its owner.

2.19 At first sight this seems illogical and unrealistic. Nevertheless, it is an idea which you must try to appreciate. It is the basis of a fundamental rule of accounting, which is that the assets and liabilities of a business must always be equal. You looked at this rule in your earlier studies, but we re-cap below.

2.20 EXAMPLE: THE BUSINESS AS A SEPARATE ENTITY

On 1 July 20X6, Courtney Spice decided to open up a stall in the market, to sell herbs and spices. She had saved up some money in her building society account, and had £2,500 to put into her business.

2.21 When the business is set up, an accountant's picture can be drawn of what it **owns** and what it **owes**.

The business begins by owning the cash that Courtney has put into it, £2,500. But does it owe anything? The answer is yes.

The business is a separate entity in accounting terms. It has obtained its assets, in this example cash, from its owner, Courtney Spice. It therefore owes this amount of money to its owner. If Courtney changed her mind and decided not to go into business after all, the business would be dissolved by the 'repayment' of the cash by the business to Courtney.

The amount owed by a business to its owners is often known as **capital**.

The need for accounts

2.22 Why do businesses need to produce accounts? If a business is being run efficiently, why should it have to go through all the bother of accounting procedures in order to produce financial information?

2.23 The answer is simple. A business should produce information about its activities because there are **various groups** of people who **want or need to know** that information. This sounds rather vague: to make it clearer, we should look more closely at the classes of people who might need information about a business. We need also to think about what information in particular is of interest to the members of each class.

2.24 Because large businesses are usually of interest to a greater variety of people than small businesses we will consider the case of a large public company whose shares can be purchased and sold on the Stock Exchange.

Users of accounting information

2.25 The people who might be interested in financial information about a large public company may be classified as follows.

(a) **Employees of the company**. These should have a right to information about the company's financial situation, because their future careers and the size of their wages and salaries depend on it.

(b) **Lenders**. These might include a bank which permits the company to operate an overdraft, or provides longer-term finance by granting a loan. The bank will want to ensure that the company is able to keep up with interest payments, and eventually to repay the amounts advanced.

(c) **Suppliers and other creditors** will want to know about the company's ability to pay its debts.

(d) **Customers** need to know that the company is a secure source of supply and is in no danger of having to close down.

(e) **Government and their agencies.** Governments and their agencies are interested in the allocation of resources and therefore in the activities of enterprises. They also require information in order to provide a basis for national statistics.

(f) **The public.** Enterprises affect members of the public in a variety of ways. For example, enterprises may make a substantial contribution to a local economy by providing employment and using local suppliers. Another important factor is the effect of an enterprise on the environment, for example as regards pollution.

(g) **Shareholders of the company,** ie the company's owners. These will want to assess how effectively management is performing its stewardship function. They will want to know how profitably management is running the company's operations and how much profit they can afford to withdraw from the business for their own use.

(h) **The Inland Revenue,** who will want to know about business profits in order to assess the tax payable by the company, and also the **Customs and Excise**.

(i) **Managers of the company.** These are people appointed by the company's owners to supervise the day-to-day activities of the company. They need information about the company's financial situation as it is currently and as it is expected to be in the future. This is to enable them to manage the business efficiently and to take effective control and planning decisions.

(j) **Financial analysts and advisers,** who need information for their clients or audience. For example, stockbrokers will need information to advise investors in stocks and shares; credit agencies will want information to advise potential suppliers of goods to the company; and journalists need information for their reading public.

2.26 Users (a) – (f) are also specified in the *Statement of Principles*, the conceptual framework of accounting, covered in Chapter 10.

2.27 Accounting information is prepared in financial statements to satisfy the **information needs** of these different groups. Not all will be equally satisfied.

2.28 **Managers** of a business need the most information, to help them take their planning and control decisions; and they obviously have 'special' access to information about the business, because they can get people to give them the types of statements they want. When managers want a large amount of information about the costs and profitability of individual products, or different parts of their business, they can arrange to obtain it through a system of cost and management accounting.

Activity 1.1

It is easy to see how 'internal' people get hold of accounting information. A manager, for example, can just go along to the accounts department and ask the staff there to prepare whatever accounting statements he needs. But external users of accounts cannot do this. How, in practice, can a business contact or a financial analyst access accounting information about a company?

2.29 In addition to management information, financial statements are prepared and perhaps published for the benefit of other user groups.

(a) The **law** provides for the provision of some information. The Companies Acts require every company to publish accounting information for its shareholders; and companies must also file a copy of their accounts with the Registrar of Companies, so that any member of the public who so wishes can go and look at them.

(b) The **Inland Revenue** authorities will receive the information they need to make tax assessments.

(c) A **bank** might demand a forecast of a company's expected future cash flows as a pre-condition of granting an overdraft.

(d) The **professional accountancy bodies** have been jointly responsible for issuing **accounting standards** and some standards require companies to publish certain additional information. Accountants, as members of these professional bodies, are placed under a strong obligation to ensure that company accounts conform to the requirements of the standards.

(e) Some companies provide, voluntarily, specially prepared financial information for issue to their employees. These statements are known as **employee reports**.

2.30 **Section summary**

A **business** exists to make a **profit**. In accounting, though not in law, it is a **separate entity** from its owner(s).

Accounts are prepared so that owners, managers, lenders and other interested parties can see how the business is doing.

3 THE ACCOUNTING EQUATION

3.1 We will start by showing how to account for a business's transactions from the time that trading first begins. We will use an example to illustrate the 'accounting equation', ie the rule that the assets of a business will at all times equal its liabilities. This is also known as the **balance sheet equation.**

3.2 **EXAMPLE: THE ACCOUNTING EQUATION**

Liza Doolittle starts a business selling flowers. She puts in £2,500. The business begins by **owning** the cash that Liza has put into it, £2,500. The business is a separate entity in accounting terms and so it owes the money to Liza as **capital**.

> **KEY TERM**
>
> In accounting, **capital** is an investment of money (funds) with the intention of earning a return. A business proprietor invests capital with the intention of earning profit. As long as that money is invested, accountants will treat the capital as money owed to the proprietor by the business.

3.3 Capital is also called **ownership interest**. This is the term used in the *Statement of Principles*.

> **KEY TERM**
>
> **Ownership interest** is the residual amount found by deducting all of the entity's liabilities from the entity's assets.

3.4 When Liza Doolittle sets up her business:

Part A: Introduction to financial reporting

Capital invested	=	£2,500
Cash	=	£2,500

Capital invested is a form of liability, because it is an amount owed by the business to its owner(s). Adapting this to the idea that assets and liabilities are always equal amounts, we can state the accounting equation as follows.

Assets = *Capital (ownership interest)* + *Liabilities*

For Liza Doolittle, as at 1 July 20X6:

£2,500 (cash) = £2,500 + £0

3.5 EXAMPLE CONTINUED

Liza Doolittle purchases a market stall from Len Turnip, who is retiring from his fruit and vegetables business. The cost of the stall is £1,800.

She also purchases some flowers and potted plants from a trader in the wholesale market, at a cost of £650.

This leaves £50 in cash, after paying for the stall and goods for resale, out of the original £2,500. Liza kept £30 in the bank and drew out £20 in small change. She was now ready for her first day of market trading on 3 July 20X6.

3.6 The assets and liabilities of the business have now altered, and at 3 July before trading begins, the state of her business is as follows.

Assets		–	*Liabilities*	=	*Ownership interest*
	£				
Stall	1,800	–	£0	=	£2,500
Flower and plants	650				
Cash at bank	30				
Cash in hand	20				
	2,500				

The stall and the flowers and plants are physical items, but they must be given a money value. This money value is usually what they cost the business (called **historical cost** in accounting terms).

Profit introduced into the accounting equation

3.7 On 3 July Liza has a very successful day. She sells all of her flowers and plants for £900 cash.

Since Liza has sold goods costing £650 to earn revenue of £900, we can say that she has **earned a profit of £250 on the day's trading.**

Profits belong to the owners of a business. In this case, the £250 belongs to Liza Doolittle. However, so long as the business retains the profits and does not pay anything out to its owners, the **retained profits** are accounted for as an addition to the ownership interest.

1: Introduction to financial statements

	Assets	– Liabilities	= Ownership interest	
	£			£
Stall	1,800		Original investment	2,500
Flower and plants	0			
Cash in hand and at bank				
(30+20+900)	950		Retained profit	
			(900 – 650)	250
	2,750	– £0		2,750

3.8 Assets less liabilities are often called **net assets**.

Assets – liabilities = Ownership interest, which is the same as
Net assets = Ownership interest

3.9 At the beginning and end of 3 July 20X6, Liza Doolittle's financial position was as follows.

		Net assets	Ownership interest
(a)	At the beginning of the day:	£(2,500 – 0) = £2,500 =	£2,500
(b)	At the end of the day:	£(2,750 – 0) = £2,750 =	£2,750

There has been an increase of £250 in net assets, which is the amount of profits earned during the day.

Activity 1.2

Fill in the missing words. (Don't cheat!)

Assets . . . . less . . . . = ownership interest

4 THE MAIN FINANCIAL STATEMENTS

4.1 In this section we look briefly at the two principal financial statements drawn up by accountants: the balance sheet and the profit and loss account.

KEY TERM

The **balance sheet** is simply a list of all the assets owned by a business and all the liabilities owed by a business as at a particular date. It is a snapshot of the financial position of the business at a particular moment.

4.2 **Assets** are the business's **resources** so, for example, a business may buy buildings to operate from, plant and machinery, stock to sell and cars for its employees. These are all resources which it uses in its operations. Additionally, it may have bank balances, cash and amounts of money owed to it. These provide the **funds** it needs to carry out its operations, and are also assets. On the other hand, it may **owe money** to the bank or to suppliers. These are **liabilities**.

KEY TERM

A **profit and loss account** is a record of income generated and expenditure incurred over a given period. The profit and loss account shows whether the business has had more income than expenditure (a profit) or vice versa (a loss).

Part A: Introduction to financial reporting

4.3 The period chosen will depend on the purpose for which the statement is produced. The profit and loss account which forms part of the published annual accounts of a **limited company** will be made up for the period of a **year**, commencing from the date of the previous year's accounts. On the other hand, **management** might want to keep a closer eye on a company's profitability by making up **quarterly or monthly** profit and loss accounts. Organisations which are not run for profit (charities etc) produce a similar statement called an income and expenditure account which shows the surplus of income over expenditure (or a deficit where expenditure exceeds income).

Accruals basis

4.4 It is very important to grasp the principle, which is applied in nearly all businesses' accounts, that accounts are not prepared on a cash basis but on an **accruals** (or earnings) basis. That is, a sale or purchase is dealt with in the year in which it is made, even if cash changes hands in a later year. This is important because most businesses, even if they do not sell on credit, make purchases on credit. If cash accounting is used, then accounts do not present a true picture of the business's activities in any given period. Accountants call this convention an application of the accruals concept. This is discussed in more detail in Chapter 2 of this Interactive Text, but in the meantime is explained briefly by means of the example below.

4.5 **EXAMPLE: ACCRUALS CONCEPT**

Emma has a business printing and selling T-shirts. In May 20X7 she makes the following purchases and sales.

Invoice date	Numbers bought/sold	Amount £	Date paid
Purchases			
7.5.X7	20	100	1.6.X7
Sales			
8.5.X7	4	40	1.6.X7
12.5.X7	6	60	1.6.X7
23.5.X7	10	100	1.7.X7

What is Emma's profit for May?

4.6 **SOLUTION**

	£
Cash basis	
Sales	0
Purchases	0
Profit/loss	0
Accruals basis	
Sales (£40 + £60 + £100)	200
Purchases	100
Profit	100

4.7 Obviously, the accruals basis gives a truer picture than the cash basis. Emma has no cash to show for her efforts until June but her customers are legally bound to pay her and she is legally bound to pay for her purchases.

4.8 Her balance sheet as at 31 May 20X7 would therefore show her assets and liabilities as follows.

	£
Assets	
Debtors (£40 + £60 + £100)	200
Liabilities	
Creditors	100
Net assets	100
Proprietor's capital (ownership interest)	100

4.9 **Capital** is a special form of liability, representing the amount owed by the business to its proprietor(s). In Emma's case it represents the profit earned in May, which she, as sole proprietor of the business, is entitled to in full. Usually, however, capital will also include the proprietor's initial capital, introduced as cash and perhaps equipment or other assets.

4.10 For example, if Emma had begun her business on 30 April 20X7 by opening a business bank account and paying in £100, her balance sheet immediately after this transaction would look like this.

	£
Assets	
Bank	100
Proprietor's capital	100

On 31 May 20X7 the balance sheet would look like this.

	£
Assets	
Debtors	200
Bank	100
	300
Liabilities	
Creditors	100
Net assets	200
Proprietor's capital	
Brought forward	100
Profit for the period	100
Carried forward	200

4.11 This simple example shows that both the balance sheet and the profit and loss account are summaries of a great many transactions. In later chapters we will look in detail at the ways in which these transactions are recorded and financial statements prepared.

Articulation of the income statement and the balance sheet

4.12 At the end of the accounting period, the profit for the year is added to the profit brought forward in the balance sheet to arrive at the profit carried forward in the balance sheet. You can see this in the example of Emma above.

Look at the example below. This is another illustration of the link between the profit and loss account and the balance sheet.

Part A: Introduction to financial reporting

PROFIT AND LOSS ACCOUNT		BALANCE SHEET	
Sales	100	Assets	200
Cost of sales	(60)	Liability	(100)
Gross profit	40	Net assets	100
Expenses	(10)	Capital	30
Net profit	30	Profits brought forward	40
		Profit for the year	30
			100

4.13 Accountancy textbooks often write 20X3 or 20X4 and so on for dates instead of 2001 etc. You will find both conventions in this Interactive Text, but in the exam only 'real dates' (2003 etc) will be used.

4.14 Try the activity below. It will familiarise you with some of the ideas you have just studied.

Activity 1.3

(a) State one type of profit-making organisation.

For this organisation:

(i) Give an example of an external user of the financial statements.

(ii) Describe one type of decision which would be made by the users with the assistance of the financial statements of the organisation.

(b) The accounting equation is often expressed as:

ASSETS – LIABILITIES = OWNERSHIP INTEREST

(i) Explain what each of the terms 'assets', 'liabilities' and 'ownership interest' means.

(ii) Identify, in general terms only, the balances that would appear in the 'ownership interest' section of the balance sheet of a profit-making organisation.

5 QUALITIES OF GOOD ACCOUNTING INFORMATION

5.1 Below are some features that accounting information should have if it is to be useful.

(a) **Relevance**. The information provided should satisfy the needs of information users. In the case of company accounts, clearly a wide range of information will be needed to satisfy a wide range of users.

(b) **Comprehensibility**. Information may be difficult to understand because it is skimpy or incomplete; but too much detail is also a defect which can cause difficulties of understanding.

(c) **Reliability**. Information will be more reliable if it is independently verified. The law requires that the accounts published by limited companies should be verified by auditors, who must be independent of the company and must hold an approved qualification.

(d) **Completeness**. A company's accounts should present a rounded picture of its economic activities.

(e) **Objectivity**. Information should be as objective as possible. This is particularly the case where conflicting interests operate and an unbiased presentation of information is needed. In the context of preparing accounts, where many decisions must be based on judgement rather than objective facts, this problem often arises. Management are often inclined to paint a rosy picture of a company's profitability to make their own performance look impressive. By contrast, auditors responsible for verifying the accounts are inclined to take a more prudent view so that they cannot be held liable by, say, a supplier misled into granting credit to a shaky company.

(f) **Timeliness**. The usefulness of information is reduced if it does not appear until long after the period to which it relates, or if it is produced at unreasonably long intervals. What constitutes a long interval depends on the circumstances: management of a company may need very frequent (perhaps daily) information on cash flows to run the business efficiently; but shareholders are normally content to see accounts produced annually.

(g) **Comparability**. Information should be produced on a consistent basis so that valid comparisons can be made with information from previous periods and with information produced by other sources (for example the accounts of similar companies operating in the same line of business).

6 ORGANISATIONAL STRUCTURE

6.1 All types of enterprise, large and small, will produce profit and loss accounts and balance sheets. However, you can imagine that the balance sheet of a multinational company will be a more complex document than that of a sole trader. Also, while the sole trader will be producing accounts once a year in order to meet the requirements of his personal tax affairs, the accountant working in a large company will have to meet a number of **reporting deadlines** throughout the year and the accounts he produces will be subject to external scrutiny by a number of users.

6.2 Organisational structure will also determine the complexity and structure of the accounting system.

6.3 A self-employed plumber may keep just an invoice book and a pile of paid bills, and present the whole lot to his accountant in a carrier bag at the end of the year.

6.4 A typical small business will run a simple accounting package, probably with a sales ledger and either a purchase ledger system or an analysed cash book. This business will probably produce monthly management accounts as the owners will want to know whether they are making any profit and where the money is going. There will be a simple coding system involving customer account codes and general ledger codes. Probably one person will run all the accounting functions.

6.5 A large company listed on the Stock Exchange will run a rather more sophisticated system, probably backed up by an IT department. There will be an accounts department with division of sales ledger, purchase ledger and general ledger functions. The coding system will be more extensive, probably with cost centres, and there may also be the results of subsidiaries to consolidate. In addition to monthly management accounts, financial accounts will have to be prepared twice a year, and there will be a lot of pressure to get them prepared on time.

Part A: Introduction to financial reporting

Key learning points

- Businesses of whatever size or nature exist to make a **profit**.
- An **asset** is something which a business owns. A **liability** is something which a business owes.
- A business is a **separate entity** from its owner (for accounting purposes).
- There are various groups of people who need information about the activities of a business. You should be fully aware of these different **user groups** and their varying needs.
- The main financial statements of a business are the **balance sheet** and the **profit and loss account**.
  - The balance sheet is a 'snapshot' of the business position at a given point in time.
  - The profit and loss account is a record of income and expenditure over a period
- Both financial statements are prepared on an **accruals basis**, not a cash basis.
- You should be able to identify the qualities of **good accounting information**. These are:
  - Relevance
  - Comprehensibility
  - Reliability
  - Completeness
  - Objectivity
  - Timeliness
  - Comparability

Quick quiz

1. What is an asset? Give three examples.
2. What is a liability? Give three examples
3. Identify seven user groups who need accounting information.
4. What are the two main financial statements drawn up by accountants?
5. What is the qualities of good accounting information?

Answers to quick quiz

1. An asset is something which a business owns or has the use of, eg a factory, a delivery van or a piece of machinery.
2. A liability is something which is owed to somebody else, eg a bank overdraft, amounts owed to suppliers or taxation owed to the government.
3. Managers; shareholders; trade contacts; providers of finance; the Inland Revenue; employees; financial analysts and advisers; the public.
4. The balance sheet and the profit and loss account.
5. Relevance, reliability, comprehensibility, objectivity, timeliness, completeness, comparability.

Answers to activities

Answer 1.1

The answer is that limited companies (though not other forms of business such as partnerships) are required to make certain accounting information public. They do so by sending copies of the required information to the Registrar of Companies at Companies House. The information filed at Companies House is available, at a fee, to any member of the public who asks for it. Other sources include financial comment in the press and company brochures.

Answer 1.2

Assets less liabilities = ownership interest

Answer 1.3

> **Tutorial note.** You were asked for only one example – our answer gives three for completeness. Other reasonable types of organisation and user would also be acceptable.

(a) (i)

Type of organisation	Example of user
Sole trader	Supplier
Partnership	Bank
Limited company	Shareholder

(ii)

User	Possible decisions
Supplier	Whether to carry on supplying goods on credit (eg by looking at liquidity position)
Bank	Whether to continue an overdraft facility (by assessing profitability and liquidity)
Shareholders	Whether to increase or decrease holding or whether to remove directors. They will assess liquidity, profitability, gearing and the stewardship of management.

(b) (i) Each of the items in the accounting equation is defined in the ASB's *Statement of Principles.*

 (1) *Assets* are 'rights or other access to future economic benefits controlled by an entity as a result of past transactions or events'.

 (2) *Liabilities* are 'obligations of an entity to transfer economic benefits as a result of past transactions or events'.

 (3) *Ownership interest* is the residual amount found by deducting all of the entity's liabilities from all of the entity's assets.

 More simply, assets are owned by an entity, liabilities are owed by an entity and ownership interest is capital, which is owed to the owner.

 (ii) In the balance sheet of a profit making organisation, for example, a limited company, the ownership interest section would consist of share capital (originally paid in by the owners) and reserves (profits made by the company and owed to the owners.

Now try Question 1 in the Exam Question Bank at the end of the Text.

Chapter 2 Fixed assets and stocks

Chapter topic list

1. Capital and revenue expenditure
2. Depreciation
3. Fixed asset disposals
4. Fixed assets: statutory requirements
5. FRS 15 Tangible fixed assets
6. Revaluations
7. Stock valuation: revision

The following study sessions are covered in this chapter.

		Syllabus reference
4 & 5 (a)	Distinguish between capital and revenue expenditure	2
4 & 5 (b)	Explain, calculate and demonstrate the inclusion of the profit or loss on disposal in the profit and loss account	2
4 & 5 (c)	Account for the revaluation of fixed assets	2
4 & 5 (d)	Account for gains and losses on the disposal of revalued assets	2
4 & 5 (e)	Account for depreciation – definition, reasons and methods, including straight line, reducing balance and sum of digits	2
4 & 5 (f)	Account for changes in the useful economic life or residual value of assets	2
4 & 5 (g)	Explain how fixed asset balances and movements are disclosed in the financial statements	2

Part A: Introduction to financial reporting

1 CAPITAL AND REVENUE EXPENDITURE

1.1 In order to tackle the subject of fixed assets you need to be familiar with an important distinction, the distinction between **capital and revenue expenditure**.

> **KEY TERMS**
>
> **Capital expenditure** is expenditure which results in the acquisition of fixed assets, or an improvement in their earning capacity.
>
> (a) Capital expenditure is not charged as an expense in the profit and loss account, although a depreciation charge will usually be made to write off the capital expenditure gradually over time. Depreciation charges are expenses in the profit and loss account.
>
> (b) Capital expenditure on fixed assets results in the appearance of a fixed asset in the balance sheet of the business.
>
> **Revenue expenditure** is expenditure which is incurred for either of the following reasons.
>
> (a) For the purpose of the trade of the business. This includes expenditure classified as selling and distribution expenses, administration expenses and finance charges.
>
> (b) To maintain the existing earning capacity of fixed assets.

1.2 Revenue expenditure is charged to the profit and loss account of a period, if it relates to the trading activity and sales of that particular period. For example, a business buys ten widgets for £200 (£20 each) and sells eight of them during an accounting period. It has two widgets left at the end of the period. The full £200 is revenue expenditure but only £160 is a cost of goods sold during the period. The remaining £40 (cost of two units) will be included in the balance sheet as a current asset valued at £40.

1.3 A business purchases a building for £30,000. It then adds an extension to the building at a cost of £10,000. The building needs to have a few broken windows mended, its floors polished and some missing roof tiles replaced. These cleaning and maintenance jobs cost £900.

In this example, the original purchase (£30,000) and the cost of the extension (£10,000) are capital expenditure, because they are incurred to acquire and then improve a fixed asset. The other costs of £900 are revenue expenditure, because these merely maintain the building and thus the 'earning capacity' of the building.

Capital income and revenue income

1.4 **Capital income** is the proceeds from the sale of non-trading assets (ie proceeds from the sale of fixed assets, including fixed asset investments). The profits (or losses) from the sale of fixed assets are included in the profit and loss account of a business, for the accounting period in which the sale takes place.

1.5 **Revenue income** is income derived from the following sources.

(a) The sale of trading assets
(b) Interest and dividends received from investments held by the business

Capital transactions

1.6 The categorisation of capital and revenue items given above does not mention raising additional capital from the owner(s) of the business, or raising and repaying loans. These are transactions which:

(a) Add to the cash assets of the business, thereby creating a corresponding liability (capital or loan).

(b) When a loan is repaid, reduce the liabilities (loan) and the assets (cash) of the business.

None of these transactions would be reported through the profit and loss account.

Why is the distinction between capital and revenue items important?

1.7 Revenue expenditure results from the purchase of goods and services that will:

(a) Be used fully in the accounting period in which they are purchased, and so be a cost or expense in the trading, profit and loss account.

(b) Result in a current asset as at the end of the accounting period because the goods or services have not yet been consumed or made use of. The current asset would be shown in the balance sheet and is not yet a cost or expense in the trading, profit and loss account.

1.8 Capital expenditure results in the **purchase or improvement** of fixed assets, which are assets that will provide benefits to the business in more than one accounting period, and which are not acquired with a view to being resold in the normal course of trade. The cost of purchased fixed assets is not charged in full to the trading, profit and loss account of the period in which the purchase occurs. Instead, the fixed asset is gradually depreciated over a number of accounting periods.

1.9 Since revenue items and capital items are accounted for in different ways, the correct and consistent calculation of profit for any accounting period depends on the correct and consistent classification of items as revenue or capital.

1.10 This may seem rather confusing at the moment, but things will become clearer in the next few chapters. In the meantime just get used to the terminology. These words appear in the accounts standards themselves, as we will see.

Activity 2.1

State whether each of the following items should be classified as 'capital' or 'revenue' expenditure or income for the purpose of preparing the trading, profit and loss account and the balance sheet of the business.

(a) The purchase of leasehold premises.
(b) The annual depreciation of leasehold premises.
(c) Solicitors' fees in connection with the purchase of leasehold premises.
(d) The costs of adding extra storage capacity to a mainframe computer used by the business.
(e) Computer repairs and maintenance costs.
(f) Profit on the sale of an office building.
(g) Revenue from sales by credit card.
(h) The cost of new machinery.
(i) Customs duty charged on the machinery when imported into the country.

Part A: Introduction to financial reporting

(j) The 'carriage' costs of transporting the new machinery from the supplier's factory to the premises of the business purchasing the machinery.

(k) The cost of installing the new machinery in the premises of the business.

(l) The wages of the machine operators.

2 DEPRECIATION

2.1 This section is a detailed look at depreciation and how it is calculated. Depreciation is also discussed in Section 4 when we will see how FRS 15 affects the use of depreciation.

2.2 A fixed asset is acquired for use within a business with a view to earning profits. Its life extends over more than one accounting period, and so it earns profits over more than one period. In contrast, a current asset is used and replaced many times within the period eg stock is sold and replaced, debtors increase with sales and decrease with payments received.

2.3 With the exception of land held on freehold or very long leasehold, every fixed asset eventually wears out over time. Machines, cars and other vehicles, fixtures and fittings, and even buildings do not last for ever. When a business acquires a fixed asset, it will have some idea about how long its useful life will be, and it might decide:

(a) To keep on using the fixed asset until it becomes completely worn out, useless, and worthless.

(b) To sell off the fixed asset at the end of its useful life, either by selling it as a second-hand item or as scrap.

2.4 Since a fixed asset has a cost, and a limited useful life, and its value eventually declines, it follows that a charge should be made in the trading, profit and loss account to reflect the use that is made of the asset by the business. This charge is called **depreciation**.

Definition of depreciation

2.5 Suppose that a business buys a machine for £40,000. Its expected life is four years, and at the end of that time it is expected to be worthless.

2.6 Since the fixed asset is used to make profits for four years, it would be reasonable to charge the cost of the asset over those four years (perhaps by charging £10,000 per annum) so that at the end of the four years the total cost of £40,000 would have been charged against profits.

2.7 Indeed, one way of defining depreciation is to describe it as **a means of spreading the cost of a fixed asset over its useful life**, and so matching the cost against the full period during which it earns profits for the business. Depreciation charges are an example of the application of the accruals (or matching) concept to calculate profits.

2.8 Depreciation has two important aspects.

(a) Depreciation is a **measure of the wearing out** or depletion of a fixed asset through use, time or obsolescence.

(b) Depreciation charges should be **spread fairly** over a fixed asset's life, and so allocated to the accounting periods which are expected to benefit (ie make profits) from the asset's use.

22

The total charge for depreciation: the depreciable amount

2.9 The total amount to be charged over the life of a fixed asset ('the depreciable amount') is usually its cost less any expected 'residual' sales value or disposal value at the end of the asset's life.

(a) A fixed asset costing £20,000, which has an expected life of five years and an expected residual value of nil, should be depreciated by £20,000 in total over the five year period.

(b) A fixed asset costing £20,000, which has an expected life of five years and an expected residual value of £3,000, should be depreciated by £17,000 in total over the five years.

Depreciation in the accounts of a business

2.10 When a fixed asset is depreciated, two things must be accounted for.

(a) The **charge for depreciation** is a **cost or expense** of the accounting period. Depreciation is an expense in the profit and loss account.

(b) At the same time, the fixed asset is wearing out and diminishing in value. So the value of the fixed asset in the balance sheet must be reduced by the amount of depreciation charged. The balance sheet value of the fixed asset will be its '**net book value**', which is the value after depreciation in the books of account of the business.

2.11 The amount of depreciation will build up (or 'accumulate') over time, as more depreciation is charged in each successive accounting period. This accumulated depreciation is a 'provision' because it provides for the fall in value in use of the fixed asset. The term 'provision for depreciation' means the 'accumulated depreciation' of a fixed asset.

2.12 For example, if a fixed asset costing £40,000 has an expected life of four years and an estimated residual value of nil, it might be depreciated by £10,000 per annum.

	Depreciation charge for the year (P & L a/c) (A) £	Accumulated depreciation at end of year (B) £	Cost of the asset (C) £	Net book value at end of year (C-B) £
At beginning of its life	-	-	40,000	40,000
Year 1	10,000	10,000	40,000	30,000
Year 2	10,000	20,000	40,000	20,000
Year 3	10,000	30,000	40,000	10,000
Year 4	10,000	40,000	40,000	0

2.13 So each year, £10,000 depreciation is charged as an expense in the profit and loss account. Also each year, the net book value (NBV) recorded in the balance sheet reduces by £10,000 until the NBV reaches the residual value (nil in this case).

Methods of depreciation

2.14 There are several different methods of depreciation. Of these, the ones you need to know about are:

- Straight line method
- Reducing balance method
- Sum of the digits method

The straight line method

2.15 This is the most commonly used method of all. The total depreciable amount is charged in equal instalments to each accounting period over the expected useful life of the asset. So the net book value of the fixed asset declines at a steady rate, or in a 'straight line' over time.

2.16 The annual depreciation charge is calculated as:

$$\frac{\text{Cost of asset minus residual value}}{\text{Expected useful life of the asset}}$$

2.17 EXAMPLE: STRAIGHT LINE DEPRECIATION

(a) A fixed asset costing £20,000 with an estimated life of 10 years and no residual value would be depreciated at the rate of:

$$\frac{£20,000}{10 \text{ years}} = £2,000 \text{ per annum}$$

(b) A fixed asset costing £60,000 has an estimated life of 5 years and a residual value of £7,000. The annual depreciation charge using the straight line method would be:

$$\frac{£(60,000 - 7,000)}{5 \text{ years}} = £10,600 \text{ per annum}$$

The net book value of the fixed asset would be:

	After 1 year £	After 2 years £	After 3 years £	After 4 years £	After 5 years £
Cost of the asset	60,000	60,000	60,000	60,000	60,000
Accumulated depreciation	10,600	21,200	31,800	42,400	53,000
Net book value	49,400	38,800	28,200	17,600	7,000 *

* ie its estimated residual value.

2.18 Since the depreciation charge per annum is the same amount every year with the straight line method, it is often convenient to state that depreciation is charged at the rate of x per cent per annum on the cost of the asset. In the example in paragraph 1.17(a) above, the depreciation charge per annum is 10% of cost (ie 10% of £20,000 = £2,000).

Examination questions often describe straight line depreciation in this way.

2.19 The straight line method of depreciation is a fair allocation of the total depreciable amount between the different accounting periods, provided the business enjoys equal benefits from the use of the asset in every period throughout its life.

Assets acquired in the middle of an accounting period

2.20 A business can purchase new fixed assets at any time during the course of an accounting period. So it might seem fair to charge a reduced amount for depreciation in the period when the purchase occurs.

2.21 EXAMPLE: ASSETS ACQUIRED IN THE MIDDLE OF AN ACCOUNTING PERIOD

A business which has an accounting year which runs from 1 January to 31 December purchases a new fixed asset on 1 April 20X1, at a cost of £24,000. The expected life of the asset is 4 years, and its residual value is nil. What should be the depreciation charge for 20X1?

2.22 SOLUTION

The annual depreciation charge will be $\frac{24,000}{4 \text{ years}}$ = £6,000 per annum

However, since the asset was acquired on 1 April 20X1, the business has only benefited from the use of the asset for 9 months instead of a full 12 months. It would therefore seem fair to charge depreciation in 20X1 of only

$\frac{9}{12} \times £6,000 = £4,500$

> **Exam alert**
>
> If an examination question gives you the purchase or disposal date of a fixed asset, part way through an accounting period, you should assume that depreciation is calculated as a 'part-year' amount, unless told to the contrary in the question. However, you will only be given such a problem when the straight line method of depreciation is used.

2.23 In practice, many businesses ignore the niceties of part-year depreciation, and charge a full year's depreciation on fixed assets in the year of their purchase and/or disposal, regardless of the time of year they were acquired.

The reducing balance method

2.24 The **reducing balance method** of depreciation calculates the depreciation charge as a fixed percentage of the net book value of the asset, as at the end of the accounting period.

2.25 For example, a business purchases a fixed asset at a cost of £10,000. Its expected useful life is 3 years and its estimated residual value is £2,160. The business wishes to use the reducing balance method to depreciate the asset, and calculates that the rate of depreciation should be 40% of the reducing balance (NBV) of the asset. (The method of deciding that 40% is a suitable annual percentage is a problem of mathematics, not financial accounting, and is not described here.)

The total depreciable amount is £(10,000 − 2,160) = £7,840.

The depreciation charge per annum and the net book value of the asset as at the end of each year will be as follows:

	NBV £	Accumulated depreciation £	
Asset at cost	10,000		
Depreciation in year 1 (40% × £10,000)	4,000	4,000	
Net book value at end of year 1	6,000		
Depreciation in year 2			
(40% × £6,000)	2,400	6,400	(4,000 + 2,400)
Net book value at end of year 2	3,600		
Depreciation in year 3 (40% × £3,600)	1,440	7,840	(6,400 + 1,440)
Net book value at end of year 3	2,160		

2.26 With the reducing balance method, the annual charge for depreciation is higher in the earlier years of the asset's life, and lower in the later years. In the example above, the annual charges for years 1, 2 and 3 are £4,000, £2,400 and £1,440 respectively. The reducing balance method, therefore, is used when it is considered fair to allocate a greater proportion of the total depreciable amount to the earlier years and a lower proportion to later years, on the assumption that the benefits obtained by the business from using the asset decline over time.

Sum of the digits method

2.27 This is a variant of the reducing balance method, based on the estimated useful life of an asset. If an asset has an estimated useful life of five years, then the digits 1, 2, 3, 4 and 5 are added together, giving a total of 15. Depreciation of 5/15, 4/15, 3/15, and so on, of the depreciable amount is charged in the respective years.

2.28 EXAMPLE: SUM OF THE DIGITS METHOD

A van cost £20,000 and is expected to be sold for £4,000 after four years. Calculate the depreciation to be provided in each of the years 1 to 4 using the sum of the digits method.

2.29 SOLUTION

Sum of digits = 1+2+3+4 = 10. Depreciable amount = £20,000 − £4,000 = £16,000

		£
Year 1	Cost	20,000
	Depreciation at 4/10 of £16,000	6,400
	Net book value	13,600
Year 2	Depreciation at 3/10 of £16,000	4,800
	Net book value	8,800
Year 3	Depreciation at 2/10 of £16,000	3,200
	Net book value	5,600
Year 4	Depreciation at 1/10 of £16,000	1,600
	Net book value	4,000*
	*The residual value	

> **Exam alert**
> Any of the above three methods could be tested in the exam.

Revaluation method

2.30 This is used when depreciation is charged on a value other than cost, ie a revalued amount. Revaluations are dealt with in Section 5 of this chapter.

Applying a depreciation method consistently

2.31 It is up to the business concerned to decide which method of depreciation to apply to its fixed assets. Once that decision has been made, however, it should not be changed - the chosen method of depreciation should be applied **consistently from year to year**. This is an instance of the consistency concept, which we will look at later in Chapter 14.

2.32 Similarly, it is up to the business to decide what a sensible life span for a fixed asset should be. Again, once that life span has been chosen, it should not be changed unless something unexpected happens to the fixed asset.

2.33 It is permissible for a business to depreciate different categories of fixed assets in different ways. For example, if a business owns three cars, then each car would normally be depreciated in the same way (eg by the straight line method); but another category of fixed asset, say, photocopiers, can be depreciated using a different method (eg by the sum of digits method).

Activity 2.2

A lorry bought for a business cost £17,000. It is expected to last for five years and then be sold for scrap for £2,000.

Required

Work out the depreciation to be charged each year under:

(a) The straight line method
(b) The reducing balance method (using a rate of 35%)
(c) The sum of digits method

A fall in the value of a fixed asset

2.34 When the 'market' value of a fixed asset falls so that it is worth less than the amount of its net book value, the asset should be **written down to its new low market value**. The charge in the profit and loss account for the fall in the value of the asset during the accounting period should then be:

	£
Net book value at the beginning of the period	X
Less new reduced value	(X)
Equals the charge for the diminution in the asset's value in the period	X

2.35 EXAMPLE: FALL IN ASSET VALUE

A business purchased a leasehold property on 1 January 20X1 at a cost of £100,000. The lease has a 20 year life. After 5 years' use, on 1 January 20X6, the business decides that since property prices have fallen sharply, the leasehold is now worth only £60,000, and that the value of the asset should be reduced in the accounts of the business.

The leasehold was being depreciated at the rate of 5% per annum on cost.

2.36 Before the asset is reduced in value, the annual depreciation charge is:

$$\frac{£100,000}{20 \text{ years}} = £5,000 \text{ per annum } (= 5\% \text{ of } £100,000)$$

After 5 years, the accumulated depreciation would be £25,000, and the net book value of the leasehold £75,000, which is £15,000 more than the new asset value. This £15,000 should be written off as a charge for depreciation or fall in the asset's value in year 5, so that the total charge in year 5 is:

	£
Net book value of the leasehold after 4 years (£100,000 – 20,000)	80,000
Revised asset value at end of year 5	60,000
Charge against profit in year 5	20,000

Part A: Introduction to financial reporting

An alternative method of calculation is:

	£
'Normal' depreciation charge per annum	5,000
Further fall in value, from net book value at end of year 5 to revised value	15,000
Charge against profit in year 5	20,000

2.37 The leasehold has a further 15 years to run, and its value is now £60,000. From year 6 to year 20, the annual charge for depreciation will be:

$$\frac{£60,000}{15 \text{ years}} = £4,000 \text{ per annum}$$

Change in expected life of an asset

2.38 The depreciation charge on a fixed asset depends not only on the cost (or value) of the asset and its estimated residual value, but also on its **estimated useful life**.

2.39 A business purchased a fixed asset costing £12,000 with an estimated life of four years and no residual value. If it used the straight line method of depreciation, it would make an annual provision of 25% of £12,000 = £3,000.

Now what would happen if the business decided after two years that the useful life of the asset has been underestimated, and it still had five more years in use to come (making its total life seven years)?

For the first two years, the asset was depreciated by £3,000 per annum, so that its net book value after two years is £(12,000 − 6,000) = £6,000. If the remaining life of the asset is now revised to five more years, the remaining amount to be depreciated (£6,000) is spread over the remaining life, giving an annual depreciation charge for the final five years of:

$$\frac{\text{Net book value at time of life readjustment, minus residual value}}{\text{New estimate of remaining useful life}}$$

$$= \frac{£6,000}{5 \text{ years}} = £1,200 \text{ per annum}$$

> **FORMULA TO LEARN**
>
> $$\text{New depreciation} = \frac{\text{NBV less residual value}}{\text{Revised useful life}}$$

2.40 The same formula is used if there is a **revision of residual value**.

2.41 In the example in paragraph 1.39, the business also decides that the fixed asset will have a residual value of £1,000 at the end of the five years. The new depreciation is calculated as follows:

$$\text{New depreciation} = \frac{\text{NBV less new residual value}}{\text{Revised useful life}}$$

$$= \frac{£6,000 - £1,000}{5}$$

$$= £1,000 \text{ per annum}$$

Depreciation is not a cash expense

2.42 Depreciation spreads the cost of a fixed asset (less its estimated residual value) over the asset's life. The cash payment for the fixed asset will be made when, or soon after, the asset is purchased. Therefore, annual depreciation of the asset in subsequent years is **not a cash expense**.

2.43 For example, a business purchased some shop fittings for £6,000 on 1 July 20X5 and paid for them in cash on that date.

Subsequently, depreciation may be charged at £600 pa for ten years. So each year £600 is deducted from profits and the net book value of the fittings goes down, but no actual cash is being paid. The cash was all paid on 1 July 20X5. So annual depreciation is not a cash expense, but rather an allocation of the original cost to later years.

Provision for depreciation

> **KEY TERM**
>
> A **provision for depreciation** is the amount written off for the wearing out of fixed assets.

2.44 There are two basic aspects of the provision for depreciation to remember:

(a) A depreciation charge (provision) is made in the profit and loss account in each accounting period for every depreciable fixed asset. Nearly all fixed assets are depreciable, the most important exceptions being freehold land and long-term investments.

(b) The total accumulated depreciation on a fixed asset builds up as the asset gets older. Unlike a provision for doubtful debts, therefore, the total provision for depreciation is always getting larger, until the fixed asset is fully depreciated.

2.45 If you understand these points, the similarity in the accounting treatment of the provision for doubtful debts and the provision for depreciation may become apparent to you.

2.46 The ledger accounting entries for the provision for depreciation are as follows.

(a) There is a provision for depreciation account for each separate category of fixed assets, for example, plant and machinery, land and buildings, fixtures and fittings.

(b) The depreciation charge for an accounting period is a charge against profit. It is an increase in the provision for depreciation and is accounted for as follows:

DEBIT   P & L account (depreciation expense)
CREDIT   Provision for depreciation account

with the depreciation charge for the period.

(c) The balance on the provision for depreciation account is the **total accumulated depreciation**. This is always a credit balance brought forward in the ledger account for depreciation.

(d) The fixed asset accounts are unaffected by depreciation. Fixed assets are recorded in these accounts at cost (or, if they are revalued, at their revalued amount).

(e) In the balance sheet of the business, the total balance on the provision for depreciation account (ie accumulated depreciation) is set against the value of fixed asset accounts (ie fixed assets at cost or revalued amount) to derive the net book value of the fixed assets.

2.47 EXAMPLE: PROVISION FOR DEPRECIATION

Brian Box set up his own computer software business on 1 March 20X6. He purchased a computer system on credit from a manufacturer, at a cost of £16,000. The system has an expected life of three years and a residual value of £2,500. Using the straight line method of depreciation, the fixed asset account, provision for depreciation account and P & L account (extract) and balance sheet (extract) would be as follows, for each of the next three years ended 28 February 20X7, 20X8 and 20X9.

FIXED ASSET - COMPUTER EQUIPMENT

	Date		£	Date		£
(a)	1.3.X6	Creditor	16,000	28.2.X7	Balance c/f	16,000
(b)	1.3.X7	Balance b/f	16,000	28.2.X8	Balance c/f	16,000
(c)	1.3.X8	Balance b/f	16,000	28.2.X9	Balance c/f	16,000
(d)	1.3.X9	Balance b/f	16,000			

In theory, the fixed asset has completed its expected useful life. However, until it is sold off or scrapped, the asset will still appear in the balance sheet at cost (less accumulated depreciation) and it should remain in the ledger account for computer equipment until it is eventually disposed of.

PROVISION FOR DEPRECIATION

	Date		£	Date		£
(a)	28.2.X7	Balance c/f	4,500	28.2.X7	P & L account	4,500
(b)	28.2.X8	Balance c/f	9,000	1.3.X7	Balance b/f	4,500
				28.2.X8	P & L account	4,500
			9,000			9,000
(c)	28.2.X9	Balance c/f	13,500	1.3.X8	Balance b/f	9,000
				28.2.X9	P & L account	4,500
			13,500			13,500
				1 Mar 20X9 Balance b/f		13,500

The annual depreciation charge is $\dfrac{(£16,000 - 2,500)}{3 \text{ years}}$ = £4,500 pa

At the end of three years, the asset is fully depreciated down to its residual value. If it continues to be used by Brian Box, it will not be depreciated any further (unless its estimated residual value is reduced).

P & L ACCOUNT (EXTRACT)

	Date		£
(a)	28 Feb 20X7	Provision for depreciation	4,500
(b)	28 Feb 20X8	Provision for depreciation	4,500
(c)	28 Feb 20X9	Provision for depreciation	4,500

BALANCE SHEET (EXTRACT) AS AT 28 FEBRUARY

	20X7 £	20X8 £	20X9 £
Computer equipment at cost	16,000	16,000	16,000
Less accumulated depreciation	4,500	9,000	13,500
Net book value	11,500	7,000	2,500

2.48 EXAMPLE: PROVISION FOR DEPRECIATION WITH ASSETS ACQUIRED PART-WAY THROUGH THE YEAR

Brian Box prospers in his computer software business, and before long he purchases a car for himself, and later for his chief assistant Bill Ockhead. Relevant data is as follows:

	Date of purchase	Cost	Estimated life	Estimated residual value
Brian Box car	1 June 20X6	£20,000	3 years	£2,000
Bill Ockhead car	1 June 20X7	£8,000	3 years	£2,000

The straight line method of depreciation is to be used.

Prepare the motor vehicles account and provision for depreciation of motor vehicle account for the years to 28 February 20X7 and 20X8. (You should allow for the part-year's use of a car in computing the annual charge for depreciation.)

Calculate the net book value of the motor vehicles as at 28 February 20X8.

2.49 SOLUTION

(a) (i) Brian Box car   Annual depreciation $\frac{£(20,000 - 2,000)}{3 \text{ years}}$ =   £6,000 pa

Monthly depreciation £500

Depreciation   1 June 20X6 - 28 February 20X7 (9 months)   £4,500
               1 March 20X7 - 28 February 20X8   £6,000

(ii) Bill Ockhead car   Annual depreciation $\frac{£(8,000 - 2,000)}{3 \text{ years}}$ =   £2,000 pa

Depreciation   1 June 20X7 - 28 February 20X8 (9 months)   £1,500

(b)

MOTOR VEHICLES

Date		£	Date		£
1 Jun 20X6	Creditors (or cash) (car purchase)	20,000	28 Feb 20X7	Balance c/f	20,000
1 Mar 20X7	Balance b/f	20,000			
1 Jun 20X7	Creditors (or cash) (car purchase)	8,000	28 Feb 20X8	Balance c/f	28,000
		28,000			28,000
1 Mar 20X8	Balance b/f	28,000			

Part A: Introduction to financial reporting

PROVISION FOR DEPRECIATION OF MOTOR VEHICLES

Date		£	Date		£
28 Feb 20X7	Balance c/f	4,500	28 Feb 20X7	P & L account	4,500
			1 Mar 20X7	Balance b/f	4,500
28 Feb 20X8	Balance c/f	12,000	28 Feb 20X8	P & L account (6,000+1,500)	7,500
		12,000			12,000
			1 March 20X8	Balance b/f	12,000

BALANCE SHEET (WORKINGS) AS AT 28 FEBRUARY 20X8

	Brian Box car		Bill Ockhead car		Total
	£	£	£	£	£
Asset at cost		20,000		8,000	28,000
Accumulated depreciation:					
Year to:					
28 Feb 20X7	4,500		-		
28 Feb 20X8	6,000		1,500		
		10,500		1,500	12,000
Net book value		9,500		6,500	16,000

2.50 In practice the provision for depreciation account is usually known as the **accumulated depreciation** account.

3 FIXED ASSET DISPOSALS

The disposal of fixed assets

3.1 Fixed assets are not purchased by a business with the intention of reselling them in the normal course of trade. However, they might be sold off at some stage, eg when their useful life is over. A business may sell off a fixed asset long before its useful life has ended, eg to get more a more up to date model.

3.2 Whenever a business sells something, it makes a profit or a loss. So when fixed assets are disposed of, there is a profit or loss on disposal. This is a **capital gain** or a **capital loss**.

3.3 These gains or losses are reported in the profit and loss account of the business (and not as a trading profit in the trading account). They are commonly referred to as '**profit on disposal of fixed assets**' or '**loss on disposal**'.

3.4 Examination questions on the disposal of fixed assets usually ask for ledger accounts to be prepared, showing the entries in the accounts to record the disposal. But before we look at the ledger accounting for disposing of assets, we had better look at the principles behind calculating the profit (or loss) on disposing of assets.

The principles behind calculating the profit or loss on disposal

3.5 The profit or loss on the disposal of a fixed asset is the difference between:

(a) The net book value of the asset at the time of its sale.
(b) Its net sale price, which is the price minus any costs of making the sale.

A profit is made when the sale price exceeds the net book value, and a loss is made when the sale price is less than the net book value.

3.6 EXAMPLE: DISPOSAL OF A FIXED ASSET

A business purchased a fixed asset on 1 January 20X1 for £25,000. It had an estimated life of six years and an estimated residual value of £7,000. The asset was eventually sold after three years on 1 January 20X4 to another trader who paid £17,500 for it.

What was the profit or loss on disposal, assuming that the business uses the straight line method for depreciation?

3.7 SOLUTION

Annual depreciation $= \dfrac{£(25{,}000 - 7{,}000)}{6 \text{ years}}$

$= £3{,}000$ per annum

	£
Cost of asset	25,000
Less accumulated depreciation (three years)	9,000
Net book value at date of disposal	16,000
Sale price	17,500
Profit on disposal	1,500

This profit will be shown in the profit and loss account of the business, where it will be an item of other income added to the gross profit brought down from the trading account, as shown below.

	£
Gross profit	30,000
Profit on disposal of fixed assets	1,500
	31,500
Expenses	21,500
Net profit	10,000

3.8 SECOND EXAMPLE: DISPOSAL OF A FIXED ASSET

A business purchased a machine on 1 July 20X1 at a cost of £35,000. The machine had an estimated residual value of £3,000 and a life of eight years. The machine was sold for £18,600 on 31 December 20X4, the last day of the accounting year of the business. To make the sale, the business had to incur dismantling costs and costs of transporting the machine to the buyer's premises. These amounted to £1,200.

The business uses the straight line method of depreciation. What was the profit or loss on disposal of the machine?

3.9 SOLUTION

Annual depreciation $\dfrac{£(35{,}000 - 3{,}000)}{8 \text{ years}} = £4{,}000$ per annum

It is assumed that in 20X1 only one-half year's depreciation was charged, because the asset was purchased six months into the year.

Part A: Introduction to financial reporting

		£	£
Fixed asset at cost			35,000
Depreciation in 20X1 (6 months)		2,000	
20X2, 20X3 and 20X4 (3 years)		12,000	
Accumulated depreciation			14,000
Net book value at date of disposal			21,000
Sale price		18,600	
Costs incurred in making the sale		(1,200)	
Net sale price			17,400
Loss on disposal			(3,600)

This loss will be shown as an expense in the profit and loss account of the business. It is a capital loss, not a trading loss, and it should not therefore be shown in the trading account.

Profit and loss account (extract)		£
Gross profit		30,000
Expenses	21,500	
Loss on sale of fixed assets	3,600	25,100
Net profit		4,900

The disposal of fixed assets: ledger accounting entries

3.10 A profit on disposal is an item of 'other income' in the P & L account, and a loss on disposal is an item of expense in the P & L account.

3.11 It is customary in ledger accounting to record the disposal of fixed assets in a **disposal of fixed assets** account.

(a) The profit or loss on disposal is the difference between:

  (i) The sale price of the asset (if any).
  (ii) The net book value of the asset at the time of sale.

(b) The relevant items which must appear in the disposal of fixed assets account are therefore:

  (i) The value of the asset (at cost, or revalued amount*).
  (ii) The accumulated depreciation up to the date of sale.
  (iii) The sale price of the asset.

  *To simplify the explanation of the rules, we will assume now that the fixed assets disposed of are valued at cost.

(c) The ledger accounting entries are:

  (i) DEBIT   Disposal of fixed asset account
      CREDIT Fixed asset account

  With the cost of the asset disposed of.

  (ii) DEBIT   Provision for depreciation account (or accumulated depreciation account)
       CREDIT Disposal of fixed asset account

  With the accumulated depreciation on the asset as at the date of sale.

  (iii) DEBIT   Debtor account or cash book
        CREDIT Disposal of fixed asset account

  With the sale price of the asset. The sale is therefore not recorded in a sales account, but in the disposal of fixed asset account itself.

  (iv) The balance on the disposal account is the profit or loss on disposal and the corresponding double entry is recorded in the P & L account itself.

Exam alert

Calculation of profit or loss on disposal is likely to come up in an exam.

3.12 EXAMPLE: DISPOSAL OF ASSETS: LEDGER ACCOUNTING ENTRIES

A business has £110,000 worth of machinery at cost. Its policy is to make a provision for depreciation at 20% per annum straight line. The total provision now stands at £70,000. The business now sells for £19,000 a machine which it purchased exactly two years ago for £30,000.

Show the relevant ledger entries.

3.13 SOLUTION

PLANT AND MACHINERY ACCOUNT

	£		£
Balance b/f	110,000	Plant disposals account	30,000
		Balance c/f	80,000
	110,000		110,000
Balance b/f	80,000		

PLANT AND MACHINERY ACCUMULATED DEPRECIATION

	£		£
Plant disposals (20% of £30,000 for 2 years)	12,000	Balance b/f	70,000
Balance c/f	58,000		
	70,000		70,000
		Balance b/f	58,000

PLANT DISPOSALS

	£		£
Plant and machinery account	30,000	Accumulated depreciation	12,000
Profit and loss a/c (profit on sale)	1,000	Cash	19,000
	31,000		31,000

Check:

	£
Asset at cost	30,000
Accumulated depreciation at time of sale	12,000
Net book value at time of sale	18,000
Sale price	19,000
Profit on sale	1,000

3.14 EXAMPLE CONTINUED

Taking the example above assume that, instead of the machine being sold for £19,000, it was exchanged for a new machine costing £60,000, a credit of £19,000 being received upon exchange. In other words £19,000 is the trade-in price of the old machine. Now what are the relevant ledger account entries?

Part A: Introduction to financial reporting

3.15 SOLUTION

PLANT AND MACHINERY ACCOUNT

	£		£
Balance b/f	110,000	Plant disposal	30,000
Cash (60,000 - 19,000)	41,000	Balance c/f	140,000
Plant disposals	19,000		
	170,000		170,000
Balance b/f	140,000		

The new asset is recorded in the fixed asset account at cost £(41,000 + 19,000) = £60,000.

PLANT AND MACHINERY ACCUMULATED DEPRECIATION

	£		£
Plant disposals (20% of £30,000 for 2 years)	12,000	Balance b/f	70,000
Balance c/f	58,000		
	70,000		70,000
		Balance b/f	58,000

PLANT DISPOSALS

	£		£
Plant and machinery	30,000	Accumulate depreciation	12,000
Profit transferred to P & L	1,000	Plant and machinery	19,000
	31,000		31,000

Activity 2.3

A business purchased two widget-making machines on 1 January 20X5 at a cost of £15,000 each. Each had an estimated life of five years and a nil residual value. The straight line method of depreciation is used.

Owing to an unforeseen slump in market demand for widgets, the business decided to reduce its output of widgets, and switch to making other products instead. On 31 March 20X7, one widget-making machine was sold (on credit) to a buyer for £8,000.

Later in the year, however, it was decided to abandon production of widgets altogether, and the second machine was sold on 1 December 20X7 for £2,500 cash.

Prepare the machinery account, provision for depreciation of machinery account and disposal of machinery account for the accounting year to 31 December 20X7.

4 FIXED ASSETS: STATUTORY REQUIREMENTS

4.1 This section acts as an introduction to the Companies Act requirements for all fixed assets.

Statutory provisions relating to all fixed assets

4.2 The standard balance sheet format of CA 1985 divides fixed assets into three categories:

  (a) **Intangible assets**
  (b) **Tangible assets**
  (c) **Investments**

4.3 Companies Act requirements in regard to fixed assets may be considered under two headings.

  (a) **Valuation:** the amounts at which fixed assets should be stated in the balance sheet.

(b) **Disclosure:** the information which should be disclosed in the accounts as to valuation of fixed assets and as to movements on fixed asset accounts during the year.

Valuation of fixed assets

4.4 Where an asset is **purchased**, its cost is simply the **purchase price plus any expenses incidental to its acquisition**.

4.5 Where an asset is **produced by a company for its own use**, its 'production cost' **must** include the cost of **raw materials, consumables** and **other attributable direct costs** (such as labour). Production cost may additionally include a reasonable proportion of indirect costs, together with the interest on any capital borrowed to finance production of the asset.

4.6 The 'cost' of any fixed asset having a limited economic life, whether purchase price or production cost, must be reduced by provisions for depreciation calculated to write off the cost, less any residual value, systematically over the period of the asset's useful life. This very general requirement is supplemented by the more detailed provisions of FRS 15 *Tangible fixed assets*.

4.7 Provision for a permanent reduction in value (now called impairment) of a fixed asset must be made in the profit and loss account and the asset should be disclosed at the reduced amount in the balance sheet. Any such provision should be disclosed on the face of the profit and loss account or by way of note. Where a provision becomes no longer necessary, because the conditions giving rise to it have altered, it should be written back, and again disclosure should be made.

Fixed assets valuation: alternative accounting rules

4.8 Although the Companies Act 1985 maintains historical cost principles as the normal basis for the preparation of accounts, **alternative bases** allowing for revaluations and current cost accounting are permitted provided that:

(a) The **items affected** and the **basis of valuation** are **disclosed** in a note to the accounts.

(b) The **historical cost** in the current and previous years is **separately disclosed** in the balance sheet or in a note to the accounts. Alternatively, the difference between the revalued amount and historical cost may be disclosed.

> **KEY TERM**
>
> Using the **alternative accounting rules** the appropriate value of any fixed asset (its current cost or market value), rather than its purchase price or production cost, may be included in the balance sheet.

4.9 Where appropriate, depreciation may be provided on the basis of the new valuation(s), such depreciation being referred to in the Companies Act 1985 as the 'adjusted amount' of depreciation. For profit and loss account purposes it is acceptable under the Companies Act to calculate (and disclose) depreciation in respect of any such fixed asset on the basis of historical cost. If the 'historical cost amount' rather than the 'adjusted amount' of depreciation were to be used in the profit and loss account, the difference between the two would be shown separately in the profit and loss account or in a note to the accounts.

Revaluation reserve

4.10 Where the value of any fixed asset is determined by using the alternative accounting rules the amount of profit or loss arising must be credited or (as the case may be) debited to a separate reserve, the revaluation reserve. The calculation of the relevant amounts should be based on the written down values of the assets prior to revaluation.

4.11 The revaluation reserve must be reduced to the extent that the amounts standing to the credit of the reserves are, in the opinion of the directors of the company, no longer necessary for the purposes of the accounting policies adopted by the company. However, an amount may only be transferred from the reserve to the profit and loss account if either:

(a) The amount in question was previously charged to that account
(b) It represents realised profit (for example on disposal of a fixed asset).

The **only other** transfer possible from the revaluation reserve is on capitalisation, that is, when a bonus issue is made.

4.12 The amount of a revaluation reserve must be shown under a separate sub-heading on the balance sheet. However, the reserve need not necessarily be called a 'revaluation reserve'.

Fixed assets: disclosure

4.13 Notes to the accounts must show, for each class of fixed assets, an analysis of the movements on both costs and depreciation provisions.

4.14 The following format (with notional figures) is commonly used to disclose fixed assets movements.

	Total £	Land and buildings £	Plant and machinery £
Cost or valuation			
At 1 January 20X4	50,000	40,000	10,000
Revaluation surplus	12,000	12,000	–
Additions in year	4,000	–	4,000
Disposals in year	(1,000)	–	(1,000)
At 31 December 20X4	65,000	52,000	13,000
Depreciation			
At 1 January 20X4	6,000	10,000	6,000
Charge for year	4,000	1,000	3,000
Elimination on revaluation	–	(10,000)	–
Eliminated on disposals	(500)	–	(500)
At 31 December 20X4	9,500	1,000	8,500
Net book value			
At 31 December 20X4	55,500	51,000	4,500
At 1 January 20X4	34,000	30,000	4,000

4.15 Where any fixed assets of a company (other than listed investments) are included in the accounts at an alternative accounting valuation, the following information must also be given.

(a) The years (so far as they are known to the directors) in which the assets were severally valued and the several values

(b) In the case of assets that have been valued during the financial period, the names of the persons who valued them or particulars of their qualifications for doing so and (whichever is stated) the bases of valuation used by them.

4.16 A note to the accounts must classify land and buildings under the headings of:

(a) Freehold property

(b) Leasehold property, distinguishing between:

(i) Long leaseholds, in which the unexpired term of the lease at the balance sheet date is not less than 50 years.

(ii) Short leaseholds which are all leaseholds other than long leaseholds.

5 FRS 15 TANGIBLE FIXED ASSETS

5.1 FRS 15 *Tangible fixed assets* was published in February 1999. It goes into a lot more detail than the Companies Act.

Objective

5.2 FRS 15 deals with accounting for the initial measurement, valuation and depreciation of tangible fixed assets. It also sets out the information that should be disclosed to enable readers to understand the impact of the accounting policies adopted in relation to these issues.

Initial measurement

5.3 A tangible fixed asset should **initially be measured at cost**.

> **KEY TERM**
>
> **Cost** is purchase price and any costs directly attributable to bringing the asset into working condition for its intended use.

5.4 Examples of directly attributable costs are:

- **Acquisition costs**, eg stamp duty, import duties
- Cost of **site preparation** and clearance
- Initial **delivery and handling** costs
- **Installation** costs
- **Professional fees** eg legal fees
- The estimated cost of **dismantling and removing** the asset and restoring the site, to the extent that it is recognised as a provision under FRS 12 *Provisions, contingent liabilities and contingent assets* (discussed in Chapter 11).

Part A: Introduction to financial reporting

5.5 Any abnormal costs, such as those arising from design error, industrial disputes or idle capacity are not directly attributable costs and therefore should not be capitalised as part of the cost of the asset.

Finance costs

5.6 The **capitalisation of finance costs**, including interest, is **optional**. However, if an entity does capitalise finance costs they must do so **consistently**.

5.7 All finance costs that are **directly attributable** to the construction of a tangible fixed asset should be capitalised as part of the cost of the asset.

KEY TERM

Directly attributable finance costs are those that would have been avoided if there had been no expenditure on the asset.

5.8 If finance costs are capitalised, capitalisation should start when:
- Finance costs are being incurred
- Expenditure on the asset is being incurred
- Activities necessary to get the asset ready for use are in progress

5.9 Capitalisation of finance costs should cease when the asset is ready for use.

Subsequent expenditure

5.10 Subsequent expenditure on a tangible fixed asset should only be capitalised in the following three circumstances.

(a) It enhances the economic benefits over and above those previously estimated. An example might be modifications made to a piece of machinery that increases its capacity or useful life.

(b) A component of an asset that has been treated separately for depreciation purposes (because it has a substantially different useful economic life from the rest of the asset) has been restored or replaced.

(c) It relates to a major inspection or overhaul that restores economic benefits that have been consumed and reflected in the depreciation charge.

Activity 2.4

Can you think of examples for (b) and (c) above?

Valuation

5.11 FRS 15 supplements and clarifies the rules on revaluation of fixed assets which the Companies Act allows. Revaluation is discussed in the next section.

Depreciation

5.12 As noted earlier, the Companies Act 1985 requires that all fixed assets having a limited economic life should be depreciated. FRS 15 gives a useful discussion of the purpose of depreciation and supplements the statutory requirements in important ways.

> **KEY TERM**
>
> **Depreciation** is defined in FRS 15 as the measure of the cost or revalued amount of the economic benefits of the tangible fixed asset that have been consumed during the period. Consumption includes the wearing out, using up or other reduction in the useful economic life of a tangible fixed asset, whether arising from use, effluxion of time or obsolescence through either changes in technology or demand for the goods and services produced by the asset.

5.13 This definition covers the amortisation of assets with a pre-determined life, such as a leasehold, and the depletion of wasting assets such as mines.

5.14 The need to depreciate fixed assets arises from the accruals concept. If money is expended in purchasing an asset then the amount expended must at some time be charged against profits. If the asset is one which contributes to an enterprise's revenue over a number of accounting periods it would be inappropriate to charge any single period (for example the period in which the asset was acquired) with the whole of the expenditure. Instead, some method must be found of spreading the cost of the asset over its useful economic life.

5.15 This view of depreciation as a process of **allocation** of the cost of an asset over several accounting periods is the view adopted by FRS 15. It is worth mentioning here two common **misconceptions** about the purpose and effects of depreciation.

(a) It is sometimes thought that the net book value (NBV) of an asset is equal to its net realisable value and that the object of charging depreciation is to reflect the fall in value of an asset over its life. This misconception is the basis of a common, but incorrect, argument which says that freehold properties (say) need not be depreciated in times when property values are rising. It is true that historical cost balance sheets often give a misleading impression when a property's NBV is much below its market value, but in such a case it is open to a business to incorporate a revaluation into its books, or even to prepare its accounts on the current cost convention. This is a separate problem from that of allocating the property's cost over successive accounting periods.

(b) Another misconception is that depreciation is provided so that an asset can be replaced at the end of its useful life. This is not the case.

(i) If there is no intention of replacing the asset, it could then be argued that there is no need to provide for any depreciation at all.

(ii) If prices are rising, the replacement cost of the asset will exceed the amount of depreciation provided.

5.16 FRS 15 contains **no detailed guidance** on the calculation of depreciation or the suitability of the various depreciation methods, merely stating the following two **general principles**.

> 'The depreciable amount of a tangible fixed asset should be allocated on a **systematic** basis over its useful economic life. The depreciation method used should reflect as fairly as possible the pattern in which the asset's economic benefits are consumed by the entity. The depreciation charge for each period should be recognised as an expense in the profit and loss account unless it is permitted to be included in the carrying amount of another asset.'

'A variety of methods can be used to allocate the depreciable amount of a tangible fixed asset on a systematic basis over its useful economic life. The method chosen should result in a **depreciation charge throughout the asset's useful** economic life and not just towards the end of its useful economic life or when the asset is falling in value.'

We will therefore consider first the factors affecting depreciation and then proceed to an analysis of the main depreciation methods available.

Factors affecting depreciation

5.17 FRS 15 states that the following factors need to be considered in determining the useful economic life, residual value and depreciation method of an asset.

(a) The **expected usage** of the asset by the entity, assessed by reference to the asset's expected capacity or physical output

(b) The **expected physical deterioration** of the asset through use or effluxion of time; this will depend upon the repair and maintenance programme of the entity both when the asset is in use and when it is idle

(c) **Economic or technological obsolescence**, for example arising from changes or improvements in production, or a change in the market demand for the product or service output of that asset

(d) **Legal or similar limits** on the use of the asset, such as the expiry dates of related leases

5.18 If it becomes clear that the **original estimate** of an asset's useful life was **incorrect**, it should be **revised**. Normally, no adjustment should be made in respect of the depreciation charged in previous years; instead the remaining net book value of the asset should be depreciated over the new estimate of its remaining useful life. If future results could be materially distorted, the adjustment to accumulated depreciation should be recognised in the accounts in accordance with FRS 3 (usually as an exceptional item). FRS 3 is discussed in Chapter 9.

Methods of depreciation

5.19 The **cost of an asset less its residual value is known as the depreciable amount** of the asset. For example, if plant has a five year expected life and the anticipated capital costs are:

	£
Purchase cost	19,000
Delivery	1,500
Installation by own employees	2,700
	23,200

while the residual value at the end of the fifth year is expected to be £3,200, the depreciable amount would be £20,000. Any repair and maintenance costs incurred during the period are written off as running costs in the year in which they are incurred.

5.20 However, if major improvements are made to an asset, thereby increasing its expected life, the depreciable amount should be adjusted. For example, if at the beginning of year 3, £11,000 was spent on technological improvements to the plant so prolonging its expected life by three years (with a residual value of £1,200 at the end of the eighth year), the depreciable amount would be adjusted.

	£
Original depreciable amount	20,000
Less amount already depreciated (say 2 × £4,000)	8,000
	12,000
Add fall in residual value £(3,200 – 1,200)	2,000
	14,000
Add further capital expenditure	11,000
New depreciable amount	25,000

The new depreciable amount would be written off over the remaining useful life of the asset, 6 years.

5.21 There are a number of different methods of calculating the depreciation charge for an accounting period, each giving a different result. The most common are:

- Straight line method
- Reducing balance method
- Sum of digits method
- Machine hour method
- Revaluation

5.22 The **straight line method** is the simplest and the most commonly used in practice. The **reducing balance** and **sum of digits** methods are accelerated methods which lead to a higher charge in earlier years. Since repair and maintenance costs tend to increase as assets grow older these methods lead to a more even allocation of total fixed asset costs (depreciation plus maintenance).

5.23 The **machine hour method** is suited to assets which depreciate primarily through use rather than through passing of time. Such assets might include mines and quarries, which are subject to gradual exhaustion of the minerals that they contain, and also delivery lorries, which may be argued to depreciate in accordance with the number of miles travelled.

5.24 Neither the CA nor FRS 15 prescribes which method should be used. **Management** must **exercise its judgement**. Furthermore, FRS 15 states:

> 'The useful economic life of a tangible fixed asset should be **reviewed at the end of each reporting period** and revised if expectations are significantly different from previous estimates. If a useful economic life is revised, the carrying amount of the tangible fixed asset at the date of revision should be **depreciated over the revised remaining useful economic life.**'

5.25 FRS 15 also states that a **change from one method** of providing depreciation **to another** is permissible only on the grounds that the new method will give a **fairer presentation** of the results and of the financial position. Such a change does **not**, however, constitute a **change of accounting policy**; the carrying amount of the tangible fixed asset is depreciated using the revised method over the remaining useful economic life, beginning in the period in which the change is made.

5.26 Tangible fixed assets other than non depreciable land, should be **reviewed for impairment** at the end of the reporting period where:

- No depreciation is charged on the grounds that it would immaterial
- The estimated remaining useful economic life exceeds 50 years.

The review should be in accordance with FRS 11 *Impairment of fixed assets and goodwill* (this is not within the scope of your Paper 6 syllabus).

Part A: Introduction to financial reporting

5.27 Many companies carry fixed assets in their balance sheets at revalued amounts, particularly in the case of freehold buildings. When this is done, the **depreciation charge** should be calculated **on the basis of the revalued amount** (not the original cost), in spite of the alternative accounting rules in CA 1985.

5.28 Where the tangible fixed asset comprises two or more major components with substantially different useful economic lives, each component should be accounted for separately for depreciation purposes and depreciated over its individual useful economic life.

5.29 You still need to charge depreciation if there is subsequent expenditure on a tangible fixed asset that maintains or enhances the previously assessed standard of performance of the asset.

Disclosure requirements of FRS 15

5.30 The following information should be disclosed separately in the financial statements for each class of tangible fixed assets.

(a) The depreciation methods used

(b) The useful economic lives or the depreciation rates used

(c) Total depreciation charged for the period

(d) Where material, the financial effect of a change during the period in either the estimate of useful economic lives or the estimate of residual values

(e) The cost or revalued amount at the beginning of the financial period and at the balance sheet date

(f) The cumulative amount of provisions for depreciation or impairment at the beginning of the financial period and at the balance sheet date

(g) A reconciliation of the movements, separately disclosing additions, disposals, revaluations, transfers, depreciation, impairment losses, and reversals of past impairment losses written back in the financial period

(h) The net carrying amount at the beginning of the financial period and at the balance sheet date

5.31 Where there has been a change in the depreciation method used, the effect, if material, should be disclosed in the period of change. The reason for the change should also be disclosed.

Activity 2.5

The Furrow Manufacturing Company has recently purchased a machine for £256,000 and expects to use it for three years at the end of which period it will be sold as scrap for £4,000.

Required:

(a) Calculate in respect of each of the three years the annual depreciation charge using each of the following methods:

 (i) Straight line
 (ii) Reducing balance (at 75% per annum).

(b) Suppose that the Furrow Manufacturing Company adopted the reducing balance method and depreciated the machine for one year; then at the end of the following year the company decided to change from the reducing balance method to the straight line method. Indicate how the machine should appear in the balance sheet at the end of its second year (including any notes relating thereto) assuming that all the original estimates had proved accurate, and bearing in mind the requirements of FRS 15.

Activity 2.6

Annette Book is the financial controller of a medium-sized publishing company. The managing director, Eddie Torial, is a man of sound literary judgement and marketing instinct, but has no accountancy training. Annette has received from him the following note.

'I understand that we have to provide "depreciation" on all our fixed assets except land. This is going to come out of our profit, so there has to be a reason for it. Could you answer the following questions?'

(a) Why do we provide depreciation?

(b) What exactly is net book value? (I think I know roughly what it is.)

(c) Why do we sometimes use the reducing balance method and not the straight line method?

Required

Write Annette's reply to Eddie, addressing each of the above queries.

---

6 REVALUATIONS

6.1 For freehold property which is in operational use, the principle laid down in FRS 15 is that since **buildings have a finite useful life**, a part of their **cost must be charged against profit each year,** in order to be consistent with the accruals concept.

6.2 Although **freehold land does not normally require a provision for depreciation** (unless it is subject to depletion, for example where mineral resources are extracted) **buildings on that land have a limited life** which may be affected by technological and environmental changes. **Buildings should therefore be depreciated.**

6.3 Where there is a freehold property this means that the land element in its cost will not be depreciated, but the building element of cost must be depreciated.

6.4 As previously discussed, a property's NBV may be well below its market value. A business may, therefore, decide to revalue the property to its market value. When a property is revalued, depreciation should be charged to write off the new valuation over the estimated remaining useful life of the building (see paragraph 2.39).

6.5 The gain on revaluation cannot go to the profit and loss account, as it has not been realised. Therefore the 'gain' is transferred to a revaluation reserve (see paragraphs 4.10 to 4.12).

6.6 EXAMPLE: REVALUATION OF A FREEHOLD BUILDING

A freehold building is purchased on 1 January 20X4 for £20,000. Its estimated useful life is 20 years and it is depreciated at the rate of £1,000 per annum in each of the years ending 31 December 20X4 and 20X5. On 1 January 20X6 a professional valuer estimates the value of the building at £54,000.

On the assumption that the revaluation is to be incorporated into the books of account, and that the original estimate of useful life was correct, show the relevant ledger accounts for the period 1 January 20X4 to 31 December 20X6.

Part A: Introduction to financial reporting

6.7 SOLUTION

FREEHOLD BUILDING AT COST

		£			£
1.1.X4	Purchase	20,000	31.12.X4	Balance c/d	20,000
1.1.X5	Balance b/d	20,000	31.12.X5	Balance c/d	20,000
1.1.X6	Balance b/d	20,000			
	Revaluation	34,000	31.12.X6	Balance c/d	54,000
		54,000			54,000

DEPRECIATION ON FREEHOLD BUILDINGS

		£			£
31.12.X4	Balance c/d	1,000	31.12.X4	P & L account	1,000
			1.1.X5	Balance b/d	1,000
31.12.X5	Balance c/d	2,000	31.12.X5	P & L account	1,000
		2,000			2,000
1.1.X6	Revaluation	2,000	1.1.X6	Balance b/d	2,000
			31.12.X6	P & L account	
31.12.X6	Balance c/d	3,000		(£54,000/18 years)	3,000
		5,000			5,000

REVALUATION RESERVE

		£			£
			1.1.X6	Freehold building	34,000
31.12.X6	Balance c/d	36,000		Dep'n on freehold	2,000
		36,000			36,000

Note that the revaluation surplus is the difference between valuation (£54,000) and net book value at the time of revaluation (£20,000 – £2,000 = £18,000). The revalued amount, £54,000, must then be depreciated over the asset's remaining estimated useful life of 18 years, ie £3,000 per annum.

BALANCE SHEET AS AT 31.12.X6 (EXTRACTS)

(a) **Revaluation**

		£
Fixed assets		
Freehold buildings:	valuation	54,000
	accumulated depreciation	(3,000)
	NBV	51,000
Capital and reserves		
Revaluation reserves		36,000

(b) **If revaluation had not taken place**

		£
Fixed assets		
Freehold buildings:	cost	20,000
	accumulated depreciation (3 years)	(3,000)
	NBV	17,000

Note that the balance sheet under (a) is effectively £15,000 (£51,000 – £36,000), compared to £17,000 under (b). This difference of £2,000 is due to the increased depreciation after the revaluation (old rate of depreciation £1,000 pa, new rate £3,000 pa).

FRS 15 rules

6.8 An entity may adopt a policy of **revaluing tangible fixed assets**. Where this policy is adopted **it must be applied consistently** to all assets of the same class.

2: Fixed assets and stocks

> **KEY TERM**
>
> A **class of fixed assets** is 'a category of tangible fixed assets having a similar nature, function or use in the business of an entity'. (FRS 15)

6.9 Where an asset is revalued its carrying amount should be its **current value** as at the balance sheet date, current value being the **lower of replacement cost and recoverable amount**.

6.10 To achieve the above, the standard states that a **full valuation** should be carried out **at least every five years** with an **interim valuation in year 3**. If it is likely that there has been a material change in value, interim valuations in years 1, 2 and 4 should also be carried out.

6.11 A full valuation should be conducted by either a **qualified external valuer** or a **qualified internal valuer**, provided that the valuation has been subject to review by a qualified external valuer. An interim valuation may be carried out by either an external or internal valuer.

6.12 For certain types of assets (other than properties) eg company cars, there may be an active second hand market for the asset or appropriate indices may exist, so that the directors can establish the asset's value with reasonable reliability and therefore avoid the need to use the services of a qualified valuer.

Valuation basis

6.13 The following valuation bases should be used for properties that are not impaired.

(a) **Specialised properties** should be valued on the basis of **depreciated replacement cost**.

Specialised properties are those which, due to their specialised nature, are rarely, if ever, sold on the open market for single occupation for a continuation of their existing use, except as part of a sale of the business in occupation. Eg oil refineries, chemical works, power stations, or schools, colleges and universities where there is no competing market demand from other organisations using these types of property in the locality.

(b) **Non-specialised properties** should be valued on the basis of **existing use value** (EUV).

(c) **Properties surplus** to an entity's requirements should be valued on the basis of **open market value** (OMV).

6.14 Where there is an indication of impairment, an impairment review should be carried out in accordance with FRS 11. (FRS 11 is outside the scope of the Paper 6 syllabus.) The asset should be recorded at the lower of revalued amount (as above) and recoverable amount.

6.15 Tangible fixed assets other than properties should be valued using market value or, if not obtainable, depreciated replacement cost.

> **Exam alert**
>
> For your exam, you should be able to discuss the FRS 15 rules. Practically, you only need to know how to treat revaluations in the ledger accounts, how to set up a revaluation reserve and how to calculate revised depreciation.

Part A: Introduction to financial reporting

7 STOCK VALUATION: REVISION

7.1 This area should be familiar to you from your Paper 3 (B1) studies.

> **Exam alert**
>
> SSAP 9 *Stocks and long-term contracts* is examinable but long-term contracts will not be examined.

7.2 There are **several methods** which, in theory, might be used for the valuation of stock items.

(a) Stocks might be valued at their **expected selling price**.

(b) Stocks might be valued at their expected selling price, less any costs still to be incurred in getting them ready for sale and then selling them. This amount is referred to as the **Net Realisable Value** (NRV) of the stocks.

(c) Stocks might be valued at their **historical cost** (the cost at which they were originally bought).

(d) Stocks might be valued at the amount it would cost to replace them. This amount is referred to as the **current replacement cost** of stocks.

7.3 Current replacement costs are not used in the type of accounts dealt with in this Interactive Text, and so are not considered further.

7.4 The use of selling prices in stock valuation is ruled out because this would create a profit for the business before the stock has been sold.

7.5 A simple example might help to explain this. Suppose that a trader buys two items of stock, each costing £100. He can sell them for £140 each, but in the accounting period we shall consider, he has only sold one of them. The other is closing stock in hand.

7.6 Since only one item has been sold, you might think it is common sense that profit ought to be £40. But if closing stock is valued at selling price, profit would be £80 as profit would be taken on the closing stock as well.

	£	£
Sales		140
Opening stock	-	
Purchases (2 × 100)	200	
	200	
Less closing stock (at selling price)	140	
Cost of sale		60
Profit		80

This would contradict the accounting concept of prudence, as it involves claiming a profit before the item has actually been sold.

7.7 The same objection *usually* applies to the use of NRV in stock valuation. Say that the item purchased for £100 requires £5 of further expenditure in getting it ready for sale and then selling it (for example, £5 of processing costs and distribution costs). If its expected selling price is £140, its NRV is £(140 – 5) = £135. To value it at £135 in the balance sheet would still be to anticipate a profit of £35.

7.8 We are left with historical cost as the normal basis of stock valuation. The only times when historical cost is not used is in the exceptional cases when the prudence concept requires a lower value to be used.

7.9 Staying with the example in paragraph 9.6, suppose that the market in this kind of product suddenly slumps and the item's expected selling price is only £90. The item's NRV is then £(90 − 5) = £85 and the business has in effect made a loss of £15 (£100 − £85). The prudence concept requires that losses should be recognised as soon as they are foreseen. This can be achieved by valuing the stock item in the balance sheet at its NRV of £85.

7.10 The argument developed above suggests that the rule to follow is that stocks should be valued at cost, or if lower, net realisable value.

> **RULE TO LEARN**
>
> SSAP 9 *Stocks and long-term contracts* states that **stock should be valued at the lower of cost and net realisable value.**

(a) **Cost** is that expenditure which has been incurred in the normal course of business in bringing the product or service to its present location and condition. This expenditure should include:

   (i) Cost of purchase (including import duties, transport and handling costs and any other directly attributable costs, less trade discounts, rebates and subsidies)

   (ii) Any costs of conversion appropriate to that location and condition (including direct labour and expenses, and attributable production overheads)

(b) **Net realisable value** is the actual or estimated selling price (net of trade but before settlement discounts) less:

   (i) All further costs to completion; an
   (ii) All costs to be incurred in marketing, selling and distributing

Applying the basic valuation rule

7.11 If a business has many stock items on hand, the comparison of cost and NRV should theoretically be carried out for each item separately. It is not sufficient to compare the total cost of all stock items with their total NRV. An example will show why.

7.12 Suppose a company has four items of stock on hand at the end of its accounting period. Their cost and NRVs are as follows.

Stock item	Cost	NRV	Lower of cost/NRV
	£	£	£
1	27	32	27
2	14	8	8
3	43	55	43
4	29	40	29
	113	135	107

7.13 It would be incorrect to compare total costs (£113) with total NRV (£135) and to state stocks at £113 in the balance sheet. The company can foresee a loss of £6 on item 2 and this should be recognised. If the four items are taken together in total the loss on item 2 is masked by the anticipated profits on the other items. By performing the cost/NRV comparison for each item separately, the prudent valuation of £107 can be derived. This is the value which should appear in the balance sheet. This is an example of the fifth accounting principle introduced by CA 1985 and mentioned in Chapter 4: the **separate valuation principle**.

Part A: Introduction to financial reporting

7.14 However, for a company with large amounts of stock this procedure may be impracticable. In this case it is acceptable to group similar items into categories and perform the comparison of cost and NRV category by category, rather than item by item.

7.15 So have we now solved the problem of how a business should value its stocks? It seems that all the business has to do is to choose the lower of cost and net realisable value. This is true as far as it goes, but there is one further problem, perhaps not so easy to foresee: for a given item of stock, what was the cost?

Determining the purchase cost

7.16 Stock may be raw materials or components bought from suppliers, finished goods which have been made by the business but not yet sold, or work in the process of production, but only part-completed (this type of stock is called **work in progress** or WIP). It will simplify matters, however, if we think about the historical cost of purchased raw materials and components, which ought to be their purchase price.

7.17 A business may be continually purchasing consignments of a particular component. As each consignment is received from suppliers it is stored in the appropriate bin or on the appropriate shelf or pallet, where it will be mingled with previous consignments. When the storekeeper issues components to production he will simply pull out from the bin the nearest components to hand, which may have arrived in the latest consignment or in an earlier consignment or in several different consignments. Our concern is to devise a pricing technique, a rule of thumb which we can use to attribute a cost to each of the components issued from stores.

7.18 There are several techniques which are used in practice.

  (a) **FIFO (first in, first out).** Using this technique, we assume that components are used in the order in which they are received from suppliers. The components issued are deemed to have formed part of the oldest consignment still unused and are costed accordingly.

  (b) **LIFO (last in, first out).** This involves the opposite assumption, that components issued to production originally formed part of the most recent delivery, while older consignments lie in the bin undisturbed.

  (c) **Average cost.** As purchase prices change with each new consignment, the average price of components in the bin is constantly changed. Each component in the bin at any moment is assumed to have been purchased at the average price of all components in the bin at that moment.

  (d) **Standard cost.** A pre-determined standard cost is applied to all stock items. If this standard price differs from prices actually paid during the period it will be necessary to write off the difference as a 'variance' in the profit and loss account.

  (e) **Replacement cost.** The arbitrary assumption is made that the cost at which a stock unit was purchased is the amount it would cost to replace it. This is often (but not necessarily) the unit cost of stocks purchased in the next consignment *following* the issue of the component to production. For this reason, a method which produces similar results to replacement costs is called NIFO (next in, first out).

7.19 Any or all of these methods might provide a suitable basis for valuing stocks. But it is worth mentioning here that if you are preparing financial accounts you would normally expect to use FIFO or average cost for the balance sheet valuation of stock. SSAP 9 specifically discourages the use of LIFO and replacement costs. Nevertheless, you should know about all of the methods so that you can discuss the differences between them.

> **Key learning points**
>
> - **Capital expenditure** is expenditure which results in the acquisition of fixed assets.
>
> - **Revenue expenditure** is expenditure incurred for the purpose of the business or for maintenance of fixed assets.
>
> - This has been a long chapter with a lot to take in, so do not be surprised if it has taken you longer than you expected to work through it. Now that you have finally reached the end, you should understand the following points.
>
> - The cost of a fixed asset, less its estimated residual value, is allocated fairly between accounting periods by means of **depreciation**. The provision for depreciation is both:
>   - Charged against profit
>   - Deducted from the value of the fixed asset in the balance sheet.
>
> - There are several different methods of depreciation, but the **straight line method** and the **reducing balance method** are most commonly used in practice. You also need to know how to use the **sum of the digits method** of depreciation. Every method described in this chapter allocates the total depreciable amount between accounting periods, although in different ways.
>
> - When a fixed asset is **revalued**, depreciation is charged on the residual amount.
>
> - When a fixed asset is sold, there is likely to be a **profit or loss on disposal**. This is the difference between the net sale price of the asset and its net book value at the time of disposal.
>
> - You should also know how to handle the double entry bookkeeping for providing for depreciation, and for the disposal of fixed assets.
>
> - A number of accounting regulations on the valuation and disclosure of fixed assets are contained in the Companies Act 1985. In the case of tangible fixed assets, these regulations are supplemented by the provisions of FRS 15 on tangible fixed assets.
>
> - SSAP 9 requires that stock be valued at the lower of cost and net realisable value.

Quick quiz

1 Which of the following is an item of capital expenditure?

    A   Cost of goods sold
    B   Purchase of a machine
    C   Repairs to a machine
    D   Wages cost

2 Which of the following statements regarding fixed asset accounting is correct?

    A   All fixed assets should be revalued each year.

    B   Fixed assets may be revalued at the discretion of management. Once revaluation has occurred it must be repeated regularly for all fixed assets in a class.

    C   Management can choose which fixed assets in a class of fixed assets should be revalued.

    D   Fixed assets should be revalued to reflect rising prices.

3 Which of the following statements regarding depreciation is correct?

    A   All fixed assets must be depreciated.

    B   Straight line depreciation is usually the most appropriate method of depreciation.

    C   A change in the chosen depreciation method is a change in accounting policy which should be disclosed.

    D   Depreciation charges must be based upon the depreciable amount.

Part A: Introduction to financial reporting

4 What is an asset's net book value?

5 Give three common depreciation methods.

6 A fixed asset (cost £10,000, depreciation £7,500) is given in part exchange for a new asset costing £20,500. The agreed trade-in value was £3,500. The profit and loss account will include?

    A   A loss on disposal £1,000
    B   A profit on disposal £1,000
    C   A loss on purchase of a new asset £3,500
    D   A profit on disposal £3,500

7 SSAP 9 encourages LIFO for valuing stocks. *True or false?*

Answers to quick quiz

1   B.   This results in the acquisition of a fixed asset. All the others are revenue expenditure.

2   B   Correct.
       A   Fixed assets may be revalued, there is no requirement to do so in FRS 15.
       C   Incorrect, all fixed assets in a class must be revalued.
       D   Incorrect, fixed assets may be reduced in value as well as being increased.

3   D   Correct.
       A   Incorrect, some fixed assets are not depreciated eg land.
       B   Incorrect, management should choose the most appropriate method.
       C   Incorrect, a method change is not a change in accounting policy.

4   Its cost less accumulated depreciation.

5   Straight-line, reducing balance and sum of the digits.

6   B

	£
Net book value at disposal	2,500
Trade-in allowance	3,500
Profit	1,000

7   False.

Answers to activities

Answer 2.1

(a) Capital expenditure.

(b) Depreciation of a fixed asset is a revenue expenditure.

(c) The legal fees associated with the purchase of a property may be added to the purchase price and classified as capital expenditure. The cost of the leasehold premises in the balance sheet of the business will then include the legal fees.

(d) Capital expenditure (enhancing an existing fixed asset).

(e) Revenue expenditure.

(f) Capital income (net of the costs of sale).

(g) Revenue income.

(h) Capital expenditure.

(i) If customs duties are borne by the purchaser of the fixed asset, they may be added to the cost of the machinery and classified as capital expenditure.

(j) Similarly, if carriage costs are paid for by the purchaser of the fixed asset, they may be included in the cost of the fixed asset and classified as capital expenditure.

(k) Installation costs of a fixed asset are also added to the fixed asset's cost and classified as capital expenditure.

(l) Revenue expenditure.

Answer 2.2

(a) Under the straight line method, depreciation for each of the five years is: $\dfrac{£17,000 - £2,000}{5} = £3,000$ pa

(5 × £3,000 = £15,000).

(b) Under the reducing balance method, depreciation for each of the five years is:

Year	Depreciation		
1	35% × £17,000	=	£5,950
2	35% × (£17,000 – £5,950) = 35% × £11,050	=	£3,868
3	35% × (£11,050 – £3,868) = 35% × £7,182	=	£2,514
4	35% × (£7,182 – £2,514) = 35% × £4,668	=	£1,634
5	Balance to bring book value down to £2,000 = £4,668 – £1,634 – £2,000	=	£1,034
			£15,000

(c) The sum of digits is 5+4+3+2+1=15 and the depreciable amount is £15,000 (£17,000 – £2,000).

Year		Depreciation (£)
1	5/15 x £15,000	5,000
2	4/15 x £15,000	4,000
3	3/15 x £15,000	3,000
4	2/15 x £15,000	2,000
5	1/15 x £15,000	1,000
		15,000

Answer 2.3

MACHINERY ACCOUNT

20X7		£	20X7		£
1 Jan	Balance b/f	30,000	31 Mar	Disposal of machinery account	15,000
			1 Dec	Disposal of machinery account	15,000
		30,000			30,000

PROVISION FOR DEPRECIATION OF MACHINERY

20X7		£	20X7		£
31 Mar	Disposal of machinery account*	6,750	1 Jan	Balance b/f	12,000
1 Dec	Disposal of machinery account**	8,750	31 Dec	P & L account***	3,500
		15,500			15,500

* Depreciation at date of disposal £6,000 + £750
** Depreciation at date of disposal £6,000 + £2,750
*** Depreciation charge for the year = £750 + £2,750

Part A: Introduction to financial reporting

DISPOSAL OF MACHINERY

20X7			£	20X7		£
31 Mar	Machinery account		15,000	31 Mar	Debtor account (sale price)	8,000
				31 Mar	Provision for depreciation	6,750
1 Dec	Machinery		15,000	1 Dec	Cash (sale price)	2,500
				1 Dec	Provision for depreciation	8,750
				31 Dec	P & L account (loss on disposal)	4,000
			30,000			30,000

You should be able to calculate that there was a loss on the first disposal of £250, and on the second disposal of £3,750, giving a total loss of £4,000.

Workings

1. At 1 January 20X7, accumulated depreciation on the machines will be

    2 machines × 2 years × $\dfrac{£15,000}{5}$ per machine pa = £12,000,

    or £6,000 per machine

2. Monthly depreciation is $\dfrac{£3,000}{12}$ = £250 per machine per month

3. The machines are disposed of in 20X7.

    (a) On 31 March - after 3 months of the year.
    Depreciation for the year on the machine = 3 months × £250 = £750.

    (b) On 1 December - after 11 months of the year.
    Depreciation for the year on the machine = 11 months × £250 = £2,750

Answer 2.4

(b) A factory building may require a new roof every 10 years, whereas the factory itself may have a useful economic life of 50 years. In this case the roof will be treated as a separate asset and depreciated over 10 years and the expenditure incurred in replacing the roof will be accounted for as an addition and the carrying amount of the replaced asset removed from the balance sheet.

(c) An aircraft may be required by law to be overhauled every three years. Unless the overhaul is carried out the aircraft will not be licensed to fly. The entity will reflect the need to overhaul the aircraft by depreciating an amount equivalent to the estimated cost of the overhaul over the three year period. The cost of the overhaul will then be capitalised because it restores the economic value of the aircraft.

Answer 2.5

(a) The depreciable amount of the machine is £(256,000 – 4,000) = £252,000

   (i) The annual depreciation charge $\dfrac{£252,000}{3}$ = £84,000

   (ii) The annual depreciation charge is as follows.

		NBV £'000	Charge for year £'000
Year 1:	cost	256	
	depreciation (75%)	(192)	192
	net book value	64	
Year 2:	depreciation (75%)	(48)	48
	net book value	16	
Year 3:	depreciation (75%)	(12)	12
	net book value	4	
			252

(b) FRS 15 states that if the depreciation method is changed it is unnecessary to adjust amounts charged in previous years. Instead, the new method is simply applied to the unamortised cost of the asset over its remaining useful life.

At the end of year 1, the machine's net book value (after one year's depreciation on the reducing balance method) is £64,000 (see part (a)). For year 2, it is decided to use the straight line method over the remaining two years of useful life. The charge for depreciation in year 2 will therefore be £30,000 ((£64,000 – £4,000) ÷ 2) and the asset's net book value at the end of year 2 will be £34,000.

FURROW MANUFACTURING COMPANY
BALANCE SHEET AT END OF YEAR 2 (EXTRACT)

		£
Fixed assets		
Tangible assets		
Plant and machinery:	cost	256,000
	depreciation	(222,000)
		34,000

Answer 2.6

To: Eddie Torial
    Managing Director
From: Annette Book
Date: 5 March 1997
Subject: Depreciation

(a) The accounts of a business try to recognise that the cost of a fixed asset is gradually consumed as the asset wears out. This is done by gradually writing off the asset's cost in the profit and loss account over several accounting periods. This process is known as depreciation, and is an example of the matching concept. FRS 15 *Tangible fixed assets* requires that depreciation should be allocated to charge against income a fair proportion of cost or valuation of the asset to each accounting period expected to benefit from its use.

With regard to the matching principle, it is fair that the profits should be reduced by the depreciation charge; this is not an arbitrary exercise. Depreciation is not, as is sometime supposed, an attempt to set aside funds to purchase new fixed assets when required. Depreciation is not generally provided on freehold land because it does not 'wear out' (unless it is held for mining etc).

(b) In simple terms the net book value of an asset is the cost of an asset less the 'accumulated depreciation', that is all depreciation charged so far. It should be emphasised that the main purpose of charging depreciation is to ensure that profits are fairly reported. Thus depreciation is concerned with the profit and loss account rather than the balance sheet. In consequence the net book value figure in the balance sheet can be quite arbitrary. In particular, it does not necessarily bear any relation to the market value of an asset and is of little use for planning and decision making.

An obvious example of the disparity between net book value and market value is found in the case of buildings, which may be worth more than ten times as much as their net book value.

(c) The reducing balance method of depreciation is used instead of the straight line method when it is considered fair to allocate a greater proportion of the total depreciable amount to the earlier years and a lower proportion to the later years on the assumption that the benefits obtained by the business from using the asset decline over time.

In favour of this method it may be argued that it links the depreciation charge to the costs of maintaining and running the asset. In the early years these costs are low and the depreciation charge is high, while in later years this is reversed.

Now try Question 2 in the Exam Question Bank at the end of the Text.

Chapter 3 Review of basic financial accounts

Chapter topic list

1   Revision of bad and doubtful debts
2   Revision of sole trader accounts preparation

This chapter is background and revision for the other topics.

Part A: Introduction to financial reporting

1 REVISION OF BAD AND DOUBTFUL DEBTS

> **Exam alert**
>
> You have covered bad and doubtful debts in detail in Paper 3 (or B1), so only a summary is given here. Look back to your earlier studies if you're in doubt.

Bad debts written off: ledger accounting entries

1.1 For bad debts written off, there is a bad debts account. The double-entry bookkeeping is fairly straightforward, but there are two separate transactions to record.

  (a) When it is decided that a particular debt will not be paid, the customer is no longer called an outstanding debtor, and becomes a bad debt. We therefore:

  DEBIT   Bad debts account (expense)
  CREDIT Debtors account

  (b) At the end of the accounting period, the balance on the bad debts account is transferred to the P & L ledger account (like all other expense accounts):

  DEBIT   P & L account
  CREDIT Bad debts account.

1.2 Where a bad debt is subsequently recovered in the same accounting period, you simply reverse the entries in (a) above and so there will be no need to carry out the entries in (b) above.

  DEBIT   Debtors account
  CREDIT Bad debts account (expense)

1.3 However, where a bad debt is subsequently recovered in a later accounting period the accounting entries will be as follows.

  DEBIT   Debtors account
  CREDIT Bad debts recovered (income in the P & L a/c)

1.4 EXAMPLE: BAD DEBTS WRITTEN OFF

At 1 October 20X5 a business had total outstanding debts of £8,600. During the year to 30 September 20X6:

(a) Credit sales amounted to £44,000.

(b) Payments from various debtors amounted to £49,000.

(c) Two debts, for £180 and £420, were declared bad and the customers are no longer purchasing goods from the company. These are to be written off.

Required

Prepare the debtors account and the bad debts account for the year.

1.5 SOLUTION

DEBTORS

	£		£
Opening balance b/f	8,600	Cash	49,000
Sales	44,000	Bad debts	180
		Bad debts	420
		Closing balance c/f	3,000
	52,600		52,600
Opening balance b/f	3,000		

BAD DEBTS

	£		£
Debtors	180	P & L a/c: bad debts written off	600
Debtors	420		
	600		600

1.6 In the sales ledger, personal accounts of the customers whose debts are bad will be taken off the ledger. The business should then take steps to ensure that it does not sell goods on credit to those customers again.

Provision for doubtful debts: ledger accounting entries

1.7 A provision for doubtful debts is rather different. A business might know from past experience that, say 2% of debtors' balances are unlikely to be collected. It would then be considered prudent to make a general provision of 2%. It may be that no particular customers are regarded as suspect and so it is not possible to write off any individual customer balances as bad debts. The procedure is then to leave the total debtors balances completely untouched, but to open up a provision account by the following entries:

DEBIT   Doubtful debts account (expense)
CREDIT   Provision for doubtful debts

> **IMPORTANT!**
> When preparing a balance sheet, the credit balance on the provision account is deducted from the total debit balances in the debtors ledger.

1.8 **In subsequent years, adjustments may be needed to the amount of the provision.** The procedure to be followed then is as follows.

(a) Calculate the new provision required.

(b) Compare it with the existing balance on the provision account (ie the balance b/f from the previous accounting period).

(c) Calculate increase or decrease required.

   (i) If a higher provision is required now:

   CREDIT   Provision for doubtful debts
   DEBIT   P & L account

   with the amount of the increase.

   (ii) If a lower provision is needed now than before:

   DEBIT   Provision for doubtful debts
   CREDIT   P & L account

   with the amount of the decrease.

Part A: Introduction to financial reporting

1.9 EXAMPLE: ACCOUNTING ENTRIES FOR PROVISION FOR DOUBTFUL DEBTS

Alex Gullible has total debtors' balances outstanding at 31 December 20X2 of £28,000. He believes that about 1% of these balances will not be collected and wishes to make an appropriate provision. Before now, he has not made any provision for doubtful debts at all.

On 31 December 20X3 his debtors balances amount to £40,000. His experience during the year has convinced him that a provision of 5% should be made.

What accounting entries should Alex make on 31 December 20X2 and 31 December 20X3, and what figures for debtors will appear in his balance sheets as at those dates?

1.10 SOLUTION

At 31 December 20X2

Provision required = 1% × £28,000
= £280

Alex will make the following entries:

DEBIT	P & L account (doubtful debts)	£280	
CREDIT	Provision for doubtful debts		£280

In the balance sheet debtors will appear as follows under current assets.

	£
Sales ledger balances	28,000
Less provision for doubtful debts	280
	27,720

At 31 December 20X3

Following the procedure described above, Alex will calculate as follows.

	£
Provision required now (5% × £40,000)	2,000
Existing provision	(280)
∴ Additional provision required	1,720

He will make the following entries:

DEBIT	P & L account (doubtful debts)	£1,720	
CREDIT	Provision for doubtful debts		£1,720

The provision account will by now appear as follows.

PROVISION FOR DOUBTFUL DEBTS

20X2			£	20X2		£
31 Dec	Balance c/f		280	31 Dec	P & L account	280
20X3				20X3		
31 Dec	Balance c/f		2,000	1 Jan	Balance b/f	280
				31 Dec	P & L account	1,720
			2,000			2,000
				20X4		
				1 Jan	Balance b/f	2,000

For the balance sheet debtors will be valued as follows.

	£
Sales ledger balances	40,000
Less provision for doubtful debts	2,000
	38,000

1.11 In practice, it is unnecessary to show the total debtors balances and the provision as separate items in the balance sheet. A balance sheet would normally show only the net figure

(**£27,720 in 20X2, £38,000 in 20X3**). **If you do show the net figure show the set off of the provision as a working.**

1.12 Now try the following activity on provision for doubtful debts for yourself. At this level, you should get it completely correct.

Activity 3.1

Horace Goodrunning fears that his business will suffer an increase in defaulting debtors in the future and so he decides to make a provision for doubtful debts of 2% of outstanding debtors at the balance sheet date from 28 February 20X6. On 28 February 20X8, Horace decides that the provision has been over-estimated and he reduces it to 1% of outstanding debtors. Outstanding debtors balances at the various balance sheet dates are as follows.

	£
28.2.20X6	15,200
28.2.20X7	17,100
28.2.20X8	21,400

You are required to show extracts from the following accounts for each of the three years above.

(a) Debtors
(b) Provision for doubtful debts
(c) Profit and loss

Show how debtors would appear in the balance sheet at the end of each year.

---

2 REVISION OF SOLE TRADER ACCOUNTS PREPARATION

2.1 Paper 6 assumes knowledge of double entry bookkeeping and basic financial accounts preparation. Have a go at **all** the following activities. If you make any mistakes re-work those parts of the question. If you are unsure about anything, look back to your earlier study material.

Exam alert

These examples are useful for revision purposes only. Sole trader accounts will not be tested in the real exam.

Activity 3.2

James opened a shop on 1 July 20X2 and during his first month in business, the following transactions occurred.

20X2
- 1 July James contributes £20,000 in cash to the business out of his private bank account.
- 2 July He opens a business bank account by transferring £18,000 of his cash in hand.
- 5 July Some premises are rented, the rent being £500 per quarter payable in advance in cash.
- 6 July James buys some second-hand shop equipment for £300 paying by cheque.
- 9 July He purchases some goods for resale for £1,000 paying for them in cash.
- 10 July Seddon supplies him with £2,000 of goods on credit.
- 20 July James returns £200 of the goods to Seddon.
- 23 July Cash sales for the week amount to £1,500.
- 26 July James sells goods on credit for £1,000 to Frodsham.
- 28 July Frodsham returns £500 of the goods to James.
- 31 July James settles his account with Seddon by cheque, and is able to claim a cash discount of 10%.
- 31 July Frodsham sends James a cheque for £450 in settlement of his account, any balance remaining on his account being treated as a cash discount.

Part A: Introduction to financial reporting

31 July During his initial trading, James has discovered that some of his shop equipment is not suitable, but he is fortunate in being able to dispose of it for £50 in cash. There was no profit or loss on disposal.

31 July He withdraws £150 in cash as part payment towards a holiday for his wife.

Required

(a) Enter the above transactions in James' ledger accounts, balance off the accounts and bring down the balances as at 1 August 20X2.

(b) Extract a trial balance as at 31 July 20X2.

Activity 3.3

Spark has been trading for a number of years as an electrical appliance retailer and repairer in premises which he rents at an annual rate of £1,500 payable in arrears. Balances appearing in his books at 1 January 20X1 were as follows.

	£	£
Capital account		1,808
Motor van		1,200
Fixtures and fittings		806
Provision for depreciation on motor van		720
Provisions for depreciation on fixtures and fittings		250
Stock at cost		366
Debtors for credit sales		
Brown	160	
Blue	40	
Stripe	20	
		220
Cash at bank		672
Cash in hand		5
Loan from Flex		250
Creditors for supplies		
Live	143	
Negative	80	
Earth	73	
		296
Amount owing for electricity		45
Rates paid in advance		100

Although Sparks has three credit customers the majority of his sales and services are for cash, out of which he pays various expenses before banking the balance.

The following transactions took place during the first four months of 20X1.

	January £	February £	March £	April £
Suppliers' invoices				
Live	468	570	390	602
Negative	-	87	103	64
Earth	692	-	187	-
Capital introduced	-	500	-	-
Bankings of cash (from cash sales)	908	940	766	1,031
Expenditure out of cash sales before banking				
Drawings	130	120	160	150
Stationery	12	14	26	21
Travelling	6	10	11	13
Petrol and van repairs	19	22	37	26
Sundry expenses	5	4	7	3
Postage	12	10	15	19
Cleaner's wages	60	60	65	75
Goods invoiced to credit customers				
Brown	66	22	10	12
Blue	120	140	130	180
Stripe	44	38	20	48
Cheque payments (other than those to suppliers)				
Telephone	40	49	59	66
Electricity	62	47	20	106
Rates	-	-	220	-
Motor van (1 February 20X1)	-	800	-	-
Unbanked at the end of April	-	-	-	12

Spark pays for goods by cheque one month after receipt of invoice, and receives a settlement discount of 15% from each supplier.

Credit customers also pay by cheque one month after receipt of invoice, and are given a settlement discount of 10% of the invoice price.

Required

(a) Write up the ledger accounts of Spark for the four months to 30 April 20X1, and extract a trial balance after balancing off the accounts.

(b) Prepare:

   (i) A trading and profit and loss account for the four months
   (ii) A balance sheet on 30 April 20X1

   after dealing with the following matters.

   (i) The payment of £800 for a new motor van represents the balance paid to the garage after being granted a part-exchange value of £500 on the old van.

   (ii) Depreciation is provided at the rate of 20% per annum on the cost of motor vans and at the rate of 10% on the cost of fixtures and fittings. No depreciation is to be provided in the period of disposal.

   (iii) Interest on the loan from Flex is to be accrued at 10% per annum and credited to his account.

   (iv) Amounts owing at 30 April 20X1 were electricity £22, and telephone £15. The payment for rates was for six months in advance from 1 March.

   (v) Included in the payments for telephone was one of Spark's private bills of £37 which is to be charged to him.

   (vi) Stock at cost on 30 April 20X1 amounted to £390.

Activity 3.4

Donald Brown, a sole trader, extracted the following trial balance on 31 December 20X0.

TRIAL BALANCE AS AT 31 DECEMBER 20X0

	Debit £	Credit £
Capital at 1 January 20X0		26,094
Debtors	42,737	
Cash in hand	1,411	
Creditors		35,404
Fixtures and fittings at cost	42,200	
Discounts allowed	1,304	
Discounts received		1,175
Stock at 1 January 20X0	18,460	
Sales		491,620
Purchases	387,936	
Motor vehicles at cost	45,730	
Lighting and heating	6,184	
Motor expenses	2,862	
Rent	8,841	
General expenses	7,413	
Balance at bank		19,861
Provision for depreciation		
Fixtures and fitting		2,200
Motor vehicles		15,292
Drawings	26,568	
	591,646	591,646

The following information as at 31 December is also available.

(a) £218 is owing for motor expenses.

(b) £680 has been prepaid for rent.

Part A: Introduction to financial reporting

(c) Depreciation is to be provided of the year as follows.

Motor vehicles: 20% on cost
Fixtures and fittings: 10% reducing balance method

(d) Stock at the close of business was valued at £19,926.

Required

Prepare Donald Brown's trading and profit and loss account for the year ended 31 December 20X0 and his balance sheet at that date.

Activity 3.5

The following trial balance has been extracted from the ledger of Herbert Howell, a sole trader, as at 31 May 20X9, the end of his most recent financial year.

HERBERT HOWELL
TRIAL BALANCE AS AT 31 MAY 20X9

	Dr £	Cr £
Property, at cost	90,000	
Equipment, at cost	57,500	
Provisions for depreciation (as at 1 June 20X8)		
property		12,500
equipment		32,500
Stock, as at 1 June 20X8	27,400	
Purchases	259,600	
Sales		405,000
Discounts allowed	3,370	
Discounts received		4,420
Wages and salaries	52,360	
Bad debts	1,720	
Loan interest	1,560	
Carriage out	5,310	
Other operating expenses	38,800	
Trade debtors	46,200	
Trade creditors		33,600
Provision for bad debts		280
Cash on hand	151	
Bank overdraft		14,500
Drawings	28,930	
13% Loan		12,000
Capital, as at 1 June 20X8		98,101
	612,901	612,901

The following additional information as at 31 May 20X9 is available:

(a) Stock as at the close of business was valued at £25,900.

(b) Depreciation for the year ended 31 May 20X9 has yet to be provided as follows:

property - 1% using the straight line method;
equipment - 15% using the straight line method;

(c) Wages and salaries are accrued by £140.

(d) 'Other operating expenses' includes certain expenses prepaid by £500. Other expenses included under this heading are accrued by £200.

(e) The provision for bad debts is to be adjusted so that it is 0.5% of trade debtors as at 31 May 20X9.

(f) 'Purchases' includes goods valued at £1,040 which were withdrawn by Mr Howell for his own personal use.

3: Review of basic financial accounts

Required

Prepare Mr Howell's trading and profit and loss account for the year ended 31 May 20X9 and his balance sheet as at 31 May 20X9.

Activity 3.6

The following trial balance has been extracted from the accounts of Brenda Bailey, a sole trader.

BRENDA BAILEY
TRIAL BALANCE AS AT 30 JUNE 20X9

	Dr £	Cr £
Sales		427,726
Purchases	302,419	
Carriage inwards	476	
Carriage outwards	829	
Wages and salaries	64,210	
Rent and rates	12,466	
Heat and light	4,757	
Stock at 1 July 20X8	15,310	
Drawings	21,600	
Equipment at cost	102,000	
Motor vehicles at cost	43,270	
Provision for depreciation:		
Equipment		22,250
Motor vehicles		8,920
Debtors	50,633	
Creditors		41,792
Bank		3,295
Sundry expenses	8,426	
Cash	477	
Capital		122,890
	626,873	626,873

The following information as at 30 June 20X9 is also available.

(a) £350 is owing for heat and light.
(b) £620 has been prepaid for rent and rates.
(c) Depreciation is to be provided for the year as follows:

    Equipment   - 10% on cost
    Motor vehicles   - 20% on cost.

(d) Stock at the close of business was valued at £16,480.

Required

Prepare Brenda Bailey's trading and profit and loss account for the year ended 30 June 20X9 and her balance sheet at that date.

Activity 3.7

The following trial balance was extracted from the ledger of Kevin Webster, a sole trader, as at 31 May 20X1 - the end of his financial year.

KEVIN WEBSTER
TRIAL BALANCE AS AT 31 MAY 20X1

	Dr £	Cr £
Property, at cost	120,000	
Equipment, at cost	80,000	
Provisions for depreciation (as at 1 June 20X0)		
- on property		20,000
- on equipment		38,000
Purchases	250,000	
Sales		402,200
Stock, as at 1 June 20X0	50,000	
Discounts allowed	18,000	
Discounts received		4,800
Returns out		15,000
Wages and salaries	58,800	
Bad debts	4,600	
Loan interest	5,100	
Other operating expenses	17,700	
Trade creditors		36,000
Trade debtors	38,000	
Cash on hand	300	
Bank	1,300	
Drawings	24,000	
Provision for bad debts		500
17% long term loan		30,000
Capital, as at 1 June 20X0		121,300
	667,800	667,800

The following additional information as at 31 May 20X1 is available.

(a) Stock as at the close of business has been valued at cost at £42,000.
(b) Wages and salaries need to be accrued by £800.
(c) Other operating expenses are prepaid by £300.
(d) The provision for bad debts is to be adjusted so that it is 2% of trade debtors.
(e) Depreciation for the year ended 31 May 20X1 has still to be provided for as follows:

   Property: 1.5% per annum using the straight line method; and
   Equipment: 25% per annum using the diminishing balance method.

Required

Prepare Kevin Webster's trading and profit and loss account for the year ended 31 May 20X1 and his balance sheet as at that date.

2.2 How did you get on? When you feel you have mastered all aspects of accounting covered in the above activities, study and memorise the following tips.

TIPS FOR FINAL ACCOUNTS QUESTIONS

The examination paper will contain a compulsory question involving preparation of final accounts.

- You may have to prepare the final accounts of a limited company or a not-for-profit organisation, and the accounts may have to be prepared from incomplete records, all topics you will cover in this Interactive Text.

Whatever form the final accounts question takes, you should bear in mind the following tips.

- **Annotate the trial balance.** If you are given a trial balance, note the final destination of each item, for example:

    T = Trading account
    P/L = Profit and loss account
    I/E = Income and expenditure account
    B/S = Balance sheet

- **Show workings clearly.** The workings should be clearly referenced to the final accounts and should enable the marker to follow through your calculations. This is particularly important because if, as often happens under time pressure, you make minor arithmetical mistakes, you will not be heavily penalised if the marker can see that you have used the right method.

- **Present a clear, logical layout of financial accounts.** Allow plenty of space, better too much than too little. For example if you have to do a profit and loss account and balance sheet you should allow at least one page for the Profit and Loss account, one for the balance sheet and one or more for your workings. Underline any totals for columns and figures, and if you make a mistake, cross it out neatly and clearly. **You do not have time to wait for Tippex to dry.**

Key learning points

- An **increase** in the **provision for doubtful debts** is an **expense** in the profit and loss account whereas a decrease in the provision for doubtful debts is shown as 'other income' in the P & L account.
- **Debtors** are valued in the balance sheet **after deducting any provision** for doubtful debts.
- You should have been able to do **all** the activities in this chapter.
- Look back at the **mistakes** you have made. These will be your **learning points**.

Quick quiz

1 A bad debt arises in which of the following situations?

    A   A debtor pays part of the account
    B   An invoice is in dispute
    C   The debtor goes bankrupt
    D   The invoice is not yet due for payment

Part A: Introduction to financial reporting

2 A provision for doubtful debt of 2% is required. Trade debtors at the period end are £200,000 and the provision for doubtful debt brought forward from the previous period is £2,000. What movements are required this year?

    A   Increase by £4,000
    B   Decrease by £4,000
    C   Increase by £2,000
    D   Decrease by £2,000

3 If a doubtful debts provision is increased, what is the effect on the P&L a/c?

4 What is the double entry to record a bad debt written off?

5 Do you understand double entry?

6 Can you prepare final accounts from a trial balance?

7 Did you get the activities right - second time round if not first time?

Answers to quick quiz

1 C

2 C   2% of £200,000 = £4,000. Therefore the provision needs to be increased by £2,000.

3 The increase in the provision is charged as an expense in the P&L a/c.

4 DEBIT   Bad debts account (expenses)
   CREDIT   Trade debtors

5 – 7 Your answer should have been, 'Yes, no problem'! If not, you've still got a bit of work to do!

Answers to activities

Answer 3.1

The entries for the three years are denoted by (a), (b) and (c) in each account.

DEBTORS (EXTRACT)

				£
(a)		28.2.20X6	Balance	15,200
(b)		28.2.20X7	Balance	17,100
(c)		28.2.20X8	Balance	21,400

PROVISION FOR DOUBTFUL DEBTS

				£			£
(a)	28.2.20X6	Balance c/f (2% of 15,200)		304	28.2.20X6	Profit and loss	304
				304			304
(b)	28.2.20X7	Balance c/f (2% of 17,100)		342	1.3.20X6	Balance b/f	304
					28.2.20X7	Profit and loss (note (i))	38
				342			342
(c)	28.2.20X8	Profit and loss (note (ii))		128	1.3.20X7	Balance b/f	342
	28.2.20X8	Balance c/f (1% of 21,400)		214			
				342			342
					1.3.20X8	Balance b/f	214

PROFIT AND LOSS (EXTRACT)

			£			£
	28.2.20X6	Provision for doubtful debts	304			
	28.2.20X7	Provision for doubtful debts	38			
				28.2.20X8	Provision for doubtful debts	128

Notes

(i) The increase in the provision is £(342 - 304) = £38
(ii) The decrease in the provision is £(342 - 214) = £128

We calculate the net debtors figure for inclusion in the balance sheet as follows.

	20X6 £	20X7 £	20X8 £
Current assets			
Debtors	15,200	17,100	21,400
Less provision for doubtful debts	304	342	214
	14,896	16,758	21,186

Answer 3.2

(a)

CASH ACCOUNT

			£			£
1.7.X2	Capital		20,000	2.7.X2	Bank	18,000
23.7.X2	Sales		1,500	5.7.X2	Rent	500
31.7.X2	Equipment		50	9.7.X2	Purchases	1,000
				31.7.X2	Drawings	150
					Balance c/d	1,900
			21,550			21,550
1.8.X2	Balance b/d		1,900			

CAPITAL ACCOUNT

		£			£
31.7.X2	Balance c/d	20,000	1.7.X2	Cash	20,000
			1.8.X2	Balance b/d	20,000

BANK ACCOUNT

		£			£
2.7.X2	Cash	18,000	6.7.X2	Equipment	300
31.7.X2	Debtors	450	31.7.X2	Creditors	1,620
				Balance c/d	16,530
		18,450			18,450
1.8.X2	Balance b/d	16,530			

RENT ACCOUNT

		£			£
5.7.X2	Cash	500	31.7.X2	Balance c/d	500
31.7.X2	Balance b/d	500			

EQUIPMENT ACCOUNT

		£			£
6.7.X2	Bank	300	31.7.X2	Cash	50
				Balance c/d	250
		300			300
1.8.X2	Balance b/d	250			

PURCHASES ACCOUNT

		£			£
9.7.X2	Cash	1,000	31.7.X2	Balance c/d	3,000
10.7.X2	Creditors (Seddon)	2,000			
		3,000			3,000
1.8.X2	Balance b/d	3,000			

CREDITORS ACCOUNT

			£			£
20.7.X2	Purchase returns		200	10.7.X2	Purchases	2,000
31.7.X2	Bank		1,620			
	Discounts received		180			
			2,000			2,000

PURCHASES RETURNS ACCOUNT

		£			£
31.7.X2	Balance c/d	200	20.7.X2	Creditors	200
			1.8.X2	Balance b/d	200

SALES ACCOUNT

		£			£
31.7.X2	Balance c/d	2,500	23.7.X2	Cash	1,500
			26.7.X2	Debtors (Frodsham)	1,000
		2,500			2,500
			1.8.X2	Balance b/d	2,500

DEBTORS ACCOUNT

		£			£
26.7.X2	Sales	1,000	28.7.X2	Sales returns	500
			31.7.X2	Bank	450
				Discounts allowed	50
		1,000			1,000

SALES RETURNS ACCOUNT

		£			£
28.7.X2	Debtors	500	31.7.X2	Balance c/d	500
1.8.X2	Balance b/d	500			

DISCOUNTS RECEIVED ACCOUNT

		£			£
31.7.X2	Balance c/d	180	31.7.X2	Creditors	180
			1.8.X2	Balance b/d	180

DISCOUNTS ALLOWED ACCOUNT

		£			£
31.7.X2	Debtors	50	31.7.X2	Balance c/d	50
1.8.X2	Balance b/d	50			

DRAWINGS ACCOUNT

		£			£
31.7.X2	Cash	150	31.7.X2	Balance c/d	150
1.8.X2	Balance b/d	150			

(b) TRIAL BALANCE AS AT 31 JULY 20X2

	Debit £	Credit £
Cash	1,900	
Capital		20,000
Bank	16,530	
Rent	500	
Equipment	250	
Purchases	3,000	
Purchase returns		200
Sales		2,500
Sales returns	500	
Discounts received		180
Discounts allowed	50	
Drawings	150	
	22,880	22,880

Answer 3.3

(a) Check the balances on your ledger accounts with the trial balance shown below.

	Debit £	Credit £
Cash book		
Bank (note below) (W1)	1,703	
Cash (unbanked at end of period) (W2)	12	
Nominal ledger		
Drawings	560	
Postage and stationery	129	
Travelling expenses	40	
Motor expenses	104	
Cleaning expenses	260	
Sundry expenses	19	
Telephone	214	
Electricity	190	
Motor vans	2,000	
Rates	320	
Fixtures and fittings	806	
Capital		2,308
Purchases	3,163	
Discounts received		419
Credit sales		830
Cash sales		4,764
Discount allowed	81	
Provision for depreciation:		
motor van		720
fixtures and fittings		250
Stock at 1 January 20X1	366	
Loan - Flex		250
Sales ledger		
Brown	12	
Blue	180	
Stripe	48	
Purchase ledger		
Live		602
Negative		64
Earth		
	10,207	10,207

Part A: Introduction to financial reporting

Workings

1 Cash at bank

	£
Opening balance	672
Bankings of cash (908+940+766+1,031)	3,645
Capital introduced	500
Received from customers	
90% × (160+66+22+10+40+120+140+130+20+44+38+20) = 90% of 810	729
	5,546
Less cheque payments (telephone, electricity, rates, van)	(1,469)
Payments to suppliers	
85% × (143+468+570+390+80+87+103+73+692+187) = 85% × 2,793	(2,374)
Closing balance	1,703

2 Cash in hand

	£		£
Balance b/d	5	Bank	3,645
∴ Sales	4,764	Drawings	560
		Stationery	73
		Travel	40
		Petrol and van	104
		Sundry	19
		Postage	56
		Cleaner	260
		Balance c/d	12
	4,769		4,769

(b) (i) SPARK - TRADING AND PROFIT AND LOSS ACCOUNT FOR THE FOUR MONTHS ENDED 30 APRIL 20X1

	£	£	£
Sales			5,594
Opening stock		366	
Purchases		3,163	
		3,529	
Closing stock		390	
			3,139
Gross profit			2,455
Discount received			419
Profit on sale of motor van			20
			2,894
Rent (W1)		500	
Rates (W2)		174	
Electricity		212	
Telephone (W3)		192	
Motor expenses		104	
Travelling		40	
Postage and stationery		129	
Cleaning		260	
Sundry expenses		19	
Depreciation (W4)			
Motor van	65		
Fixtures and fittings	27		
		92	
Discount allowed		81	
Loan interest (W5)		8	
			1,811
Net profit			1,083

Workings

1. Rent: 4/12 × £1,500 = £500; Accrual of £500 at 30 April
2. Rates: £100 + 2/6 × £220 = £174; Prepayment of £146 at 30 April
3. Telephone: £214 + £15 - £37 = £192

3: Review of basic financial accounts

        4   Depreciation: Motor van: 20% × £1,300 × 3/12 = £65
                Fixtures: 10% × £806 × 4/12 = £27
        5   Loan interest: 10% × £250 × 4/12 = £8

(ii) SPARK - BALANCE SHEET AS AT 30 APRIL 20X1

	Cost £	Dep'n £	£
Fixed assets			
Motor van	1,300	65	1,235
Fixtures and fittings	806	277	529
	2,106	342	1,764
Current assets			
Stock at cost		390	
Debtors		240	
Payments in advance		146	
Cash at bank		1,703	
Cash in hand		12	
		2,491	
Current liabilities			
Trade creditors	666		
Accrued expenses	537		
		1,203	
			1,288
			3,052
Loan account: Flex			258
			2,794
Capital account			£
Balance at 1 January			1,808
Capital introduced			500
Profit for the four months			1,083
			3,391
Less drawings			597
			2,794

Answer 3.4

DONALD BROWN
TRADING AND PROFIT AND LOSS ACCOUNT
FOR THE YEAR ENDED 31 DECEMBER 20X0

	£	£
Sales		491,620
Less cost of sales		
Opening stock	18,460	
Purchases	387,936	
	406,396	
Closing stock	19,926	
		386,470
Gross profit		105,150
Discounts received		1,175
		106,325
Less expenses:		
discounts allowed	1,304	
lighting and heating	6,184	
motor expenses	3,080	
rent	8,161	
general expenses	7,413	
depreciation (W)	13,146	
		39,288
Net profit		67,037

Part A: Introduction to financial reporting

Working: depreciation charge

Motor vehicles: £45,730 × 20% = £9,146
Fixtures and fittings: 10% × £(42,200 – 2,200) = £4,000
Total: £4,000 + £9,146 = £13,146.

DONALD BROWN
BALANCE SHEET AS AT 31 DECEMBER 20X0

	Cost £	Depreciation £	Net £
Fixed assets			
Fixtures and fittings	42,200	6,200	36,000
Motor vehicles	45,730	24,438	21,292
	87,930	30,638	57,292
Current assets			
Stock		19,926	
Debtors		42,737	
Prepayments		680	
Cash in hand		1,411	
		64,754	
Current liabilities			
Creditors	35,404		
Accruals	218		
Bank overdraft	19,861		
		55,483	
Net current assets			9,271
Net assets			66,563
Represented by:			
Capital			26,094
Net profit for year			67,037
			93,131
Less drawings			26,568
			66,563

Answer 3.5

HERBERT HOWELL
TRADING AND PROFIT AND LOSS ACCOUNT
FOR THE YEAR ENDED 31 MAY 20X9

	£	£
Sales		405,000
Cost of sales:		
Opening stock	27,400	
Purchases (£259,600 - £1,040)	258,560	
	285,960	
Closing stock	25,900	
		260,060
Gross profit		144,940
Discounts received		4,420
		149,360
Discounts allowed	3,370	
Loan interest	1,560	
Bad and doubtful debts (W1)	1,671	
Carriage out	5,310	
Wages and salaries	52,500	
Depreciation (W2)	9,525	
Other operating expenses (W3)	38,500	
		112,436
Net profit		36,924

3: Review of basic financial accounts

HERBERT HOWELL
BALANCE SHEET AS AT 31 MAY 20X9

	Cost £	Dep'n £	Net book value £
Fixed assets			
Property (W4)	90,000	13,400	76,600
Equipment (W4)	57,500	41,125	16,375
	147,500	54,525	92,975
Current assets			
Stock		25,900	
Trade debtors	46,200		
Less provision for doubtful debts (W1)	231		
		45,969	
Prepayment		500	
Cash on hand		151	
		72,520	
Current liabilities			
Bank overdraft		14,500	
Trade creditors		33,600	
Accruals (140 + 200)		340	
		48,440	
Net current assets			24,080
Total assets less current liabilities			117,055
Long-term liabilities			
13% loan			12,000
			105,055
Capital			
Balance at 1 June 20X8			98,101
Net profit for the year			36,924
Drawings (£28,930 + £1,040)			(29,970)
Balance at 31 May 20X9			105,055

Workings

1 **Bad debts**

	£
Provision required: 0.5% × £46,200	231
Provision b/f	280
Decrease required	(49)
Add bad debts	1,720
Bad and doubtful debts expense for the year	1,671

2 **Depreciation**

	£
Property: 1% × £90,000	900
Equipment: 15% × £57,500	8,625
	9,525

3 **Other operating expenses**

	£
As trial balance	38,800
Less prepayment	(500)
Add accrual	200
	38,500

4 **Provision for depreciation**

	Property £	Equipment £
Balance b/f	12,500	32,500
Charge for the year (W2)	900	8,625
Balance c/f	13,400	41,125

Answer 3.6

BRENDA BAILEY
TRADING AND PROFIT AND LOSS ACCOUNT
FOR THE YEAR ENDED 30 JUNE 20X9

	£	£
Sales		427,726
Opening stock	15,310	
Purchases	302,419	
Carriage inwards	476	
	318,205	
Less closing stock	16,480	
Cost of sales		301,725
Gross profit		126,001
Carriage outwards	829	
Wages and salaries	64,210	
Rent and rates (12,466 - 620)	11,846	
Heat and light (4,757 + 350)	5,107	
Depreciation - equipment	10,200	
- motor vehicles	8,654	
Sundry expenses	8,426	
		109,272
Net profit for the year		16,729

BRENDA BAILEY
BALANCE SHEET AS AT 30 JUNE 20X9

	Cost £	Dep'n £	Net book value £
Fixed assets			
Equipment	102,000	32,450	69,550
Motor vehicles	43,270	17,574	25,696
	145,270	50,024	95,246
Current assets			
Stock		16,480	
Debtors		50,633	
Prepayments		620	
Cash		477	
		68,210	
Current liabilities			
Bank overdraft		3,295	
Creditors		41,792	
Accruals		350	
		45,437	
Net current assets			22,773
			118,019
Capital			
Balance at 1 July 20X8			122,890
Add profit for the year			16,729
			139,619
Less drawings			21,600
Balance at 30 June 20X9			118,019

Answer 3.7

KEVIN WEBSTER
TRADING AND PROFIT AND LOSS ACCOUNT
FOR THE YEAR ENDED 31 MAY 20X1

	£	£
Sales		402,200
Cost of sales		
Opening stock	50,000	
Purchases	250,000	
Purchases returns	(15,000)	
	285,000	
Closing stock	42,000	
		243,000
Gross profit		159,200
Other income - discounts received		4,800
		164,000
Expenses		
Operating expenses		
Wages and salaries (£58,800 + £800)	59,600	
Discounts allowed	18,000	
Bad debts (W1)	4,860	
Loan interest	5,100	
Depreciation	12,300	
Other operating expenses (£17,700 – £300)	17,400	
		117,260
Net profit for the year		46,740

KEVIN WEBSTER
BALANCE SHEET AS AT 31 MAY 20X1

	Cost £	Accumulated deprn. £	Net book value £
Fixed assets			
Property	120,000	21,800	98,200
Equipment	80,000	48,500	31,500
	200,000	70,300	129,700

Current assets		
Stock	42,000	
Trade debtors net of provision for bad debts (£38,000 less 2%)	37,240	
Prepayments	300	
Bank	1,300	
Cash in hand	300	
	81,140	
Current liabilities		
Trade creditors	36,000	
Accruals	800	
	36,800	
Net current assets		44,340
Less 17% loan		30,000
Net assets		144,040
Capital		
Balance at 1 June 20X0		121,300
Net profit for the year		46,740
		168,040
Drawings		24,000
		144,040

Part A: Introduction to financial reporting

Workings

			£
1	*Provision for bad debts*		
	Previous provision		500
	New provision (2% × 38,000)		760
	Increase		260
	Per trial balance		4,600
	Profit and loss account		4,860

			£
2	*Depreciation*		
	Property		
	Opening provision		20,000
	Provision for the year (1.5% × 120,000)		1,800
	Closing provision		21,800
	Equipment		
	Opening provision		38,000
	Provision for the year (25% × 42,000)		10,500
	Closing provision		48,500

Now try Question 3 in the Exam Question Bank at the end of the Text.

Chapter 4 Accounting conventions

Chapter topic list

1 Background
2 'Bedrock' concepts
3 Other concepts and conventions
4 Accounting policies

The following study sessions are covered in this chapter.

Syllabus reference

2(e) Discuss and apply accounting concepts and policies   1

Part A: Introduction to financial reporting

1 BACKGROUND

1.1 Accounting practice has developed gradually over a matter of centuries. Many of its procedures are operated automatically by people who have never questioned whether alternative methods exist which are just as valid. However, the procedures in common use imply the acceptance of certain **concepts** which are by no means self-evident; nor are they the only possible **concepts**. These concepts could be used to build up an accounting framework.

1.2 Our next step is to look at some of the more important concepts which are taken for granted in preparing accounts. Originally, a statement of standard accounting practice (SSAP 2 *Disclosure of accounting policies*) described four concepts as *fundamental accounting concepts*: they were **going concern, prudence, accruals** and **consistency**.

1.3 In December 2000 FRS 18 *Accounting policies* was issued. FRS 18 emphasises the importance of **going concern** and **accruals** calling them the **bedrock** of financial statements. **Prudence** and **consistency** have been relegated to **'desirable'** elements of financial statements.

> **Exam alert**
>
> You still need to learn the concepts of prudence and consistency, just put them into the correct context; going concern and accruals are **more** important concepts.

1.4 In this chapter we shall single out the following concepts for discussion.

   (a) The **going concern** concept
   (b) The **accruals** or matching concept
   (c) The **prudence** concept
   (d) The **consistency** concept
   (e) The **entity** concept
   (f) The **separate valuation** principle
   (g) The **materiality** concept
   (h) The **historical cost** convention
   (i) The **objectivity** concept
   (j) The **duality** concept
   (k) **Substance over form**

2 'BEDROCK' CONCEPTS

2.1 Below are discussed the two 'bedrocks' of financial statements as identified by FRS 18 *Accounting policies*.

The going concern concept

> **KEY TERM**
>
> The **going concern concept** implies that the business will continue in operational existence for the foreseeable future, and that there is no intention to put the company into liquidation or to make drastic cutbacks to the scale of operations.

2.2 FRS 18 states that the financial statements **must** be prepared under the going concern basis unless the entity is being (or is going to be) liquidated or if it has ceased (or is about to cease) trading. The directors of a company must also disclose any significant doubts about the company's future if and when they arise.

2.3 The main significance of the going concern concept is that the assets of the business should not be valued at their 'break-up' value, which is the amount that they would sell for if they were sold off piecemeal and the business were thus broken up.

2.4 EXAMPLE: GOING CONCERN CONCEPT

Suppose, for example, that Emma acquires a T-shirt making machine at a cost of £60,000. The asset has an estimated life of six years, and it is normal to write off the cost of the asset to the profit and loss account over this time. In this case a depreciation cost of £10,000 per annum will be charged.

2.5 Using the going concern concept, it would be presumed that the business will continue its operations and so the asset will live out its full six years in use. A depreciation charge of £10,000 will be made each year, and the value of the asset in the balance sheet will be its cost less the accumulated amount of depreciation charged to date. After one year, the **net book value** of the asset would therefore be £(60,000 − 10,000) = £50,000, after two years it would be £40,000, after three years £30,000 etc, until it has been written down to a value of 0 after 6 years.

2.6 Now suppose that this asset has no other operational use outside the business, and in a forced sale it would only sell for scrap. After one year of operation, its scrap value might be, say, £8,000.

2.7 The net book value of the asset, applying the going concern concept, would be £50,000 after one year, but its immediate sell-off value only £8,000. It might be argued that the asset is over-valued at £50,000 and that it should be written down to its break-up value (ie in the balance sheet it should be shown at £8,000 and the balance of its cost should be treated as an expense). However, provided that the going concern concept is valid, so that the asset will continue to be used and will not be sold, it is appropriate accounting practice to value the asset at its net book value.

Activity 4.1

Now try this example yourself.

A retailer commences business on 1 January and buys a stock of 20 washing machines, each costing £100. During the year he sells 17 machines at £150 each. How should the remaining machines be valued at 31 December if:

(a) He is forced to close down his business at the end of the year and the remaining machines will realise only £60 each in a forced sale?

(b) He intends to continue his business into the next year?

2.8 Entities are required to consider going concern and disclose the following.

(a) **Material uncertainties**. Conditions or events which present significant doubts about the entity's ability to continue as a going concern.

(b) **Foreseeable future**. Where the future has been restricted to less than one year from the approval of the financial statements.

Part A: Introduction to financial reporting

(c) **Going concern**. Where the financial statements are **not prepared** on a **going concern basis**, the reason for this and the method under which they have been prepared.

The accruals concept or matching concept

2.9 FRS 18 also stipulates that financial statements must be prepared under the accruals concept. This concept is a cornerstone of present day financial statements, so work through this section carefully so that you understand how it is applied during the preparation of accounts.

> **KEY TERM**
>
> The **accruals concept** states that revenue and costs must be recognised as they are earned or incurred, not as money is received or paid. They must be matched with one another so far as their relationship can be established or justifiably assumed, and dealt with in the profit and loss account of the period to which they relate.

2.10 This is illustrated in the example of Emma introduced in Chapter 1; profit of £100 was computed by matching the revenue (£200) earned from the sale of 20 T-shirts against the cost (£100) of acquiring them.

2.11 If, however, Emma had only sold eighteen T-shirts, it would have been incorrect to charge her profit and loss account with the cost of twenty T-shirts, as she still has two T-shirts in stock. If she intends to sell them in June she is likely to make a profit on the sale. Therefore, only the purchase cost of eighteen T-shirts (£90) should be matched with her sales revenue, leaving her with a profit of £90.

Her balance sheet would therefore look like this.

	£
Assets	
Stock (at cost, ie 2 × £5)	10
Debtors (18 × £10)	180
	190
Liabilities	
Creditors	100
	90
Proprietor's capital (profit for the period)	90

2.12 If, however, Emma had decided to give up selling T-shirts, then the going concern concept would no longer apply and the value of the two T-shirts in the balance sheet would be a break-up valuation rather than cost. Similarly, if the two unsold T-shirts were now unlikely to be sold at more than their cost of £5 each (say, because of damage or a fall in demand) then they should be recorded on the balance sheet at their *net realisable value* (ie the likely eventual sales price less any expenses incurred to make them saleable, eg paint) rather than cost. This shows the application of the prudence concept (see section 3 for details).

2.13 In this example, the concepts of going concern and matching are linked. Because the business is assumed to be a going concern it is possible to carry forward the cost of the unsold T-shirts as a charge against profits of the next period.

The accruals concept defined

2.14 Essentially, the accruals concept states that, in computing profit, revenue earned must be matched against the expenditure incurred in earning it.

3 OTHER CONCEPTS AND CONVENTIONS

The prudence concept

> **KEY TERM**
>
> The **prudence concept** states that where alternative procedures, or alternative valuations, are possible, the one selected should be the one which gives the most cautious presentation of the business's financial position or results.

3.1 The importance of **prudence** has diminished over time. Prudence is a **desirable quality** of financial statements but **not** a bedrock. The key reason for this change of perspective is that some firms have been over pessimistic and **over stated provisions** in times of high profits in order to 'profit-smooth'.

3.2 You should bear this in mind as you read through the explanation of prudence. On the one hand assets and profits should not be overstated, but a balance must be achieved to prevent the material overstatement of liabilities or losses.

3.3 You may have wondered why the three washing machines in Activity 1 were stated in the balance sheet at their cost (£100 each) rather than their selling price (£150 each). This is simply an aspect of the prudence concept: to value the machines at £150 would be to anticipate making a profit before the profit had been realised.

3.4 The other aspect of the prudence concept is that where a **loss** is foreseen, it **should** be anticipated and taken into account immediately. If a business purchases stock for £1,200 but because of a sudden slump in the market only £900 is likely to be realised when the stock is sold the prudence concept dictates that the stock should be valued at £900. It is not enough to wait until the stock is sold, and then recognise the £300 loss; it must be recognised as soon as it is foreseen.

3.5 A profit can be considered to be a **realised profit** when it is in the form of:

- Cash
- Another asset which has a reasonably certain cash value. This includes amounts owing from debtors, provided that there is a reasonable certainty that the debtors will eventually pay up what they owe

3.6 EXAMPLES: PRUDENCE CONCEPT

Some examples might help to explain the application of the prudence concept.

(a) A company begins trading on 1 January 20X5 and sells goods worth £100,000 during the year to 31 December. At 31 December there are debts outstanding of £15,000. Of these, the company is now doubtful whether £6,000 will ever be paid.

The company should make a **provision for doubtful debts** of £6,000. Sales for 20X5 will be shown in the profit and loss account at their full value of £100,000, but the provision for doubtful debts would be a charge of £6,000. Because there is some uncertainty that the sales will be realised in the form of cash, the prudence concept dictates that the £6,000 should not be included in the profit for the year.

(b) Samson Feeble trades as a carpenter. He has undertaken to make a range of kitchen furniture for a customer at an agreed price of £1,000. At the end of Samson's accounting year the job is unfinished (being two thirds complete) and the following data has been assembled:

	£
Costs incurred in making the furniture to date	800
Further estimated costs to completion of the job	400
Total cost	1,200

The incomplete job represents *work in progress* at the end of the year which is an asset, like stock. Its cost to date is £800, but by the time the job is completed Samson will have made a loss of £200.

The full £200 loss should be charged against profits of the current year. The value of work in progress at the year end should be its *net realisable value*, which is lower than its cost. The net realisable value can be calculated in either of two ways:

	(i)		(ii)
	£		£
Eventual sales value	1,000	Work in progress at cost	800
Less further costs to completion in order to make the sale	400	Less loss foreseen	200
Net realisable value	600		600

The consistency concept

3.7 Accounting is not an exact science. There are many areas in which judgement must be exercised in attributing money values to items appearing in accounts. Over the years certain procedures and principles have come to be recognised as good accounting practice, but within these limits there are often various acceptable methods of accounting for similar items.

> **KEY TERM**
>
> The **consistency concept** states that similar items should be accorded similar accounting treatments.

3.8 The consistency concept states that in preparing accounts consistency should be observed in two respects.

(a) Similar items within a single set of accounts should be given similar accounting treatment.

(b) The same treatment should be applied from one period to another in accounting for similar items. This enables valid comparisons to be made from one period to the next.

3.9 FRS 18 is designed to sit alongside the *Statement of Principles* framework. This helps explain the downplaying of the previously important prudence and consistency concepts.

3.10 The preparers of financial statements must now consider:

4: Accounting conventions

- Relevance
- Reliability
- Comparability
- Understandability

3.11 There is an assumption that in considering these objectives, the concepts of **prudence and consistency will be followed** in the majority of cases anyway. The objectives will need to be weighed against each other and a course of action taken which **best fits all four.**

3.12 All four objectives overlap and none of them should be compromised by the accounting policies adopted by the entity. By fulfilling the reliability and comparability objectives an accounting policy is likely to fulfil the consistency concept. If a policy provides information which is relevant and reliable then it is likely that amounts are not overstated and so the prudence concept is indirectly adhered to.

The entity concept

3.13 This concept has already been discussed in Chapter 1. Briefly, the concept is that accountants regard a business as a separate entity, distinct from its owners or managers. The concept applies whether the business is a limited company (and so recognised in law as a separate entity) or a sole proprietorship or partnership (in which case the business is not separately recognised by the law.

The separate valuation principle

> **KEY TERM**
>
> The **separate valuation principle** states that, in determining the amount to be attributed to an asset or liability in the balance sheet, each component item of the asset or liability must be determined separately.

3.14 These separate valuations must then be aggregated to arrive at the balance sheet figure. For example, if a company's stock comprises 50 separate items, a valuation must (in theory) be arrived at for each item separately; the 50 figures must then be aggregated and the total is the stock figure which should appear in the balance sheet.

The materiality concept

> **KEY TERM**
>
> The **materiality concept.** Only items material in amount or in their nature will affect the true and fair view given by a set of accounts.

3.15 An error which is too trivial to affect anyone's understanding of the accounts is referred to as **immaterial**. In preparing accounts it is important to assess what is material and what is not, so that time and money are not wasted in the pursuit of excessive detail.

Part A: Introduction to financial reporting

3.16 Determining whether or not an item is material is a **very subjective exercise**. There is no absolute measure of materiality. It is common to apply a convenient rule of thumb (for example to define material items as those with a value greater than 5% of the net profit disclosed by the accounts). But some items disclosed in accounts are regarded as particularly sensitive and even a very small misstatement of such an item would be regarded as a material error. An example in the accounts of a limited company might be the amount of remuneration paid to directors of the company.

3.17 The assessment of an item as material or immaterial may affect its treatment in the accounts. For example, the profit and loss account of a business will show the expenses incurred by the business grouped under suitable captions (heating and lighting expenses, rent and rates expenses etc); but in the case of very small expenses it may be appropriate to lump them together under a caption such as 'sundry expenses', because a more detailed breakdown would be inappropriate for such immaterial amounts.

IMPORTANT!

In assessing whether or not an item is material, it is not only the amount of the item which needs to be considered. The context is also important.

3.18 EXAMPLE: MATERIALITY

(a) If a balance sheet shows fixed assets of £2 million and stocks of £30,000 an error of £20,000 in the depreciation calculations might not be regarded as material, whereas an error of £20,000 in the stock valuation probably would be. In other words, the total of which the erroneous item forms part must be considered.

(b) If a business has a bank loan of £50,000 and a £55,000 balance on bank deposit account, it might well be regarded as a material misstatement if these two amounts were displayed on the balance sheet as 'cash at bank £5,000'. In other words, incorrect presentation may amount to material misstatement even if there is no monetary error.

Activity 4.2

Would you capitalise the following items in the accounts of a company?

(a) A box file
(b) A computer
(c) A small plastic display stand

The historical cost convention

3.19 A basic principle of accounting (some writers include it in the list of fundamental accounting concepts) is that resources are normally stated in accounts at historical cost, ie at the amount which the business paid to acquire them. An important advantage of this procedure is that the objectivity of accounts is maximised: there is usually objective, documentary evidence to prove the amount paid to purchase an asset or pay an expense.

KEY TERM

Historical cost means transactions are recorded at the cost when they occurred.

3.20 In general, accountants prefer to deal with costs, rather than with 'values'. This is because valuations tend to be subjective and to vary according to what the valuation is for. For example, suppose that a company acquires a machine to manufacture its products. The machine has an expected useful life of four years. At the end of two years the company is preparing a balance sheet and has to decide what monetary amount to attribute to the asset.

3.21 Numerous possibilities might be considered:

- The original cost (historical cost) of the machine
- Half of the historical cost, on the ground that half of its useful life has expired
- The amount the machine might fetch on the secondhand market
- The amount it would cost to replace the machine with an identical machine
- The amount it would cost to replace the machine with a more modern machine incorporating the technological advances of the previous two years
- The machine's economic value, ie the amount of the profits it is expected to generate for the company during its remaining life

3.22 All of these valuations have something to commend them, but the great advantage of the first two is that they are based on a figure (the machine's historical cost) which is objectively verifiable. (Some authors regard objectivity as an accounting concept in its own right.) The subjective judgement involved in the other valuations, particularly the last, is so great as to lessen the reliability of any accounts in which they are used.

Objectivity (neutrality)

3.23 An accountant must show objectivity in his work. This means he should try to strip his answers of any personal opinion or prejudice and should be as precise and as detailed as the situation warrants. The result of this should be that any number of accountants will give the same answer independently of each other.

KEY TERM

Objectivity means that accountants must be free from bias. They must adopt a neutral stance when analysing accounting data.

3.24 In practice, objectivity is difficult. Two accountants faced with the same accounting data may come to different conclusions as to the correct treatment. It was to combat subjectivity that accounting standards were developed.

Substance over form

> **KEY TERM**
>
> **Substance over form** means that transactions should be accounted for and presented in accordance with their economic substance, not their legal form.

3.25 An example of an application of substance over form is that of assets acquired on hire purchase. Legally the purchaser does not own the asset until the final instalment has been paid. However, the accounting treatment required is to record a fixed asset in the accounts at the start of the hire purchase agreement. The substance of the transaction is that the business owns the asset. The same could be said of fixed assets acquired under long-term leases.

4 ACCOUNTING POLICIES

4.1 FRS 18 prescribes the **regular consideration of the entity's accounting policies**. The **best** accounting policy should be adopted at all times. This is the major reason for downplaying consistency (and to a lesser extent prudence). An entity **cannot retain** an accounting policy merely because it was used last year or because it gives a prudent view.

4.2 However, the entity should consider how a **change** in accounting policy may affect **comparability**. Essentially a **balance** must be struck between selecting the **most appropriate policies** and presenting **coherent and useful** financial statements. The overriding guidance is that the financial statements should give a **true and fair view** of the entity's business. Chopping and changing accounting policies year on year is likely to jeopardise the true and fair view but so too is retaining accounting policies which do not present the most useful information to the users of the accounts.

Disclosure

4.3 FRS 18 requires the disclosure of

- A **description of each accounting policy** which is material to the entity's financial statements
- A description of any significant estimation technique
- **Changes** to accounting policies
- The effects of any material change to an estimation technique

Estimation techniques

4.4 An estimation technique is material **only where a large range** of monetary values may be arrived at. The entity should vary the assumptions it uses, to assess how sensitive monetary values are under that technique. In most cases the range of values will be relatively narrow (consider the useful life of motor vehicles for example).

Changes to accounting policies

4.5 The disclosure of new accounting policies also requires

- An explanation of the **reason for change**
- The **effects of a prior period adjustment** on the previous years results (in accordance with FRS 3)
- The **effects of the change in policy** on the previous year's results

If it is **not possible** to disclose the last two points then the **reason** for this should be disclosed instead.

> **Exam alert**
>
> You need to be confident about the application of FRS 18. Make sure that you can **identify** a change in accounting policy and the **reason** that it is a change in accounting policy as opposed to a change in estimation technique. You will have to **discuss** the decision you have reached **and justify** your conclusions.

4.6 The most complex aspect to FRS 18 is the **application of the terms and definitions** within the standard.

4.7 It is essential that you **learn the following definitions**. However, once you have read them you should **apply them** to the questions later in this section to make sure that you understand them.

> **KEY TERM**
>
> **Accounting policies.** The principles, conventions, rules and practices applied by an entity that prescribe how transactions and other events are to be reflected in its financial statements.

4.8 Accounting policies are **not** estimation techniques.

4.9 An accounting policy includes the

- Recognition
- Presentation
- And measurement basis

Of assets, liabilities, gains, losses and changes to shareholders funds.

> **KEY TERM**
>
> **Estimation technique.** The methods used by an entity to establish the estimated monetary amounts associated with the measurement bases selected for assets, liabilities, gains, losses and changes to shareholder's funds.

4.10 Estimation techniques are used to **implement the measurement basis** of an accounting policy. The accounting policy specifies the measurement basis and the estimation technique is used when there is an uncertainty over this amount.

4.11 The **method of depreciation is an estimation technique**. The accounting policy is to spread the cost of the asset over its useful economic life. Depreciation is the measurement

Part A: Introduction to financial reporting

basis. The estimation technique would be, say, straight line depreciation as opposed to reducing balance.

4.12 A change of estimation technique should **not** be accounted for as a prior period adjustment unless the following apply.

- It is the correction of a fundamental error
- The Companies Act, an accounting standard or a UITF Abstract **requires the change to be accounted** for as a prior period adjustment.

Application of FRS 18

4.13 FRS 18 gives a number of examples of its application in an appendix to the standard. When a change is required to an accounting policy then **three criteria** must be **considered** to ensure that the change is affecting the accounting policy and not an estimation technique.

1 Recognition
2 Presentation
3 Measurement basis

4.14 If **any one of the criteria apply** then a change has been made to the accounting policy. If they do **not** apply then a change to an estimation technique has taken place.

4.15 You should note that where an **accounting standard gives a choice** of treatments (i.e. SSAP 9 states that stock can be recognised on a FIFO or weighted average cost basis) then adopting the alternative treatment is a **change of accounting policy.** Also note that FRS 15 states that a **change in depreciation method is not** a change in accounting policy.

Example	Recognition	Change to Presentation	Measurement basis?	Change of Accounting Policy
1 Changing from capitalisation of finance costs associated with the construction of fixed assets to charging them through the profit and loss	Yes	Yes	No	Yes
2 A reassessment of an entity's cost centres means that all three will have production overheads allocated to them instead of just two	No	No	No	No
3 Overheads are reclassified from distribution to cost of sales	No	Yes	No	Yes
4 Change from straight-line depreciation to machine hours	No	No	No	No
5 Reallocate depreciation from administration to cost of sales	No	Yes	No	Yes
6 A provision is revised upwards and the estimates of future cash flows are now discounted in accordance with FRS 12. They were not discounted previously as the amounts involved were not material	No	No	No	No
7 Deferred tax is now reported on a discounted basis. It was previously undiscounted	No	No	Yes	Yes

4: Accounting conventions

	Example	Recognition	Change to Presentation	Change to Measurement basis?	Change of Accounting Policy
8	A foreign subsidiary's profit and loss account is now to be translated at the closing rate. It was previously translated at the average rate	No	No	Yes	Yes
9	Fungible stocks are to be measured on the weighted average cost basis instead of the previously used FIFO basis	No	No	Yes	Yes

Fungible assets

KEY TERM

Fungible assets are similar assets which are grouped together as there is no reason to view them separately in economic terms. Shares and items of stock are examples of fungible assets.

4.16 The last example (Example 9) is based on a **change to fungible assets**. The standard states that when fungible assets are considered in **aggregate** a change from weighted average cost to FIFO (or vice versa), is a change to the **measurement base**. The standard also recommends that fungible assets should **always be considered in aggregate** in order to enhance **comparability** of financial statements.

Activity 4.3

The board of Beezlebub plc decide to change the depreciation method they use on their plant and machinery from 30% reducing balance to 20% straight line to better reflect the way the assets are used within the business. Is this a change of accounting policy ?

Activity 4.4

The board of Beezlebub plc also decide to change their stock valuation. They replace their FIFO valuation method for an AVCO method to better reflect the way that stock is used within the business. Is this a change in accounting policy?

Activity 4.5

The board of Beezlebub plc decide in the following year that the development costs the business incurs should not be capitalised and presented on the balance sheet. Instead they agree that all development expenditure should be charged as an expense in the profit and loss account. Is this an accounting policy change?

Activity 4.6

Beezlebub plc's board are also considering reallocating the depreciation charges made on its large fleet of company cars to administration expenses, they were previously shown in cost of sales. Is this an accounting policy change?

Summary

4.17 FRS 18 requires an entity to conduct a review on an annual basis in order to ensure that it is using the most appropriate accounting policies.

The objectives of

- Reliability
- Relevance
- Comparability
- Understandability

Must be fulfilled by the accounting policies adopted. This requirement helps prevent entities from changing accounting policies too often.

4.18 The three criteria

- Recognition
- Presentation
- Measurement basis

4.19 Are considered in order to establish whether there has been a change of accounting policy or merely a change of estimation technique.

Key learning points

- In preparing financial statements, certain **fundamental concepts** are adopted as a framework.
- Two such concepts are identified by FRS 18 *Accounting policies* as the bedrock of accounting.
  - The **going concern concept**. Unless there is evidence to the contrary, it is assumed that a business will continue to trade normally for the foreseeable future.
  - The **accruals or matching concept**. Revenue earned must be matched against expenditure incurred in earning it.
- A number of other concepts may be regarded as fundamental.
  - The **prudence concept**. Where alternative accounting procedures are acceptable, choose the one which gives the less optimistic view of profitability and asset values.
  - The **consistency concept**. Similar items should be accorded similar accounting treatments.
  - The **entity concept**. A business is an entity distinct from its owner(s).
  - The **separate valuation principle**. Each component of an asset or liability must be valued separately.
  - The **materiality concept**. Only items material in amount or in their nature will affect the true and fair view given by a set of accounts.
  - The **historical cost convention**. Transactions are recorded at the cost when they occurred.
  - **Objectivity**. Accountants must be free from bias.
  - **Substance over form**. Transactions must be presented and accounted for in accordance with their substance and financial reality and not merely with their legal form.
- **Accounting policies** are selected from the choices provided by accounting standards to provide a true and fair view.
- Accounting estimates are the application of judgement to allocate monetary values using the criteria provided by an accounting policy.

Quick quiz

1 List five important accounting concepts.

2 What is the prudence concept?

3 What is meant by an accounting policy?

Answers to quick quiz

1 (a) Going concern
   (b) Prudence
   (c) Accruals
   (d) Consistency
   (e) Materiality

2 Where alternative procedures or alternative valuations are possible, the one selected should be the one which gives the most cautious presentation of the business's financial position or results.

3 Accounting policies are selected from the choices provided by accounting standards to provide a true and fair view.

Answers to activities

Answer 4.1

(a) If the business is to be closed down, the remaining three machines must be valued at the amount they will realise in a forced sale, ie 3 × £60 = £180.

(b) If the business is regarded as a going concern, the stock unsold at 31 December will be carried forward into the following year, when the cost of the three machines will be matched against the eventual sale proceeds in computing that year's profits. The three machines will therefore appear in the balance sheet at 31 December at cost, 3 × £100 = £300.

Answer 4.2

(a) No. You would write it off to the profit and loss account as an expense.

(b) Yes. You would capitalise the computer and charge depreciation on it.

(c) Your answer depends on the size of the company and whether writing off the item has a material effect on its profits. A larger organisation might well write this item off under the heading of advertising expenses, while a small one would capitalise it and depreciate it over time. This is because the item would be material to the small company but not to the large company.

Answer 4.3

No. This is a change to the **estimation technique**. The same measurement basis is used. The historical cost is allocated over the asset's estimated useful life.

Answer 4.4

Yes. This is a change to the **measurement basis**. The paragraphs on fungible assets discuss this further.

Answer 4.5

Yes. The choice to capitalise or not is given in SSAP 13. The criteria affected by this decision are **recognition and presentation**.

Answer 4.6

Yes. Beelzebub would be changing the way they **presented** the depreciation figure.

Now try Question 4 in the Exam Question Bank at the end of the Text.

Part B
Preparation of final accounts

Chapter 5 Partnership accounts

Chapter topic list

1 The characteristics of partnerships
2 Preparing partnership accounts
3 Retirement or death of a partner
4 Admission of a partner
5 Formation of a partnership from two or more sole traders
6 The dissolution of a partnership

The following study sessions are covered in this chapter.

		Syllabus reference
6-8(a)	Identify the key features of a partnership	2
6-8(b)	Outline the advantages and disadvantages of operating as a partnership, compared with operating as a sole trader or limited company	2
6-8(c)	Outline the conventional methods of dividing profit and maintaining equity between partners	2
6-8(d)	Draft an appropriation account for a partnership	2
6-8(e)	Distinguish between partners' capital and current accounts	2
6-8(f)	Record the partners' share of profits and losses and their drawings in the ledger accounts	2
6-8(g)	Record introductions and withdrawals in the ledger accounts	2
6-8(h)	Draft the trading and profit and loss account and appropriation account and the balance sheet for a partnership from a trial balance incorporating period end adjustments including:	2
	(i) accruals and prepayments	
	(ii) depreciation	
	(iii) bad and doubtful debts	
	(iv) closing stock	
6-8(i)	Explain why a revaluation is required after an admission, a change in the profit sharing ratio or a retirement	2
6-8(j)	Revalue the partnership after such a change and calculate the goodwill	2
6-8(k)	Make appropriate entries in the ledger accounts	2
6-8(l)	Draft the partnership balance sheet after a change in the partnership	2
6-8(m)	Draft the partnership balance sheet after a merger of two sole traders	2
6-8(n)	Account for the dissolution of a partnership	2

Part B: Preparation of final accounts

1 THE CHARACTERISTICS OF PARTNERSHIPS

1.1 So far we have considered businesses owned by one person: sole traders. Now we will consider how we can account for businesses owned by more than one person. Try this activity to get you thinking.

Activity 5.1

Try to think of reasons why a business should be conducted as a partnership, rather than:

(a) As a sole trader
(b) As a company

KEY TERM

Partnership is defined by the Partnership Act 1890 as the relationship which exists between persons carrying on a business in common with a view of profit.

1.2 In other words, a partnership is an arrangement between two or more individuals in which they undertake to share the risks and rewards of a joint business operation.

1.3 It is usual for a partnership to be established formally by means of a **partnership agreement**. However, if individuals act as though they are in partnership even if no written agreement exists, then it will be presumed in law that a partnership does exist and that its terms of agreement are the same as those laid down in the Partnership Act 1890.

The partnership agreement

1.4 The partnership agreement is a written agreement in which the terms of the partnership are set out, and in particular the financial arrangements as between partners. The items it should cover include the following.

(a) **Capital.** Each partner puts in a share of the business capital. If there is to be an agreement on how much each partner should put in and keep in the business, as a minimum fixed amount, this should be stated.

(b) **Profit-sharing ratio.** Partners can agree to share profits in any way they choose. For example, if there are three partners in a business, they might agree to share profits equally but on the other hand, if one partner does a greater share of the work, or has more experience and ability, or puts in more capital, the ratio of profit sharing might be different.

(c) **Interest on capital.** Partners might agree to pay themselves interest on the capital they put into the business. If they do so, the agreement will state what rate of interest is to be applied.

(d) **Partners' salaries.** Partners might also agree to pay themselves salaries. These are not salaries in the same way that an employee of the business will be paid a wage or salary, because partners' salaries are an appropriation of profit, and not an expense in the profit and loss account of the business. The purpose of paying salaries is to give each partner a satisfactory basic income before the residual profits are shared out.

(e) **Drawings.** Partners may draw out their share of profits from the business. However, they might agree to put a limit on how much they should draw out in any period. If so, this limit should be specified in the partnership agreement. To encourage partners to delay taking drawings out of the business until the financial year has ended, the agreement might also be that partners should be charged interest on their drawings during the year.

1.5 In the absence of a formal agreement between the partners, certain rules laid down by the **Partnership Act 1890** are presumed to apply instead.

(a) Residual profits are shared equally between the partners

(b) There are no partners' salaries

(c) Partners receive no interest on the capital they invest in the business

(d) Partners are entitled to interest of 5% per annum on any loans they advance to the business in excess of their agreed capital.

Exam alert

Don't forget that these terms only apply in the absence of any agreement to the contrary. In tackling examination questions you should look first of all for the details of a specific partnership agreement; only if none are given should you apply the provisions of the Partnership Act 1890.

1.6 EXAMPLE: PARTNERS' SALARIES AND PROFIT-SHARING

Suppose Bill and Ben are partners sharing profit in the ratio 2:1 and that they agree to pay themselves a salary of £10,000 each. If profits before deducting salaries are £26,000, how much income would each partner receive?

1.7 SOLUTION

First, the two salaries are deducted from profit, leaving £6,000 (£26,000 – £20,000).

1.8 This £6,000 has to be distributed between Bill and Ben in the ratio 2:1. In other words, Bill will receive twice as much as Ben. You can probably work this out in your head and see that Bill will get £4,000 and Ben £2,000, but we had better see how this is calculated properly.

1.9 Add the 'parts' of the ratio together. For our example, 2 + 1 = 3. Divide this total into whatever it is that has to be shared out. In our example, £6,000 ÷ 3 = £2,000. Each 'part' is worth £2,000, so Bill receives 2 × £2,000 = £4,000 and Ben will receive 1 × £2,000 = £2,000.

1.10 So the final answer to the question is that Bill receives his salary plus £4,000 and Ben his salary plus £2,000. This could be laid out as follows:

	Bill	Ben	Total
	£	£	£
Salary	10,000	10,000	20,000
Share of residual profits (ratio 2:1)	4,000	2,000	6,000
	14,000	12,000	26,000

Activity 5.2

Suppose Tom, Dick and Harry want to share out £150 in the ratio 7:3:5. How much would each get?

Advantages and disadvantages of trading as a partnership

1.11 Operating as a partnership entails certain advantages and disadvantages when compared with both sole traders and limited companies.

Partnership v sole trader

1.12 The advantages of operating as a partnership rather than as a sole trader are practical rather than legal. They include the following.

(a) Risks are spread across a larger number of people.
(b) The trader will have access to a wider network of contacts through the other partners.
(c) Partners should bring to the business not only capital but skills and experience.
(d) It may well be easier to raise finance from external sources such as banks.

1.13 Possible disadvantages include the following.

(a) While the risk is spread over a larger number of people, so are the profits!
(b) By bringing in more people the former sole trader dilutes control over his business.
(c) There may be disputes between the partners.

Partnership v limited company

1.14 Limited companies (covered in detail in the next chapter) offer limited liability to their owners. This means that the maximum amount that an owner stands to lose in the event that the company becomes insolvent and must pay off its debts is the capital in the business. In the case of partnerships (and sole traders), liability for the debts of the business is unlimited, which means that if the business runs up debts and is unable to pay, the proprietors will become personally liable for the unpaid debts and would be required, if necessary, to sell their private possessions in order to pay for them.

1.15 Limited liability is clearly a significant incentive for a partnership to incorporate (become a company). Other advantages of incorporation are that it is easier to raise capital and that the retirement or death of one of its members does not necessitate dissolution and re-formation of the firm.

1.16 In practice, however, particularly for small firms, these advantages are more apparent than real. Banks will normally seek personal guarantees from shareholders before making loans or granting an overdraft facility and so the advantage of limited liability is lost to a small owner managed business.

In addition, a company faces a greater administrative and financial burden arising from:

(a) Compliance with the Companies Act, notably in having to prepare annual accounts and have them audited, file annual returns and keep statutory books
(b) Compliance with accounting standards
(c) Formation and annual registration costs

2 PREPARING PARTNERSHIP ACCOUNTS

How does accounting for partnerships differ from accounting for sole traders?

2.1 Partnership accounts are identical in many respects to the accounts of sole traders.

(a) The assets of a partnership are like the assets of any other business, and are accounted for in the same way. The assets side of a partnership balance sheet is no different from what has been shown in earlier chapters of this Interactive Text.

(b) The net profit of a partnership is calculated in the same way as the net profit of a sole trader. The only minor difference is that if a partner makes a loan to the business (as distinct from capital contribution) then interest on the loan will be an expense in the profit and loss account, in the same way as interest on any other loan from a person or organisation who is not a partner. We will return to partner loans later in the chapter.

2.2 There are two respects in which partnership accounts are different, however.

(a) The funds put into the business by each partner are shown differently.

(b) The net profit must be **appropriated** by the partners. This appropriation of profits must be shown in the partnership accounts.

Exam alert

Appropriation of profit means sharing out profits in accordance with the partnership agreement.

Funds employed

2.3 When a partnership is formed, each partner puts in some capital to the business. These initial capital contributions are recorded in a series of **capital accounts**, one for each partner. (Since each partner is ultimately entitled to repayment of his capital it is clearly vital to keep a record of how much is owed to whom.) Partners do not have to put in the same amount.

IMPORTANT!

The balance for the capital account will always be a brought forward credit entry in the partnership accounts, because the capital contributed by proprietors is a liability of the business.

2.4 In addition to a capital account, each partner normally has:

- A **current account**
- A **drawings account**

KEY TERM

A **current account** is used to record the *profits retained in the business* by the partner.

2.5 It is therefore a sort of capital account, which increases in value when the partnership makes profits, and falls in value when the partner whose current account it is makes drawings out of the business.

2.6 The main differences between the capital and current account in accounting for partnerships are that:

(a) (i) Whereas the balance on the capital account remains static from year to year (with one or two exceptions)

Part B: Preparation of final accounts

(ii) The current account is continually fluctuating up and down, as the partnership makes profits which are shared out between the partners, and as each partner takes out drawings

(b) A further difference is that when the partnership agreement provides for interest on capital, partners receive interest on the balance in their capital account, but *not on the balance in their current account*.

2.7 The drawings accounts serve exactly the same purpose as the drawings account for a sole trader. Each partner's drawings are recorded in a separate account. At the end of an accounting period, each partner's drawings are cleared to his current account; ie

DEBIT   Current account of partner
CREDIT   Drawings account of partner

(If the amount of the drawings exceeds the balance on a partner's current account, the current account will show a debit balance. However, in normal circumstances, we should expect to find a credit balance on the current accounts.)

2.8 The partnership balance sheet will therefore consist of:

- The capital accounts of each partner
- The current accounts of each partner, net of drawings

This will be illustrated in an example later.

Loans by partners

2.9 In addition, it is sometimes the case that an existing or previous partner will make a loan to the partnership in which case he becomes a creditor of the partnership. On the balance sheet, such a loan is not included as partners' funds, but is shown separately as a long-term liability (unless repayable within twelve months in which case it is a current liability). This is the case whether or not the loan creditor is also an existing partner.

2.10 However, **interest on such loans will be credited to the partner's current account** (if he is an existing partner). This is administratively more convenient, especially when the partner does not particularly want to be paid the loan interest in cash immediately it becomes due. Remember:

(a) Interest on loans from a partner is accounted for as an expense in the P & L account, and not as an appropriation of profit, even though the interest is added to the current account of the partners.

(b) If there is no interest rate specified, the Partnership Act 1890 (section 24) provides for interest to be paid at 5% pa on loans by partners.

Appropriation of net profits

2.11 The net profit of a partnership is shared out between them according to the terms of their agreement. This sharing out is shown in a **profit and loss appropriation account**, which follows on from the profit and loss account itself.

The accounting entries are:

(a) DEBIT   Profit and loss account with net profit c/d
     CREDIT Profit and loss appropriation account with net profit b/d

(b) DEBIT   Profit and loss appropriation account
    CREDIT The current accounts of each partner

with an individual share of profits for each partner.

2.12 The way in which profit is shared out depends on the terms of the partnership agreement. The steps to take are as follows.

Step 1. Establish how much the net profit is.

Step 2. Appropriate interest on capital and salaries first. Both of these items are an appropriation of profit and are not expenses in the P & L account.

Step 3. If partners agree to pay interest on their drawings during the year

DEBIT   Current accounts
CREDIT Appropriation of profit account

Step 4. *Residual profits*: the difference between net profits (plus any interest charged on drawings) and appropriations for interest on capital and salaries is the residual profit. This is shared out between partners in the profit-sharing ratio.

Step 5. Each partner's share of profits is credited to his current account.

Step 6. The balance on each partner's drawings account is debited to his current account.

2.13 In practice each partner's capital account will occupy a separate ledger account, as will his current account etc. The examples which follow in this text use the columnar form; they might also ignore the breakdown of net assets employed (fixed, current assets etc) to help to clarify and simplify the illustrations.

Exam alert

For examination purposes, it is customary to represent the details of these accounts side by side, in columnar form, to save time.

2.14 EXAMPLE: PARTNERSHIP ACCOUNTS

Locke, Niece and Munster are in partnership with an agreement to share profits in the ratio 3:2:1. They also agree that:

(a) All three should receive interest at 12% on capital.

(b) Munster should receive a salary of £6,000 per annum.

(c) Interest will be charged on drawings at the rate of 5% (charged on the end of year drawings balances).

(d) The interest rate on the loan by Locke is 5%.

The balance sheet of the partnership as at 31 December 20X5 revealed the following.

Part B: Preparation of final accounts

	£	£
Capital accounts		
Locke	20,000	
Niece	8,000	
Munster	6,000	
		34,000
Current accounts		
Locke	3,500	
Niece	(700)	
Munster	1,800	
		4,600
Loan account (Locke)		6,000
Capital employed to finance net fixed assets and working capital		44,600

Drawings made during the year to 31 December 20X6 were:

	£
Locke	6,000
Niece	4,000
Munster	7,000

The net profit for the year to 31 December 20X6 was £24,530 before deducting loan interest.

Required

Prepare the profit and loss appropriation account for the year to 31 December 20X6, and the partners' capital accounts, and current accounts.

2.15 SOLUTION

The interest payable by each partner on their drawings during the year is:

		£
Locke	5% of £6,000	300
Niece	5% of £4,000	200
Munster	5% of £7,000	350
		850

These payments are debited to the current accounts and credited to the profit and loss *appropriation* account.

2.16 The interest payable to Locke on his loan is:

5% of £6,000 = £300

2.17 We can now begin to work out the appropriation of profits.

		£	£
Net profit, less loan interest (deducted in P & L a/c £24,530 - £300)			24,230
Add interest on drawings			850
			25,080
Less Munster salary			6,000
			19,080
Less Interest on capital			
Locke	(12% of £20,000)	2,400	
Niece	(12% of £ 8,000)	960	
Munster	(12% of £ 6,000)	720	
			4,080
			15,000
Residual profits:			
Locke	(3)	7,500	
Niece	(2)	5,000	
Munster	(1)	2,500	
			15,000

2.18 Make sure you remember what the various interest figures represent and that you understand exactly what has been calculated here.

(a) The partners can take some drawings out of the business, but if they do they will be charged interest on it.

(b) The partners have capital tied up in the business (of course, otherwise there would be no business) and they have agreed to pay themselves interest on whatever capital each has put in.

(c) Once all the necessary adjustments have been made to net profit, £15,000 remains and is divided up between the partners in the ratio 3:2:1.

2.19 Now the financial statements for the partnership can be prepared.

LOCKE NIECE MUNSTER
PROFIT AND LOSS APPROPRIATION ACCOUNT
FOR THE YEAR ENDED 31 DECEMBER 20X6

	£	£		£	£
			Net profit b/d		24,230
Salaries - Munster		6,000	Interest on drawings:		
Interest on capital			Current account of		
Locke	2,400		Locke	300	
Niece	960		Niece	200	
Munster	720		Munster	350	
		4,080			850
Residual profits					
Locke	7,500				
Niece	5,000				
Munster	2,500				
		15,000			
		25,080			25,080

Part B: Preparation of final accounts

PARTNERS' CURRENT ACCOUNTS

	Locke £	Niece £	Munster £		Locke £	Niece £	Munster £
Balance b/f		700		Balance b/f	3,500		1,800
Interest on drawings	300	200	350	Loan interest	300		
Drawings	6,000	4,000	7,000	Interest on capital	2,400	960	720
Balance c/f	7,400	1,060	3,670	Salary			6,000
				Residual profits	7,500	5,000	2,500
	13,700	5,960	11,020		13,700	5,960	11,020
				Balance b/f	7,400	1,060	3,670

PARTNERS' CAPITAL ACCOUNTS

	Locke £	Niece £	Munster £
Balance b/f	20,000	8,000	6,000

2.20 The balance sheet of the partners as at 31 December 20X6 would be:

	£	£
Capital accounts		
Locke	20,000	
Niece	8,000	
Munster	6,000	
		34,000
Current accounts		
Locke	7,400	
Niece	1,060	
Munster	3,670	
		12,130
		46,130
Net assets		
As at 31 December 20X5		44,600
Added during the year (applying the business equation, this is the difference between net profits and drawings = £24,230 - £17,000)		7,230
Add loan interest added to Locke's current account and not paid out		300
As at 31 December 20X6		52,130
Less long term creditors		
Loan: Locke		(6,000)
		46,130

2.21 Again, make sure you understand what has happened here.

(a) The partners' *capital* accounts have not changed. They were brought forward at £20,000, £8,000 and £6,000, and they are just the same in the new balance sheet.

(b) The partners' *current* accounts have changed. The balances brought forward from last year's balance sheet of £3,500, (£700) and £1,800 have become £7,400, £1,060 and £3,670 in the new balance sheet. How this came about is shown in the partners' current (ledger) accounts.

(c) The events recorded in the current accounts are a reflection of how the partnership has distributed its profit, and this was shown in the profit and loss appropriation account.

3 RETIREMENT OR DEATH OF A PARTNER

3.1 Any changes in a partnership constitution require a new partnership agreement, as the arrangements relating to appropriation of profits etc are likely to be changed. Legally, the old partnership is dissolved and a new partnership created, but from the accounting point of view it is more realistic to make appropriate adjustments in the existing partnership books, rather than to close them off and start afresh.

3.2 When an existing partner dies, or decides to retire from the partnership, his share of the partnership assets must be calculated and transferred to him (or to his personal representatives). Unless all the partnership assets and liabilities are correctly valued in the books, the partner's capital and current account total will not show his actual entitlement.

3.3 Normally, the true worth of the partnership will exceed the book figure of net assets, and so various assets/ liabilities will have to be **revalued** and goodwill taken into account, if only on a temporary basis.

3.4 When assets are revalued, any profits or losses on revaluation are entered, in profit sharing ratio, in the partners' capital accounts (rather than their current accounts) unless there is agreement to the contrary.

3.5 Usually, since a number of items may be affected, a revaluation account is used to arrive at a total balance of profit or loss on revaluation. This balance is then divided between the partners in profit sharing ratio in their capital accounts.

3.6 EXAMPLE: DEATH OF A PARTNER

Scrap, Iron and Ore are partners in a scrap metal business, sharing profits in the ratio 5:3:2 respectively. Their capital and current account balances on 1 January 20X3 were as follows.

	Capital accounts £	Current accounts £
Scrap	24,000	29,900
Iron	18,000	4,300
Ore	13,000	(200)

Driving home from a New Year Party, Iron neglected to make a necessary right turn and drove into a river and drowned. On 1 January 20X3 (the date of Iron's death) certain assets of the Scrap, Iron and Ore partnership were revalued. The breakdown of the total assets less current liabilities figure (in the 31 December 20X2 accounts), together with relevant revaluations was as follows:

	Book value £	Valuation £
Freehold property	30,000	45,000
Equipment and machinery (WDV)	25,000	20,500
Stocks	30,000	30,000
Debtors (one emigrated and could not be traced)	18,000	17,500
Bank	10,000	10,000
	113,000	123,000
Creditors	(24,000)	(24,000)
Net assets	89,000	99,000

Show the journal entries recording the above revaluations in the partnership books.

Part B: Preparation of final accounts

3.7 SOLUTION

JOURNAL

		£	£
DEBIT	Freehold property	15,000	
CREDIT	Revaluation account		15,000
	Being profit on revaluation		
DEBIT	Revaluation account	5,000	
CREDIT	Equipment and machinery		4,500
	Debtors		500
	Being loss on revaluation		
DEBIT	Revaluation account	10,000	
CREDIT	Partners' capital accounts		
	Scrap (5/10)		5,000
	Iron (3/10)		3,000
	Ore (2/10)		2,000

Being net profit on revaluation of assets divided between the partners in profit sharing ratio.

Remember that if the revaluation of the partnership assets had brought about a net decrease in value, then the partners would be debited with the loss.

Goodwill

3.8 In addition to revaluing tangible assets when there is a change in a partnership, the problem of **goodwill** may have to be considered. Goodwill, whether originally purchased or whether internally generated is dependent on a wide variety of factors, such as business location, reputation, staff personalities and the ability to earn profits or 'super profits' etc. The concept will be expanded in Chapter 12.

> **KEY TERM**
>
> **Goodwill** is the excess of the price paid for a business over the market value of its individual assets and liabilities.

3.9 Goodwill often has to be calculated when fixing the purchase (or sale) price of a business, as well as when a partnership constitution is changed. There are many ways of arriving at a value for goodwill and most of them are related to the profit record of the business.

> **Exam alert**
>
> For your examination the value of goodwill is usually either given or you are told to calculate it as an average of recent years' profits.

3.10 A partner who retires or dies must be credited with his fair share of the partnership assets, including goodwill. Just as the profit/loss on revaluation of tangible items was divided between the partners, so the goodwill figure (once calculated per the partnership agreement) has to be entered in the partnership books. The journal entry made in Scrap, Iron and Ore's books (assuming an arbitrary figure for goodwill of £32,000) would be:

JOURNAL

		£	£
DEBIT	Goodwill account	32,000	
CREDIT	Partners' capital accounts:		
	Scrap (5/10)		16,000
	Iron (3/10)		9,600
	Ore (2/10)		6,400

Being introduction of goodwill into the partnership books.

3.11 The partners' capital accounts on 1 January 20X3 are now:

CAPITAL ACCOUNTS

	Scrap £	Iron £	Ore £		Scrap £	Iron £	Ore £
Iron's estate (personal Representative's account)		30,600		Balance b/d	24,000	18,000	13,000
				Revaluation	5,000	3,000	2,000
Balances c/f	45,000		21,400	Goodwill	16,000	9,600	6,400
	45,000	30,600	21,400		45,000	30,600	21,400

3.12 The balances on the **deceased partner's** capital and current accounts (£30,600 + £4,300) are transferred to a separate loan account. The total of £34,900 is a liability of the partnership and has to be paid to Iron's personal representative.

3.13 A **retiring partner** may take his full entitlement immediately (in cash or in assets) but often will only take part of the amount due, leaving the balance as a loan to the partnership to be repaid over a period of time. Any interest paid on the loan is a chargeable expense in the profit and loss account.

Elimination of goodwill

3.14 Once goodwill appears in the books, the partners must decide what to do with it. Whether goodwill is a 'premium paid on acquisition' (when a business is acquired as a going concern) or whether it is internally generated, it is often unstable and is usually difficult to quantify. There are three principal ways to treat goodwill.

(a) Retain goodwill in the accounts indefinitely (as an intangible asset) on the basis that the total goodwill of a business tends to increase rather than decrease, and so write-off is unnecessary.

(b) Write off goodwill over a period of years, on the basis that goodwill has a limited life and is a cost to be offset against future profits.

(c) Write off goodwill immediately on the grounds of prudence. The goodwill never appears in the balance sheet and so the fact that goodwill does have some value, however difficult it is to quantify, is ignored.

3.15 EXAMPLE: GOODWILL

In Scrap, Iron and Ore the two surviving partners decide to continue in partnership sharing profits in the ratio: Scrap 2: Ore 1. If goodwill is to be retained in the books of the new partnership no further entry is required. However, if it is to be eliminated, then the 'new' partners have to bear the write-off in their new profit sharing ratio.

Part B: Preparation of final accounts

JOURNAL

		£	£
DEBIT	Partners' capital accounts:		
	Scrap (2/3)	21,333	
	Ore (1/3)	10,667	
CREDIT	Goodwill account		32,000

Being goodwill written off in the partnership books.

Activity 5.3

Putty and Glass are in partnership sharing profits 3:2. Glass decides to retire. It is agreed that the business is worth £150,000 as a whole and that the net tangible assets are worth £100,000. Glass has a debit balance on his current account of £2,000 and a credit balance on capital account of £25,000, before allowing for goodwill. How much must be paid to Glass on his retirement?

4 ADMISSION OF A PARTNER

4.1 When a prospective partner is due to be admitted to a partnership, the old partners will wish to ensure that they receive their full entitlement to partnership profits up to the date of the change in the constitution. Similarly, the 'new' partner will not wish to bear any losses which may have arisen during the period prior to his admission.

4.2 Consequently, as in the case of retirement or death of a partner, the partnership assets (including goodwill) will have to be **revalued** and the new values introduced (and possibly later eliminated) from the partnership books.

4.3 If the new partner introduces **additional capital** into the partnership, the total amount of cash/assets he brings in must be **credited** to his capital account. This account may include (in examination questions at least) an amount he brings in for goodwill.

4.4 EXAMPLE: ADMISSION OF A PARTNER

Oil and Grease, equal partners in a vehicle repair business, agree to Detergent becoming a partner on 1 January 20X1. Their capitals are Oil - £12,000; Grease - £9,000; and Detergent agrees to introduce £3,000 capital and £2,000 for his share of the partnership goodwill. The partners agree to share profits in the ratio - Oil 2: Grease 2: Detergent 1: and decide that goodwill should not be shown in the books.

The partners' capital accounts, with goodwill of £10,000 (£2,000 being a one-fifth share of the total goodwill) being introduced and eliminated are:

CAPITAL ACCOUNTS

	Oil £	Grease £	Detergent £		Oil £	Grease £	Detergent £
Goodwill:				Balances b/f	12,000	9,000	
Oil (2/5)	4,000			Bank-cash			
Grease (2/5)		4,000		introduced			5,000
Detergent (1/5)			2,000	Goodwill:			
				Oil (½)	5,000		
Balances c/f	13,000	10,000	3,000	Grease (½)		5,000	
	17,000	14,000	5,000		17,000	14,000	5,000

Should the old partners wish to withdraw their share of the premium paid by Detergent for goodwill, they can each take out £1,000 (Dr Capital accounts Cr Cash), thus restoring their capitals to the original amounts.

4.5 When tangible assets are revalued on the admission of a new partner, the profit or loss on revaluation must be divided between the old partners. Generally the new values are retained in the books (as indeed goodwill may be), but should the examination question state that 'new values are not be introduced' the profit or loss has to be apportioned between the new partners (as illustrated above).

Partnership changes during a financial period

4.6 If a change in the constitution of a partnership takes place during the financial year the profit and loss appropriation account will have to be prepared in two stages in columnar form. Generally it is assumed that profit is earned evenly over a period (unless otherwise stated), but some points to watch out for are as follows.

(a) If an employee is admitted to partnership in mid-year, his salary whilst an employee is an expense chargeable wholly against profits of the first part of the year and subsequent drawings are debited to his current account.

(b) If a partner leaves in mid-year and a loan account is created, interest on the loan account is chargeable as an expense against profits of the last part of the year only.

5 FORMATION OF A PARTNERSHIP FROM TWO OR MORE SOLE TRADERS

5.1 When two or more businesses decide to combine their operations (to expand their range of operations, achieve some economies of scale etc) the problems of accounting for the amalgamation will arise. In respect of partnership accounts typical problems are concerned with either:

- Two (or more) sole traders amalgamating to form a partnership; *or*
- A sole trader amalgamating with an existing partnership; *or*
- Two partnerships amalgamating to form a new partnership.

We are concerned with the first of these situations.

5.2 Whatever the type of amalgamation, the accounting problems are very much the same. As we have already seen, where a partner retires from, or a new partner is admitted to, a partnership, problems arise in respect of revaluing assets, valuing goodwill, establishing new profit shares, ascertaining new capital introduced, and so on. All these problems of establishing and evaluating assets which are to be brought in, and liabilities which are to be taken over by the new partnership, are relevant to amalgamations.

5.3 The old firms' assets and liabilities are **realised** by 'sale' to the new firm, not for cash, but for a share in the capital of the new business, the amount of capital being determined by the value of net assets contributed.

5.4 A **revaluation account** is used in each of the old firms' existing set of books to account for and apportion to the sole traders their share of the profit or loss on revaluation of assets and liabilities. A goodwill account (if necessary) is used to introduce (or increase) the goodwill, and to credit the sole traders with their share.

5.5 Once both firms have adjusted their asset, liability and capital accounts to take into account the agreed values, the separate books may be merged. The traders' agreed capital balances are transferred to the new firm capital accounts and goodwill written off (in new profit sharing ratio) if necessary.

5.6 EXAMPLE: TWO SOLE TRADERS BECOMING A PARTNERSHIP.

Sinner and Gee were two sole traders in the same line of business. On 1 January 20X1 the two firms were to be merged to form Sinnergee, the partners sharing the profits equally. The summarised balance sheets of the two firms on 31 December 20X0 were as follows.

BALANCE SHEETS AS AT 31 DECEMBER 20X0

	Sinner £	Gee £
Assets		
Freehold property		20,000
Plant etc	12,500	
Debtors	12,000	
Cash	8,000	2,000
	32,500	22,000
Liabilities		
Creditors	(2,500)	
	30,000	22,000
Capital		
Sinner	30,000	
Gee		22,000
	30,000	22,000

The freehold property is to be revalued at £24,000 and the plant at £11,000. Goodwill is agreed at £5,000 for Sinner and £2,500 for Gee, but is not to appear on the books. All assets and liabilities are taken over by the new firm.

Show the capital accounts of the sole traders just before the merger, the partners' capital accounts in the new partnership, and the opening balance sheet (in draft form) of Sinnergee.

5.7 SOLUTION

SINNER - CAPITAL ACCOUNT

	£		£
Revaluation a/c (12,500 - 11,000)	1,500	Balance b/f	30,000
Transfer to Sinnergee	33,500	Goodwill	5,000
	35,000		35,000

GEE - CAPITAL ACCOUNT

	£		£
		Balance b/f	22,000
		Revaluation a/c	4,000
Transfer to Sinnergee	28,500	Goodwill	2,500
	28,500		28,500

SINNERGEE - CAPITAL ACCOUNTS

	Sinner £	Gee £		Sinner £	Gee £
Goodwill w/off 1:1	3,750	3,750	Transfer: old firms	33,500	28,500
Balances c/d	29,750	24,750			
	33,500	28,500		33,500	28,500

SINNERGEE
DRAFT OPENING BALANCE SHEET

	£
Assets	
Freehold property	24,000
Plant etc	11,000
Debtors	12,000
Cash	10,000
	57,000
Liabilities	
Creditors	(2,500)
	54,500
Capital	
Sinner	29,750
Gee	24,750
	54,500

6 THE DISSOLUTION OF A PARTNERSHIP

6.1 We will now examine the sequence of events when the business does *not* continue and the partnership ceases to exist.

Step 1. All assets (except cash) and liabilities are transferred to a realisation account at their book value.

Step 2. Each partner's current account is cleared to his capital account, as the distinction between the two is irrelevant at this stage.

Step 3. As the assets are sold and liabilities are settled, double entry is made between the realisation account and the cash account. Any realisation expenses are debited to the realisation account. If partners take over assets this fact is recorded in their accounts.

Step 4. When all assets are disposed of and all liabilities met, the balance on the realisation account is transferred to the partners' accounts, in their profit sharing ratio. A credit balance on the realisation account represents a profit on dissolution, a debit balance a loss.

Step 5. At this stage the total amount due to the partners should equal the cash balance. The cash is distributed and the partnership is over.

6.2 EXAMPLE: DISSOLUTION

Hop Skip and Jump decide to dissolve their partnership on 1 January 20X2, after an ugly scene at Skip's New Year's Eve party. The balance sheet of the partnership as at 31 December 20X1, was as follows:

Part B: Preparation of final accounts

	£	£		£	£
Capital accounts			Fixed assets at net book value		
Hop	21,000		Furniture and fittings	20,000	
Skip	21,000		Motor vehicles	16,000	
Jump	10,000				36,000
		52,000			
Current accounts			Current assets		
Hop	5,750		Investments	21,000	
Skip	2,450		Debtors	37,000	
Jump	2,500		Balance at bank	3,000	
		10,700			61,000
Loan		15,000			
Creditors		19,300			
		97,000			97,000

The loan was repaid, interest already having been paid up to 31 December 20X1. The furniture and fittings were sold for £18,200 and Jump took over a motor vehicle (which had a net book value of £5,000) at an agreed valuation of £6,000. The other vehicles were sold for £13,450 after repairs had first been carried out on a faulty transit van by the Gloria Monday Service Station, at a cost of £450. Debtors realised only £34,800. Because of large discounts available, creditors were settled for £17,600. The investments realised £22,300. Dissolution expenses, excluding the transit van repair costs, totalled £750. Hop, Skip and Jump share profits and losses in the ratio 2:2:1.

You are required to show the relevant accounts and the final distribution between the partners.

Approach and solution

6.3 The first stage in accounting for the dissolution is:

(a) To combine the capital and current account for each partner, since the distinction between the two is no longer relevant

(b) To transfer all assets (except cash) and liabilities to a realisation account at their book value. A liability will appear as a credit entry in the realisation account and an asset as a debit entry

PARTNERSHIP ACCOUNTS

	Hop £	Skip £	Jump £
Capital account: balance b/f	21,000	21,000	10,000
Current account: balance b/f	5,750	2,450	2,500
	26,750	23,450	12,500

REALISATION ACCOUNT

	£		£
Furniture and fittings (NBV)	20,000	Loan account	15,000
Motor vehicles (NBV)	16,000	Creditors	19,300
Investments	21,000		
Debtors	37,000		

CASH AND BANK

	£
Balance b/f	3,000

The net result of these accounting entries is to clear all the accounts of the partnership, except for the three shown above.

6.4 The next stage is to record what happens on the sale of the business assets and settlement of the business debts.

(a) In paying creditors and redeeming loans:

DEBIT   Realisation account
CREDIT   Cash and bank account

(b) In selling assets (for cash):

DEBIT   Cash and bank account
CREDIT   Realisation account

(c) Costs incurred in the dissolution (or on realisation):

DEBIT   Realisation account
CREDIT   Cash and bank account

(d) Assets taken out by partners:

DEBIT   Partner's account, with the agreed valuation of the asset
CREDIT   Realisation account.

6.5 The accounts now appear as follows.

PARTNERS' ACCOUNTS

	Hop £	Skip £	Jump £		Hop £	Skip £	Jump £
Realisation account (vehicle)			6,000	Balance b/f	26,750	23,450	12,500

REALISATION ACCOUNT

	£		£
Furniture and fittings	20,000	Loan account	15,000
Motor vehicles	16,000	Creditors	19,300
Investments	21,000		
Debtors	37,000		
Cash and bank		Cash and bank: proceeds	
Loan account paid off	15,000	Furniture and fittings	18,200
Creditors-debts settled	17,600	Motor vehicles	13,450
Transit van repairs	450	Investments	22,300
Realisation expenses	750	Debtors	34,800
Balance (ie balancing figure)	1,250	Jump's account (motor vehicle)	6,000
	129,050		129,050

CASH AND BANK

	£		£
Balance b/f	3,000	Realisation account	
Realisation account		Loan	15,000
Furniture and fittings	18,200	Creditors	17,600
Motor vehicles	13,450	Transit van repairs	450
Investments	22,300	Expenses	750
Debtors	34,800	Balance c/f	57,950
	91,750		91,750

6.6 The balances on the various accounts are now as follows.

Part B: Preparation of final accounts

			£	£	£
CREDIT	Partners' accounts:	Hop		26,750	
		Skip		23,450	
		Jump		6,500	
					56,700
DEBIT	Cash and bank		57,950		
CREDIT	Realisation account				1,250

6.7 The balance on the realisation account is the profit or loss on realisation. In this example, there is a profit on realisation.

	Proceeds from realisation £	Book value of assets less liabilities £
Furniture and fittings	18,200	20,000
Motor vehicles (13,450 + 6,000)	19,450	16,000
Investments	22,300	21,000
Debtors	34,800	37,000
Loan	(15,000)	(15,000)
Creditors	(17,600)	(19,300)
Van repairs	(450)	
Expenses	(750)	
	60,950	59,700

6.8 Excess of proceeds over net book values £(60,950 − 59,700) = £1,250.

6.9 The next stage is to share the profit or loss on realisation between the partners in the profit sharing ratio. Having done this, the money due to each partner is established, and the partnership accounts are ended by:

- Crediting the bank account
- Debiting the partners' accounts

with the money due to and so paid to each partner.

6.10 The final accounts are as follows.

REALISATION ACCOUNT

	£	£		£
Book values			Book values	
Furniture & fittings		20,000	Loan	15,000
Motor vehicles		16,000	Creditors	19,300
Investments		21,000		
Debtors		37,000	Bank	
Bank			Furniture etc	18,200
Loan repaid		15,000	Motor vehicles	13,450
Creditors		17,600	Debtors	34,800
Repairs		450	Investment	22,300
Expenses		750		
Profit on realisation			Jump (vehicle)	6,000
Hop (2)	500			
Skip (2)	500			
Jump (1)	250			
		1,250		
		129,050		129,050

PARTNERS' ACCOUNTS

	Hop £	Skip £	Jump £		Hop £	Skip £	Jump £
Realisation a/c			6,000	Capital b/d	21,000	21,000	10,000
Cash *	27,250	23,950	6,750	Current b/d	5,750	2,450	2,500
				Realisation a/c	500	500	250
	27,250	23,950	12,750		27,250	23,950	12,750

* Balance due to each partner, and so paid out of the partnership's bank account.

CASH AND BANK

	£		£	£
Balance b/d	3,000	Realisation a/c		
		Loan		15,000
Realisation a/c		Creditors		17,600
Furniture etc	18,200	Repairs		450
Motor vehicles	13,450	Expenses		750
Debtors	34,800			
Investment	22,300	Partners' accounts:		
		Hop	27,250	
		Skip	23,950	
		Jump	6,750	
				57,950
	91,750			91,750

Insolvency of a partner: Garner v Murray

6.11 If a partner has a **debit balance** on his account at the end of the dissolution he must make the necessary **contribution to the partnership**. Suppose that the accounts of A, B and C, three partners sharing profits in the ratio 3:2:1, appeared as follows after completing the realisation account.

PARTNERS' ACCOUNTS

	A £	B £	C £		A £	B £	C £
Realisation a/c:				Capital a/c b/f	12,000	6,000	2,000
loss	9,600	6,400	3,200	Current a/c b/f	1,000	800	900
Balance c/d	3,400	400		Balance c/d			300
	13,000	6,800	3,200		13,000	6,800	3,200
Balance b/d			300	Balance b/d	3,400	400	

6.12 At this stage, the bank balance would stand at £3,500. C would be required to make good his deficit by paying £300 into the partnership bank account. A and B could then receive the amounts of £3,400 and £400 respectively which are due to them.

6.13 What happens if C is insolvent and cannot make good his deficit? In that case there will only be £3,500 to meet the claims of A and B and they will have to bear a £300 loss. It might seem fair that the loss should be shared in the ratio 3:2, since that is their profit sharing ratio.

Part B: Preparation of final accounts

> **RULE TO LEARN**
>
> The rule in the case of *Garner v Murray 1904* is that in the event of the insolvency of a partner, such losses should be shared in the ratio of the last agreed capital balances (ie the capital balances **before** the dissolution begins).

In this case, A and B would bear the loss in the proportions 12:6:

A   12/18 × £300 = £200
B   6/18 × £300 = £100

6.14   The partners' accounts can then be closed off as follows.

PARTNERS' ACCOUNTS

	A £	B £	C £		A £	B £	C £
Balance b/f			300	Balance b/f	3,400	400	
C's deficit	200	100		A and B			300
Bank	3,200	300					
	3,400	400	300		3,400	400	300

6.15   Many partnership agreements exclude the rule established in *Garner v Murray*, in which case the deficit must be borne by the other partners in their profit sharing ratio. If this was the case in the example above the £300 deficit would be borne by A and B in the ratio 3:2, so A £180, B £120.

> **Exam alert**
>
> An exam question may ask you to apply the rule in *Garner v Murray*.

Activity 5.4

Alpha and Beta are in partnership. They share profits equally after Alpha has been allowed a salary of £4,000 pa. No interest is charged on drawings or allowed on current accounts or capital accounts. The trial balance of the partnership at 31 December 20X9 before adjusting for any of the items below, is as follows:

		Dr £'000	Cr £'000
Capital	- Alpha		30
	- Beta		25
Current	- Alpha		3
	- Beta		4
Drawings	- Alpha	4	
	- Beta	5	
Sales			200
Stock 1 January 20X9		30	
Purchases		103	
Operating expenses		64	
Loan	- Beta (10%)		10
	- Gamma (10%)		20
Land and buildings		60	
Plant and machinery	- cost	70	
	- depreciation to 31 December 20X9		40
Debtors and creditors		40	33
Bank			11
		376	376

(i) Closing stock on hand at 31 December was £24,000.

(ii) On 31 December Alpha and Beta agree to take their manager, Gamma, into partnership. Gamma's loan account balance is to be transferred to a capital account as at 31 December. It is agreed that in future Alpha, Beta and Gamma will all share profits equally. Alpha will be allowed a salary of £4,000 as before, and Gamma will be allowed a salary of £5,000 per annum (half of what he received in 20X9 as manager, included in operating expenses).

The three partners agree that the goodwill of the business at 31 December should be valued at £12,000, but is not to be recorded in the books. It is also agreed that land and buildings are to be revalued to a figure of £84,000 and that this revalued figure is to be retained and recorded in the accounts.

(iii) Interest on the loan has not been paid.

(iv) Included in sales are two items sold on 'sale or return' for £3,000 each. Each item had cost the business £1,000. One of these items was in fact returned on 4 January 19Y0 and the other was one formally accepted by the customer on 6 January 19Y0.

Task

(a) Submit with appropriately labelled headings and subheadings:

 (i) partners' capital accounts in columnar form;
 (ii) partners' current accounts in columnar form;
 (iii) trading, profit and loss and appropriation account for 20X9;
 (iv) balance sheet as at 31 December 20X9.

(b) Write a brief note to Gamma, who cannot understand why his capital account balance seems so much less than those of Alpha and Beta. Explain to him the adjustments you have made.

Activity 5.5

Lucas and Lodge have been in partnership for many years running a medium-sized country hotel in Hertfordshire. When they started the business, they did not have a formal written partnership agreement, but agreed to share the profits in the ratio Lucas $^2/_5$, Lodge $^3/_5$.

Lucas has produced a summarised balance sheet as at 31 December 20X7.

	£'000
Fixed assets	
Land	100
Buildings	75
Fixtures and fittings	30
	205
Current assets	40
Current liabilities	(35)
Net assets	210
Capital accounts	
Lucas	90
Lodge	120
	210

After Lucas produced this balance sheet, the partners decided to draw up a written partnership agreement in preparation for the new accounting year, stating, amongst other things, that profits were to be shared equally. At the same time, the partners agreed to make changes to the value of certain assets as follows.

(a) The hotel buildings are to be revalued upwards to £115,000 as at 31 December 20X7. However, the revaluation is not to remain in the books of the partnership.

(b) The land is to be revalued downwards as at 31 December 20X7 to £80,000. The revaluation is to remain in the books of the partnership.

(c) The values of the fixtures and fittings, current assets and current liabilities are to stay the same as in the balance sheet prepared by Lucas. However, the value of the business as a whole (the net assets) is to be £270,000.

Part B: Preparation of final accounts

Task

(a) What are the implications for Lucas of the change in profit sharing ratio?

(b) Prepare a summarised balance sheet for the partnership as at 1 January 20X8, taking account of the new profit sharing ratio and the above revaluations.

   Note. You should present your workings clearly.

(c) How and why do each of the following affect the partners' capital accounts?

   (i)   The revaluation of the hotel
   (ii) The revaluation of the land
   (iii) The valuation of the business as a whole

(d) Account for the change in the balance on Lodge's capital account, showing how each component of the change is different in the case of Lucas. Set out your answer in a table as follows.

Effect on Lodge's capital account + (–) £'000	Explanation	Effect on Lucas' capital account + (–) £'000

To what do you attribute the different effects on each partner's capital account? Has either of the partners 'lost out'?

(e) If the aim of a balance sheet is to show the financial state of affairs of a business at a given point in time, which of the two balance sheets, the one prepared by Lucas and the one prepared by you in part (b), best fulfils this objective? Give reasons for your answer.

5: Partnership accounts

Key learning points

- Accounting for a partnership is for the most part the same as accounting for a sole trader except in the following respects.
- The initial capital put into the business by each partner is shown by means of a **capital account** for each partner.
- Each partner also has a **current account** and a drawings account.
- The net profit of the partnership is **appropriated** by the partners according to some **previously agreed ratio**.
- Partners may be charged **interest on their drawings**, and may receive interest on capital. If a partner makes a **loan** to the business, he will receive interest on it in the normal way.
- On **admission** or **retirement** of a partner one partnership ends and another begins.
- Calculate **goodwill**. Assuming, as is usual, it is to be eliminated:
  - Credit old partners in their profit sharing rates
  - Debit new partners in their profit sharing ratio
- Partnerships may be **terminated** either by closing down the business entirely or by disposing of the business as a going concern to a limited company.
- In either case the key to getting the double entry right is to begin by closing off asset and liability accounts (except cash) and transferring their balances to a single **realisation account**.
- At this stage, the balances on the realisation account and bank account are **matched** by the combined balances on the partners' personal accounts.
- As liabilities are settled, credit bank and debit realisation account.
- As assets are taken over by partners or by a limited company at agreed values, debit personal accounts and credit realisation account.
- Transfer the balance on realisation account to the partners' accounts. **Close partners' accounts** by debiting them with cash.
- Following *Garner v Murray,* if a partner is insolvent and cannot make good his deficit, losses must be shared in the ratio of the last agreed capital balances.

Quick quiz

1. What is a partnership?
2. Is a partner's salary an expense of the partnership?
3. Why might a sole trader take on a partner?
4. If a partnership does not have a written partnership agreement, what is the interest to be paid on a partnership loan?
5. What are the entries required to introduce goodwill into a partnership and subsequently to eliminate it?
6. If tangible assets are revalued on admission of a partner, how is the profit or loss on revaluation treated?
7. What is the double entry to record:
   (a) The sale of partnership assets for cash?
   (b) Dissolution costs incurred?
8. When a partner is insolvent and unable to make good his deficit, losses must be apportioned in the profit sharing ratio. True or false?

Part B: Preparation of final accounts

Answers to quick quiz

1 The relationship which exists between persons carrying on a business in common with a view of profit.

2 No. They are an appropriation of profit.

3 To spread the risk, to bring in extra capital and to widen a network of contacts.

4 5% pa.

5 To introduce goodwill:

DEBIT	Goodwill a/c
CREDIT	Partners' capital accounts (old profit sharing ratio)

To eliminate goodwill:

DEBIT	Partners' capital accounts (new profit sharing ratio)
CREDIT	Goodwill a/c

6 It is divided between the old partners. If the revaluation is to be eliminated, it is divided between the new partners.

7 (a) DEBIT   Bank
       CREDIT Realisation account

  (b) DEBIT   Realisation account
       CREDIT Bank

8 False. Losses must be shared in the ratio of the last agreed capital balances.

Answers to activities

Answer 5.1

(a) The main problem with trading as a sole trader is the limitation on resources it implies. As the business grows, there will be a need for:

  (i) Additional capital. Although some capital may be provided by a bank, it would not be desirable to have the business entirely dependent on borrowing

  (ii) Additional expertise. A sole trader technically competent in his own field may not have, for example, the financial skills that would be needed in a larger business

  (iii) Additional management time. Once a business grows to a certain point, it becomes impossible for one person to look after all aspects of it without help

(b) The main disadvantage of incorporating is the regulatory burden faced by limited companies. In addition, there are certain 'businesses' which are not allowed to enjoy limited liability; you may have read about the Lloyd's 'names' who face personal bankruptcy because the option of limited liability was not available to them.

There are also tax factors to consider, but these are beyond the scope of this book.

Answer 5.2

The sum of the ratio 'parts' is 7 + 3 + 5 = 15. Each part is therefore worth £150 ÷ 15 = £10. So the £150 would be shared as follows:

			£
(a)	Tom:	7 × £10 =	70
(b)	Dick:	3 × £10 =	30
(c)	Harry:	5 × £10 =	50
			150

Answer 5.3

Goodwill = £150,000 − £100,000 = £50,000; Glass's share is 2/5 (£20,000). Glass is therefore owed £25,000 − £2,000 + £20,000 = £43,000.

Answer 5.4

(a) (i)

PARTNERS CAPITAL ACCOUNTS

	Alpha £	Beta £	Gamma £		Alpha £	Beta £	Gamma £
Goodwill eliminated	4	4	4	Balances b/d	30	25	-
Balances c/d	44	39	16	Goodwill	6	6	-
				Land revaluation surplus	12	12	-
				Loan account	-	-	20
	48	43	20		48	43	20

(ii)

PARTNERS' CURRENT ACCOUNTS

	Alpha £	Beta £	Gamma £		Alpha £	Beta £	Gamma £
Drawings	4	5	-	Balances b/d	3	4	-
Balances c/d	11	8	2	Salary	4	-	-
				Residual profit	8	8	-
				Loan interest	-	1	2
	15	13	2		15	13	2

(*Note*. It is assumed that the adjustment for interest is DR Interest expense CR partners' current accounts. Interest could have been a cash payment, in which case you could have credited cash instead.)

(iii) TRADING, PROFIT AND LOSS AND APPROPRIATION ACCOUNTS
FOR THE YEAR ENDED 31 DECEMBER 20X9

	£'000	£'000
Sales (200 - 6)		194
Opening stock	30	
Purchases	103	
	133	
Closing stock (24 + 2)	26	
Cost of sales		107
Gross profit		87
Operating expenses	64	
Interest (10% × (10,000 + 20,000))	3	
		67
Net profit		20
Salary - Alpha		4
Residual profit		16
Residual profit appropriated		
- Alpha (½)	8	
- Beta (½)	8	
		16

Note. No adjustment has to be made in respect of Gamma's salary as manager as this relates entirely to the period *before* he became a partner and so has been properly treated as an *expense* and not as an *appropriation* of profit. However, when an employee is made a partner mid-year, an adjustment is required to differentiate between his salary as an employee and his salary as a partner in apportioning profit to each partnership.

Part B: Preparation of final accounts

(iv) BALANCE SHEET AS AT 31 DECEMBER 20X9

	£'000	£'000
Fixed assets		
Land and buildings (revalued amount)		84
Plant and machinery — cost	70	
— depreciation	40	
		30
		114
Current assets		
Stock (W)	26	
Debtors (W)	34	
	60	
Current liabilities		
Bank overdraft	11	
Creditors	33	
	44	
Net current assets		16
		130
Long-term liabilities		
10% loan - Beta		10
		120
Partners' capital accounts		
- Alpha	44	
- Beta	39	
- Gamma	16	
		99
Partners' current accounts		
- Alpha	11	
- Beta	8	
- Gamma	2	
		21
		120

Working

Sales made on sale or return can only be treated as sales once the customer accepts the goods. Up to that point, the goods 'sold' are treated as stock and valued at the lower of cost and net realisable value, as usual. The goods accepted in January will therefore be treated as sold in the next accounting period.

	£'000
∴ Sales: £200,000 - £6,000	194
Stock: £24,000 + £2,000	26
Debtors: £40,000 - £6,000	34

(b)

MEMORANDUM

TO: Gamma
FROM: A N Accountant
SUBJECT: Adjustments to partners' capital on admission of a new partner
DATE: 14 February 20Y0

You have just bought a share of the assets of the Alpha & Beta partnership. Not all of these assets were previously recorded in the partnership books. Land and buildings were recorded at cost and are now worth more than cost. Goodwill, the difference between the value of the separable net assets of a business and its worth as a whole, was not recorded at all but had a value, as you agreed with your new partners.

The adjustments made to Alpha's and Beta's capital accounts reflect the fact that they earned the goodwill and that they made the decision to retain the land and buildings, thus earning the current surplus. Although you, as an employee of the firm, participated in its activities, you took no risk and had no capital in the firm beyond your loan which had a fixed rate of interest and was guaranteed priority repayment in the event of the firm's winding up.

5: Partnership accounts

It is therefore fair that Alpha's and Beta's capital should be increased by these previously unrecognised assets. However, as it was agreed not to record goodwill as a permanent asset in the books, it was then eliminated by means of a deduction from partners' capital.

If you consider a numerical analysis, you will see that the end result is entirely equitable. If the firm were sold tomorrow, you would each now receive your capital and current account balances plus an equal share of any surplus over the firm's book value.

	£'000
Book value of net assets	120
Add: goodwill (split equally between partners)	12
	132
Alpha (44 + 11 + 4)	59
Beta (39 + 8 + 4)	51
Gamma (16 + 2 + 4)	22
	132

You can see that your original capital and the loan interest due to you would all be returned. Of course, the value of goodwill may fluctuate in the future, but that is the risk (or reward) of being a partner rather than an employee.

Answer 5.5

(a) Lucas will now receive a greater share of future profits or losses ($\frac{1}{2}$ as opposed to $\frac{2}{5}$). He will also receive a greater share of any goodwill or gains/losses on revaluation of assets.

(b) LUCAS LODGE
SUMMARISED BALANCE SHEET AS AT 1 JANUARY 20X8

	£'000
Fixed assets	
Land	80
Buildings	75
Fixtures and fittings	30
	185
Current assets	40
Current liabilities	(35)
Net assets	190
Capital accounts	
Lucas	74
Lodge	116
	190

Workings

1   Goodwill

	£'000
Value of business	270
Fair value of separable	
net assets: 115 + 80 + 30 + 40 – 35	230
∴ Goodwill	40

2   Land

LAND

	£'000		£'000
31.12.X7	100	Capital a/c (bal fig)	20
		1.1.X8	80
	100		100

3   Buildings

BUILDINGS

	£'000		£'000
31.12.X7	75	Capital: revaln eliminated	40
Capital (bal fig) revaluation	40	1.1.X8	75
	115		115

Part B: Preparation of final accounts

4   Capital accounts

CAPITAL ACCOUNTS

	Lucas £'000	Lodge £'000		Lucas £'000	Lodge £'000
Land	8	12	31.12.X7 b/d	90	120
Buildings	20	20	Buildings	16	24
Goodwill	20	20	Goodwill	16	24
1.1.X8 c/d	74	116			
	122	168		122	168

(c) (i) The hotel buildings have been revalued by £40,000 to £115,000. Because the increase in value took place before 31 December 20X7, it make sense to attribute it to the partners in their old profit sharing ratio of 2:3. Thus the capital accounts will be credited in this ratio.

The revaluation is not to remain in the books of the partnership and must therefore be removed by crediting the asset and debiting the capital accounts with the increase in value. The increase is eliminated in the new profit sharing ratio of 1:1. The logic behind doing this is that, if the building were to be sold at any time in the future, the realised gain or loss should be attributed to the partners in the profit sharing ratio used at that time. Thus any changes in value before 31 December 20X7 are attributed to the partners in the old profit sharing ratio, and any changes after that date are attributed to them in the new profit sharing ratio.

(ii) The land has fallen in value by £20,000 and this loss has occurred before 31 December 20X7. It therefore makes sense to attribute it to the partners (by debiting their capital accounts) in the old profit sharing ratio. The loss on revaluation of the land is to be retained in the books of the firm, so there is no need to eliminate it in the new profit sharing ratio as was the case with the buildings.

(iii) The business as a whole is given a higher value than the fair value of the separable net assets. This is because the business as a whole is worth more than the individual assets. The excess is an intangible asset known as goodwill.

Because this goodwill was earned before December 20X7, for example by the partners building up a good reputation, it is credited to the partners in the old profit sharing ratio of 2:3. It is then eliminated by debiting the capital accounts in the new profit sharing ratio of 1:1.

(d)

Effect on Lodge's capital account £'000	Explanation	Effect on Lucas' capital account £'000
(12)	Share of reduction in value of land	(8)
4	Net share in adjustment to value of building	(4)
4	Net share in goodwill adjustment	(4)
(4)		(16)

Thus Lodge's capital account has been reduced by £4,000 from £120,000 to £116,000 and Lucas' capital account has been reduced by £16,000 from £90,000 to £74,000.

However, Lucas should not feel aggrieved that he has 'lost out' by this adjustment; in future years he will receive an increased share of the partnership's profit and already receives a greater share of the unrecorded assets (goodwill: £40,000, building revaluation: £40,000) than he would have done under the old profit sharing ratio.

(e) A balance sheet is simply a record of a business's assets and liabilities at a given point in time. Most balance sheets are prepared under the historical cost convention, and this is certainly true of the original balance sheet as at 31 December 20X7. The fact that, when the partnership agreement was changed, certain assets were revalued, shows that this balance sheet did not place a valuation on the assets as at the accounting date, but either represented a historical cost or a previous valuation.

With regard to the balance sheet as at 1 January 20X8, this more closely reflects the value of the business in that the land is now shown at its current value. However, goodwill is not included and the increase in the value of the buildings has not been allowed to remain on the books, presumably on grounds of prudence. It would therefore be difficult to argue that this balance sheet gives a 'true' valuation of the assets.

Now try Question 5 in the Exam Question Bank at the end of the Text.

Chapter 6 Incomplete records

Chapter topic list

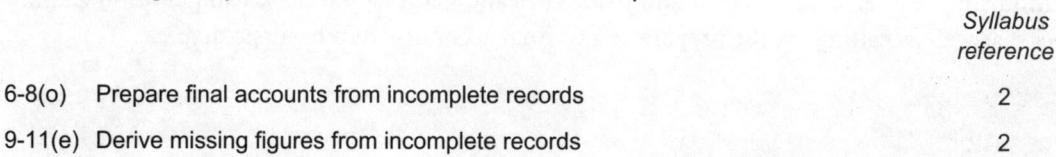

1 Incomplete records questions
2 The opening balance sheet
3 Credit sales and debtors
4 Purchases and trade creditors
5 Establishing cost of sales
6 Stolen goods or goods destroyed
7 The cash book
8 Accruals and prepayments
9 Drawings
10 Dealing with incomplete records problems in the examination

The following study sessions are covered in this chapter.

		Syllabus reference
6-8(o)	Prepare final accounts from incomplete records	2
9-11(e)	Derive missing figures from incomplete records	2

Part B: Preparation of final accounts

1 INCOMPLETE RECORDS QUESTIONS

1.1 So far in your work on preparing the final accounts for a sole trader we have assumed that a full set of records are kept. In practice many sole traders do not keep a full set of records and you must apply certain techniques to arrive at the necessary figures. Incomplete records problems occur when a business does not have a full set of accounting records, either because:

- The proprietor of the business does not keep a full set of accounts
- Some of the business accounts are accidentally lost or destroyed.

1.2 The problem for the accountant is to prepare a set of year-end accounts for the business; ie a trading, profit and loss account, and a balance sheet. Since the business does not have a full set of accounts, preparing the final accounts is not a simple matter of closing off accounts and transferring balances to the trading, P&L account, or showing outstanding balances in the balance sheet. The task of preparing the final accounts involves:

(a) Establishing the **cost of purchases** and **other expenses**

(b) Establishing the **total amount of sales**

(c) Establishing the amount of **creditors, accruals, debtors** and **prepayments** at the end of the year

1.3 Examination questions often take incomplete records problems a stage further, by introducing an 'incident' - such as fire or burglary - which leaves the owner of the business uncertain about how much stock has been destroyed or stolen.

1.4 The great merit of incomplete records problems is that they focus attention on the relationship between cash received and paid, sales and debtors, purchases and creditors, and stocks, as well as calling for the preparation of final accounts from basic principles.

Exam alert
While the incomplete records techniques in this chapter are discussed in the context of sole traders, identical techniques can be applied to both limited companies and partnerships.

1.5 To understand what incomplete records are about, it will obviously be useful now to look at what exactly might be incomplete. The items we shall consider in turn are:

(a) The opening balance sheet
(b) Credit sales and debtors
(c) Purchases and trade creditors
(d) Purchases, stocks and the cost of sales
(e) Stolen goods or goods destroyed
(f) The cash book
(g) Accruals and prepayments
(h) Drawings

Exam alert
Incomplete records questions are a good test of whether you have a really thorough grasp of double entry. Examiners are fond of them. With practice they become easier and can be very satisfying!

2 THE OPENING BALANCE SHEET

2.1 In practice there should not be any missing item in the opening balance sheet of the business, because it should be available from the preparation of the previous year's final accounts. However, an examination problem might provide information about the assets and liabilities of the business at the beginning of the period under review, but then leave the balancing figure - ie the proprietor's business capital - unspecified.

2.2 EXAMPLE: OPENING BALANCE SHEET

Suppose a business has the following assets and liabilities as at 1 January 20X3.

	£
Fixtures and fittings at cost	7,000
Provision for depreciation, fixtures and fittings	4,000
Motor vehicles at cost	12,000
Provision for depreciation, motor vehicles	6,800
Stock in trade	4,500
Trade debtors	5,200
Cash at bank and in hand	1,230
Trade creditors	3,700
Prepayment	450
Accrued rent	2,000

You are required to prepare a balance sheet for the business, inserting a balancing figure for proprietor's capital.

2.3 SOLUTION

Balance sheet as at 1 January 20X3

	£	£
Fixed assets		
Fixtures and fittings at cost	7,000	
Less accumulated depreciation	4,000	
		3,000
Motor vehicles at cost	12,000	
Less accumulated depreciation	6,800	
		5,200
		8,200
Current assets		
Stock in trade	4,500	
Trade debtors	5,200	
Prepayment	450	
Cash	1,230	
	11,380	
Current liabilities		
Trade creditors	3,700	
Accrual	2,000	
	5,700	
Net current assets		5,680
		13,880
Proprietor's capital as at 1 January 20X3 (balancing figure)		13,880

Part B: Preparation of final accounts

3 CREDIT SALES AND DEBTORS

3.1 If a business does not keep a record of its sales on credit, the value of these sales can be derived from the opening balance of trade debtors, the closing balance of trade debtors, and the payments received from trade debtors during the period.

> **FORMULA TO LEARN**
>
> | | £ |
> |---|---|
> | Credit sales are: | |
> | Payments received from trade debtors | X |
> | Plus closing balance of trade debtors (since these represent sales in the current period for which cash payment has not yet been received) | X |
> | Less opening balance of trade debtors (unless these become bad debts, they will pay what they owe in the current period for sales in a previous period) | (X) |
> | | X |

3.2 For example, suppose that a business had trade debtors of £1,750 on 1 April 20X4 and trade debtors of £3,140 on 31 March 20X5. If payments received from trade debtors during the year to 31 March 20X5 were £28,490, and if there are no bad debts, then credit sales for the period would be:

	£
Cash received from debtors	28,490
Plus closing debtors	3,140
Less opening debtors	(1,750)
Credit sales	29,880

If there are bad debts during the period, the value of sales will be increased by the amount of bad debts written off, no matter whether they relate to opening debtors or credit sales during the current period.

3.3 The same calculation could be made in a T account, with credit sales being the balancing figure to complete the account.

DEBTORS

	£		£
Opening balance b/f	1,750	Cash received	28,490
Credit sales (balancing fig)	29,880	Closing balance c/f	3,140
	31,630		31,630

3.4 The same interrelationship between credit sales, cash from debtors, and opening and closing debtors balances can be used to derive a missing figure for cash from debtors, or opening or closing debtors, given the values for the three other items. For example, if we know that opening debtors are £6,700, closing debtors are £3,200 and credit sales for the period are £69,400, then cash received from debtors during the period would be as follows.

DEBTORS

	£		£
Opening balance	6,700	Cash received (balancing figure)	72,900
Sales (on credit)	69,400	Closing balance c/f	3,200
	76,100		76,100

An alternative way of presenting the same calculation would be:

	£
Opening balance of debtors	6,700
Credit sales during the period	69,400
Total money owed to the business	76,100
Less closing balance of debtors	3,200
Equals cash received during the period	72,900

4 PURCHASES AND TRADE CREDITORS

4.1 A similar relationship exists between purchases of stock during a period, the opening and closing balances for trade creditors, and amounts paid to trade creditors during the period.

> **FORMULA TO LEARN**
>
> If we wish to calculate an unknown amount for purchases, the amount would be derived as follows:
>
> | | £ |
> |---|---:|
> | Payments to trade creditors during the period | X |
> | Plus closing balance of trade creditors | X |
> | (since these represent purchases in the current period for which payment has not yet been made) | |
> | Less opening balance of trade creditors | (X) |
> | (these debts, paid in the current period, relate to purchases in a previous period) | |
> | Purchases during the period | X |

4.2 For example, suppose that a business had trade creditors of £3,728 on 1 October 20X5 and trade creditors of £2,645 on 30 September 20X6. If payments to trade creditors during the year to 30 September 20X6 were £31,479, then purchases during the year would be:

	£
Payments to trade creditors	31,479
Plus closing balance of trade creditors	2,645
Less opening balance of trade creditors	(3,728)
Purchases	30,396

4.3 The same calculation could be made in a T account, with purchases being the balancing figure to complete the account.

CREDITORS

	£		£
Cash payments	31,479	Opening balance b/f	3,728
Closing balance c/f	2,645	Purchases (balancing figure)	30,396
	34,124		34,124

Activity 6.1

Sonia Khan does not keep full accounting records, but the following information is available in respect of her accounting year ended 31 December 20X9.

	£
Cash purchases in year	7,800
Cash paid for goods supplied on credit	55,700
Creditors at 1 January 20X9	1,940
Creditors at 31 December 20X9	1,440

In her trading account for 20X9, what will be Sonia's figure for purchases?

Part B: Preparation of final accounts

5 ESTABLISHING COST OF SALES

5.1 When the value of purchases is not known, a different approach might be required to find out what they were, depending on the nature of the information given to you.

5.2 One approach would be to use information about the cost of sales, and opening and closing stocks, in other words, to use the trading account rather than the trade creditors account to find the cost of purchases.

> **FORMULA TO LEARN**
>
> | | | £ |
> |---|---|---|
> | Since | opening stocks | X |
> | | plus purchases | X |
> | | less closing stocks | (X) |
> | | equals the cost of goods sold | X |
> | then | the cost of goods sold | X |
> | | plus closing stocks | X |
> | | less opening stocks | (X) |
> | | equals purchases | X |

5.3 Suppose that the stock in trade of a business on 1 July 20X6 has a balance sheet value of £8,400, and a stock taking exercise at 30 June 20X7 showed stock to be valued at £9,350. Sales for the year to 30 June 20X7 are £80,000, and the business makes a gross profit of $33^1/_3$% on cost for all the items that it sells. What were the purchases during the year?

5.4 The cost of goods sold can be derived from the value of sales, as follows.

		£
Sales	($133^1/_3$%)	80,000
Gross profit	($33^1/_3$%)	20,000
Cost of goods sold	(100%)	60,000

The cost of goods sold is 75% of sales value.

	£
Cost of goods sold	60,000
Plus closing stock	9,350
Less opening stocks	(8,400)
Purchases	60,950

Activity 6.2

Tarquin has budgeted sales for the coming year of £300,000. He achieves a constant gross mark-up of 50% on cost. He plans to reduce his stock level by £15,000 over the year.

What will Tarquin's purchases be for the year?

6 STOLEN GOODS OR GOODS DESTROYED

6.1 A similar type of calculation might be required to derive the value of goods stolen or destroyed. When an unknown quantity of goods is lost, whether they are stolen, destroyed in a fire, or lost in any other way such that the quantity lost cannot be counted, then the cost of the goods lost is the difference between:

(a) The **cost of goods sold**

(b) **Opening stock of the goods** (at cost) plus **purchases** less **closing stock of the goods** (at cost)

In theory (a) and (b) should be the same. However, if (b) is a larger amount than (a), it follows that the difference must be the cost of the goods purchased and neither sold nor remaining in stock - ie the cost of the goods lost.

6.2 EXAMPLE: COST OF GOODS DESTROYED

Orlean Flames is a shop which sells fashion clothes. On 1 January 20X5, it had stock in trade which cost £7,345. During the 9 months to 30 September 20X5, the business purchased goods from suppliers costing £106,420. Sales during the same period were £154,000. The shop makes a gross profit of 40% on cost for everything it sells. On 30 September 20X5, there was a fire in the shop which destroyed most of the stock in it. Only a small amount of stock, known to have cost £350, was undamaged and still fit for sale.

How much stock was lost in the fire?

6.3 SOLUTION

(a)
	£
Sales (140%)	154,000
Gross profit (40%)	44,000
Cost of goods sold (100%)	110,000

(b)
	£
Opening stock, at cost	7,345
Plus purchases	106,420
	113,765
Less closing stock, at cost	350
Equals cost of goods sold and goods lost	113,415

(c)
	£
Cost of goods sold and lost	113,415
Cost of goods sold	110,000
Cost of goods lost	3,415

6.4 EXAMPLE: COST OF GOODS STOLEN

Sam Sparkle runs a jewellery shop in the High Street. On 1 January 20X9, his stock in trade, at cost, amounted to £4,700 and his trade creditors were £3,950.

During the six months to 30 June 20X9, sales were £42,000. Sam Sparkle makes a gross profit of $33^{1}/3$% on the sales value of everything he sells.

On 30 June, there was a burglary at the shop, and all the stock was stolen.

In trying to establish how much stock had been taken, Sam Sparkle was only able to say that:

(a) He knew from his bank statements that he had paid £28,400 to creditors in the 6 month period to 30 June 20X9.

(b) He currently owed creditors £5,550.

Task

(a) Calculate the amount of stock stolen.
(b) Prepare a trading account for the 6 months to 30 June 20X9.

Part B: Preparation of final accounts

6.5 SOLUTION

Step 1. The first 'unknown' is the amount of purchases during the period. This is established by the method previously described in this chapter.

CREDITORS

	£		£
Payments to creditors	28,400	Opening balance b/f	3,950
Closing balance c/f	5,550	Purchases (balancing figure)	30,000
	33,950		33,950

Step 2. The cost of goods sold is also unknown, but this can be established from the gross profit margin and the sales for the period.

		£
Sales	(100%)	42,000
Gross profit	($33^1/_3$%)	14,000
Cost of goods sold	($66^2/_3$%)	28,000

Step 3. The cost of the goods stolen is:

	£
Opening stock at cost	4,700
Purchases	30,000
	34,700
Less closing stock (after burglary)	0
Cost of goods sold and goods stolen	34,700
Cost of goods sold (see (b) above)	28,000
Cost of goods stolen	6,700

Step 4. The cost of the goods stolen will not be a charge in the trading account, and so the trading account for the period is as follows:

SAM SPARKLE
TRADING ACCOUNT FOR THE SIX MONTHS TO 30 JUNE 20X9

	£	£
Sales		42,000
Less cost of goods sold		
Opening stock	4,700	
Purchases	30,000	
	34,700	
Less stock stolen	6,700	
		28,000
Gross profit		14,000

Accounting for stock destroyed, stolen or otherwise lost

6.6 When stock is stolen, destroyed or otherwise lost, the loss must be accounted for somehow. The procedure was described briefly in the earlier chapter on accounting for stocks. Since the loss is not a trading loss, the cost of the goods lost is not included in the trading account, as the previous example showed. The accounting double entry is therefore

DEBIT	See below
CREDIT	Trading account (although instead of showing the cost of the loss as a credit, it is usually shown as a deduction on the debit side of the trading account, which is the same as a 'plus' on the credit side).

6.7 The account that is to be debited is one of two possibilities, depending on whether or not the lost goods were insured against the loss.

(a) If the lost goods were not insured, the business must bear the loss, and the loss is shown in the P & L account: ie

DEBIT   Profit and loss
CREDIT Trading account

(b) If the lost goods were insured, the business will not suffer a loss, because the insurance will pay back the cost of the lost goods. This means that there is no charge at all in the P&L account, and the appropriate double entry is:

DEBIT   Insurance claim account (debtor account)
CREDIT Trading account

with the cost of the loss. The insurance claim will then be a current asset, and shown in the balance sheet of the business as such. When the claim is paid, the account is then closed by

DEBIT   Cash
CREDIT Insurance claim account

7 THE CASH BOOK

7.1 The construction of a cash book, largely from bank statements showing receipts and payments of a business during a given period, is often an important feature of incomplete records problems.

> **Exam alert**
>
> In an examination, the purpose of an incomplete records question is largely to test the understanding of candidates about how various items of receipts or payments relate to the preparation of a final set of accounts for a business.

7.2 We have already seen in this chapter that information about cash receipts or payments might be needed to establish one of two things.

(a) The amount of purchases during a period
(b) The amount of credit sales during a period

Other items of receipts or payments might be relevant to establishing one of the following.

(a) The amount of cash sales
(b) The amount of certain expenses in the P & L account
(c) The amount of drawings by the business proprietor

7.3 It might therefore be helpful, if a business does not keep a cash book day-to-day, to construct a cash book at the end of an accounting period. A business which typically might not keep a day-to-day cash book is a shop, where:

(a) Many sales, if not all sales, are cash sales (ie with payment by notes and coins, cheques, or credit cards at the time of sale)

(b) Some payments are made in notes and coins out of the till rather than by payment out of the business bank account by cheque

7.4 Where there appears to be a sizeable volume of receipts and payments in cash (ie notes and coins), then it is also helpful to construct a two column cash book.

Part B: Preparation of final accounts

> **KEY TERM**
>
> **A two column cash book** is a cash book with one column for receipts and payments, and one column for money paid into and out of the business bank account.

An example will illustrate the technique and the purpose of a two column cash book.

7.5 EXAMPLE: TWO COLUMN CASH BOOK

Mr Splash owns and runs a shop selling bathroom fittings, making a gross profit of 25% on the cost of everything he sells. He does not keep a cash book.

On 1 January 20X7 the balance sheet of his business was as follows.

	£	£
Net fixed assets		20,000
Stock	10,000	
Cash in the bank	3,000	
Cash in the till	200	
	13,200	
Trade creditors	1,200	
		12,000
		32,000
Proprietor's capital		32,000

In the year to 31 December 20X7:

(a) there were no sales on credit;
(b) £41,750 in receipts were banked;
(c) the bank statements of the period show the payments:

			£
(i)	to trade creditors		36,000
(ii)	sundry expenses		5,600
(iii)	in drawings		4,400

(d) payments were also made in cash out of the till:

			£
(i)	to trade creditors		800
(ii)	sundry expenses		1,500
(iii)	in drawings		3,700

At 31 December 20X7, the business had cash in the till of £450 and trade creditors of £1,400. The cash balance in the bank was not known and the value of closing stock has not yet been calculated. There were no accruals or prepayments. No further fixed assets were purchased during the year. The depreciation charge for the year is £900.

Task

(a) Prepare a two column cash book for the period

(b) Prepare the trading, profit and loss account for the year to 31 December 20X7 and the balance sheet as at 31 December 20X7.

7.6 DISCUSSION AND SOLUTION

A two column cash book is completed as follows.

Step 1. Enter the opening cash balances.

Step 2. Enter the information given about cash payments (and any cash receipts, if there had been any such items given in the problem).

Step 3. The cash receipts banked are a 'contra' entry, being both a debit (bank column) and a credit (cash in hand column) in the same account.

Step 4. Enter the closing cash in hand (cash in the bank at the end of the period is not known).

CASH BOOK

	Cash in hand £	Bank £		Cash in hand £	Bank £
Balance b/f	200	3,000	Trade creditors	800	36,000
Cash receipts banked (contra)		41,750	Sundry expenses	1,500	5,600
Sales*	48,000		Drawings	3,700	4,400
			Cash receipts banked (contra)		41,750
			Balance c/f	450	
Balance c/f		*1,250			
	48,200	46,000		48,200	46,000

* Balancing figure

Step 5. The closing balance of money in the bank is a balancing figure.

Step 6. Since all sales are for cash, a balancing figure that can be entered in the cash book is sales, in the cash in hand (debit) column.

7.7 It is important to notice that since not all receipts from cash sales are banked, the value of cash sales during the period is:

	£
Receipts banked	41,750
Plus expenses and drawings paid out of the till in cash £(800 + 1,500 + 3,700)	6,000
Plus any cash stolen (here there is none)	0
Plus the closing balance of cash in hand	450
	48,200
Less the opening balance of cash in hand	(200)
Equals cash sales	48,000

7.8 The cash book constructed in this way has enabled us to establish both the closing balance for cash in the bank and also the volume of cash sales. The trading, profit and loss account and the balance sheet can also be prepared, once a value for purchases has been calculated.

CREDITORS

	£		£
Cash book:		Balance b/f	1,200
Payments from bank	36,000	Purchases (balancing figure)	37,000
Cash book:			
Payments in cash	800		
Balance c/f	1,400		
	38,200		38,200

The gross profit margin of 25% on cost indicates that the cost of the goods sold is £38,400, ie:

	£
Sales (125%)	48,000
Gross profit (25%)	9,600
Cost of goods sold (100%)	38,400

Part B: Preparation of final accounts

The closing stock amount is now a balancing figure in the trading account.

MR SPLASH
TRADING, PROFIT AND LOSS ACCOUNT
FOR THE YEAR ENDED 31 DECEMBER 20X7

	£	£
Sales		48,000
Less cost of goods sold		
Opening stock	10,000	
Purchases	37,000	
	47,000	
Less closing stock (balancing figure)	8,600	
		38,400
Gross profit (25/125 × £48,000)		9,600
Expenses		
Sundry £(1,500 + 5,600)	7,100	
Depreciation	900	
		8,000
Net profit		1,600

MR SPLASH
BALANCE SHEET AS AT 31 DECEMBER 20X7

	£	£
Net fixed assets £(20,000 – 900)		19,100
Stock	8,600	
Cash in the till	450	
	9,050	
Bank overdraft	1,250	
Trade creditors	1,400	
	2,650	
Net current assets		6,400
		25,500
Proprietor's capital		
Balance b/f		32,000
Net profit for the year		1,600
		33,600
Drawings £(3,700 + 4,400)		(8,100)
Balance c/f		25,500

Theft of cash from the till

7.9 When cash is stolen from the till, the amount stolen will be a credit entry in the cash book, and a debit in either the P&L account or insurance claim account, depending on whether the business is insured. The missing figure for cash sales, if this has to be calculated, must not ignore cash received but later stolen - see above.

8 ACCRUALS AND PREPAYMENTS

8.1 Where there is an accrued expense or a prepayment, the charge to be made in the P&L account for the item concerned should be found from the opening balance b/f, the closing balance c/f, and cash payments for the item during the period. The charge in the P&L account is perhaps most easily found as the balancing figure in a T account.

8.2 For example, suppose that on 1 April 20X6 a business had prepaid rent of £700 which relates to the next accounting period. During the year to 31 March 20X7 it pays £9,300 in rent, and at 31 March 20X7 the prepayment of rent is £1,000. The cost of rent in the P&L

account for the year to 31 March 20X7 would be the balancing figure in the following T account. (Remember that a prepayment is a current asset, and so is a debit balance b/f.)

RENT

	£		£
Prepayment: balance b/f	700	P & L account (balancing figure)	9,000
Cash	9,300	Prepayment: balance c/f	1,000
	10,000		10,000
Balance b/f	1,000		

8.3 Similarly, if a business has accrued telephone expenses as at 1 July 20X6 of £850, pays £6,720 in telephone bills during the year to 30 June 20X7, and has accrued telephone expenses of £1,140 as at 30 June 20X7, then the telephone expense to be shown in the P&L account for the year to 30 June 20X7 is the balancing figure in the following T account. (Remember that an accrual is a current liability, and so is a credit balance b/f.)

TELEPHONE EXPENSES

	£		£
Cash	6,720	Balance b/f (accrual)	850
Balance c/f (accrual)	1,140	P&L a/c (balancing figure)	7,010
	7,860		7,860
		Balance b/f	1,140

9 DRAWINGS

9.1 Drawings would normally represent no particular problem at all in preparing a set of final accounts from incomplete records, but it is not unusual for examination questions to introduce a situation in which:

(a) the business owner pays income into his bank account which has nothing whatever to do with the business operations. For example, the owner might pay dividend income, or other income from investments into the bank, from stocks and shares which he owns personally, separate from the business itself. (In other words, there are no investments in the business balance sheet, and so income from investments cannot possibly be income of the business);

(b) the business owner pays money out of the business bank account for items which are not business expenses, such as life insurance premiums or a payment for his family's holidays etc.

9.2 Where such **personal items of receipts or payments** are made:

(a) receipts should be set off against drawings. For example, if a business owner receives £600 in dividend income and pays it into his business bank account, although the dividends are from investments not owned by the business, then the accounting entry is:

DEBIT   Cash
CREDIT Drawings;

(b) payments should be charged to drawings; ie

DEBIT   Drawings
CREDIT Cash

Part B: Preparation of final accounts

Drawings: beware of the wording in an examination question

9.3 You should note that:

(a) If a question states that a proprietor's drawings during a given year are 'approximately £40 per week' then you should assume that drawings for the year are £40 × 52 weeks = £2,080.

(b) However, if a question states that drawings in the year are 'between £35 and £45 per week', do not assume that the drawings average £40 per week and so amount to £2,080 for the year. You could not be certain that the actual drawings did average £40, and so you should treat the drawings figure as a missing item that needs to be calculated.

10 DEALING WITH INCOMPLETE RECORDS PROBLEMS IN THE EXAMINATION

10.1 A suggested approach to dealing with incomplete records problems brings together the various points described so far in this chapter. The nature of the 'incompleteness' in the records will vary from problem to problem, but the approach, suitably applied, should be successful in arriving at the final accounts whatever the particular characteristics of the problem might be.

10.2 The approach is as follows.

Step 1. If possible, and if it is not already known, establish the opening balance sheet and the proprietor's interest.

Step 2. Open up four accounts.

- **Trading account** (if you wish, leave space underneath for entering the P&L account later)
- A **cash book**, with two columns if cash sales are significant and there are payments in cash out of the till
- A **debtors account**
- A **creditors account**

Step 3. Enter the opening balances in these accounts.

Step 4. Work through the information you are given line by line; and each item should be entered into the appropriate account if it is relevant to one or more of these four accounts.

You should also try to recognise each item as a 'P&L account income or expense item' or a 'closing balance sheet item'.

It may be necessary to calculate an amount for drawings and an amount for fixed asset depreciation.

Step 5. Look for the balancing figures in your accounts. In particular you might be looking for a value for credit sales, cash sales, purchases, the cost of goods sold, the cost of goods stolen or destroyed, or the closing bank balance. Calculate these missing figures, and make any necessary double entry (eg to the trading account from the creditors account for purchases, to the trading account from the cash book for cash sales, and to the trading account from the debtors account for credit sales).

Step 6. Now complete the P&L account and balance sheet. Working T accounts might be needed where there are accruals or prepayments.

10.3 An example will illustrate this approach.

10.4 EXAMPLE: AN INCOMPLETE RECORDS PROBLEM

Edgar and Cook, a partnership, is the sole distribution agent in the London area for Milly's wallpaper. Under an agreement with the manufacturers, Edgar and Cook purchases the wallpaper at a trade discount of 20% off list price and annually in May receives an agency commission of 1% of his purchases for the year ended on the previous 31 March.

For several years, the partnership has obtained a gross profit of 40% on all sales. In a burglary in January 20X1 the partnership lost stock costing £4,000 as well as many of his accounting records. However, after careful investigations, the following information has been obtained covering the year ended 31 March 20X1.

(a) Assets and liabilities at 31 March 20X0 were as follows:

		£
Buildings:	at cost	10,000
	provision for depreciation	6,000
Motor vehicles:	at cost	5,000
	provision for depreciation	2,000
Stock: at cost		3,200
Trade debtors (for sales)		6,300
Agency commission due		300
Prepayments (trade expenses)		120
Balance at bank		4,310
Trade creditors		4,200
Accrued vehicle expenses		230

(b) The partners have been notified that the firm will receive an agency commission of £440 on 1 May 20X1.

(c) Stock, at cost, at 31 March 20X1 was valued at an amount £3,000 more than a year previously.

(d) In October 20X0 stock costing £1,000 was damaged by fire and had to be scrapped as worthless.

(e) Trade creditors at 31 March 20X1 related entirely to goods received whose list prices totalled £9,500.

(f) Discounts allowed amounted to £1,620 whilst discounts received were £1,200.

(g) Trade expenses prepaid at 31 March 20X1 totalled £80.

(h) Vehicle expenses for the year ended 31 March 20X1 amounted to £7,020.

(i) Trade debtors (for sales) at 31 March 20X1 were £6,700.

(j) All receipts are passed through the bank account.

(k) Depreciation is provided annually at the following rates.

    Buildings 5% on cost
    Motor vehicles 20% on cost.

(l) Commissions received are paid directly to the bank account.

(m) In addition to the payments for purchases, the bank payments were:

Part B: Preparation of final accounts

	£
Vehicle expenses	6,720
Drawings	4,300
Trade expenses	7,360

(n) The firm is not insured against loss of stock owing to burglary or damage to stock caused by fire.

Task

Prepare the trading and profit and loss account of the partnership for the year ended 31 March 20X1 and a balance sheet on that date.

Note. You are not given detail of the profit-sharing ratio, so there is no need to deal with the partnership aspects.

10.5 DISCUSSION AND SOLUTION

This is an incomplete records problem because we are told that Edgar Cook has lost many of his accounting records. In particular we do not know sales for the year, purchases during the year, or all the cash receipts and payments.

10.6 The first step is to find the opening balance sheet, if possible. In this case, it is. The capital is the balancing figure.

EDGAR COOK
BALANCE SHEET AS AT 31 MARCH 20X0

	Cost £	Dep'n £	NBV £
Fixed assets			
Buildings	10,000	6,000	4,000
Motor vehicles	5,000	2,000	3,000
	15,000	8,000	7,000
Current assets			
Stock		3,200	
Trade debtors		6,300	
Commission due		300	
Prepayments		120	
Balance at hand		4,310	
		14,230	
Current liabilities			
Trade creditors		4,200	
Accrued expenses		230	
		4,430	
			9,800
			16,800
Partners' capital as at 31 March 20X0			16,800

10.7 The next step is to open up a trading account, cash book, debtors account and creditors account and to insert the opening balances, if known. Cash sales and payments in cash are not a feature of the problem, and so a single column cash book is sufficient.

10.8 The problem should then be read line by line, identifying any transactions affecting those accounts.

TRADING ACCOUNT

	£	£
Sales (note (f))		60,000
Opening stock	3,200	
Purchases (note (a))	44,000	
	47,200	
Less: damaged stock written off (note (c))	(1,000)	
stock stolen (note (e))	(4,000)	
	42,200	
Less closing stock (note (b))	6,200	
Cost of goods sold		36,000
Gross profit (note (f))		24,000

CASH BOOK

	£		£
Opening balance	4,310	Trade creditors	
Trade debtors (see below)	57,980	(see creditors a/c)	39,400
Agency commission (note (g))	300	Trade expenses	7,360
		Vehicle expenses	6,720
		Drawings	4,300
		Balance c/f	4,810
	62,590		62,590

TRADE DEBTORS

	£		£
Opening balance b/f	6,300	Discounts allowed (note (d))	1,620
Sales (note (f))	60,000	Cash received (balancing figure)	57,980
		Closing balance c/f	6,700
	66,300		66,300

TRADE CREDITORS

	£		£
Discounts received (note (d))	1,200	Opening balance b/f	4,200
Cash paid (balancing figure)	39,400	Purchases (note (a))	44,000
Closing balance c/f	7,600		
	48,200		48,200

VEHICLE EXPENSES

	£		£
Cash	6,720	Accrual b/f	230
Accrual c/f (balancing figure)	530	P & L account	7,020
	7,250		7,250

10.9 The trading account is complete already, but now the P&L account and balance sheet can be prepared. Remember not to forget items such as the stock losses, commission earned on purchases, discounts allowed and discounts received.

Part B: Preparation of final accounts

EDGAR AND COOK - TRADING, PROFIT AND LOSS ACCOUNT
FOR THE YEAR ENDED 31 MARCH 20X1

	£	£
Sales (note (f))		60,000
Opening stock	3,200	
Purchases (note (a))	44,000	
	47,200	
Less: damaged stock written off (note (c))	(1,000)	
stock stolen	(4,000)	
	42,200	
Less closing stock (note (b))	6,200	
Cost of goods sold		36,000
Gross profit (note (f))		24,000
Add: commission on purchases		440
discounts received		1,200
		25,640
Expenses		
Trade expenses (note (h))	7,400	
Stock damaged	1,000	
Stock stolen	4,000	
Vehicle expenses	7,020	
Discounts allowed	1,620	
Depreciation		
Buildings	500	
Motor vehicles	1,000	
		22,540
Net profit (to be appropriated and apportioned to capital accounts)		3,100

EDGAR AND COOK
BALANCE SHEET AS AT 31 MARCH 20X1

	Cost £	Dep'n £	NBV £
Fixed assets			
Buildings	10,000	6,500	3,500
Motor vehicles	5,000	3,000	2,000
	15,000	9,500	5,500
Current assets			
Stock		6,200	
Trade debtors		6,700	
Commission due		440	
Prepayments (trade expenses)		80	
Balance at bank		4,810	
		18,230	
Current liabilities			
Trade creditors		7,600	
Accrued expenses		530	
		8,130	
			10,100
			15,600
Proprietor's capital			
As at 31 March 20X0			16,800
Net profit for year to 31 March 20X1		3,100	
Less drawings		(4,300)	
Retained deficit			(1,200)
As at 31 March 20X1			15,600

Notes

(a) The agency commission due on 1 May 20X1 indicates that purchases for the year to 31 March 20X1 were

100%/1% × £440 = £44,000

(b) Closing stock at cost on 31 March 20X1 was £(3,200 + 3,000) = £6,200.

(c) Stock scrapped (£1,000) is accounted for by:

CREDIT   Trading account
DEBIT   P&L account

(d) Discounts allowed are accounted for by:

DEBIT   Discounts allowed account
CREDIT   Debtors

Similarly, discounts received are:

DEBIT   Creditors
CREDIT   Discounts received

Note. Discounts received represents settlement discounts, not *trade* discounts, which are not usually accounted for as they are given automatically at source.

(e) Stocks lost in the burglary are accounted for by:

CREDIT   Trading account
DEBIT   P&L account

(f) The trade discount of 20% has already been deducted in arriving at the value of the purchases. The gross profit is 40% on sales, so with cost of sales = £36,000

		£
Cost	(60%)	36,000
Profit	(40%)	24,000
Sales	(100%)	60,000

(It is assumed that trade expenses are not included in the trading account, and so should be ignored in this calculation.)

(g) The agency commission of £300 due on 1 May 20X0 would have been paid to Edgar Cook at that date.

(h) The P&L account expenditure for trade expenses and closing balance on vehicle expenses account are as follows:

TRADE EXPENSES

	£		£
Prepayment	120	P&L account (balancing figure)	7,400
Cash	7,360	Prepayment c/f	80
	7,480		7,480

Using a debtors account to calculate both cash sales and credit sales

10.10 A final point which needs to be considered is how a missing value can be found for cash sales and credit sales, when a business has both, but takings banked by the business are not divided between takings from cash sales and takings from credit sales.

10.11 EXAMPLE: USING A DEBTORS ACCOUNT

Suppose, for example, that a business had, on 1 January 20X8, trade debtors of £2,000, cash in the bank of £3,000, and cash in hand of £300.

During the year to 31 December 20X8 the business banked £95,000 in takings.

It also paid out the following expenses in cash from the till:

| Drawings | £1,200 |
| Sundry expenses | £800 |

Part B: Preparation of final accounts

On 29 August 20X8 a thief broke into the shop and stole £400 from the till.

At 31 December 20X8 trade debtors amounted to £3,500, cash in the bank £2,500 and cash in the till £150.

What was the value of sales during the year?

10.12 SOLUTION

If we tried to prepare a debtors account and a two column cash book, we would have insufficient information, in particular about whether the takings which were banked related to cash sales or credit sales.

DEBTORS

	£		£
Balance b/f	2,000	Payments from debtors (credit sales)	Unknown
Credit sales	Unknown	Balance c/f	3,500

CASH BOOK

	Cash £	Bank £		Cash £	Bank £
Balance b/f	300	3,000	Drawings	1,200	
			Sundry expenses	800	
Debtors-payments		Unknown	Cash stolen	400	
Cash sales	Unknown		Balance c/f	150	2,500

All we do know is that the combined sums from debtors and cash takings banked is £95,000.

The value of sales can be found instead by using the debtors account, which should be used to record cash takings banked as well as payments by debtors. The balancing figure in the debtors account will then be a combination of credit sales and some cash sales. The cash book only needs to be a single column.

DEBTORS

	£		£
Balance b/f	2,000	Cash banked	95,000
Sales-to trading account	96,500	Balance c/f	3,500
	98,500		98,500

CASH (EXTRACT)

	£		£
Balance in hand b/f	300	Payments in cash:	
Balance in bank c/f	3,000	Drawings	1,200
Debtors a/c	95,000	Expenses	800
		Other payments	?
		Cash stolen	400
		Balance in hand c/f	150
		Balance in bank c/f	2,500

The remaining 'undiscovered' amount of cash sales is now found as follows.

6: Incomplete records

	£	£
Payments in cash out of the till		
Drawings		1,200
Expenses		800
		2,000
Cash stolen		400
Closing balance of cash in hand		150
		2,550
Less opening balance of cash in hand		(300)
Further cash sales		2,250

(This calculation is similar to the one described above for calculating cash sales.)

Total sales for the year are:

	£
From debtors account	96,500
From cash book	2,250
Total sales	98,750

Activity 6.3

Anna Forbes, retail fruit and vegetable merchant, does not keep a full set of accounting records. However, the following information has been produced from the business's records.

(a) Summary of the bank account for the year ended 31 August 20X8

	£		£
1 Sept 20X7 balance brought forward	1,970	Payment to suppliers	72,000
		Purchase of motor van (E471 KBR)	13,000
Receipts from trade debtors	96,000	Rent and rates	2,600
Sale of private yacht	20,000	Wages	15,100
Sale of motor van (A123 BWA)	2,100	Motor vehicle expenses	3,350
		Postages and stationery	1,360
		Drawings	9,200
		Repairs and renewals	650
		Insurances	800
		31 August 20X8 balance c/fwd	2,010
	120,070		120,070
1 Sept 20X8 balance b/fwd	2,010		

(b) Assets and liabilities, other than balance at bank as at:

		1 Sept 20X7	31 Aug 20X8
		£	£
Trade creditors		4,700	2,590
Trade debtors		7,320	9,500
Rent and rates accruals		200	260
Motor vans:			
A123 BWA:	At cost	10,000	-
	Provision for depreciation	8,000	-
E471 KBR:	At cost	-	13,000
	Provision for depreciation	-	To be determined
Stock in trade		4,900	5,900
Insurance prepaid		160	200

(c) All receipts are banked and all payments are made from the business bank account.

(d) A trade debt of £300 owing by Warren Jones and included in the trade debtors at 31 August 20X8 (see (b) above), is to be written off as a bad debt.

Part B: Preparation of final accounts

(e) It is Anna Forbes' policy to provide depreciation at the rate of 20% on the cost of motor vans held at the end of each financial year; no depreciation is provided in the year of sale or disposal of a motor van.

(f) Discounts received during the year ended 31 August 20X8 from trade creditors amounted to £1,100.

Task

(a) Prepare Anna Forbes' trading and profit and loss account for the year ended 31 August 20X8.
(b) Prepare Anna Forbes' balance sheet as at 31 August 20X8.

Activity 6.4

Miss Anne Teek runs a market stall selling old pictures, china, copper goods and curios of all descriptions. Most of her sales are for cash, although regular customers are allowed credit. No double entry accounting records have been kept, but the following information is available.

SUMMARY OF NET ASSETS AT 31 MARCH 20X8

	£	£
Motor van		
Cost		3,000
Depreciation		2,500
Net book value		500
Current assets		
Stock	500	
Debtors	170	
Cash at bank	2,800	
Cash in hand	55	
	3,525	
Current liabilities		
Creditors	230	
Net current assets		3,295
Net assets		3,795

Additional information

(a) Anne bought a new motor van in January 20X9 receiving a part-exchange allowance of £1,800 for her old van. A full year's depreciation is to be provided on the new van, calculated at 20% on cost.

(b) Anne has taken £50 cash per week for her personal use. She also estimates that petrol for the van, paid in cash, averages £10 per week.

(c) Other items paid in cash were:

Sundry expenses	£24
Repairs to stall canopy	£201

(d) Anne makes a gross profit of 40% on selling prices. She is certain that no goods have been stolen but remembers that she appropriated a set of glasses and some china for her own use. These items had a total selling price of £300.

(e) Trade debtors and creditors at 31.3.X9 are £320 and £233 respectively, and cash in hand amounts to £39. No stock count has been made and there are no accrued or prepaid expenses.

A summary of bank statements for the twelve months in question shows:

	£
Credits	
Cash banked (all cash sales)	7,521
Cheques banked (all credit sales)	1,500
Dividend income	210
	9,231

Debits	£
Purchase of motor van	3,200
Road fund licence	80
Insurance on van	323
Creditors for purchases	7,777
Rent	970
Sundry	31
Accountancy fees (re current work)	75
Bank overdraft interest (6 months to 1.10.X8)	20
Returned cheque (bad debt)	29
	12,505

The bank statement for 1 April 20X9 shows an interest charge of £27.

Task

Prepare Anne's trading and profit and loss account for the year to 31 March 20X9 and a balance sheet as at that date.

(Assume a 52 week year)

Activity 6.5

A Highton is in business as a general retailer. He does not keep a full set of accounting records; however it has been possible to extract the following details from the few records that are available.

	1 April 20X1 £	31 March 20X2 £
Freehold land and buildings at cost	10,000	10,000
Motor vehicle (cost £3,000)	2,250	
Stock, at cost	3,500	4,000
Trade debtors	500	1,000
Prepayments: motor vehicle expenses	200	300
property insurance	50	100
Cash at bank	550	950
Cash in hand	100	450
Loan from Highton's father	10,000	
Trade creditors: accruals	1,500	1,800
electricity	200	400
motor vehicle expenses	200	100

Extract from a rough cash book for the year to 31 March 20X2

	£
Receipts	
Cash sales	80,400
Payments	£
Cash purchases	17,000
Drawings	7,000
General shop expenses	100
Telephone	100
Wages	3,000

Extract from the bank pass sheets for the year to 31 March 20X2

	£
Receipts	
Cash banked	52,850
Cheques from trade debtors	8,750

Part B: Preparation of final accounts

	£
Payments	
Cheques to suppliers	47,200
Loan repayment (including interest)	10,100
Electricity	400
Motor vehicle expenses	1,000
Property insurance	150
Rates	300
Telephone	300
Drawings	1,750

Note. Depreciation is to be provided on the motor vehicle at a rate of 25% per annum on cost.

You are required to prepare a trading and profit and loss account for the year to 31 March 20X2, and a balance sheet as at that date.

Activity 6.6

The summarised balance sheet of Richard Church, photographic retailer, as at 31 March 20X2, is as follows.

	Cost £	Dep'n £	NBV £
Fixed assets			
Shop equipment and fittings	15,000	3,000	12,000
Motor vehicles	6,000	1,500	4,500
	21,000	4,500	16,500
Current assets			
Stock		10,420	
Debtors		6,260	
Rent prepaid		650	
Bank		6,690	
		24,020	
Current liabilities			
Trade creditors		4,740	
Accrued expenses: heating and lighting		380	
		5,120	
Net current assets			18,900
			35,400
Long term liabilities			
Loan from S Chappell			3,000
			32,400
Capital			32,400

Despite professional advice, Richard Church has not maintained an accounting system, but produces the following information regarding the financial year ended 31 March 20X3.

(a) Total sales and sales returns were £152,600 and £3,500 respectively. An average gross profit to sales ratio of 30 per cent is maintained during the year.

(b) The trade debtors figure at 31 March 20X3 was £5,620, on which figure it has been decided to make a provision for doubtful debts of 5 per cent at the year end. During the course of the year trade debts amounting to £470 had been written off.

(c) The trade creditors figure at 31 March 20X3 was £6,390. Discounts received from suppliers amounted to £760.

(d) Stock at 31 March 20X3 indicates an increased investment of £4,000 in stock over that one year earlier. Drawings from stock by Richard Church during the year amounted to £600 and were included in payments made to suppliers; otherwise no records of these drawings were made.

(e) Payments for shop salaries for the year were £15,840, and for heating, lighting, rent and rates and other administration expenses amounted to £3,460. At 31 March 20X3 rent paid in advance amounted to £480, and heating bills outstanding were £310.

(f) Shop fittings acquired during the year, and paid for, amounted to £2,000. Depreciation on shop equipment and fittings is provided annually at the rate of 10 per cent on the original cost of assets held at the year end. Similarly, depreciation on the motor vehicle is to be provided at the rate of 25% on original cost.

(g) On 31 March 20X3 the loan from S Chappell was repaid.

(h) Cash drawings by Richard Church amounted to £9,000.

Task

(a) Prepare a trading, profit and loss account for the year ended 31 March 20X3.
(b) Prepare a balance sheet as at 31 March 20X3.

Key learning points

- **Incomplete records** questions may test your ability to prepare accounts in the following situations.
    - A business might not maintain a ledger and therefore has no continuous double entry record of transactions.
    - Accounting records are destroyed by accident, such as fire.
    - Some essential figure is unknown and must be calculated as a balancing figure. This may occur as a result of stock being damaged or destroyed, or because of misappropriation of assets.

- The approach to incomplete records questions is to build up the information given so as to complete the necessary double entry. This may involve reconstructing **control accounts** for:
    - Cash and bank (often in columnar format);
    - Debtors and creditors

- Where stock, sales or purchases is the unknown figure it will be necessary to use information on **gross profit percentages** so as to construct a trading account in which the unknown figure can be inserted as a balance.

Quick quiz

1 In the absence of a sales account or sales day book, how can a figure of sales for the year be computed?

2 In the absence of a purchases account or purchases day book, how can a figure of purchases for the year be computed?

3 What is the accounting double entry to record the loss of stock by fire or burglary?

4 If a business proprietor pays his personal income into the business bank account, what is the accounting double entry to record the transaction?

Answers to quick quiz

1 Using the following formula:

	£
Payments from trade debtors	X
Add closing debtors	X
Deduct opening debtors	(X)
Credit sales	X

2 By using the formula:

	£
Payments to creditors	X
Add closing creditors	X
Deduct opening creditors	(X)
Credit purchases	X

Part B: Preparation of final accounts

3 If insured:

    DEBIT   Insurance claim (debtor account)
    CREDIT   Trading account

If not insured:

    DEBIT   Profit and loss account
    CREDIT   Trading account

4 DEBIT   Cash
   CREDIT   Drawings

Answers to activities

Answer 6.1

Credit purchases = £(55,700 + 1,440 − 1,940) = £55,200. Therefore total purchases = £(55,200 + 2,800) = £63,000.

Answer 6.2

Cost of sales = 100/150 × £300,000
                   = £200,000

Since the stock level is being allowed to fall, it means that purchases will be £15,000 less than £200,000, ie £185,000.

Answer 6.3

(a) TRADING AND PROFIT AND LOSS ACCOUNT
FOR THE YEAR ENDED 31 AUGUST 20X8

	£	£
Sales (W1)		98,180
Opening stock	4,900	
Purchases (W2)	70,990	
	75,890	
Less closing stock	5,900	
		69,990
Gross profit		28,190
Discounts received		1,100
Profit on sale of motor vehicle £2,100 − £(10,000 − 8,000)		100
		29,390
Rent and rates (W3)	2,660	
Wages	15,100	
Motor vehicle expenses	3,350	
Postages and stationery	1,360	
Repairs and renewals	650	
Insurances (W4)	760	
Bad debt	300	
Depreciation of van (20% × £13,000)	2,600	
		26,780
		2,610

(b) BALANCE SHEET AS AT 31 AUGUST 20X8

	£	£
Fixed assets		
Motor van: cost	13,000	
depreciation	2,600	
		10,400
Current assets		
Stock	5,900	
Debtors (£9,500 - £300 bad debt)	9,200	
Prepayment	200	
Cash at bank	2,010	
	17,310	
Current liabilities		
Creditors	2,590	
Accrual	260	
	2,850	
Net current assets		14,460
		24,860
Capital account		
Balance at 1 September 20X7 (W5)		11,450
Additional capital: proceeds on sale of yacht		20,000
Net profit for the year	2,610	
Less drawings	9,200	
Retained loss for the year		(6,590)
Balance at 31 August 20X8		24,860

Workings

1. Sales

	£
Cash received from customers	96,000
Add debtors balances at 31 August 20X8	9,500
	105,500
Less debtors balances at 1 September 20X7	7,320
Sales in year	98,180

2. Purchases

	£	£
Payments to suppliers		72,000
Add: creditors balances at 31 August 20X8	2,590	
discounts granted by creditors	1,100	
		3,690
		75,690
Less creditors balances at 1 September 20X7		4,700
		70,990

3. Rent and rates

	£
Cash paid in year	2,600
Add accrual at 31 August 20X8	260
	2,860
Less accrual at 1 September 20X7	200
Charge for the year	2,660

4. Insurances

	£
Cash paid in year	800
Add prepayment at 1 September 20X7	160
	960
Less prepayment at 31 August 20X8	200
	760

Workings 1-4 could also be presented in ledger account format as follows.

Part B: Preparation of final accounts

TOTAL DEBTORS

	£		£
Balance b/f	7,320	Bank	96,000
∴ Sales	98,180	Balance c/f	9,500
	105,500		105,500

TOTAL CREDITORS

	£		£
Bank	72,000	Balance b/f	4,700
Discounts received	1,100	∴ Purchases	70,990
Balance c/f	2,590		
	75,690		75,690

RENT AND RATES

	£		£
Bank	2,600	Balance b/f	200
Balance c/f	260	∴ P & L charge	2,660
	2,860		2,860

INSURANCES

	£		£
Balance b/f	160	∴ P & L charge	760
Bank	800	Balance c/f	200
	960		960

5 **Capital at 1 September 20X7**

	£	£
Assets		
Bank balance		1,970
Debtors		7,320
Motor van £(10,000 − 8,000)		2,000
Stock		4,900
Prepayment		160
		16,350
Liabilities		
Trade creditors	4,700	
Accrual	200	
		4,900
		11,450

Answer 6.4

MISS TEEK
TRADING AND PROFIT AND LOSS ACCOUNT
FOR THE YEAR ENDED 31 MARCH 20X9

	£	£
Sales: cash (W1)		10,850
credit (W2)		1,650
		12,500
Opening stock	500	
Purchases (W3)	7,600	
	8,100	
Closing stock (W4)	(600)	
Cost of sales		7,500
Gross profit		5,000
Expenses		
Rent	970	
Repairs to canopy	201	
Van running expenses (520 + 80 + 323)	923	
Depreciation	1,000	
Sundry expenses (24 + 31)	55	
Bank interest	47	
Accounting fees	75	
Bad debts	29	
		3,300
		1,700
Profit on disposal of van		1,300
		3,000

MISS TEEK
BALANCE SHEET AS AT 31 MARCH 20X9

	£	£	£
Fixed assets			
Motor van: cost (W5)			5,000
depreciation (W5)			1,000
net book value			4,000
Current assets			
Stock (W4)		600	
Debtors (W2)		320	
Cash in hand (W1)		39	
		959	
Current liabilities			
Bank overdraft (W1)	474		
Bank interest (presumably not paid until 1 April)	27		
Creditors (W3)	233		
		734	
Net current assets			225
			4,225
Proprietor's capital			
Balance at 31 March 20X8			3,795
Profit for the year		3,000	
Less drawings		2,570	
Retained profit for the year			430
Balance at 31 March 20X9			4,225

Part B: Preparation of final accounts

Workings

1   CASH BOOK

	Cash £	Bank £		Cash £	Bank £
Balance b/d	55	2,800	Drawings (52 × £50)	2,600	
Cash takings banked (contra entry)		7,521	Petrol (52 × £10)	520	
Cheques banked		1,500	Sundry expenses	24	
Dividend income - drawings a/c		210	Repairs to canopy	201	
Cash takings (balancing figures)	10,850		Taking banked (contra entry)	7,521	
			Purchase of van		3,200
			Road fund licence		80
			Insurance on van		323
			Creditors		7,777
			Rent		970
			Sundry		31
			Accounting work		75
			Bank interest		20
			Returned cheque - bad debt		29
Balance c/d (overdraft)		474	Balance c/d	39	
	10,905	12,505		10,905	12,505
Balance b/d	39		Balance b/d		474

2   DEBTORS

	£		£
Balance b/d	170	Cash	1,500
Credit sales - balancing figure	1,650	Balance c/d	320
	1,820		1,820

3   CREDITORS

	£		£
Bank	7,777	Balance b/d	230
Balance c/d	233	Purchases (balancing figure)	7,780
	8,010		8,010

Goods taken as drawings:

		£
Selling price	(100%)	300
Gross profit	(40%)	120
Cost	(60%)	180

Therefore, purchases taken to the trading account = £7,780 - £180 = £7,600.

4   *Closing stock*

		£
Sales (10,850 + 1,650)	(100%)	12,500
Gross profit	(40%)	5,000
Cost of goods sold	(60%)	7,500
Opening stock		500
Purchases (W3)		7,600
		8,100
Cost of goods sold		7,500
Closing stock (balancing figure)		600

5   *New van*

The bank statement shows that the cash paid for the new van was £3,200. Since there was a part exchange of £1,800 on the old van, the cost of the new van must be £5,000 with first year depreciation (20%) £1,000.

6   *Disposal of van*

	£		£
Van at cost	3,000	Provision for depreciation at	
Profit on disposal	1,300	date of sale	2,500
		Asset account (trade in value for new van)	1,800
	4,300		4,300

7   *Drawings*

	£		£
Cash	2,600	Dividend income	210
Stock	180	Capital account (balance)	2,570
	2,780		2,780

Since there are no investments in the business balance sheet, the dividend income must be separate from the business. However, since it is paid into the business bank account, it should be accounted for, in effect, as a reduction in drawings.

Answer 6.5

TRADING PROFIT AND LOSS ACCOUNT
FOR THE YEAR ENDED 31 MARCH 20X2

	£	£
Sales: cash	80,400	
credit (W1)	9,250	
		89,650
Cost of sales		
Opening stock	3,500	
Purchases: cash	17,000	
credit (W2)	47,500	
	68,000	
Less closing stock	4,000	
		64,000
Gross profit		25,650
Expenses		
Depreciation of motor vehicle (25% × £3,000)	750	
Motor vehicle expenses (W3)	800	
Property insurance £(50 + 150 - 100)	100	
Loan interest	100	
Electricity £(400 + 400 - 200)	600	
General shop expenses	100	
Telephone £(100 + 300)	400	
Wages	3,000	
Rates	300	
		6,150
Net profit		19,500

Part B: Preparation of final accounts

BALANCE SHEET AS AT 31 MARCH 20X2

	£	£
Fixed assets		
Freehold land and buildings at cost		10,000
Motor vehicle: cost	3,000	
accumulated depreciation	1,500	
		1,500
		11,500
Current assets		
Stock	4,000	
Trade debtors	1,000	
Prepayments	400	
Cash at bank	950	
Cash in hand	450	
	6,800	
Current liabilities		
Trade creditors	1,800	
Accruals	500	
	2,300	
Net current assets		4,500
		16,000
Proprietor's capital		
At 1 April 20X4 (W4)*		5,250
Net profit for the year	19,500	
Less drawings £(7,000 + 1,750)	8,750	
Profit retained in business		10,750
		16,000

*The opening capital could be inserted as a balancing figure; W4 is included merely to prove the figure.

Workings

1 DEBTORS CONTROL ACCOUNT

	£		£
Opening balance	500	Bank	8,750
∴ Credit sales	9,250	Closing balance	1,000
	9,750		9,750

2 CREDITORS CONTROL ACCOUNT

	£		£
Bank	47,200	Opening balance	1,500
Closing balance	1,800	∴ Credit purchases	47,500
	49,000		49,000

3 MOTOR VEHICLE EXPENSES

	£		£
Prepayment b/f	200	Accrual b/f	200
Bank	1,000	∴ P & L account	800
Accrual b/f	100	Prepayment c/f	300
	1,300		1,300

4 PROPRIETOR'S CAPITAL AT 1 APRIL 20X1

	£	£
Assets		
Freehold land and buildings	10,000	
Motor vehicle	2,250	
Stock	3,500	
Debtors and prepayments	750	
Cash at bank and in hand	650	
		17,150
Liabilities		
Loan	10,000	
Creditors and accruals	1,900	
		11,900
		5,250

Answer 6.6

(a) TRADING PROFIT AND LOSS ACCOUNT
FOR THE YEAR ENDED 31 MARCH 20X3

	£	£
Sales (less returns)		149,100
Opening stock	10,420	
Purchases (balancing figure)	108,370	
	118,790	
Closing stock £(10,420 + 4,000)	14,420	
Cost of goods sold		104,370
Gross profit (30% × £149,100)		44,730
Add discounts received		760
		45,490
Expenses		
Bad debts	470	
Provision for doubtful debts (5% × £5,620)	281	
Salaries	15,840	
Heat, light etc (W5)	3,560	
Depreciation:		
shop fittings 10% × £(15,000 + 2,000)	1,700	
motor vehicle 25% × £6,000	1,500	
		23,351
Net profit		22,139

Part B: Preparation of final accounts

(b) BALANCE SHEET AS AT 31 MARCH 20X3

	Cost £	Depreciation £	Net £
Fixed assets			
Shop equipment and fittings	17,000	4,700	12,300
Motor vehicle	6,000	3,000	3,000
	23,000	7,700	15,300
Current assets			
Stock		14,420	
Trade debtors less provision		5,339	
Rent paid in advance		480	
Bank		16,100	
		36,339	
Current liabilities			
Trade creditors		6,390	
Accrued expenses		310	
		6,700	
Net current assets			29,639
			44,939
Proprietor's capital			
Balance at 31 March 20X2			32,400
Profit for year		22,139	
Less drawings £(9,000 + 600)		9,600	
			12,539
			44,939

Workings

Note. No distinction is made in the question between cash transactions and bank transactions. A 'total cash account' must therefore be constructed instead of the more usual columnar bank and cash account.

1   CASH ACCOUNT

	£		£
Balance b/f	6,690	Creditors (Working 3)	106,560
Debtors (W2)	149,270	Salaries	15,840
		Heat, light etc	3,460
		Shop fittings	2,000
		Loan - repayment	3,000
		Drawings	9,000
		Balance c/d	16,100
	155,960		155,960
Balance b/d	16,100		

2   DEBTORS CONTROL ACCOUNT

	£		£
Balance b/f	6,260	Bad debts	470
Sales	152,600	Returns inwards	3,500
		Cash (balancing figure)	149,270
		Balance c/d	5,620
	158,860		158,860
Balance b/d	5,620		

3   CREDITORS CONTROL ACCOUNT

	£		£
Discounts received	760	Balance b/f	4,740
Cash (balancing figure)	106,560	Purchases (W4)	108,970
Balance c/d	6,390		
	113,710		113,710
		Balance b/d	6,390

4   PURCHASES ACCOUNT
                                £   £
         Creditors   108,970   Trading account   108,370
                                         Drawings   600
                            _____   _____
                            108,970   108,970
                            =======   =======

5   *Heat, light etc*
                                                              £   £
     Amounts paid in year   3,460
     Add: rent prepayment at 31 March 20X2   650
            heating accrual at 31 March 20X3   310
                                                           ____
                                                                          960
                                                                       _____
                                                                        4,420
     Less: rent prepayment at 31 March 20X3   480
            heating accrual at 31 March 20X2   380
                                                           ____
                                                                          860
                                                                       _____
     P & L charge for year   3,560
                                                                       ======

Now try Question 6 in the Exam Question Bank at the end of the Text.

Chapter 7 Limited companies

Chapter topic list

1. What are limited companies?
2. The accounting records of limited companies
3. The capital of limited companies
4. The board of directors
5. Dividends
6. Ordinary shares and preference shares
7. The final accounts of limited companies: internal use
8. Fixed assets
9. Current liabilities
10. Debenture loans
11. Taxation
12. Ledger accounts and limited companies
13. Share capital and reserves
14. Example: company accounts for internal purposes

The following study sessions are covered in this chapter.

		Syllabus reference
9-11(a)	Prepare the financial statements for a limited company from a trial balance, including adjustments for items including: (i) corporation tax (ii) dividends (iii) depreciation (iv) bad and doubtful debts (v) closing stock (vi) share capital (vii) accruals and prepayments (viii) revaluation of assets (ix) provisions	2
15 & 16(a)	Distinguish between issued and authorised share capital and between called up and paid up share capital	2
15 & 16(b)	Distinguish between ordinary and preference shares	2
15 & 16(c)	Account for a share issue	2
15 & 16(d)	Explain the share premium account	2
15 & 16(e)	Define and account for a bonus issue	2

Part B: Preparation of final accounts

15 & 16(f)	Define and account for a rights issue	2
15 & 16(g)	Outline the advantages and disadvantages of a rights issue and a bonus issue	2
15 & 16(h)	Distinguish between the market value and nominal value of a share	2
15 & 16(i)	Explain why companies will be concerned with the value of their shares	2
15 & 16(j)	Define and account for debentures	2
15 & 16(k)	Explain the advantages and disadvantages of raising finance by issuing debentures rather than issuing ordinary or preference shares	2

1 WHAT ARE LIMITED COMPANIES?

1.1 As we should expect, the accounting rules and conventions for recording the business transactions of limited companies and then preparing their final accounts are much the same as for sole traders. For example, companies will have a cash book, sales day book, purchase day book, journal, sales ledger, purchase ledger and nominal ledger. They will also prepare a profit and loss account annually and a balance sheet at the end of the accounting year.

1.2 There are, however, some **differences** in the accounts of limited companies, of which the following are perhaps the most significant.

(a) The **legislation** governing the activities of limited companies is very extensive. Amongst other things, the Companies Acts define certain minimum accounting records which must be maintained by companies.

   (i) They specify that the **annual accounts** of a company must be filed with the Registrar of Companies and so available for public inspection

   (ii) They contain detailed requirements on the **minimum information** which must be disclosed in a company's accounts. Businesses which are not limited companies (non-incorporated businesses) enjoy comparative freedom from statutory regulation.

(b) The owners of a company (its **members** or **shareholders**) may be very numerous. Their capital is shown differently from that of a sole trader; and similarly the 'appropriation account' of a company is different.

Limited liability

> **KEY TERM**
>
> **Unlimited liability** means that if the business runs up debts that it is unable to pay, the proprietors will become personally liable for the unpaid debts, and would be required, if necessary, to sell their private possessions in order to repay them.

1.3 Sole traders and partnerships are, with some significant exceptions, generally fairly small concerns. The amount of capital involved may be modest, and the proprietors of the business usually participate in managing it. Their liability for the debts of the business is unlimited. For example, if a sole trader has some capital in his business, but the business now owes £40,000 which it cannot repay, the trader might have to sell his house to raise the money to pay off his business debts.

1.4 Limited companies offer limited liability to their owners.

> **KEY TERM**
>
> **Limited liability** means that the maximum amount that an owner stands to lose in the event that the company becomes insolvent and cannot pay off its debts, is his share of the capital in the business.

Thus limited liability is a major advantage of turning a business into a limited company. However, in practice, banks will normally seek personal guarantees from shareholders before making loans or granting an overdraft facility and so the advantage of limited liability is lost to a small owner managed business.

1.5 There are other disadvantages too. In comparison with sole trader businesses and partnerships, there is a significantly increased administrative and financial burden. This arises from:

(a) Compliance with the Companies Act 1985, notably in having to prepare annual accounts and have them audited, in keeping statutory registers and having to publish accounts etc

(b) Having to comply with all SSAPs and FRSs

(c) Formation and annual registration costs

1.6 As a business grows, it needs more capital to finance its operations, and significantly more than the people currently managing the business can provide themselves. One way of obtaining more capital is to invite **investors from outside** the business to invest in the ownership or equity of the business. These new co-owners would not usually be expected to help with managing the business. To such investors, **limited liability is very attractive**.

1.7 Investments are always risky undertakings, but with limited liability the investor knows the maximum amount that he stands to lose when he puts some capital into a company.

Public and private companies

1.8 There are two classes of limited company.

(a) **Private companies**. These have the word 'limited' at the end of their name. Being private, they cannot invite members of the public to invest in their equity (ownership).

(b) **Public companies**. These are much fewer in number than private companies, but are generally much larger in size. They have the words 'public limited company' - shortened to PLC or plc (or the Welsh language equivalent) at the end of their name. Public limited companies can invite members of the general public to invest in their equity, and the 'shares' of these companies may be traded on The Stock Exchange.

Activity 7.1
Limited liability means that the directors do not have to account for their mistakes. True or false?

Part B: Preparation of final accounts

2 THE ACCOUNTING RECORDS OF LIMITED COMPANIES

2.1 There is a legal requirement for companies in the UK to keep **accounting records** which are sufficient to show and explain the company's transactions. The records should:

(a) Disclose the company's current financial position at any time;

(b) Contain:

  (i) Day-to-day entries of money received and spent;

  (ii) A record of the company's assets and liabilities;

  (iii) Where the company deals in goods:

   (1) A statement of stocks held at the year end, and supporting stocktaking sheets

   (2) With the exception of retail sales, statements of goods bought and sold which identify the sellers and buyers of those goods

(c) Enable the directors of the company to ensure that the final accounts of the company give a true and fair view of the company's profit or loss and balance sheet position.

Registers: the statutory books

2.2 A company must also keep a number of registers. These include:

- Register of members
- Register of shareholders' 3 per cent interests
- Register of charges and a register of debenture holders
- Register of directors and company secretaries
- Register of directors' interests (in shares or debentures of the company)

These registers are known collectively as the non-accounting **statutory books** of the company.

3 THE CAPITAL OF LIMITED COMPANIES

3.1 The proprietors' capital in a limited company consists of **share capital**. When a company is set up for the first time, it issues shares, which are paid for by investors, who then become shareholders of the company. Shares are denominated in units of 25 pence, 50 pence, £1 or whatever seems appropriate. The 'face value' of the shares is called their nominal value.

3.2 For example, when a company is set up with a share capital of, say, £100,000, it may be decided to issue:

(a) 100,000 shares of £1 each nominal value; or
(b) 200,000 shares of 50p each; or
(c) 400,000 shares of 25p each; or
(d) 250,000 shares of 40p each etc.

The amount at which the shares are issued may exceed their nominal value. For example, a company might issue 100,000 £1 shares at a price of £1.20 each. Subscribers will then pay a total of £120,000. The issued share capital of the company would be shown in its accounts at nominal value, £100,000; the excess of £20,000 is described not as share capital, but as **share premium**.

Authorised, issued, called-up and paid-up share capital

3.3 A distinction must be made between authorised, issued, called-up and paid-up share capital.

(a) **Authorised (or nominal) capital** is the maximum amount of share capital that a company is empowered to issue. The amount of authorised share capital varies from company to company, and can change by agreement.

For example, a company's authorised share capital might be 5,000,000 ordinary shares of £1 each. This would then be the maximum number of shares it could issue, unless the maximum were to be changed by agreement.

(b) **Issued capital** is the nominal amount of share capital that has been issued to shareholders. The amount of issued capital cannot exceed the amount of authorised capital.

Continuing the example above, the company with authorised share capital of 5,000,000 ordinary shares of £1 might have issued 4,000,000 shares. This would leave it the option to issue 1,000,000 more shares at some time in the future.

When share capital is issued, shares are allotted to shareholders. The term 'allotted' share capital means the same thing as issued share capital.

(c) **Called-up capital**. When shares are issued or allotted, a company does not always expect to be paid the full amount for the shares at once. It might instead call up only a part of the issue price, and wait until a later time before it calls up the remainder.

For example, if a company allots 400,000 ordinary shares of £1, it might call up only, say, 75 pence per share. The issued share capital would be £400,000, but the called up share capital would only be £300,000.

(d) **Paid-up capital**. Like everyone else, investors are not always prompt or reliable payers. When capital is called up, some shareholders might delay their payment (or even default on payment). Paid-up capital is the amount of called-up capital that has been paid.

For example, if a company issues 400,000 ordinary shares of £1 each, calls up 75 pence per share, and receives payments of £290,000, we would have:

	£
Allotted or issued capital	400,000
Called-up capital	300,000
Paid-up capital	290,000
Called-up capital not paid	10,000

The balance sheet of the company would then include called up capital not paid on the assets side, as follows:

	£
Called-up capital not paid	10,000
Cash (called-up capital paid)	290,000
	300,000
Called-up share capital	
400,000 ordinary shares of £1, with 75p per share called up.	300,000

4 THE BOARD OF DIRECTORS

4.1 A company might have a large number of **shareholders**, or only a few. No matter how many there are, they delegate authority for the day-to-day management of the company to its **directors**, who are directly responsible to the shareholders for what they do. (In some companies, the directors of the company and its shareholders might be the same people.)

Part B: Preparation of final accounts

There must also be a company secretary. Company policy is decided at regular meetings of the board of directors.

> **IMPORTANT!**
>
> Whereas the salary of a sole trader or a partner in a partnership is not a charge in the P & L account, but is an appropriation of profit, the salary of a director is a P & L account expense, even when the director is also a shareholder of the company.

4.2 It would be wrong to give the impression that all companies are large-scale with many shareholders. The vast majority of UK companies are in fact small and family-owned.

> **Case example**
>
> There are many good reasons why a sole trader, say Alfred Newbegin Tools might choose to set up his own company (Newbegin Tools Ltd). These include limited personal liability and various tax advantages. Such a company would typically have one director (Alf) and his wife (Mabel) would be the company secretary. There would be two shareholders (Alf and Mabel) and board meetings would tend to be held during the commercial breaks on television or over breakfast. In this case it would be true to say that the providers of capital would also be running the business (as is normal with a sole trader) but Alf and Mabel as individuals would now be distinct from the business, because a company is a 'person' in its own right in the eyes of the law. Alf's salary, formerly an appropriation of profit, would now be a charge against company profits.

5 DIVIDENDS

5.1 Shareholders who, in common with all the other shareholders, are also directors of their company will receive a salary as a director. They are also entitled to a share of the profits made by the company.

> **KEY TERM**
>
> **Dividends** are appropriations of profit after tax.

5.2 A company might pay dividends in two stages during the course of their accounting year.

(a) In **mid year**, after the half-year financial results are known, the company might pay an **interim dividend.**

(b) At the **end of the year**, the company might pay a further **final dividend.**

5.3 The total dividend for the year is the sum of the interim and the final dividend. (Not all companies by any means pay an interim dividend. Interim dividends are, however, commonly paid out by public limited companies.)

5.4 At the end of an accounting year, a company's directors will have proposed a final dividend payment, but this will not yet have been paid. This means that the final dividend should be appropriated out of profits and shown as a current liability in the balance sheet.

5.5 The terminology of dividend payments can be confusing, since they may be expressed either in the form, as 'x pence per share' or as 'y per cent'. In the latter case, the meaning is always 'y per cent of the nominal value of the shares in issue'. For example, suppose a company's issued share capital consists of 100,000 50p ordinary shares which were issued at a premium of 10p per share. The company's balance sheet would include the following:

		£
Called up share capital:	100,000 50p ordinary shares	50,000
Share premium account	(100,000 × 10p)	10,000

If the directors wish to pay a dividend of £5,000, they may propose either:

(a) a dividend of 5p per share (100,000 × 5p = £5,000); or
(b) a dividend of 10% (10% × £50,000 = £5,000).

Profits re-invested

5.6 Not all profits are distributed as dividends; some will be retained in the business to finance future projects. The 'market value' (see below) of the share should, all other things being equal, be increased if these projects are profitable.

Activity 7.2

A company has authorised share capital of 1,000,000 50p ordinary shares and an issued share capital of 800,000 50p ordinary shares. If an ordinary dividend of 5% is declared, what is the amount payable to shareholders?

6 ORDINARY SHARES AND PREFERENCE SHARES

6.1 At this stage it is relevant to distinguish between the two types of shares most often encountered, **preference shares** and **ordinary shares**.

KEY TERM

Preference shares are shares which confer certain preferential rights on their holder.

6.2 **Preference shares** are now rather old-fashioned and are rarely issued, although they do have occasional resurgences of popularity.

6.3 They carry the right to a final dividend which is expressed as a percentage of their nominal value: eg a 6% £1 preference share carries a right to an annual dividend of 6p. Preference dividends have priority over ordinary dividends; in other words, if the directors of a company wish to pay a dividend (which they are not obliged to do) they must pay any preference dividend first. Otherwise, no ordinary dividend may be paid.

6.4 The rights attaching to preference shares are set out in the company's constitution. They may vary from company to company, but typically:

(a) Preference shareholders have a **priority right** over ordinary shareholders to a **return of their capital** if the company goes into liquidation.

(b) Preference shares do **not carry a right to vote**.

(c) If the preference shares are cumulative, it means that before a company can pay an ordinary dividend it must not only pay the current year's preference dividend, but must also make good any arrears of preference dividends unpaid in previous years.

Part B: Preparation of final accounts

6.5 **Ordinary shares** are by far the most common. They carry no right to a fixed dividend but are entitled to all profits left after payment of any preference dividend. Generally however, only a part of such remaining profits is distributed, the rest being kept in reserve (see below).

> **KEY TERM**
>
> **Ordinary shares** are shares which are not preferential with regard to dividend payments. Thus a holder only receives a dividend after fixed dividends have been paid to preference shareholders.

6.6 The amount of ordinary dividends fluctuates although there is a general expectation that it will increase from year to year. Should the company be wound up, any surplus not distributed is shared between the ordinary shareholders. Ordinary shares normally carry voting rights.

6.7 Ordinary shareholders are thus the effective owners of a company. They own the 'equity' of the business, and any reserves of the business (described later) belong to them. Ordinary shareholders are sometimes referred to as equity shareholders. Preference shareholders are in many ways more like creditors (although legally they are members, not creditors).

6.8 It should be emphasised however that the precise rights attached to preference and ordinary shares vary from company to company; the distinctions noted above are generalisations.

6.9 EXAMPLE: DIVIDENDS, ORDINARY SHARES AND PREFERENCE SHARES: EXAMPLE

Garden Gloves Ltd has issued 50,000 ordinary shares of 50 pence each and 20,000 7% preference shares of £1 each. Its profits after taxation for the year to 30 September 20X5 were £8,400. The board of directors has decided to pay an ordinary dividend (ie a dividend on ordinary shares) which is 50% of profits after tax and preference dividend.

Task

Show the amount in total of dividends and of retained profits, and calculate the dividend per share on ordinary shares.

6.10 SOLUTION

Profits after tax and preference dividend are called *earnings*, and an important measure of company performance is the *earnings per share*. Although not required by the problem, the earnings per share (EPS) is also shown below.

	£
Profit after tax	8,400
Preference dividend (7% of £1 × 20,000)	1,400
Earnings (profit after tax and preference dividend)	7,000
Earnings per share (÷ 50,000) 14 pence	
Ordinary dividend (50% of earnings)	3,500
Retained profit (also 50% of earnings)	3,500

The ordinary dividend is 7 pence per share (£3,500 ÷ 50,000 ordinary shares).

7: Limited companies

The appropriation of profit would be shown as follows:

	£	£
Profit after tax		8,400
Dividends: preference	1,400	
ordinary	3,500	
		4,900
Retained profit		3,500

The market value of shares

6.11 The nominal value of shares will be different from their market value, which is the price at which someone is prepared to purchase shares in the company from an existing shareholder. If Mr A owns 1,000 £1 shares in Z Ltd he may sell them to B for £1.60 each.

6.12 This transfer of existing shares does not affect A Ltd's own financial position in any way whatsoever, and apart from changing the register of members, Z Ltd does not have to bother with the sale by Mr A to Mr B at all. There are certainly no accounting entries to be made for the share sale.

6.13 Shares in private companies do not change hands very often, hence their market value is often hard to estimate. Public companies are usually (not always) quoted; a quoted company is one whose shares are traded on The Stock Exchange and it is the market value of the shares which is quoted.

7 THE FINAL ACCOUNTS OF LIMITED COMPANIES: INTERNAL USE

7.1 The preparation and publication of the final accounts of limited companies in the UK are governed by the Companies Act 1985 as amended by the Companies Act 1989. At this stage we are concerned with the preparation of limited company accounts for *internal use*. If you are asked to produce such a set of final accounts, you need not follow the detailed regulations laid down by the Act. However, the general format of the balance sheet and profit and loss account of a limited company will be shown below with some simplifications, in order to introduce certain assets and liabilities which we have not come across before in earlier chapters of this Interactive Text.

7.2 The format of a limited company balance sheet is shown on the next page.

Part B: Preparation of final accounts

TYPICAL COMPANY LIMITED BALANCE SHEET
AS AT....

	£	£	£
Fixed assets			
Intangible assets			
Development costs		X	
Concessions, patents, licences, trademarks		X	
Goodwill		X	
			X
Tangible assets			
Land and buildings		X	
Plant and machinery		X	
Fixtures, fittings, tools and equipment		X	
Motor vehicles		X	
			X
Investments			X
			X
Current assets			
Stocks		X	
Debtors and prepayments		X	
Investments		X	
Cash at bank and in hand		X	
		X	
Creditors: amounts falling due within one year (ie current liabilities)			
Debenture loans (nearing their redemption date)	X		
Bank overdraft and loans	X		
Trade creditors	X		
Bills of exchange payable	X		
Taxation	X		
Accruals	X		
Proposed dividend	X		
		(X)	
Net current assets			X
Total assets less current liabilities			X
Creditors: amounts falling due after more than one year			
Debenture loans		X	
Taxation		X	
			(X)
			X
Capital and reserves			
Called up share capital			
Ordinary shares		X	
Preference shares		X	
			X
Reserves			
Share premium account		X	
Revaluation reserve		X	
Other reserves		X	
Profit and loss account (retained profits)		X	
			X
			X

7.3 The profit and loss account of a company might have a format roughly similar to the one below.

TYPICAL COMPANY LIMITED
PROFIT AND LOSS ACCOUNT FOR THE YEAR ENDED...

	£	£
Turnover		X
Cost of sales		(X)
Gross profit		X
Distribution costs	X	
Administrative expenses	X	
		(X)
		X
Other operating income	X	
Income from fixed asset investments	X	
Other interest receivable and similar income	X	
		X
		X
Interest payable		(X)
Profit before taxation		X
Tax		(X)
Profit after tax		X
Dividends: preference	X	
ordinary	X	
		(X)
Retained profit for the year		X
Profit and loss account as at the beginning of the year		X
Profit and loss account as at the end of the year		X

7.4 You may be asked to produce a set of accounts for **external use**, in which case you will have to follow the statutory format in all respects. This is covered in Chapter 8.

8 FIXED ASSETS

Intangible fixed assets

8.1 Intangible fixed assets represent amounts of money paid by a business to acquire benefits of a long-term nature. **Goodwill** and **deferred development expenditure** are two intangible assets which were discussed in detail in an earlier chapter.

8.2 If a company purchases some **patent rights**, or a concession from another business, or the right to use a trademark, the cost of the purchase can be accounted for as the purchase of an intangible fixed asset. These assets must then be **amortised** (depreciated) over their economic life.

Tangible fixed assets

8.3 As with any other type of business, tangible fixed assets are shown in the balance sheet at their net book value (ie at cost less provision for depreciation). Sometimes, a fixed asset, such as a building, might be revalued to a current market value. Depreciation would then be based on the revalued amount, and the balance sheet value of the asset would be the revalued amount less provision for depreciation on the revalued amount.

Investments

8.4 Investments are fixed assets if the company intends to hold on to them for a long time, and current assets if they are only likely to be held for a short time before being sold.

9 CURRENT LIABILITIES

9.1 The term '**creditors: amounts falling due within one year**' is used in the Companies Act 1985 as an alternative phrase meaning 'current liabilities'. You will therefore come across this term increasingly often as you progress through your accountancy studies.

10 DEBENTURE LOANS

10.1 Limited companies may issue **debenture stock** (debentures) or loan stock. These are **long-term liabilities** described on the balance sheet as loan capital. They are different from share capital in the following ways.

  (a) **Shareholders** are **members** of a company, while **providers of loan capital** are **creditors**.

  (b) **Shareholders** receive **dividends** (appropriations of profit) whereas the holders of loan capital are entitled to a **fixed rate of interest** (an expense charged against revenue).

  (c) Loan capital holders can take legal action against a company if their interest is not paid when due, whereas **shareholders cannot enforce the payment of dividends**.

  (d) **Debentures** or loan stock are often **secured on company assets**, whereas shares are not.

10.2 The holder of loan capital is generally in a less risky position than the shareholder. He has greater security, although his income is fixed and cannot grow, unlike ordinary dividends. As remarked earlier, preference shares are in practice very similar to loan capital, not least because the preference dividend is normally fixed.

10.3 Interest is calculated on the nominal value of loan capital, regardless of its market value. If a company has £700,000 (nominal value) 12% debentures in issue, interest of £84,000 will be charged in the profit and loss account per year. Interest is usually paid half-yearly; examination questions often require an accrual to be made for interest due at the year-end.

10.4 For example, if a company has £700,000 of 12% debentures in issue, pays interest on 30 June and 31 December each year, and ends its accounting year on 30 September, there would be an accrual of three months' unpaid interest (3/12 × £84,000) = £21,000 at the end of each accounting year that the debentures are still in issue.

11 TAXATION

11.1 Companies pay **corporation tax** on the profits they earn. Currently (2004), small companies pay tax at the rate of 19% on their taxable profits, and large companies pay 30%. Note that because a company has a separate legal personality, its tax is included in its accounts. An unincorporated business would not show income tax in its accounts, as it would not be a business expense but the personal affair of the proprietors.

  (a) The **charge** for corporation tax on profits for the year is shown as a **deduction** from **net profit**, before appropriations.

  (b) In the balance sheet, **tax payable** to the government is generally shown as a **current liability** as it is usually due nine months after the year end.

  (c) For various reasons, the tax on profits in the P & L account and the tax payable in the balance sheet are not usually the same amount.

12 LEDGER ACCOUNTS AND LIMITED COMPANIES

12.1 Limited companies keep ledger accounts, and the only difference between the ledger accounts of companies and sole traders is the nature of some of the transactions, assets and liabilities for which accounts need to be kept.

For example, there will be an account for each of the following items:

(a) *Taxation*

(i) Tax charged against profits will be accounted for by:

DEBIT   P & L account
CREDIT   Taxation account.

(ii) The outstanding balance on the taxation account will be a liability in the balance sheet, until eventually paid, when the accounting entry would be:

DEBIT   Taxation account
CREDIT   Cash

(b) *Dividends*

A separate account will be kept for the dividends for each different class of shares (eg preference, ordinary).

(i) Dividends declared out of profits will be accounted for by

DEBIT   P & L appropriation account
CREDIT   Dividends payable account

Dividends payable (but not yet paid) are a current liability.

(ii) When dividends are paid, we then have

DEBIT   Dividends payable account
CREDIT   Cash

(c) *Debenture loans*

Debenture loans being a long-term liability will be shown as a credit balance in a debenture loan account.

Interest payable on such loans is not credited to the loan account, but is credited to a separate creditors' account for interest until it is eventually paid: ie

DEBIT   Interest account (an expense, chargeable against profits)
CREDIT   Interest payable (creditors, and a current liability until eventually paid)

(d) *Share capital and reserves*

There will be a separate account for:

(i) each different class of share capital (always a credit balance b/f);
(ii) each different type of reserve (nearly always a credit balance b/f).

We shall now turn our attention to these items in more detail.

13 SHARE CAPITAL AND RESERVES

13.1 The net fixed assets of a company, plus the working capital (ie current assets minus current liabilities) minus the long-term liabilities, are 'financed' by the shareholders' capital.

13.2 Shareholders' capital consists of:

(a) The nominal value of issued capital (minus any amounts not yet called up on issued shares)

(b) Reserves

13.3 The share capital itself might consist of both ordinary shares and preference shares. All reserves, however, are owned by the ordinary shareholders, who own the 'equity' in the company.

Called-up share capital

13.4 A company's issued share capital is its called-up share capital, provided that there are no shares in issue which have so far only been partly called up.

This means that if a company has issued 200,000 ordinary shares of 50 pence each, and 50,000 10% preference shares of £1 each, all fully called up, the called up share capital in the balance sheet will be

	£
200,000 ordinary shares of 50p each	100,000
50,000 10% preference shares of £1 each	50,000
	150,000

Reserves

13.5 In the case of a sole trader, the proprietor's interest = net assets of the business, and in the case of a partnership, partners' funds = net assets. For a company the equation is:

> Shareholders' funds = net assets
>
> Furthermore:
>
> Shareholders' funds = share capital and reserves

A company's share capital will remain fixed from year to year, unless new shares are issued. Reserves are difficult to define neatly since different reserves arise for different reasons, but it follows from the above that:

Reserves = net assets minus share capital

The total amount of reserves in a company varies, according to changes in the net assets of the business.

13.6 The typical balance sheet in paragraph 7.2 lists a number of reserves, although the list is not comprehensive.

13.7 A distinction should be made between:

(a) **Statutory reserves**, which are reserves which a company is required to set up by law, and which are not available for the distribution of dividends

(b) **Non-statutory reserves**, which are reserves consisting of profits which are distributable as dividends, if the company so wishes

Profit and loss reserve (retained profits)

13.8 The most significant **non-statutory reserve** is variously described as:

- Revenue reserve
- Retained profits
- Retained earnings

- Undistributed profits
- Profit and loss account
- Unappropriated profits

13.9 These are **profits** earned by the company and **not appropriated** by dividends, taxation or transfer to another reserve account.

13.10 Provided that a company is earning profits, this reserve generally increases from year to year, as most companies do not distribute all their profits as dividends. Dividends can be paid from it: even if a loss is made in one particular year, a dividend can be paid from previous years' retained profits.

13.11 For example, if a company makes a loss of £100,000 in one year, yet has unappropriated profits from previous years totalling £250,000, it can pay a dividend not exceeding £150,000. One reason for retaining some profit each year is to enable the company to pay dividends even when profits are low (or non-existent). Another reason is usually shortage of cash.

13.12 Very occasionally, you might come across a debit balance on the profit and loss account. This would indicate that the company has accumulated losses.

Other non-statutory reserves

13.13 The company directors may choose to set up other reserves. These may have a specific purpose (eg plant and machinery replacement reserve) or not (eg general reserve). The creation of these reserves usually indicates a general intention not to distribute the profits involved at any future date, although legally any such reserves, being non-statutory, remain available for the payment of dividends.

Appropriation of profit

13.14 Profits are transferred to these reserves by making an appropriation out of profits, usually profits for the year. Typically, you might come across the following:

	£	£
Profit after taxation		100,000
Appropriations of profit		
Dividend	60,000	
Transfer to general reserve	10,000	
		70,000
Retained profits for the year		30,000
Profit and loss reserve b/f		250,000
Profit and loss reserve c/f		280,000

The share premium account

13.15 There are a number of statutory (or capital) reserves, the most important of which at this stage is the **share premium account**. Section 130 of the Companies Act 1985 states that 'where a company issues shares at a premium, whether for cash or otherwise, a sum equal to.... the premiums on those shares shall be transferred to the share premium account'.

13.16 By '**premium**' is meant the difference between the issue price of the share and its nominal value. When a company is first incorporated (set up) the issue price of its shares will probably be the same as their nominal value and so there would be no share premium. If the company does well the market value of its shares will increase, but not the nominal value. The price of any new shares issued will be approximately their market value.

13.17 The difference between cash received by the company and the nominal value of the new shares issued is transferred to the share premium account. For example, if X Ltd issues 1,000 £1 ordinary shares at £2.60 each the book entry will be:

		£	£
DEBIT	Cash	2,600	
CREDIT	Ordinary share capital		1,000
	Share premium account		1,600

13.18 A **share premium account** only comes into being when a company issues shares at a price in excess of their nominal value. The market price of the shares, once they have been issued, has no bearing at all on the company's accounts, and so if their market price goes up or down, the share premium account would remain unaltered.

> **KEY TERM**
>
> A **share premium account** is an account into which sums received as payment for shares in excess of their nominal value must be placed.

13.19 Once established, the share premium account constitutes capital of the company which cannot be paid out in dividends. The share premium account will increase in value if and when new shares are issued at a price above their nominal value.

13.20 The share premium account can be 'used' - and so decrease in value - only in certain very limited ways. One use of the share premium account, however, is to 'finance' the issue of bonus shares, which are described later in this chapter.

> **IMPORTANT!**
>
> The share premium account cannot be distributed as dividend under any circumstances.

13.21 The reason for creating statutory reserves is to **maintain the capital** of the company. This capital 'base' provides some security for the company's creditors, bearing in mind that the liability of shareholders is limited in the event that the company cannot repay its debts. It would be most unjust - and illegal - for a company to pay its shareholders a dividend out of its base capital when it is not even able to pay back its debts.

Activity 7.3

What are the ledger entries needed to record the issue of 200,000 £1 ordinary shares at a premium of 30p and paid for by cheque in full.

7: Limited companies

Distinction between reserves and provisions

> **KEY TERMS**
>
> A **reserve** is an appropriation of distributable profits for a specific purpose (eg plant replacement) while a provision is an amount charged against revenue as an expense. A provision relates either to a diminution in the value of an asset (eg doubtful debtors) or a known liability (eg audit fees), the amount of which cannot be established with any accuracy.
>
> **Provisions** (for depreciation, doubtful debts etc) are dealt with in company accounts in the same way as in the accounts of other types of business.

Bonus issues

13.22 A company may wish to increase its share capital without needing to raise additional finance by issuing new shares. For example, a profitable company might expand from modest beginnings over a number of years. Its profitability would be reflected in large balances on its reserves, while its original share capital might look like that of a much smaller business.

13.23 It is open to such a company to **re-classify some of its reserves as share capital**. This is purely a paper exercise which raises no funds. Any reserve may be re-classified in this way, including a share premium account or other statutory reserve. Such a re-classification increases the capital base of the company and gives creditors greater protection.

13.24 EXAMPLE: BONUS ISSUE

BUBBLES LIMITED
BALANCE SHEET (EXTRACT)

	£'000	£'000
Funds employed		
Share capital		
£1 ordinary shares (fully paid)		1,000
Reserves		
Share premium	500	
Undistributed profit	2,000	
Shareholders' funds		2,500
		3,500

Bubbles decided to make a '3 for 2' bonus issue (ie 3 new shares for every 2 already held).

The double entry is	£'000	£'000
DEBIT Share premium	500	
Undistributed profit	1,000	
CREDIT Ordinary share capital		1,500

After the issue the balance sheet is as follows	£'000
Share capital	
£1 ordinary shares (fully paid)	2,500
Reserves	
Undistributed profit	1,000
Shareholders' funds	3,500

Part B: Preparation of final accounts

13.25 1,500,000 new ('bonus') shares are issued to existing shareholders, so that if Mr X previously held 20,000 shares he will now hold 50,000. The total value of his holding should theoretically remain the same however, since the net assets of the company remain unchanged and his share of those net assets remains at 2% (ie 50,000/2,500,000; previously 20,000/1,000,000).

Rights issues

13.26 A rights issue (unlike a bonus issue) is an issue of shares for cash. The 'rights' are offered to existing shareholders, who can sell them if they wish.

13.27 EXAMPLE: RIGHTS ISSUE

Bubbles Ltd (above) decides to make a rights issue, shortly after the bonus issue. The terms are '1 for 5 @ £1.20' (ie one new share for every five already held, at a price of £1.20). Assuming that all shareholders take up their rights (which they are not obliged to) the double entry is:

		£'000	£'000
DEBIT	Cash	600	
CREDIT	Ordinary share capital		500
	Share premium		100

13.28 Mr X who previously held 50,000 shares will now hold 60,000, and the value of his holding should increase (all other things being equal) because the net assets of the company will increase. The new balance sheet will show:

	£'000	£'000
Share capital		
£1 ordinary shares		3,000
Reserves		
Share premium	100	
Undistributed profit	1,000	
		1,100
Shareholders' funds		4,100

The increase in funds of £600,000 represents the cash raised from the issue of 500,000 new shares at a price of £1.20 each.

13.29 Rights issues are a popular way of raising cash by issuing shares and they are cheap to administer. In addition, shareholders retain control of the business as their holding is not diluted.

14 EXAMPLE: COMPANY ACCOUNTS FOR INTERNAL PURPOSES

14.1 We can now try to draw together several of the items described in this chapter into an illustrative example. Study it carefully: it is a typical examination-style problem.

14.2 The accountant (unqualified) of Megatec Ltd has prepared the following trial balance as at 31 December 20X7.

	£'000
50p ordinary shares (fully paid)	350
7% £1 preference shares (fully paid)	100
10% debentures (secured)	200
Retained profit 1.1.X7	242
General reserve 1.1.X7	171
Freehold land and buildings 1.1.X7 (cost)	430
Plant and machinery 1.1.X7 (cost)	830
Provision for depreciation:	
Freehold buildings 1.1.X7	20
Plant and machinery 1.1.X7	222
Stock 1.1.X7	190
Sales	2,695
Purchases	2,152
Preference dividend	7
Ordinary dividend (interim)	8
Debenture interest	10
Wages and salaries	254
Light and heat	31
Sundry expenses	113
Suspense account	135
Debtors	179
Creditors	195
Cash	126

Notes

(a) Sundry expenses include £9,000 paid in respect of insurance for the year ending 1 September 20X8. Light and heat does not include an invoice of £3,000 for electricity for the three months ending 2 January 20X8, which was paid in February 20X8. Light and heat also includes £20,000 relating to salesmen's commission.

(b) The suspense account is in respect of the following items:

	£'000
Proceeds from the issue of 100,000 ordinary shares	120
Proceeds from the sale of plant	300
	420
Less consideration for the acquisition of Minitec & Co	285
	135

(c) The net assets of Minitec & Co were purchased on 3 March 20X7. Assets were valued as follows:

	£'000
Investments	230
Stock	34
	264

All the stock acquired was sold during 20X7. The investments were still held by Megatec at 31.12.X7.

(d) The freehold property was acquired some years ago. The buildings element of the cost was estimated at £100,000 and the estimated useful life of the assets was fifty years at the time of purchase. As at 31 December 20X7 the property is to be revalued at £800,000.

(e) The plant which was sold had cost £350,000 and had a net book value of £274,000 as on 1.1.X7. £36,000 depreciation is to be charged on plant and machinery for 20X7.

(f) The debentures have been in issue for some years. The 50p ordinary shares all rank for dividends at the end of the year.

Part B: Preparation of final accounts

    (g) The directors wish to provide for:

        (i) debenture interest due;
        (ii) a final ordinary dividend of 2p per share;
        (iii) a transfer to general reserve of £16,000;
        (iv) audit fees of £4,000.

    (h) Stock as at 31 December 20X7 was valued at £220,000 (cost).

    (i) Taxation is to be ignored.

Task

Prepare the final accounts of Megatec Ltd in a form suitable for internal purposes.

Approach and suggested solution

14.3 (a) Normal adjustments are needed for accruals and prepayments (insurance, light and heat, debenture interest and audit fees). The debenture interest accrued is calculated as follows:

	£'000
Charge needed in P & L account (10% × £200,000)	20
Amount paid so far, as shown in trial balance	10
Accrual - presumably six months' interest now payable	10

	£'000
The accrued expenses shown in the balance sheet comprise:	
Debenture interest	10
Light and heat	3
Audit fee	4
	17

    (b) The misposting of £20,000 to light and heat is also adjusted, by reducing the light and heat expense, but charging £20,000 to salesmen's commission.

    (c) Depreciation on the freehold building is calculated as $\frac{£100,000}{50} = £2,000$.

The NBV of the freehold property is then £430,000 - £20,000 - £2,000 = £408,000 at the end of the year. When the property is revalued a reserve of £800,000 - £408,000 = £392,000 is then created.

    (d) The profit on disposal of plant is calculated as proceeds £300,000 (per suspense account) less NBV £274,000, ie £26,000. The cost of the remaining plant is calculated at £830,000 – £350,000 = £480,000. The depreciation provision at the year end is:

	£'000
Balance 1.1.X7	222
Charge for 20X7	36
Less depreciation on disposals (350 – 274)	(76)
	182

    (e) Goodwill arising on the purchase of Minitec & Co is:

	£'000
Consideration (per suspense account)	285
Assets at valuation	264
Goodwill	21

In the absence of other instructions, this is shown as an asset on the balance sheet. The investments, being owned by Megatec at the year end, are also shown on the balance sheet, whereas Minitec's stock, acquired and then sold, is added to the purchases figure for the year.

(f) The other item in the suspense account is dealt with as follows:

	£'000
Proceeds of issue of 100,000 ordinary shares	120
Less nominal value 100,000 × 50p	50
Excess of consideration over nominal value (= share premium)	70

(g) Appropriations of profit must be considered. The final ordinary dividend, shown as a current liability in the balance sheet, is

(700,000 + 100,000 ordinary shares) × 2p = £16,000

(h) The transfer to general reserve increases that reserve to £171,000 + £16,000 = £187,000.

14.4 MEGATEC LIMITED
TRADING AND PROFIT AND LOSS ACCOUNT
FOR THE YEAR ENDED 31 DECEMBER 20X7

	£'000	£'000	£'000
Sales			2,695
Less cost of sales			
Opening stock		190	
Purchases		2,186	
		2,376	
Less closing stock		220	
			2,156
Gross profit			539
Profit on disposal of plant			26
			565
Less expenses			
Wages, salaries and commission		274	
Sundry expenses		107	
Light and heat		14	
Depreciation: freehold buildings		2	
plant		36	
Audit fees		4	
Debenture interest		20	
			457
Net profit			108
Appropriations			
Transfer to general reserve		16	
Dividends: preference (paid)	7		
ordinary: interim (paid)	8		
final (proposed)	16		
		31	
			47
Retained profit for the year			61
Retained profit brought forward			242
Retained profit carried forward			303

Part B: Preparation of final accounts

14.5 MEGATEC LIMITED
BALANCE SHEET AS AT 31 DECEMBER 20X7

	Cost/val'n £'000	Dep'n £'000	£'000
Fixed assets			
Intangible assets			
Goodwill			21
Tangible assets			
Freehold property	800	-	800
Plant and machinery	480	182	298
	1,280	182	
Investments			230
			1,349
Current assets			
Stock		220	
Debtors		179	
Prepayment		6	
Cash		126	
		531	
Creditors: amounts falling due within one year			
Creditors	195		
Accrued expenses	17		
Proposed dividend	16		
		228	
Net current assets			303
Total assets less current liabilities			1,652
Creditors: amounts falling due after more than one year			
10% debentures (secured)			(200)
			1,452
Capital and reserves			
Called up share capital			
50p ordinary shares		400	
7% £1 preference shares		100	
			500
Reserves			
Share premium		70	
Revaluation reserve		392	
General reserve		187	
Profit and loss account		303	
			952
			1,452

Activity 7.4

You are the assistant to the financial controller of Hanoi Ltd, a manufacturing company. The company's year end is 31 March 20X4. The following balances have been extracted as at that date.

	£'000
Freehold land	200
Leasehold premises: cost	150
accumulated amortisation	96
Plant and equipment: cost	120
accumulated depreciation	48
Trade debtors	100
Provision for doubtful debts	2
Trade creditors	76
Operating expenses accrual	10
Stocks	62
Bank balance (positive)	20

	£'000
10% debentures	110
8% preference shares	100
Share capital (ordinary £1 shares)	200
Profit and loss account	100

The following information is also available.

(a) During the year, a boring machine was found to be past its best. It was decided to write down the machine from its net book value of £20,000 to its scrap value of £5,000. The original cost of the machine was £40,000.

(b) On 31 March 20X4 the preference dividend for the year was paid. Debenture interest was also all paid on 31 March 20X4.

(c) On 1 April 20X3 50,000 £1 ordinary shares were issued at a premium of 50p per share.

(d) An ordinary dividend of 10p per share was paid on 31 March 20X4.

(e) In the year ended 31 March 20X4, the following transactions took place.

	£
Sales	305,000
Purchases	108,000
Contras between debtors and creditors accounts	25,000
Operating expenses paid	58,000
Bad debts written off	12,000

(f) The lease on the premises, when originally taken out, was for fifty years. The premises are to be amortised over the period of the lease. Plant and equipment is depreciated at 20% pa on the straight line basis.

(g) Stock at 31 March 20X4 amounted to £45,000.

(h) The following balances were available as at 31 March 20X4.

	£
Accrued operating expenses	15,000
Trade creditors	58,000
Trade debtors	96,000

Task

Prepare the profit and loss account of Hanoi Ltd for the year ended 31 March 20X4 and a balance sheet at that date.

Note. While you are not required to comply with all statutory disclosure requirements, your financial statements should be clearly and informatively presented and be in accordance with generally accepted principles.

Activity 7.5

Butthead Ltd is a small trading company. From the information below, you are required to prepare a trading, profit and loss account and a balance sheet in a form suitable for presentation to the directors. You should show all your workings and your financial statements should provide as much information as is helpful. Taxation is to be ignored.

Part B: Preparation of final accounts

(a) BUTTHEAD LIMITED
TRIAL BALANCE AS AT 31 DECEMBER 20X7

	£	£
Sales		160,800
Purchases	82,400	
Stock at 1 January 20X7	10,800	
Suspense account	2,800	
Freehold building	56,000	
Fixtures and fittings: cost	52,000	
depreciation 31.12.X7		18,800
Ordinary shares of 25p each		20,000
10% debentures		16,000
5% preference shares of 25p each		8,000
Profit and loss reserve at 1.1.X7		15,200
Cash at bank	1,200	
Cash in hand	1,200	
Sundry expenses*	37,600	
New issue account		12,000
Debtors control account	21,200	
Creditors control account		14,400
	265,200	265,200

*Note. This figure includes depreciation for the year.

(b) The following details relate to the company's bank reconciliation.

(i) The balance per the bank statement was £1,200 overdrawn.

(ii) A cheque for £2,000 had been accepted by the bank as being for £2,000, but had been entered in the cash book as £1,600.

(iii) Bank charges appear on the bank statement, but are not shown in the cash book.

(iv) On 31 December 20X7 there were unpresented cheques totalling £800, all of which cleared in the first week of the next accounting period.

(c) Stock at 31 December 20X7 was £13,600.

(d) In January 20X7 12,000 25p shares were issued at £1 each. The cash received was treated correctly, but the corresponding credit was made to a 'share issue account', as the bookkeeper was unsure of the correct treatment.

(e) As at 31 December 20X7, the building is to be revalued to £60,000.

(f) The directors propose a dividend on the ordinary share capital as at 31 December 20X7 of 20p per share. No dividends were paid during the year.

(g) Debenture interest for the six months to 30 June 20X7 has been paid and is included in the figure for sundry expenses.

(h) The debtors and creditors ledgers do not reconcile with the debtors and creditors control accounts. Balance totals are as follows.

Debtors ledger
Debit balances £20,000
Credit balances £1,200

Creditors ledger
Credit balances £16,000
Debit balances £800

In reconciling the accounts you discover the following errors.

(i) The total on the debtors control account should be £22,400, not £21,200.

(ii) Contras of £1,600 have been correctly entered in the individual ledger accounts but not in the control accounts.

(iii) The list of debit balances on the sales ledger has been understated by £400.

(iv) The balance owed to Beavis plc of £800 has not been included in the list of ledger balances.

(v) During the year, a credit note was issued for £800. This has been treated like an invoice in both the individual ledger account and the control account.

After adjusting for the above errors, any remaining differences should be dealt with by transferring from the control accounts to the suspense account. If there is still a balance on the suspense account, this must be transferred to sundry expenses.

Exam alert

The June 2004 and Pilot Paper had a question similar in approach and standard to the above activity.

Key learning points

- Limited companies have **limited liability,** which means that their members' liability in the event of insolvency is limited to the amount of capital they put in.
- You should be able to distinguish:
  - **Private companies**
  - **Public companies**
- Limited companies must keep **accounting records**.
- Limited companies have a **share capital**. Distinguish:
  - Authorised share capital
  - Issued share capital
  - Called up share capital
  - Paid up share capital
- **Dividends** are **appropriations of profit**.
- **Ordinary shares** are different from **preference shares**, mainly because they carry no right to a fixed dividend.
- **Revenue reserves** are available for distribution. **Capital reserves** are not.
- **Debentures** are long term liabilities, not capital. Unlike dividends, debenture interest must be paid.
- Companies pay **corporation tax** on their profits.

Quick quiz

1. What is the meaning of limited liability?
2. List four of the statutory books which companies must maintain.
3. What is the difference between issued capital and called-up capital?
4. What are the differences between ordinary shares and preference shares?
5. What are the differences between debentures and share capital?
6. How does a share premium account arise?
7. Distinguish between a bonus issue and a rights issue.

Answers to quick quiz

1. The maximum an owner stands to lose if the company becomes insolvent is his share of the capital in the business.
2. Register of members; register of charges; register of directors and secretaries; register of directors' interests.

Part B: Preparation of final accounts

3   Issued capital is the nominal amount of share capital that has been issued to shareholders. Only part of the issue price may be called up.

4   Preference shares are shares which confer certain preferential rights on their owner. Preference dividends have priority over ordinary dividends. Ordinary shares are more common and carry no such rights.

5   (a)   Shareholders are members; debenture holders are creditors.

    (b)   Shareholders receive dividends; debenture holders receive interest, to which they are legally entitled.

    (c)   Debentures are often secured on company assets. Shares are not.

6   The share premium is the difference between the issue price of a share and its nominal value. It must be credited to a share premium account.

7   A bonus issue is a way of re-classifying reserves as share capital. A rights issue is an issue of shares for cash to existing shareholders.

Answers to activities

Answer 7.1

False. But what *does* it mean? Look back to paragraph 1.4.

Answer 7.2

800,000 × 50p × 5% = £20,000.

Answer 7.3

		£	£
DEBIT	Bank	260,000	
CREDIT	Share capital		200,000
CREDIT	Share premium		60,000

Answer 7.4

HANOI LIMITED
TRADING, PROFIT AND LOSS ACCOUNT
FOR THE YEAR ENDED 31 MARCH 20X4

	£'000	£'000
Sales		305
Cost of sales		
Opening stock	62	
Purchases	108	
	170	
Closing stock	45	
		125
Gross profit		180
Operating expenses (W4)	63	
Plant depreciation (W5)	31	
Lease amortisation	3	
Bad debt expense	12	
		109
Operating profit		71
Debenture interest		11
		60
Dividends: ordinary		25
preference		8
Retained profit for the year		27

7: Limited companies

HANOI LIMITED
BALANCE SHEET AS AT 31 MARCH 20X4

	Cost £'000	Depn £'000	NBV £'000
Fixed assets			
Freehold land	200	-	200
Leasehold premises	150	9	141
Plant and equipment	85	44	41
		(W6)	
	435	53	382

	£'000	£'000
Current assets		
Stocks		45
Debtors (96 – 2)		94
Bank (W1)		164
		303
Current liabilities		
Trade creditors	58	
Accrual	15	
	73	
Net current assets		230
		612
10% debentures		110
		502
Capital and reserves		
Ordinary £1 shares		250
Share premium		25
8% preference shares		100
Profit and loss a/c (100 + 27)		127
		502

Workings

1   Bank balance

BANK A/C

	£'000		£'000
Balance b/d	20	Creditors (W3)	101
Debtors (W2)	272	Dividends: ordinary	25
Share capital	50	preference	8
Share premium	25	Debenture interest	11
		Operating expenses	58
		Balance c/d	164
	367		367

2   Receipts from debtors

DEBTORS CONTROL A/C

	£'000		£'000
Balance b/d	100	Contra with CCA	25
Sales	305	Bad debts written off	12
		Bank (bal fig)	272
		Balance c/d	96
	405		405

3   Payments to creditors

CREDITORS CONTROL A/C

	£'000		£'000
Contras with DCA	25	Balance b/d	76
Bank (bal fig)	101	Purchases	108
Balance c/d	58		
	184		184

Part B: Preparation of final accounts

4 Operating expenses

	£'000
Owed 1.4.X3	10
Paid during year	58
Owed 31.3.X4	15
P & L charge	63

5 Plant cost and depreciation

	£'000
Plant at cost b/d	120
Less fully depreciated item	40
Depreciable amount	80

Depreciation charge £80,000 × 20% = £16,000

(*Note*. Plant at cost for balance sheet includes fully depreciated item £(80 + 5) = £85,000.)

Write down on machine (20 – 5) = £15,000.
∴ Total depreciation charge on plant (16 + 15) = £31,000.

6 Plant: accumulated depreciation

	£'000
B/d	48
Less fully depreciated item	20
	28
Add charge for year	16
	44

Answer 7.5

BUTTHEAD LIMITED
TRADING, PROFIT AND LOSS ACCOUNT
FOR THE YEAR ENDED 31 DECEMBER 20X7

	£	£
Sales (160,800 – 1,600)		159,200
Cost of goods sold		
Opening stock	10,800	
Purchases	82,400	
	93,200	
Closing stock	(13,600)	
		(79,600)
Gross profit		79,600
Sundry expenses (W1)		(46,400)
Operating profit		33,200
Debenture interest		(1,600)
Net profit		31,600
Dividends: preference	400	
ordinary (92,000 × 0.20)	18,400	
		(18,800)
Retained profit for the year		12,800
Retained profit brought forward		15,200
Retained profit carried forward		28,000

7: Limited companies

BUTTHEAD LIMITED
BALANCE SHEET AS AT 31 DECEMBER 20X7

	£	£
Fixed assets		
Freehold building		60,000
Fixtures and fittings: cost	52,000	
depreciation	18,800	
		33,200
		93,200
Current assets		
Stock	13,600	
Debtors	17,600	
Cash in hand	1,200	
	32,400	
Current liabilities		
Creditors	16,000	
Debenture interest ($^6/_{12} \times 1,600$)	800	
Dividends	18,800	
Bank overdraft	2,000	
	37,600	
Net current liabilities		(5,200)
Total assets less current liabilities		88,000
10% debentures		(16,000)
		72,000
Share capital and reserves		
Ordinary shares of 25p		23,000
5% preference shares of 25p		8,000
Share premium		9,000
Revaluation reserve		4,000
Profit and loss reserve		28,000
		72,000

Workings

1 Sundry expenses

	£
Per trial balance	37,600
Less debenture interest ($16,000 \times 10\% \times ^6/_{12}$)	(800)
Suspense account (W4)	6,400
Bank (2,800 + 400)	3,200
	46,400

2 *Debtors control account and debtors ledger*

DEBTORS CONTROL ACCOUNT

	£		£
Balance b/d	21,200	Sales	1,600
Suspense	1,200	Contra	1,600
		Suspense	1,600
		Balance c/d	17,600
	22,400		22,400

Debtors ledger

	Dr	Cr
	£	£
Balances b/d	20,000	1,200
Understatement	400	
Sales		1,600
	20,400	2,800

Net corrected balance: £17,600

Part B: Preparation of final accounts

3   *Creditors control account and creditors ledger*

CREDITORS CONTROL ACCOUNT

	£		£
Contra	1,600	Balance b/d	14,400
Balance c/d	16,000	Suspense a/c	3,200
	17,600		17,600

Creditors ledger

	Dr	Cr
	£	£
	800	16,000
Beavis plc		800
	800	16,800

Net credit balances: £16,000

4   *Suspense account*

SUSPENSE ACCOUNT

	£		£
Balance b/d	2,800	Debtors control	1,200
Creditors control	3,200	Sundry expenses (bal fig)	6,400
Debtors control	1,600		
	7,600		7,600

5   Bank

	£	
Balance per bank statement	(1,200)	o/d
Unpresented cheques	(800)	
	(2,000)	o/d
Cash book balance per t/b	1,200	
Cheque difference (to sundry expenses)	(400)	
Bank charges (bal fig)	(2,800)	
	(2,000)	

Now try Question 7 in the Exam Question Bank at the end of the Text.

Part C

The regulatory and conceptual framework

Chapter 8 The regulatory framework

Chapter topic list

1. The standard setting process
2. Published accounts
3. Small and medium sized companies
4. The role of the Stock Exchange
5. Generally accepted accounting practice (GAAP)
6. Accounting standards and choice

The following study sessions are covered in this chapter.

		Syllabus reference
3(a)	Explain the legal framework and obligations of directors	1
3(b)	Explain the standard setting process and the role of the:	1
	(i) Financial Reporting Council	
	(ii) Accounting Standards Board	
	(iii) Urgent Issues Task Force	
	(iv) Financial Reporting Review Panel	
12(a)	State the requirements of the Companies Act regarding:	1
	(i) the duty to prepare annual accounts	
	(ii) the form and content of prescribed formats	

Part C: The regulatory and conceptual framework

1 THE STANDARD SETTING PROCESS

1.1 **Limited companies** are required by law (the Companies Act 1985 or CA 1985) to **prepare** and **publish accounts annually**. The form and content of the accounts are regulated primarily by CA 1985, but must also comply with **accounting standards**.

Accounting Standards Board and Financial Reporting Council

1.2 Accounting standards are produced by the Accounting Standards Board (ASB). They are called **Financial Reporting Standards** (FRSs). The standard-setting processes, including the ASB is overseen by the **Financial Reporting Council** (FRC).

1.3 An important offshoot of the ASB is an Urgent Issues Task Force, whose function is 'to tackle urgent matters not covered by existing standards, and for which, given the urgency, the normal standard-setting process would not be practicable' (Sir Ron Dearing, Chairman of the FRC). This was established in March 1991.

1.4 The **Review Panel**, chaired by a barrister, is concerned with the examination and questioning of departures from accounting standards by large companies. The Review Panel will be alerted to most cases for investigation by the results of the new CA 1985 requirement that companies must include in the notes to the accounts a statement that they have been prepared in accordance with applicable accounting standards or, alternatively, giving details of material departures from those standards, with reasons.

1.5 Although it is expected that most such referrals will be resolved by discussion, the Panel (and the Secretary of State for Trade and Industry) have the power to apply to the court for revision of the accounts, with all costs potentially payable (if the court action is successful) by the company's directors. The auditors may also be disciplined if the audit report on the defective accounts was not qualified with respect to the departure from standards. Revised accounts, whether prepared voluntarily or under duress, will have to be circulated to all persons likely to rely on the previous accounts. The Review Panel was set up in early 1991.

Current accounting standards

1.6 The following standards are in force at the date of writing (June 2004). The SSAPs (Statements of Standard Accounting Practice) which were in force at the date the ASB was formed have been adopted by the Board. They have largely been superseded by Financial Reporting Standards.

UK accounting standards

Title		Issue date
	Foreword to accounting standards	Jun 93
FRS 1	Cash flow statements (revised Oct 96)	Sep 91
FRS 2	Accounting for subsidiary undertakings	July 92
FRS 3	Reporting financial performance	Oct 92
FRS 4	Capital instruments	Dec 93
FRS 5	Reporting the substance of transactions	Apr 94
FRS 6	Acquisitions and mergers	Sep 94
FRS 7	Fair values in acquisition accounting	Sep 94
FRS 8	Related party disclosures	Oct 95
	Financial Reporting Standard for Smaller Entities	Dec 99
FRS 9	Associates and joint ventures	Nov 97
FRS 10	Goodwill and intangible assets	Dec 97
		Cont'd

Title		*Issue date*
FRS 11	Impairment of fixed assets and goodwill	July 98
FRS 12	Provisions, contingent liabilities and contingent assets	Sept 98
FRS 13	Derivatives and other financial instruments: disclosures	Sept 98
FRS 14	Earnings per share	Oct 98
FRS 15	Tangible fixed assets	Feb 99
FRS 16	Current tax	Dec 99
FRS 17	Retirement benefits	Nov 00
FRS 18	Accounting policies	Dec 00
FRS 19	Deferred tax	Dec 00
FRS 20	Share-based payment	Apr 04
FRS 21	Events after the balance sheet date	May 04
SSAP 4	Accounting for government grants	Jul 90
SSAP 5	Accounting for value added tax	Apr 74
SSAP 9	Stocks and long-term contracts	Sep 88
SSAP 13	Accounting for research and development	Jan 89
SSAP 19	Accounting for investment properties	Nov 81
SSAP 20	Foreign currency translation	Apr 83
SSAP 21	Accounting for leases and hire purchase contracts	Aug 84
SSAP 25	Segmental reporting	Jun 90

Notes

Exposure drafts are *not* on your syllabus. The *Statement of Principles for Financial Reporting*, which is covered in Chapter 10, is examinable. The *Statement* was published in December 1999.

2 PUBLISHED ACCOUNTS

2.1 **Statutory accounts** are part of the price to be paid for the benefits of limited liability. Limited companies must produce such accounts annually and they must appoint an independent person to audit and report on them. Once prepared, a copy of the accounts must be sent to the Registrar of Companies, who maintains a separate file for every company. The Registrar's files may be inspected for a nominal fee, by any member of the public. This is why the statutory accounts are often referred to as published accounts.

> **KEY TERM**
>
> **Statutory accounts** are accounts which limited companies are obliged by law to publish in a particular form.

2.2 It is the responsibility of the company's directors to produce accounts which show a **true and fair view** of the company's results for the period and its financial position at the end of the period. The board evidence their approval of the accounts by the signature of one director on the balance sheet (formerly two signatures were required). Once this has been done, and the auditors have completed their report, the accounts are laid before the members of the company in general meeting. When the members have adopted the accounts they are sent to the Registrar for filing.

2.3 The requirement that the accounts show a true and fair view is paramount.

Part C: The regulatory and conceptual framework

> **IMPORTANT!**
> Although statute lays down numerous rules on the information to be included in the published accounts and the format of its presentation, any such rule may be **overridden** if compliance with it would prevent the accounts from showing a **true and fair view**.

2.4 The documents which must be included by law in the accounts laid before a general meeting of the members are:

(a) A **profit and loss account** (or an income and expenditure account in the case of a non-trading company)

(b) A **balance sheet** as at the date to which the profit and loss account is made up

(c) A **directors' report**

(d) An **auditors' report** addressed to the members (not to the directors) of the company

(e) The **group accounts** in the case of a company which has subsidiaries at the year end date

2.5 FRS 1 requires the inclusion of a cash flow statement. This statement is discussed in Chapter 13; here we will look at the legally required accounting statements, the profit and loss account and balance sheet.

2.6 The following example shows a *pro forma* profit and loss account and balance sheet with selected notes.

STANDARD PLC
PROFIT AND LOSS ACCOUNT FOR THE YEAR ENDED
31 DECEMBER 20X5

	Notes	£'000	£'000
Turnover			X
Cost of sales			X
Gross profit			X
Distribution costs			X
Administrative expenses			X
Operating profit	1		X
Income from fixed asset investments			X
			X
Interest payable and similar charges			X
Profit on ordinary activities before taxation			X
Tax on profit on ordinary activities			X
Profit on ordinary activities after taxation			X
Dividend paid and proposed		X	
Transfer to general reserve		X	
			X
Retained profit for the financial year			X

STANDARD PLC
BALANCE SHEET AS AT 31 DECEMBER 20X5

	Notes	£'000	£'000
Fixed assets			
Intangible assets	2		X
Tangible assets	3		X
Fixed asset investments			X
			X̄
Current assets			
Stocks		X	
Debtors		X	
Cash at bank and in hand		X	
		X̄	
Creditors: amounts falling due within one year		X	
Net current assets			X
Total assets less current liabilities			X̄
Creditors: amounts falling due after more than one year			X
Accruals and deferred income			X
			X̄
Capital and reserves			
Called up share capital			X
Share premium account	4		X
Revaluation reserve	4		X
General reserve	4		X
Profit and loss account	4		X
			X̄

Approved by the board on ....

.... Director

The notes on pages XX to XX form part of these accounts.

Exam alert

On the basis of recent exam papers, it is very unlikely that published accounts questions will require anything more complicated than the above proforma.

NOTES TO THE ACCOUNTS

1 *Operating profit*

   Operating profit is stated after charging:

	£'000
Depreciation (see Chapter 2)	X
Amortisation	X
Auditors' remuneration	X
Exceptional items (see Chapter 9)	X
Directors' emoluments	X
Staff costs	X
Research and development (see Chapter 12)	X

   Notes

   Separate totals are required to be disclosed for:

   (a) Audit fees and expenses
   (b) Fees paid to auditors for non-audit work

   This disclosure is not required for small or medium-sized companies.

Part C: The regulatory and conceptual framework

Activity 8.1

Arco Ltd receives an invoice in respect of the current year from its auditors made up as follows.

	£
Audit of accounts	10,000
Taxation computation and advice	1,500
Travelling expenses: audit	1,100
Consultancy fees charged by another firm of accountants	1,600
	14,200

What figure should be disclosed as auditors' remuneration in the notes to the profit and loss account?

---

2 *Intangible fixed assets*

	Development expenditure £'000
Cost	
At 1 January 20X5	X
Expenditure	X
At 31 December 20X5	X
Amortisation	
At 1 January 20X5	X
Charge for year	X
At 31 December 20X5	X
Net book value at 31 December 20X5	X
Net book value 31 December 20X4	X

Note

The above disclosure should be given for each intangible asset.

3 *Tangible fixed assets*

	Freehold land and buildings £'000	Leasehold land and buildings Long leases £'000	Leasehold land and buildings Short leases £'000	Plant and machinery £'000	Fixtures and fittings £'000	Total £'000
Cost (or valuation)						
At 1 Jan 20X5	X	X	X	X	X	X
Additions	X	-	X	-	X	X
Revaluation	X	-	-	-	-	X
Disposals	(X)	-	-	(X)	(X)	(X)
At 31 Dec 20X5	X	X	X	X	X	X
Depreciation						
At 1 Jan 20X5	X	X	X	X	X	X
Charge for year	X	X	X	X	X	X
Revaluation	(X)	-	-	-	-	(X)
Disposals	(X)	-	-	(X)	(X)	(X)
At 31 Dec 20X5	X	X	X	X	X	X
Net book value						
At 31 Dec 20X5	X	X	X	X	X	X
At 31 Dec 20X4	X	X	X	X	X	X

Notes

(a) Long leases are ≥ 50 years unexpired at balance sheet date.

8: The regulatory framework

(b) Classification by asset type represents Arabic numbers from formats.

(c) Motor vehicles (unless material) are usually included within plant and machinery.

(d) Revaluations in the year: state for each asset revalued:

(i) method of valuation;

(ii) date of valuation; and

(iii) the historical cost equivalent of the above information as if the asset had not been revalued.

4   *Reserves*

	Share premium £'000	Revaluation £'000	General £'000	Profit and loss £'000
At 1 January 20X5	X	X	X	X
Retained profit for the year	-	-	-	X
Revaluation	-	X	-	-
Transfers	-	-	X	X
At 31 December 1995	X̄	X̄	X̄	X̄

Activity 8.2

The best way to learn the format and content of published accounts and notes is to practise questions. However, you must start somewhere, so try to learn the above formats, then close this text and write out on a piece of paper:

(a) A standard layout for a balance sheet and profit and loss account
(b) A standard layout for the notes to these accounts specified by your Teaching Guide

3   SMALL AND MEDIUM SIZED COMPANIES

3.1 Small and medium sized companies are allowed certain **filing exemptions**: the accounts they lodge with the registrar of companies, and which are available for public inspection, need not contain all the information which must be published by large companies. This concession allows small and medium-sized companies to reduce the amount of information about themselves available to, say, trading rivals. It does not relieve them of their obligation to prepare full statutory accounts, because all companies, regardless of their size, must prepare full accounts for approval by the shareholders.

3.2 Small and medium-sized companies must therefore balance the expense of preparing two different sets of accounts against the advantage of publishing as little information about themselves as possible. Many such companies may decide that the risk of assisting their competitors is preferable to the expense of preparing accounts twice over, and will therefore not take advantage of the filing exemptions.

Definitions

3.3 A company qualifies as a **small company** in a particular financial year if, for that year, two or more of the following conditions are satisfied.

(a) The amount of its turnover for the year should not exceed £5.6 million. This amount must be adjusted proportionately in the case of an accounting period greater or less than twelve months.

(b) Its balance sheet total should not exceed £2.8 million. Balance sheet total means the total of assets disclosed under headings A to D in the statutory balance sheet format, ie total assets before deduction of any liabilities.

(c) Its average number of employees should not exceed 50.

3.4 For a **medium-sized company**, the corresponding conditions are:

(a) Turnover not more than £22.8 million
(b) Balance sheet total not more than £11.4 million
(c) Average number of employees not more than 250

Again, a minimum of two of these conditions must be satisfied.

3.5 Public companies can never be entitled to the filing exemptions whatever their size; nor can banking and insurance companies; nor can companies which are authorised persons under the Financial Services Act 1986; nor can members of groups containing any of these exceptions.

4 THE ROLE OF THE STOCK EXCHANGE

4.1 The Stock Exchange is a market for stocks and shares, and a company whose securities are traded on the main market is known as being 'quoted' as a 'listed' company.

4.2 When a share is granted a quotation on The Stock Exchange, it appears on the *Official List* which is published in London for each business day. The Official List shows the 'official quotation' or price for the share for that particular day; it is drawn up by the Quotations Department of The Stock Exchange, which derives its prices from those actually ruling in this market. In practice, the buying and selling prices used by member firms will be within the prices quoted on the Official List.

4.3 In order to receive a listing for its securities, a company must conform with Stock Exchange regulations contained in the **Listing Rules** issued by the Council of The Stock Exchange. The company commits itself to certain procedures and standards, including matters concerning the disclosure of accounting information, which are more extensive than the disclosure requirements of the Companies Acts.

Activity 8.3

To ensure you understand which regulations apply to which type of business, fill in the table below with a 'yes' where compliance is required and 'no' where it is not.

Type of Business	Companies Act	FRSs/ SSAPs	IASs	Stock Exchange Listing Rules
Public Listed Company				
Private Limited Company				
Sole Tradership				

5 GENERALLY ACCEPTED ACCOUNTING PRACTICE (GAAP)

5.1 This term has sprung up in recent years and its signifies all the rules, from whatever source, which govern accounting. In the UK this is seen primarily as a combination of:

(a) **Company law** (mainly CA 1985)
(b) **Accounting standards**
(c) **Stock Exchange requirements**

8: The regulatory framework

5.2 Although those sources are the basis for **UK GAAP**, the concept also includes the effects of non-mandatory sources such as:

(a) **International accounting standards**
(b) **Statutory requirements in other countries**, particularly the US

5.3 In the UK, GAAP does not have any statutory or regulatory authority or definition (unlike other countries, such as the US). The term is mentioned rarely in legislation, and only then in fairly limited terms.

5.4 GAAP is in fact a dynamic concept: it changes constantly as circumstances alter through new legislation, standards and practice. this idea that GAAP is constantly changing is recognised by the ASB in its *Statement of aims* where it states that it expects to issue new standards and amend old ones in response to 'evolving business practices, new economic developments and deficiencies identified in current practice.' The emphasis has shifted from 'principles' to 'practice' in UK GAAP.

5.5 The problem of what is 'generally accepted' is not easy to settle, because new practices will obviously not be generally adopted yet. The criteria for a practice being 'generally accepted' will depend on factors such as whether the practice is addressed by UK accounting standards or legislation, or their international equivalents, and whether other companies have adopted the practice. Most importantly perhaps, the question should be whether the practice is consistent with the needs of users and the objectives of financial reporting and whether it is consistent with the 'true and fair' concept.

6 ACCOUNTING STANDARDS AND CHOICE

6.1 It is sometimes argued that companies should be given a **choice** in matters of financial reporting on the grounds that accounting standards are detrimental to the quality of such reporting. There are arguments on both sides.

6.2 **In favour** of accounting standards, the following points can be made.

(a) They reduce or eliminate confusing variations in the methods used to prepare accounts.

(b) They provide a focal point for debate and discussions about accounting practice.

(c) They oblige companies to disclose the accounting policies used in the preparation of accounts.

(d) They are a less rigid alternative to enforcing conformity by means of legislation.

(e) They have obliged companies to disclose more accounting information than they would otherwise have done if accounting standards did not exist. FRS 3 *Reporting financial performance* and FRS 12 *Provisions, contingent liabilities and contingent assets* are examples. The reluctance of companies to disclose information is perhaps evident in the fact that very few companies chose to report the cost of sales in their accounts until legislation enforced the disclosure.

6.3 However, the following arguments may be put forward **against** standardisation and in favour of choice.

(a) A set of rules which give backing to one method of preparing accounts might be inappropriate in some circumstances. For example, the old SSAP 12 on depreciation was inappropriate for investment properties (in this case, pressure from the property

Part C: The regulatory and conceptual framework

industry secured an exemption from SSAP 12, and SSAP 19 was later issued to deal with this specific case).

(b) Standards may be subject to lobbying or government pressure. For example, an early draft on accounting for research and development (ED 14) was revised (ED 17, subsequently SSAP 13) as a result of pressure from the aerospace and electronics industries. SSAP 16 emerged partly as a result of government pressure. In the USA, the accounting standard FAS 19 on the accounts of oil and gas companies led to a powerful lobby of oil companies, which persuaded the SEC (Securities and Exchange Commission) to step in. FAS 19 was then suspended.

(c) They are not currently based on a conceptual framework of accounting.

(d) There may a trend towards rigidity, and away from flexibility in applying the rules. Michael Alexander, Director of Research and Technical Activities at the FASB in the USA, was quoted as saying (in *Accountancy* Magazine) 'The demand for rule-making...comes largely from an insatiable appetite for rules...I am very concerned about this. The reliance on judgement in technical accounting matters seems to have gone.'

Activity 8.4

'The going concern concept is fundamental to the preparation of financial statements. If a company cannot be assumed to be a going concern, the effect on those statements is dramatic.'

Discuss and illustrate your arguments with an example.

Key learning points

- In this chapter we have looked at the **legal and professional** framework governing the preparation of limited companies' **published accounts**. We also considered the role of the **Stock Exchange**, **GAAP** and the **conceptual framework** of accounting.

- Accounting standards were formerly published by the **Accounting Standards Committee** and called **SSAPs** (statements of standard accounting practice). In future, they will be published by the **Accounting Standards Board** and called **FRSs** (financial reporting standards). Make sure you know the differences between the old system and the new.

- You should also be able to discuss the role of the **Urgent Issues Task Force** and the **Review Panel**.

- All companies must prepare full **statutory accounts** for approval by their shareholders. For large companies, a copy of these accounts must also be made available to the public by filing with the registrar of companies.

- **Small and medium-sized companies** may, if they wish, prepare an additional set of accounts disclosing less information.

- The only **notes to the accounts** which you need to know are fixed assets, disclosable expenses and reserves.

- Listed companies must comply with **Stock Exchange regulations** contained in the *Listing Rules*. The requirements are more stringent than for non-listed companies.

- You should ensure that you understand what is meant by **GAAP**.

- Arguments may be put forward in favour of **choice** in financial reporting as against accounting standards.

Quick quiz

1. What body currently produces accounting standards?
2. What is the relationship between accounting standards and the Companies Act requirement to show a true and fair view?
3. What are 'filing exemptions'? Which companies can benefit from them?
4. What do you understand by GAAP?

Answers to quick quiz

1. The Accounting Standards Board.
2. Compliance with accounting standards is likely to be held necessary in order to meet the statutory 'true and fair' requirement.
3. The accounts lodged with the Registrar of Companies need not contain all the information required by large companies. The exemptions are available to 'small' and 'medium sized' companies as defined by the Companies Act.
4. Rules governing accounting deriving principally from:
   (a) Company law
   (b) Accounting standards
   (c) Stock Exchange requirements

Answers to activities

Answer 8.1

	£
Audit of accounts	10,000
Expenses	1,100
Taxation computation and advice	1,500
	12,600

The consultancy fees are not received by the auditors.

Answer 8.3

Your table should look like this.

Type of Business	Companies Act	FRSs/ SSAPs	IASs	Stock Exchange Listing Rules
Public Listed Company	YES	YES	NO	YES
Private Limited Company	YES	YES	NO	NO
Sole Tradership	NO	NO	NO	NO

Answer 8.4

The going concern concept is that an enterprise will continue in operational existence for the foreseeable future. This means that the financial statements of an enterprise are prepared on the assumption that the enterprise will continue trading. If this were not the case, various adjustments would have to be made to the accounts: provisions for losses; revaluation of assets to their possible market value and so forth.

Unless it can be assumed that the business is a going concern, the other three fundamental accounting concepts cannot apply. This can be seen by considering each concept in turn as follows.

Consistency

It is meaningless to speak of consistency from one accounting period to the next when this is the final accounting period.

Part C: The regulatory and conceptual framework

Accruals

The accruals or matching concept states that revenue and expenses which are related to each other are matched, so as to be dealt with in the same accounting period, without regard to when the cash is actually paid or received. This is particularly relevant to the purchase of fixed assets. The cost of a fixed asset is spread over the accounting periods expected to benefit from it, thus matching costs and revenues. In the absence of the going concern convention, this cannot happen, as an example will illustrate.

Suppose a company has a machine which cost £10,000 two years ago and now has a net book value of £6,000. The machine can be used for another three years, but as it is obsolete, there is no possibility of selling it, and so it has no market value.

If the going concern concept applies, the machine will be shown at cost less depreciation in the accounts, as it still has a part to play in the continued life of the enterprise. However, if the assumption cannot be applied the machine will be given a nil value and other assets and liabilities will be revalued on the basis of winding down the company's operations.

Prudence

The prudence concept as we normally understand it cannot apply if the business is no longer a going concern. A more drastic approach than mere caution is required when it is known that the business must cease trading.

Now try Question 8 in the Exam Question Bank at the end of the Text.

Chapter 9 Reporting financial performance

Chapter topic list

1. The need for FRS 3
2. Exceptional and extraordinary items
3. Structure of the profit and loss account
4. FRS 3 statements and notes
5. Earnings per share (EPS)
6. Prior period adjustments

The following study sessions are covered in this chapter.

		Syllabus reference
9-11(b)	Prepare a statement of total recognised gains and losses	2
9-11(c)	Prepare the following notes to the financial statements: (i) statement of movements in reserves (iii) exceptional items	2
9-11(d)	Distinguish between extraordinary and exceptional items, including their accounting treatment and disclosure requirements	2

Part C: The regulatory and conceptual framework

> **Exam alert**
> The Study Guide requires you to outline, explain and draft financial statements in a format suitable for publication in accordance with FRS 3.

1 THE NEED FOR FRS 3

1.1 The introduction of FRS 3 *Reporting financial performance* has meant significant changes to company published accounts. All the changes were intended to improve the quality of information provided to shareholders.

1.2 Before we launch into the details of FRS 3, it is worth considering briefly why the changes were necessary. In other words, what was wrong with the profit and loss account before FRS 3?

Comparisons

1.3 Before FRS 3, it was difficult to make comparisons between one year and another because there was no information about the turnover and profit drawn from activities that ceased during the year (and so will not continue next year) and new activities that did not exist last year.

1.4 To try to deal with this problem, FRS 3 requires an analysis of the profit and loss account as far as the figure of profit on ordinary activities before interest into three elements.

 (a) **Continuing operations**
 (b) **New acquisitions**
 (c) **Discontinued operations**

 This is discussed in more detail in Section 3 below.

1.5 Someone needing to make comparisons between this year's and last year's turnover and profit, will thus be **comparing like with like**. Similarly, someone needing to forecast next year's turnover and profit can now see how much of this year's operations will continue into the future.

1.6 To facilitate the comparison with previous years, FRS 3 requires the comparative figures for the previous year (which have to be disclosed alongside those for the current year in published accounts) to be **restated** so as to show as continuing activities only those which are still continuing in the current year.

Manipulation

1.7 Another reason for introducing FRS 3 was to put an end to the **manipulation** of the profit and loss account by means of **exceptional and extraordinary items**. These, and the changes introduced in FRS 3 are discussed in more detail in Section 2 of this chapter, but here we just look briefly at the problem which FRS 3 needed to remedy.

Effect on profit after tax

1.8 The forerunner to FRS 3, SSAP 6 *Extraordinary items and prior year adjustments* recognised that large and unusual 'one-off' items in a profit and loss account could distort results and make year-on-year comparisons difficult. It identified two such items, defined informally here, and prescribed two kinds of accounting treatment for the items in question.

(a) **Exceptional items**. These are part of the normal course of a company's business, but hardly ever happen. They were to be disclosed separately but *included* in the calculation of profit on *ordinary* activities before tax.

(b) **Extraordinary items**. These hardly ever happen and are *not* part of a company's ordinary activities. They are to be disclosed separately and *excluded* from the calculation of profit on ordinary activities before, and hence after, tax.

1.9 On occasions there was a fine line between extraordinary and exceptional items. An obvious temptation is to show 'plus points' as exceptional and 'minus points' as extraordinary. Thus good news appears above the line and bad news below it.

Effect on earnings per share

1.10 Earnings per share is a way of calculating the return on each ordinary share in the year. It is basically earnings (profit after tax and preference dividends) divided by number of shares. Users of accounts place a great deal of faith in this figure. There is an incentive to make it appear as high as possible.

1.11 Because in pre-FRS 3 times 'earnings' excluded extraordinary items but included exceptional items, there was again an incentive to make 'bad news' extraordinary and 'good news' exceptional, so the earnings per share figure was as high as possible.

1.12 By defining exceptional items very precisely and all **but outlawing extraordinary items** (see Section 3), it was hoped to deal with the above abuse, both as regards the profit and loss account, and as regards earnings per share. It was hoped, furthermore, that earnings per share would decline in importance as an indicator of financial performance.

Main elements of FRS 3

1.13 The main elements of FRS 3 are as follows.

(a) Structure of the profit and loss account
(b) Extraordinary items
(c) Statement of total recognised gains and losses
(d) Other new disclosures
(e) Earnings per share

2 EXCEPTIONAL AND EXTRAORDINARY ITEMS

2.1 FRS 3 lays down the rules for dealing with 'out of the ordinary' items and how they are shown in the P & L account. FRS 3 restricts the way companies could manipulate the figures.

Exceptional items

> **KEY TERM**
>
> FRS 3 defines **exceptional items** as:
>
> Material items which derive from events or transactions that fall within the ordinary activities of the reporting entity and which individually or, if of a similar type, in aggregate, need to be disclosed by virtue of their *size or incidence* if the financial statements are to give a true and fair view.'

2.2 The definition of ordinary activities is important.

> 'Any activities which are undertaken by a reporting entity as part of its business and such related activities in which the reporting entity engages in furtherance of, incidental to, or arising from these activities. Ordinary activities include the effects on the reporting entity of any event in the various environments in which it operates including the political, regulatory, economic and geographical environments irrespective of the frequency or unusual nature of the event.'

2.3 There are two types of exceptional item and their accounting treatment is as follows.

(a) Firstly, there are **three categories** of exceptional items which must be **shown separately** on the face of the profit and loss account after operating profit and before interest and allocated appropriately to discontinued and continued activities.

   (i) Profit or loss on the sale or termination of an operation.

   (ii) Costs of a fundamental reorganisation or restructuring that has a material effect on the nature and focus of the reporting entity's operations.

   (iii) Profit or loss on disposal of fixed assets.

   For both items (i) and (iii) profit and losses may not be offset within categories.

(b) **Other items** should be allocated to the **appropriate statutory format heading** and attributed to continuing or discounted operations as appropriate. If the item is sufficiently material that it is needed to show a true and fair view it must be disclosed on the face of the profit and loss account.

2.4 In both (a) and (b) an adequate description must be given in the notes to the accounts.

2.5 FRS 3 does not give examples of the type of transaction which is likely to be treated as exceptional. However, its predecessor on the subject, SSAP 6, gave a useful list of examples of items which if of a sufficient size might normally be treated as exceptional.

(a) Abnormal charges for bad debts and write-offs of stock and work in progress.
(b) Abnormal provisions for losses on long-term contracts.
(c) Settlement of insurance claims.

Extraordinary items

2.6 The term extraordinary item was once one of great significance. However, the ASB publicly stated that it does not envisage such items to appear on a company's profit and loss account. Its decline in importance has been achieved by tightening of the definition of an extraordinary item.

9: Reporting financial performance

> **KEY TERM**
>
> **Extraordinary items** are defined as material items possessing a high degree of abnormality which arise from events or transactions that fall outside the ordinary activities of the reporting entity and which are not expected to recur.

2.7 Extraordinary items should be shown on the face of profit and loss account before dividends. Tax on the extraordinary item should be shown separately. A description of the extraordinary items should be given in the notes to the accounts.

3 STRUCTURE OF THE PROFIT AND LOSS ACCOUNT

3.1 All statutory headings from turnover to operating profit must be subdivided between that arising from continuing operations and that arising from discontinued operations. In addition, turnover and operating profit must be further analysed between that from existing and that from newly acquired operations. Only figures for turnover and operating profit need be shown on the face of the P & L account; all additional information regarding costs may be relegated to a note. The example below is a simplified version of the example in FRS 3.

PROFIT AND LOSS EXAMPLE 1	20X3 £m	20X3 £m	20X2 as restated £m
Turnover			
Continuing operations	550		500
Acquisitions	50		
	600		
Discontinued operations	175		190
		775	690
Cost of sales		(620)	(555)
Gross profit		155	135
Net operating expenses		(104)	(83)
Operating profit			
Continuing operations	50		40
Acquisitions	6		
	56		
Discontinued operations	(15)		12
Less 20X2 provision	10		
		51	52
Profit on sale of properties in continuing operations		9	6
Provision for loss on operations to be discontinued			(30)
Loss on disposal of discontinued operations	(17)		
Less 20X2 provision	20		
		3	
Profit on ordinary activities before interest		63	28
Interest payable		(18)	(15)
Profit on ordinary activities before taxation		45	13
Tax on profit on ordinary activities		(16)	(6)
Profit on ordinary activities after taxation		29	7
Extraordinary items - included only to show positioning		-	-
Profit for the financial year		29	7
Dividends		(8)	(1)
Retained profit for the financial year		21	6
Earnings per share		39p	10p

Part C: The regulatory and conceptual framework

PROFIT AND LOSS ACCOUNT EXAMPLE 2 (to operating profit line)

	Continuing operations 20X3 £m	Acquisitions 20X3 £m	Discontinued of operations 20X3 £m	Total 20X3 £m	Total 20X2 as restated £m
Turnover	550	50	175	775	690
Cost of sales	(415)	(40)	(165)	(620)	(555)
Gross profit	135	10	10	155	135
Net operating expenses	(85)	(4)	(25)	(114)	(83)
Less 1992 provision			10	10	
Operating profit	50	6	(5)	51	52
Profit on sale of properties	9			9	6
Provision for loss on operations to be discontinued					(30)
Loss on disposal of the discontinued operations			(17)	(17)	
Less 20X2 provision			20	20	
Profit on ordinary activities before interest	59	6	(2)	63	28

Thereafter example 2 is the same as example 1.

3.2 A note to the profit and loss account will give the analysis of distribution and administrative expenses between continuing and discontinued operations.

3.3 Examples 1 and 2 give slightly different information. It would be difficult to combine the two without producing a profit and loss account so complicated that nobody would understand it.

Discontinued operations

3.4 A discontinued operation is one which meets all of the following conditions.

(a) The sale or termination must have been completed before the earlier of 3 months after the year end or the date the financial statements are approved. (Terminations not completed by this date may be disclosed in the notes.)

(b) Former activity must have ceased permanently.

(c) The sale or termination has a material effect on the nature and focus of the entity's operations and represents a material reduction in its operating facilities resulting either from one of two things.

    (i) Its withdrawal from a particular market (class of business or geographical)
    (ii) A material reduction in turnover in its continuing markets

(d) The assets, liabilities, results of operations and activities are clearly distinguishable, physically, operationally and for financial reporting purposes.

Accounting for the discontinuation

3.5 (a) **Results**. The results of the discontinued operation up to the date of sale or termination or the balance sheet date should be shown under each of the relevant profit and loss account headings.

(b) **Profit/loss on discontinuation**. The profit or loss on discontinuation or costs of discontinuation should be disclosed separately as an exceptional item after operating profit and before interest.

(c) **Comparative figures.** Figures for the previous year must be adjusted for any activities which have become discontinued in the current year.

Activity 9.1

B&C plc's profit and loss account for the year ended 31 December 20X2, with comparatives, is as follows.

	20X2 £'000	20X1 £'000
Turnover	200,000	180,000
Cost of sales	(60,000)	(80,000)
Gross profit	140,000	100,000
Distribution costs	(25,000)	(20,000)
Administration expenses	(50,000)	(45,000)
Operating profit	65,000	35,000

During the year the company sold a material business operation with all activities ceasing on 14 February 20X3. The loss on the sale of the operation amounted to £2.2m. The results of the operation for 20X1 and 20X2 were as follows.

	20X2 £'000	20X1 £'000
Turnover	22,000	26,000
Profit/(loss)	(7,000)	(6,000)

In addition, the company acquired a business which contributed £7m to turnover and an operating profit of £1.5m.

Task

Prepare the profit and loss account for the year ended 31 December 20X2 complying with the requirements of FRS 3 as far as possible.

---

4 FRS 3 STATEMENTS AND NOTES

4.1 FRS 3 introduced a new statement and a variety of new notes to expand the information required in published accounts which we saw in Chapter 8.

Statement of total recognised gains and losses

> **KEY TERM**
>
> The **statement of total recognised gains and losses** brings together the profit as shown in the profit and loss account and other gains or losses.

4.2 It is important to understand that the profit and loss account can only deal with *realised* profits. An example of realised profits might be profits resulting from the sale proceeds already received or about to be received.

4.3 A company can also make substantial **unrealised profits** and losses, for example through changes in the *value* of its fixed assets. These are **recognised**, in the case of asset revaluation, by increasing the value or the assets in the balance sheet, the double entry being to a revaluation reserve included in shareholders' funds.

Part C: The regulatory and conceptual framework

> **Activity 9.2**
>
> Can you think of two other types of gains and losses which might be recognised during a period but which are not realised and do not pass through the profit and loss account?

4.4 Generally speaking, realised profits and losses have been recognised in the profit and loss account; unrealised profits and loses may be recognised in the balance sheet. FRS 3 argues that users of accounts need to know about the unrealised movements. The statement brings all the information together.

4.5 The ASB regards the statement of total recognised gains and losses as very important, and accords it the status of a **primary statement**. This means that it must be presented with the same prominence as the balance sheet, the profit and loss account and the cash flow statement. Below is a specimen statement.

STATEMENT OF TOTAL RECOGNISED GAINS AND LOSSES

	£m
Profit for the financial year	
(ie profit after tax and extraordinary items if any)	29
Unrealised surplus on revaluation of properties	4
Unrealised loss on trade investment	(3)
	30
Foreign currency translation differences	(2)
Total gains and losses recognised since last annual report	28

4.6 The statement is, as you can see, fairly brief, but it is useful in that it brings together information from different sources: the profit and loss account, the balance sheet and the supporting notes for the asset revaluations. The ASB's *Statement of Principles*, discussed in the next chapter, envisages an even more significant role for the statement of total recognised gains and losses.

Reconciliation of movements in shareholders' funds

4.7 This reconciliation is required by FRS 3 to be included in the notes to the accounts. What the statement aims to do is to clarify exactly what has caused shareholders' funds to change during the period. The statement will include anything which causes share capital or reserves to change, ie:

(a) the profit and loss account;

(b) other movements in shareholders' funds as determined by the statement of total recognised gains and losses; and

(c) all other changes in shareholders' funds not recognised in either of the above such as goodwill immediately written off to reserves, or a new issue of shares

4.8 The typical contents of the reconciliation would be as follows.

	£
Profit for the financial year	29
* Dividends	(8)
	21
Other recognised gains and losses (per statement of total recognised gains and losses)	(1)
* New share capital	20
Net addition to shareholders' funds	40
Opening shareholders' funds	365
Closing shareholders' funds	403

* Items not appearing in the statement of recognised gains and losses.

Activity 9.3

Extracts from Z Ltd's profit and loss account for the year ended 31 December 20X1 were as follows.

	£'000
Profit after tax	512
Dividend	(120)
Retained profit	392

During the year the following important events took place.

(a) Assets were revalued upward by £110,000.
(b) £300,000 share capital was issued during the year.
(c) Certain stock items were written down by £45,000.
(d) Opening shareholders' funds at 1 January 20X1 were £3,100,000.

Show how the events for the year would be shown in the statement of recognised gains and losses and the reconciliation of movements in shareholders funds.

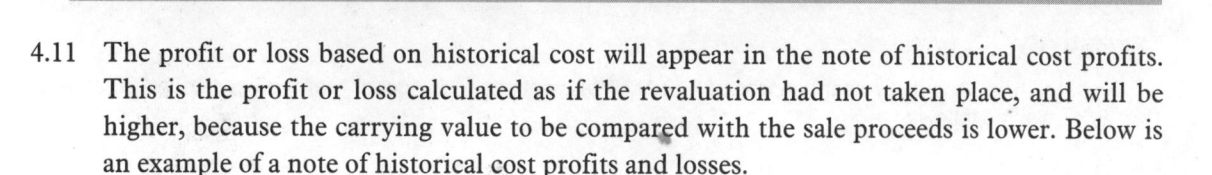

Note of historical cost profits and losses

4.9 If a company has adopted any of the alternative accounting rules as regards revaluation of assets then the reported profit figure per the profit and loss account may deviate from the historical cost profit figure. If this deviation is material then the financial statements must include a reconciliation statement after the statement of recognised gains and losses or the profit and loss account.

4.10 The profit figure to be reconciled is profit before tax; however, the retained profit for the year must also be restated.

> **IMPORTANT!**
>
> Note that FRS 3 **requires** the profit or loss on the disposal of a revalued asset to be calculated by reference to the difference between proceeds and the net carrying amount (revalued figure less depreciation on revalued figure).

4.11 The profit or loss based on historical cost will appear in the note of historical cost profits. This is the profit or loss calculated as if the revaluation had not taken place, and will be higher, because the carrying value to be compared with the sale proceeds is lower. Below is an example of a note of historical cost profits and losses.

NOTE OF HISTORICAL COST PROFITS AND LOSSES

	£m
Reported profit on ordinary activities before taxation	45
Realisation of property revaluation gains of previous years	9
Difference between historical cost depreciation charge and the actual depreciation charge of the period calculated on revalued amounts	5
Historical cost profit on ordinary activities before taxation	59

Activity 9.4

A Ltd reported a profit before tax of £162,000 for the year ended 31 December 20X1. During the year the following transactions in fixed assets took place.

Part C: The regulatory and conceptual framework

(a) An asset with a book value of £40,000 was revalued to £75,000. The remaining useful life is estimated to be five years.

(b) An asset (with a five year useful life at the date of revaluation) was revalued by £20,000 (book value £30,000) was sold one year after revaluation for £48,000.

Show the reconciliation or profit to historical cost profit for the year ended 31 December 20X1.

5 EARNINGS PER SHARE (EPS)

5.1 Earnings per share (EPS) is widely used by investors as a measure of a company's performance and is of particular importance in:

(a) Comparing the results of a company over a period of time

(b) Comparing the performance of one company's equity shares against the performance of another company's equity, and also against the returns obtainable from loan stock and other forms of investment

The purpose of any earnings yardstick is to achieve as far as possible clarity of meaning, comparability between one company and another, one year and another, and attributability of profits to the equity shares. FRS 14 *Earnings per share* goes some way to ensuring that all these aims are achieved.

KEY TERM

FRS 14 *Earnings per share* states the following with regard to **earnings per share**.

'Basic earnings per share should be calculated by dividing the net profit or loss for the period attributable to ordinary shareholders by the weighted average number of ordinary shares outstanding during the period.

For the purpose of calculating basic earnings per share, the net profit or loss for the period attributable to ordinary shareholders should be the net profit or loss for the period after deducting dividends and other appropriations in respect of non-equity shares.'

Activity 9.5

Pulp plc has 100,000 ordinary shares of £1 each. Its profit and loss account for the year ended 30 June 20X7 was as follows,

	£	£
Gross profit		250,000
Less exceptional items		50,000
Profit on ordinary activities before tax		200,000
Tax on profit on ordinary activities		66,000
Profit on ordinary activities after tax		134,000
Extraordinary charges	50,000	
Tax on extraordinary charges	16,500	
		33,500
Profit for the financial year		100,500
Less dividends:		
Preference	2,000	
Ordinary	22,000	
		24,000
Retained profit		76,500

Required

Calculate earnings per share.

6 PRIOR PERIOD ADJUSTMENTS

6.1 When the financial statements of a company are compiled, certain items (eg accruals, provisions) represent best estimates at a point in time. Further evidence received in the following year may suggest that previous estimates were incorrect. In most cases the 'error' will not be significant in size and so as a result the difference should be dealt with in the current year's accounts.

6.2 There are two situations where a **prior period adjustment** is necessary:

(a) **Fundamental errors** - evidence is found to suggest last year's accounts were wrong
(b) **A change in accounting policy**

6.3 The following accounting treatment should be used.

(a) Restate the prior year profit and loss account and balance sheet.

(b) Restate the opening reserves balance.

(c) Include the adjustment in the reconciliation of movements in shareholders' funds.

(d) Include a note at the foot of the statement of total recognised gains and losses of the current period.

> **KEY TERM**
>
> **Prior period adjustments** are therefore defined by FRS 3 as:
>
> 'Material adjustments applicable to prior periods arising from changes in accounting policy or from the correction of fundamental errors. They do not include normal recurring adjustments or corrections of accounting estimates made in prior periods.'

6.4 A **fundamental error** is an error which is so significant that the truth and fairness of the financial statements is not achieved.

6.5 A **change in accounting policy** requires a prior period adjustment based on the fundamental accounting concept of **consistency**. For users of the financial statements to make meaningful comparisons of a company's results it is important that the current year's and the last year's comparatives are prepared on the same basis. Therefore if for any reason a company changes its accounting policy they must go back and represent last year's accounts on the same basis.

6.6 Reasons for a change in accounting policy were discussed in Chapter 4.

Activity 9.6

Wick Ltd was established on 1 January 20X0. In the first three years' accounts deferred development expenditure was carried forward as an asset in the balance sheet. During 20X3 the directors decided that for the current and future years, all development expenditure should be written off as it is incurred. This decision has not resulted from any change in the expected outcome of development projects on hand, but rather from a desire to favour the prudence concept. The following information is available.

Part C: The regulatory and conceptual framework

(a) Movements on the deferred development account.

Year	Deferred development expenditure incurred during year £'000	Transfer from deferred development expenditure account to P & L account £'000
20X0	525	–
20X1	780	215
20X2	995	360

(b) The 20X2 accounts showed the following.

	£'000
Retained reserves b/f	2,955
Retained profit for the year	1,825
Retained profits carried forward	4,780

(c) The retained profit for 20X3 after charging the actual development expenditure for the year was £2,030,000.

Required

Show how the change in accounting policy should be reflected in the statement of reserves in the company's 20X3 accounts.

Ignore taxation.

Activity 9.7

Stud-U-Like Ltd is a publisher of Study Packs for various accountancy bodies. The packs are printed in-house and contained in ring binders which are made to a distinctive design in a small factory at the company's main site near Wormwood Scrubs, London. During the year ended 30 June 20X7, it was found necessary to shut down this factory and the workers were made redundant. The binders were to be bought in from an external supplier.

The following trial balance is available as at 30 June 20X7.

	£'000	£'000
Share capital - £1 ordinary shares		20
10% preference shares, 25p nominal value		20
Profit and loss account		38
Sales and purchases	85	300
Sales/purchase returns	4	8
Land and buildings (cost)	80	
Plant: cost/depn to 1 July 20X6	100	20
10% debentures		60
Opening stock	30	
Operating expenses	18	
Cost of factory closure (including redundancy)	75	
Sales/purchase ledger control	40	18
Provision for doubtful debts		2
Bank	54	
	486	486

In preparing the financial statements, the following information needs to be taken into account.

(a) No debenture interest has been accrued for.
(b) The provision for doubtful debts is to be 2½% of debtors.
(c) Depreciation at 10% on cost should be provided on plant.
(d) Sales returns of £2,000 were entered in the sales day book as if they were sales.
(e) Closing stock was valued at £35,000.
(f) The corporation tax charge for the year is £30,000.

Required

(a) Prepare a profit and loss account for the year ended 30 June 20X7. Your profit and loss account should be in good form, although it need not conform to the exact requirements of the Companies Act 1985. It must show clearly the items: gross profit, net operating profit, net profit before tax and profit for the year available to ordinary shareholders. Your workings should be set out clearly.

(b) 'FRS 3 *Reporting financial performance* aimed to improve the quality of financial information provided to shareholders.'

  (i) How might FRS 3 be applied to the profit and loss account you prepared in part (a)?

  (ii) What further information would you need in order to prepare the profit and loss account in accordance with FRS 3?

Key learning points

- FRS 3 *Reporting financial performance* has introduced radical changes to the profit and loss account of large and medium sized companies.

- You should be aware of the **FRS 3 definitions** of:
  - Extraordinary items
  - Exceptional items
  - Prior year adjustments
  - Discontinued operations
  - Total recognised gains and losses

- You should be aware of the format of the statement of total recognised gains and losses, the reconciliation of movements in shareholders' funds and the note on historical cost profits and losses, and understand their contents. It is not yet clear what type of question will be set concerning these statements.

- Earnings per share is a measure of the amount of profits earned by a company for each ordinary share. Earnings are profits after tax, preference dividends and extraordinary items.

- Prior period adjustments will only occur in two types of situation. Make sure that you can account for a prior period adjustment.

Quick quiz

1. Which exceptional items must be shown on the face of the P & L account?

2. Define extraordinary items.

3. What components of financial performance should be shown in the profit and loss account according to FRS 3?

4. A discontinued operation is one where the sale or termination must have been completed within the accounting year. True or false?

5. How should the profit or loss on discontinued activities be shown?

6. What is shown in the statement of total recognised gains and losses?

7. What is shown in the reconciliation of movements in shareholders' funds?

8. When is a prior period adjustment necessary?

Answers to quick quiz

1. (a) Profit or loss on sale or termination of an operation
   (b) Costs of a material fundamental reorganisation or restructuring
   (c) Profit or loss on disposal of fixed assets

2. Material items possessing a high degree of abnormality which arise from events or transactions that fall outside the ordinary activities of the reporting entity and which are not expected to recur.

3. All statutory headings from turnover to operating profit must be subdivided between that arising from continuing operations and that arising from discontinued operations. Turnover and operating profit must be further analysed between that from existing and that from newly acquired operations.

4. False. The sale or termination must have been completed before the earlier of three months after the year end or the date the financial statements are approved.

Part C: The regulatory and conceptual framework

5   As an exceptional item after operating profit and before interest.

6   The statement brings together realised and unrealised gains and losses from both the profit and loss account and the balance sheet.

7   Anything which causes capital or reserves to change.

8   (a) Fundamental errors
    (b) Change in accounting policies

Answers to activities

Answer 9.1

	20X2		20X1	
	£'000	£'000	£'000	£'000
Turnover				
Continuing operations				
(200 - 22 - 7)/(180 - 26)		171.0		154
Acquisitions		7.0		-
		178.0		154
Discontinued		22.0		26
		200.0		180
Cost of sales		(60.0)		(80)
Gross profit		140.0		100
Distribution costs		(25.0)		(20)
Administration expenses (50 - 2.2)		(47.8)		(45)
Operating profit				
Continuing operations* (bal)	72.7		41	
Acquisitions	1.5		-	
	74.2		41	
Discontinued	(7.0)		(6)	
		67.2		35
Exceptional item		(2.2)		-
		65.0		35

* ie 65.0 + 2.2 + 7.0 = 72.7, 35 + 6 = 41

Answer 9.2

(a) Gains or losses arising on the translation of foreign currency, for example with overseas investments
(b) Gains or losses on long-term trade investments

Answer 9.3

STATEMENT OF RECOGNISED GAINS AND LOSSES

	£'000
Profit after tax	512
Asset revaluation	110
	622

RECONCILIATION OF MOVEMENTS IN SHAREHOLDERS' FUNDS

	£'000
Profit after tax	512
Dividend	(120)
	392
Other recognised gains and losses (622 – 512)	110
New share capital	300
Net addition to shareholders' funds	802
Opening shareholders' funds	3,100
Closing shareholders' funds	3,902

Answer 9.4

RECONCILIATION OF PROFIT TO HISTORICAL COST PROFIT
FOR THE YEAR ENDED 31 DECEMBER 20X1

	£'000
Reported profit on ordinary activities before taxation	162
Realisation of property revaluation gains	20
Difference between historical cost depreciation charge and the actual depreciation charge of the year calculated on the revalued amount (75,000 - 40,000)/5	7
	189

Answer 9.5

Earnings = 100,500 – 2,000 = 98,500

No of shares = 100,000

$$\text{EPS} = \frac{98,500}{100,000} = 98.5p$$

Note. This exercise (and perhaps an exam question you might meet) contains an extraordinary item to test whether you know you should deduct it for the EPS calculation. In practice, FRS 3 has made such items more or less redundant.

Answer 9.6

If the new accounting policy had been adopted since the company was incorporated, the additional profit and loss account charges for development expenditure would have been:

	£'000
20X0	525
20X1 (780 – 215)	565
	1,090
20X2 (995 – 360)	635
	1,725

This means that the reserves brought forward at 1 January 20X3 would have been £1,725,000 less than the reported figure of £4,780,000; while the reserves brought forward at 1 January 20X2 would have been £1,090,000 less than the reported figure of £2,955,000.

The statement of reserves in Wick Ltd's 20X3 accounts should, therefore, appear as follows.

STATEMENT OF RESERVES (EXTRACT)

	20X3 £'000	Comparative (previous year) figures 20X2 £'000	
Retained profits at the beginning of year			
Previously reported	4,780	2,955	
Prior year adjustment (note 1)	1,725	1,090	
Restated	3,055	1,865	
Retained profits for the year	2,030	1,190	(note 2)
Retained profits at the end of the year	5,085	3,055	

Notes

1. The accounts should include a note explaining the reasons for and consequences of the changes in accounting policy. (See above workings for 20X3 and 20X2.)

2. The retained profit shown for 20X2 is after charging the additional development expenditure of £635,000.

Answer 9.7

(a) STUD-U-LIKE LIMITED
PROFIT AND LOSS ACCOUNT FOR THE YEAR ENDED 30 JUNE 20X7

	£'000	£'000
Turnover (W1)		292
Cost of sales (W2)		72
Gross profit		220
Operating expenses	18	
Decrease in doubtful debt provision (W3)	(1)	
Depreciation (10% × 100)	10	
		27
Net operating profit		193
Closure and redundancy costs	75	
Debenture interest (10% × 60)	6	
		81
Net profit before tax		112
Tax		30
Net profit after tax		82
Preference dividend (10% × 20,000)		2
Profit for the year available to ordinary shareholders		80

Workings

1 Turnover

	£'000
Sales per trial balance	300
Less returns incorrectly included	2
	298
Sales returns per trial balance	4
Add returns incorrectly excluded	2
	6

Turnover = sales less returns = 298 – 6 = 292

2 Cost of sales

	£'000
Opening stock	30
Purchases less returns (85 – 8)	77
	107
Closing stock	35
	72

3 Decrease in doubtful debt provision

	£'000
Provision as at 1 July 20X6	2
Provision required: 2½% × 40	1
∴ Decrease needed	1

(b) (i) The major change to the profit and loss account brought in by FRS 3 *Reporting financial performance* was to highlight certain key aspects of financial performance. It does this by requiring the following.

(1) All statutory headings from turnover to operating profit must be subdivided between that arising from continuing operations and that arising from discontinued operations.

(2) The following categories of exceptional items must be shown separately on the face of the profit and loss account after operating profit and before interest and allocated appropriately to discontinued and continued activities.

- Profit or loss on the sale or termination of an operation.
- Costs of a fundamental re-organisation or restructuring that has a material effect on the nature and focus of the reporting entity's operations.
- Profit or loss on disposal of a fixed asset.

9: Reporting financial performance

The item to which FRS 3 could apply in the profit and loss account of Stud-U-Like is the closure/redundancy costs. The figure of £75,000 is material in the context of the accounts. If the factory making the ring binders is to be regarded as a discontinued operation, it will be necessary to separate out revenues and expenses associated with it from other revenues and expenses and show them separately as required by FRS 3. It will, in any case, be necessary to separate the profit or loss on the sale of fixed assets from the other costs as, if material, this is required to be shown separately as an exceptional item.

(ii) It is not clear, however, whether the manufacture of the special ring binders can be regarded as a separate operation which has now been discontinued. It appears that the ring binders were not sold separately, giving rise to separate revenues and costs, but were part of the cost of the Study Pack products. Further information on this point would be needed to determine exactly how FRS 3 should be applied.

Now try Question 9 in the Exam Question Bank at the end of the Text.

Chapter 10 Conceptual framework

Chapter topic list

1   Criticisms of historical cost accounting
2   Alternatives to historical cost accounting
3   Conceptual framework and *Statement of Principles*

The following study sessions are covered in this chapter.

		Syllabus reference
1(d)	Describe and explain the following elements of the financial statements and their interaction: (i) assets (ii) liabilities (iii) ownership interest (iv) gains (v) losses (vi) contributions from owners	1
1(e)	Identify the three stages of recognising elements for inclusion in financial statements	1
2(a)	Discuss the nature and purpose of a conceptual framework	1
2(b)	Explain the potential benefits and drawbacks of an agreed conceptual framework	1
2(c)	Explain the role and general issues covered by the *Statement of Principles*	1
2(d)	Identify and explain the qualitative characteristics of financial information	1
2(f)	Discuss the shortcomings of historical cost accounting and how they might be overcome	1

Part C: The regulatory and conceptual framework

1 CRITICISMS OF HISTORICAL COST ACCOUNTING

1.1 Traditionally, there have been two main reasons for the preparation of accounts:

(a) To fulfil the needs of the owners of a business.

(b) To assist the managers of a business in controlling that business and in making decisions about its future.

1.2 Although the information needs of internal and external users differ considerably, it has become increasingly clear that accounts prepared on a traditional historical cost basis can present financial information in a misleading manner. The greatest criticisms of traditional accounting concepts have stemmed from their inability to reflect the effects of changing price levels.

1.3 Before mentioning the various alternatives, we should first consider the criticisms of historical cost accounting in more detail.

Fixed asset values are unrealistic

1.4 The most striking example is **property**. Although it is a statutory requirement that the market value of an interest in land should be disclosed in the directors' report if it is significantly different from the balance sheet figure, and although some companies have periodically updated the balance sheet values, revaluation's have not been reported consistently.

1.5 If fixed assets are retained in the books at their historical cost, **unrealised holding gains are not recognised**. This means that the total holding gain, if any, will be brought into account during the year in which the asset is realised, rather than spread over the period during which it was owned.

1.6 There are, in essence, two points to be considered.

(a) Although it has long been accepted that a balance sheet prepared under the historical cost concept is an historical record and not a statement of current worth, many people now argue that the balance sheet should at least give an indication of the current value of the company's tangible net assets.

(b) The prudence concept requires that profits should only be recognised when realised in the form either of cash or of other assets the ultimate cash realisation of which can be assessed with reasonable certainty. It may be argued that recognising unrealised holding gains on fixed assets is contrary to this concept.

1.7 On balance, the weight of opinion is now in favour of restating asset values. It is felt that the criticism based on prudence can be met by ensuring that valuations are made as objectively as possible (eg in the case of property, by having independent expert valuations) and by not taking unrealised gains through the profit and loss account.

Depreciation is inadequate to finance the replacement of fixed assets

1.8 Depreciation is not provided for in order to enforce retention of profits and thus ensure that funds are available for asset replacement. It is intended as a measure of the contribution of fixed assets to the company's activities in the period. However, an incidental effect of providing for depreciation is that not all liquid funds can be paid out to investors and so funds for asset replacement are on hand. What is important is not the replacement of one asset by an identical new one (something that rarely happens) but the replacement of the operating capability represented by the old asset.

1.9 Another criticism of historical cost depreciation is that it does not fully reflect the value of the asset consumed during the accounting year. Whilst this point is obviously closely related to the first, it can be overcome whilst still retaining insufficient profits to finance replacement.

Holding gains on stocks are included in profit

1.10 During a period of high inflation the monetary value of stocks held may increase significantly while they are being processed. The conventions of historical cost accounting lead to the unrealised part of this holding gain (known as stock appreciation) being included in profit for the year. It is estimated that in the late 1970s nearly half the declared profits of companies were due to stock appreciation.

1.11 EXAMPLE: HOLDING GAINS

This problem can be illustrated using a simple example. At the beginning of the year a company has 100 units of stock and no other assets. Its trading account for the year is shown below:

TRADING ACCOUNT

	Units	£		Units	£
Opening stock	100	200	Sales (made 31	100	500
Purchases (made 31 December)	100	400	(December)		
	200	600			
Closing stock (FIFO basis)	100	400			
	100	200			
Gross profit	-	300			
	100	500		100	500

Apparently the company has made a gross profit of £300. But, at the beginning of the year the company owned 100 units of stock and at the end of the year it owned 100 units of stock and £100 (sales £500 - purchases £400). From this it would seem that a profit of £100 is more reasonable. The remaining £200 is stock appreciation arising as the purchase price increased from £2 to £4.

1.12 The criticism can be overcome by using a *capital maintenance concept* based on physical units rather than money values.

Profits (or losses) on holdings of net monetary items are not shown

1.13 In periods of inflation the purchasing power, and thus the value, of money falls. It follows that an investment in money will have a lower real value at the end of a period of time than it did at the beginning. A loss has been incurred. Similarly, the real value of a monetary liability will reduce over a period of time and a gain will be made.

The true effect of inflation on capital maintenance is not shown

1.14 To a large extent this follows from the points already mentioned. It is a widely held principle that distributable profits should only be recognised after full allowance has been made for any erosion in the capital value of a business. In historical cost accounts, although capital is maintained in nominal money terms, it may not be in real terms. In other words, profits may be distributed to the detriment of the long-term viability of the business. This

Part C: The regulatory and conceptual framework

criticism may be made by those who advocate capital maintenance in physical terms and those who prefer money capital maintenance as measured by pounds of current purchasing power (see below).

Comparisons over time are unrealistic

1.15 This will tend to an exaggeration of growth. For example, if a company's profit in 1966 was £100,000 and in 1999 £500,000, a shareholder's initial reaction might be that the company had done rather well. If, however, it was then revealed that with £100,000 in 1966 he could buy exactly the same goods as with £500,000 in 1999, the apparent growth would seem less impressive.

1.16 The points mentioned in the last paragraph have demonstrated some of the accounting problems which arise in times of severe and prolonged inflation. Of the various possible systems of accounting for price changes most can be divided into two categories.

   (a) **General price** change bases and in particular current purchasing power (CPP)

   (b) **Current value** bases: the basic principles of all these are:

   (i) To show balance sheet items at some form of current value rather than historical cost

   (ii) To compute profits by matching the current value of costs at the date of consumption against revenue

   The current value of an item will normally be based on replacement cost, net realisable value or economic value.

2 ALTERNATIVES TO HISTORICAL COST ACCOUNTING

2.1 In the UK an attempt was made to implement a system of **current purchasing power** (SSAP 7). The principal feature of the system was that profit for the year was calculated after an **adjustment** designed to reflect the effect of **general price inflation** on the purchasing power of equity shareholders' funds.

2.2 CPP accounting did not catch on and in 1980 a decisive step was taken in the direction of a current value basis of accounting. SSAP 16 *Current cost accounting* was published for a trial period of three years beginning in March 1980. The system of **current cost accounting** (CCA) advocated by SSAP 16 did not attempt to cater for general price inflation; instead, profit for the year was to be calculated after allowing for the effects of price increases specifically on the operating capability of the particular business.

2.3 The principal features of CCA are as follows.

   (a) In the balance sheet, **assets** are stated at their '**value to the business**'. This may be a replacement cost, net realisable value or economic value depending on the circumstances.

   (b) In the profit and loss account **holding gains** are **excluded from profit**. A holding gain is the difference between value to the business of an asset and its original cost. If X buys an item for £100 and sells it for £150 there will be an HC profit of £150 - £100 = £50. If the replacement cost of the item at the date of sale is £130, in CC terms there will be an operating gain of £150 - £130 = £20 and a holding gain of £130 - £100 = £30. Current cost accounting recognises operating gains only as profit; historical cost accounting does not differentiate between holding and operating gains, and recognises both as profit.

2.4 SSAP 16 encountered a good deal of criticism on both practical and theoretical grounds. In 1985 the mandatory status of the standard was withdrawn; compliance with its provisions then became only voluntary. The standard itself was finally withdrawn in April 1988.

3 CONCEPTUAL FRAMEWORK AND STATEMENT OF PRINCIPLES

The search for a conceptual framework

> **KEY TERM**
>
> A **conceptual framework**, is a statement of generally accepted theoretical principles which form the frame of reference for financial reporting. These theoretical principles provide the basis for the development of new reporting standards and the evaluation of those already in existence.

3.1 The financial reporting process is concerned with providing information that is useful in the business and economic decision-making process. Therefore a conceptual framework will form the theoretical basis for determining which events should be accounted for, how they should be measured and how they should be communicated to the user.

3.2 Although it is theoretical in nature, a conceptual framework for financial reporting has highly practical final aims.

3.3 The need for a conceptual framework is demonstrated by the way UK standards have developed over recent years. Standards were produced in a haphazard and fire-fighting approach. Had an agreed framework existed, the ASC could have acted as an architect or designer, rather than a fire-fighter, building accounting rules on the foundation of sound, agreed basic principles.

3.4 The lack of a conceptual framework also meant that fundamental principles were tackled more than once in different standards, thereby producing contradictions and inconsistencies in basic concepts, such as those of prudence and matching. This led to ambiguity and it has affected the true and fair concept of financial reporting.

3.5 Another problem with the lack of a conceptual framework has become apparent in the USA. The large number of highly detailed standards produced by the Financial Accounting Standards Board (FASB) has created a financial reporting environment governed by specific rules rather than general principles. This would be avoided if a cohesive set of principles were in place.

3.6 A conceptual framework would also bolster the standard setters against political pressure from various 'lobby groups' and interested parties. Such pressure would only prevail if it was acceptable under the conceptual framework.

3.7 Towards the end of its existence, the ASC recognised the IASC's *Framework* on the preparation and presentation of financial statements, as a set of guidelines to help it develop proposals for new standards and revisions to existing standards. This represented a significant shift from the previous approach of developing SSAPs in a haphazard manner as working solutions to practical problems.

Part C: The regulatory and conceptual framework

3.8 The *Framework* deals with:

(a) the objective of financial statements;

(b) the qualitative characteristics that determine the usefulness of information in financial statements;

(c) the definition, recognition and measurement of the elements from which financial statements are constructed;

(d) concepts of capital and capital maintenance.

The IASC believes that further international harmonisation of accounting methods can best be promoted by focusing on these four topics since they will then lead to producing financial statements that meet the common needs of most users.

3.9 The ASB has gone further than the ASC in that it has already incorporated the IASC's *Framework* into its *Statement of Principles*.

3.10 Another publication which has a bearing on the area of a conceptual framework is Professor David Solomons' 1989 discussion paper, *Guidelines for Financial Reporting Standards*. The Solomons report deals with:

(a) The purpose of financial reporting
(b) Financial statements and their elements
(c) The qualitative characteristics of accounting information
(d) Recognition and measurement
(e) The choice of a general purpose accounting model

The report thus followed the same route as the IASC's *Framework*.

Advantages and disadvantages of a conceptual framework

3.11 The advantages arising from using a conceptual framework may be summarised as follows.

(a) The old SSAPs were being developed on a 'patchwork quality' basis where a particular accounting problem was recognised by the old ASC as having emerged, and resources were then channelled into standardising accounting practice in that area, without regard to whether that particular issue was necessarily the most important issue remaining at that time without standardisation.

(b) As stated above, the development of certain SSAPs (for example SSAP 13) has been subject to considerable political interference from interested parties. Where there is a conflict of interest between user groups on which policies to choose, policies deriving from a conceptual framework will be less open to criticism that the ASC buckled to external pressure.

(c) Some accounting standards seem to concentrate on the income statement (profit and loss account), some to concentrate on the valuation of net assets (balance sheet). For instance, FRS 15 and its predecessor SSAP 12 ensures that depreciation is charged on a systematic basis through the profit and loss account to comply with the accruals concept, but the net book value figure in the balance sheet has little meaning.

3.12 A counter-argument to supporters of a conceptual framework might be as follows.

(a) Financial statements are intended for a variety of users, and it is not certain that a single conceptual framework can be devised which will suit all users.

(b) Given the diversity of user requirements, there may be a need for a variety of accounting standards, each produced for a different purpose (and with different concepts as a basis).

(c) It is not clear that a conceptual framework will make the task of preparing and then implementing standards any easier than it is now.

ASB Statement of Principles

3.13 The Accounting Standards Board (ASB) published (in December 1999) its *Statement of Principles for Financial Reporting*. The statement consists of eight chapters.

(1) The objective of financial statements
(2) The reporting entity
(3) The qualitative characteristics of financial information
(4) The elements of financial statements
(5) Recognition in financial statements
(6) Measurement in financial statements
(7) Presentation of financial information
(8) Accounting for interests in other entities

> **Exam alert**
> It is expected that candidates will have a good understanding of the *Statement of Principles*.

Purpose of the *Statement of Principles*

3.14 Here are the main reasons why the Accounting Standards Board (ASB) developed the *Statement of Principles*.

(a) To assist the ASB by providing a basis for **reducing** the **number of alternative** accounting treatments permitted by accounting standards and company law

(b) To provide a **framework** for the future development of accounting standards

(c) To **assist auditors** in forming an opinion as to whether financial statements conform with accounting standards

(d) To **assist users** of accounts in interpreting the information contained in them

(e) To provide **guidance in applying accounting standards**

(f) To give **guidance** on **areas** which are **not yet covered by accounting standards**

(g) To **inform interested parties** of the approach taken by the ASB in formulating accounting standards

The role of the *Statement* can thus be summed up as being to provide **consistency, clarity and information**.

Chapter 1 The objective of financial statements

3.15 **Main points**

(a) 'The objective of financial statements is to provide information about the **financial position, performance** and **financial adaptability** of an enterprise that is useful to a wide range of users for assessing the stewardship of management and for making economic decisions.'

(b) It is acknowledged that while all not all the information needs of users can be met by financial statements, there are needs that are common to all users. Financial statements that meet the needs of providers of risk capital to the enterprise will also meet most of the needs of other users that financial statements can satisfy.

Users of financial statements other than investors include:

   (i)   Employees
   (ii) Lenders
   (iii) Suppliers and other creditors
   (iv) Customers
   (v)   Government and their agencies
   (vi) The public

(c) The **limitations** of financial statements are emphasised as well as the strengths.

(d) All of the **components** of financial statements (balance sheet, profit and loss account, cash flow statement) are **interrelated** because they reflect different aspects of the same transactions.

(e) The *Statement* emphasises the ways financial statements provide information about the financial position of an enterprise. The main elements which affect the position of the company are:

   (i)   The economic resources it controls
   (ii) Its financial structure
   (iii) Its liquidity and solvency
   (iv) Its capacity to adapt to changes in the environment in which it operates (called **financial adaptability**)

The *Statement* discusses the importance of each of these elements and how they are **disclosed** in the financial statements.

Chapter 2 The reporting entity

3.16 It is important that entities that ought to prepare financial statements, in fact do so. The entity must be a **cohesive economic unit**. It has a **determinable boundary** and is held to account for all the things it **can control**.

Chapter 3 Qualitative characteristics of financial information

3.17 The *Statement* gives a diagrammatic representation of the discussion, shown below.

   (a) Qualitative characteristics that relate to **content** are **relevance** and **reliability**.
   (b) Qualitative characteristics that relate to **presentation** are **comparability** and **understandability**.

The diagram shown here is reasonably explanatory.

What makes financial information useful?

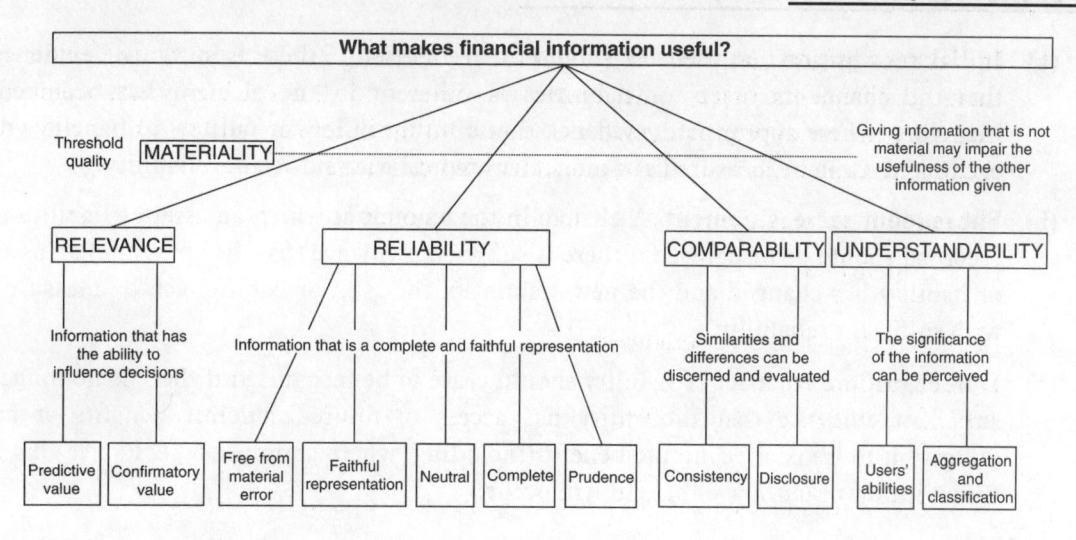

```
                    What makes financial information useful?
                                        |
    Threshold  ─── MATERIALITY ─────────────────────── Giving information that is not
    quality                                             material may impair the
                                                        usefulness of the other
                                                        information given
    
    RELEVANCE          RELIABILITY        COMPARABILITY    UNDERSTANDABILITY
    
    Information        Information that is a          Similarities and        The significance
    that has the       complete and faithful          differences can be      of the information
    ability to         representation                 discerned and           can be perceived
    influence                                         evaluated
    decisions
    
    Predictive  Confirmatory   Free from   Faithful    Neutral  Complete  Prudence   Consistency  Disclosure   Users'    Aggregation
    value       value          material    representation                                                      abilities  and
                               error                                                                                      classification
```

Chapter 4 Elements of financial statements

3.18 These are:

- Assets
- Liabilities
- Ownership interest
- Gains
- Losses
- Contributions from owners
- Distributions to owners

3.19 Any item that does not fall within one of the definitions of elements should not be included in financial statements. The definitions are as follows.

(a) **Assets** are rights or other access to future economic benefits controlled by an entity as a result of past transactions or events.

(b) **Liabilities** are obligations of an entity to transfer economic benefits as a result of past transactions or events.

(c) **Ownership interest** is the residual amount found by deducting all of the entity's liabilities from all of the entity's assets.

(d) **Gains** are increases in ownership interest, other than those relating to contributions from owners.

(e) **Losses** are decreases in ownership interest, other than those relating to distributions to owners.

(f) **Contributions from owners** are increases in ownership interest resulting from investments made by owners in their capacity as owners.

(g) **Distributions to owners** are decreases in ownership interest resulting from transfers made to owners in their capacity as owners.

Chapter 5 Recognition in financial statements

3.20 This chapter explains what is meant by recognition and discusses the three stages of recognition of assets and liabilities.

- Initial recognition
- Subsequent remeasurement
- Derecognition

3.21 The chapter goes on to describe the criteria which determine each of these stages.

Part C: The regulatory and conceptual framework

(a) **Initial recognition.** An element should be recognised if there is sufficient evidence that the change in assets or liabilities is inherent in the element has occurred, including, where appropriate, evidence that a future inflow or outflow of benefit will occur, and it can be measured at a monetary amount with sufficient reliability.

(b) **Subsequent remeasurement.** A change in the amount at which an asset or liability is recorded should be recognised if there is sufficient evidence that the amount of an asset or liability has changed and the new amount of the asset or liability can be measured with sufficient reliability.

(c) **Derecognition.** An asset or liability should cease to be recognised if there is no longer sufficient evidence that the entity has access to future economic benefits or an obligation to transfer economic benefit (including, where appropriate, evidence that a future inflow or outflow of benefit will occur.

3.22 In practice, entities operate in an uncertain environment and this **uncertainty** may sometimes make it necessary to delay the recognition process. The uncertainty is twofold.

- **Element uncertainty** - does the item exist and meet the definition of elements?
- **Measurement uncertainty** - at what monetary amount should the item be recognised?

Activity 10.1

Consider the following situations. In each case, do we have an asset or liability within the definitions given by the *Statement of Principles?* Give reasons for your answer.

(a) Pat Ltd has purchased a patent for £20,000. The patent gives the company sole use of a particular manufacturing process which will save £3,000 a year for the next five years.

(b) Baldwin Ltd paid Don Brennan £10,000 to set up a car repair shop, on condition that priority treatment is given to cars from the company's fleet.

(c) Deals on Wheels Ltd provides a warranty with every car sold.

(d) Monty Ltd has signed a contract with a human resources consultant. The terms of the contract are that the consultant is to stay for six months and be paid £3,000 per month.

(e) Rachmann Ltd owns a building which for many years it had let out to students. The building has been declared unsafe by the local council. Not only is it unfit for human habitation, but on more than one occasion slates have fallen off the roof, nearly killing passers-by. To rectify all the damage would cost £300,000; to eliminate the danger to the public would cost £200,000. The building could then be sold for £100,000.

Chapter 6 Measurement in financial statements

3.23 This chapter, with its emphasis on current values, is fairly radical and controversial. The following approach is taken.

(a) **Initially**, when an asset is purchased or a liability incurred, the asset/liability is recorded at the **transaction cost**, that is historical cost, which at that time is equal to current replacement cost.

(b) An asset/liability may subsequently be '**remeasured**'. In a historical cost system, this can involve writing down an asset to its recoverable amount. For a liability, the corresponding treatment would be amendment of the monetary amount to the amount ultimately expected to be paid.

(c) Such re-measurements will, however, only be recognised if there is **sufficient evidence** that the monetary amount of the asset/liability has changed and the new amount can be reliably measured.

Chapter 7 Presentation of financial information

3.24 Aspects of this chapter have also given rise to some **controversy**. The chapter begins by making the general point that financial information is presented in the form of a structured set of financial statements comprising primary statements and supporting notes and, in some cases, supplementary information.

Components of financial statements

3.25 The primary financial statements are as follows.

(a) Profit and loss account
(b) Statement of total recognised gains and losses
(c) Balance sheet
(d) Cash flow statement

(a) and (b) are the 'statements of financial performance'.

3.26 The notes to the financial statements 'amplify and explore' the primary statements; together they form an 'integrated whole'. Disclosure in the notes does not correct or justify non-disclosure or misrepresentation in the primary financial statements.

3.27 'Supplementary information' embraces voluntary disclosures and information which is too subjective for disclosure in the primary financial statement and the notes.

Chapter 8 Accounting for interests in other entities

3.28 Financial statements need to reflect the effect on the reporting entity's financial performance and financial position of its interests in other entities. This involves various measurement, presentation and consolidation issues which are dealt with in this chapter of the *Statement*.

Summary

3.29 The *Statement of Principles* will not have direct effect. It is **not an accounting standard** with which companies have to comply. Having said that, it may well be **influential**, especially where there is no specific standard dealing with an issue. There is still a great deal of controversy surrounding this document.

Activity 10.2

What is the purpose of the ASB's *Statement of Principles?*

Part C: The regulatory and conceptual framework

> **Key learning points**
>
> - **Historical cost accounts** have a number of **deficiencies** in times of rising prices.
>
> - In the UK attempts to deal with the problem have centred mainly on a system of **current cost accounting** introduced by SSAP 16 in 1980. Compliance with SSAP 16 was never widespread even amongst the companies (mainly public companies) within its scope.
>
> - Whereas in the past accounting standards were produced on an *ad hoc* basis, in recent years attempts have been made to develop a **conceptual framework** of accounting, on which future accounting standards should be based.
>
> - The ASB's **Statement of Principles** should provide the backbone of the conceptual framework in the UK.
>
> - Key elements in the *Statement* are as follows.
>   - Financial statements should give financial information useful for assessing stewardship of management and for making economic decisions.
>   - Financial information should be relevant, reliable, comparable and understandable.
>   - Assets and liabilities have conceptual priority over the profit and loss account.
>   - Accounts should move towards current cost valuations.
>   - Statement of total recognised gains and losses is for assets held for the business to continue trading.

Quick quiz

1. What criticisms can be made of traditional historical cost accounting?
2. What is the principal feature of CCP accounting?
3. State the principal features of CCA.
4. Why is a conceptual framework necessary?
5. What are the eight chapters of the *Statement of Principles*?
6. How does the *Statement* define 'gains' and 'losses'?

Answers to quick quiz

1. (a) Depreciation is inadequate to finance the replacement of fixed assets.
   (b) Holding gains on stocks are included in profit.
   (c) The true effect of inflation on capital maintenance is not shown.
   (d) Profits or losses on holdings of net monetary items are not shown.
   (e) Comparisons over time are unrealistic.

2. Profit for the year was calculated after an adjustment designed to reflect the effect of general price inflation on the purchasing power of equity shareholders' funds.

3. (a) In the balance sheet, assets are stated at their value to the business.
   (b) In the profit and loss account, holding gains are excluded from profit.

4. To form the theoretical basis for the provision of information that is useful in the business and economic decision making process.

5. (1) The objective of financial statements
   (2) The reporting entity
   (3) The qualitative characteristics of financial statements
   (4) The elements of financial statements
   (5) Recognition in financial statements
   (6) Measurement in financial statements
   (7) Presentation of financial information
   (8) Accounting for interests in other entities

6   (a)   Gains are increases in ownership interest other than those relating to contributions from owners.
    (b)   Losses are decreases in ownership interest other than those relating to distributions to owners.

Answers to activities

Answer 10.1

(a) This is an asset, albeit an intangible one. There is a past event, control and future economic benefit (through cost savings).

(b) This cannot be classified as an asset. Baldwin Ltd has no control over the car repair shop and it is difficult to argue that there are 'future economic benefits'.

(c) This is a liability; the business has taken on an obligation. It would be recognised when the warranty is issued rather than when a claim is made.

(d) As a firm financial commitment, this has all the appearance of a liability. However, as the consultant has not done any work yet, there has been no past event which could give rise to a liability. Similarly, because there has been no past event there is no asset.

(e) The situation is not clear cut. It could be argued that there is a liability, depending on the whether the potential danger to the public arising from the building creates a legal obligation to do the repairs. If there is such a liability, it might be possible to set off the sale proceeds of £100,000 against the cost of essential repairs of £200,000, giving a net obligation to transfer economic benefits of £100,000.

The building is clearly not an asset, because although there is control and there has been a past event, there is no expected access to economic benefit.

Answer 10.2

The following are the main reasons why the ASB developed the *Statement of Principles*.

(a) To assist the ASB by providing a basis for reducing the number of alternative accounting treatments permitted by accounting standards and company law

(b) To provide a framework for the future development of accounting standards

(c) To assist auditors in forming an opinion as to whether financial statements conform with accounting standards

(d) To assist users of accounts in interpreting the information contained in them

(e) To provide guidance in applying accounting standards

(f) To give guidance on areas which are not yet covered by accounting standards

(g) To inform interested parties of the approach taken by the ASB in formulating accounting standards

The role of the *Statement* can thus be summed up as being to provide consistency, clarity and information.

Now try Question 10 in the Exam Question Bank at the end of the Text.

Part D
Accounting standards

Chapter 11 Contingencies and events after the balance sheet date

---

Chapter topic list

1   Timing and disclosure
2   FRS 21 Events after the balance sheet date
3   FRS 12 Provisions, contingent liabilities and contingent assets

---

The following study sessions are covered in this chapter.

		Syllabus reference
17&18(a)	Define a post balance sheet event*	2
17&18(b)	Distinguish between adjusting and non-adjusting post balance sheet events	2
17&18(c)	Account for each category of post balance sheet event in the financial statements	2
17&18(d)	Define a provision, contingent liability and contingent asset	2
17&18(e)	Understand the general recognition principle	2
17&18(f)	Account for provisions, contingent liabilities and contingent assets	2
12(b)	Prepare the financial statements of limited companies in accordance with the prescribed formats and relevant accounting standards	2
12(c)	Discuss relevant accounting standards and be able to apply them	2

*Note. The term 'post balance sheet event' appears in the syllabus. Since the publication of FRS 21, the term now used is 'event after the balance sheet date'. They mean the same thing!

Part D: Accounting standards

1 TIMING AND DISCLOSURE

1.1 The financial statements are significant indicators of a company's success or failure. It is important, therefore, that they include all the information necessary for an understanding of the company's position.

1.2 FRS 21 *Events after the balance sheet date* and FRS 12 *Provisions, contingent liabilities and contingent assets* both require the provision of additional information in order to facilitate such an understanding. FRS 21 deals with events *after* the balance sheet date which may affect the position at the balance sheet date. FRS 12 *Provisions, contingent liabilities and contingent assets* deals with matters which are **uncertain** at the balance sheet date.

2 FRS 21 EVENTS AFTER THE BALANCE SHEET DATE

2.1 The standard gives the following definition.

> **KEY TERMS**
>
> **Events after the balance sheet date** are those events, both favourable and unfavourable, that occur between the balance sheet date and the date on which the financial statements are authorised for issue. Two types of events can be identified.
> - Those that provide further evidence of conditions that existed at the balance sheet date (adjusting events after the balance sheet date)
> - Those that are indicative of conditions that arose after the balance sheet date (non-adjusting events after the balance sheet date) *(FRS 21)*

Events after the balance sheet date

2.2 Between the balance sheet date and the date the financial statements are authorised (ie for issue outside the organisation), events may occur which show that assets and liabilities at the balance sheet date should be adjusted, or that disclosure of such events should be given.

Events requiring adjustment

2.3 The standard requires entities to **adjust** the amounts recognised in its financial statements to reflect adjusting events after the balance sheet date.

2.4 An **example** of additional evidence which becomes available after the balance sheet date is where a **customer goes bankrupt, thus confirming that the trade account receivable balance at the year end is uncollectable.**

2.5 In relation to going concern, the standard states that, where operating results and the financial position have deteriorated after the balance sheet date, it may be necessary to reconsider whether the going concern assumption is appropriate in the preparation of the financial statements.

Examples of adjusting events

2.6 The following examples of adjusting events are given in FRS 21.

(a) The resolution after the balance sheet date of a court case giving rise to a liability

(b) Evidence of impairment of assets, such as news that a major customer is going into liquidation, or the sale of inventories (stocks) below cost

(c) Determination of the price of assets bought or sold before the balance sheet date

(d) Determination of employee bonuses or profit shares

(e) Discovery of fraud or errors showing that the financial statements were incorrect

Events not requiring adjustment

2.7 The standard then looks at events which do **not** require adjustment. Entities **must not adjust** the amounts recognised in their financial statements to reflect these non-adjusting events.

2.8 The **example** given by the standard of such an event is where the **value of an investment falls between the balance sheet date and the date the financial statements are authorised** for issue. The fall in value represents circumstances during the current period, not conditions existing at the previous balance sheet date, so it is not appropriate to adjust the value of the investment in the financial statements. Disclosure is an aid to users, however, indicating 'unusual changes' in the state of assets and liabilities after the balance sheet date.

2.9 The rule for **disclosure** of events occurring after the balance sheet date which relate to conditions that arose after that date, is that disclosure should be made if non-disclosure would hinder the user's ability to made **proper evaluations** and decision based on the financial statements. An example might be the acquisition of another business.

Examples of non-adjusting events

2.10 The following examples of non-adjusting events are given in FRS 21.

(a) Major business combination

(b) Announcement of a plan to discontinue an operation

(c) Major purchases and disposals of assets

(d) Destruction of a major production plant by a fire

(e) Announcement of or beginning of major restructuring

(f) Major share transactions

(g) Abnormally large changes in asset prices or foreign exchange rates

(h) Changes in tax rates having a significant effect on current and deferred tax assets and liabilities

(i) Entering into significant guarantees

(j) Commencing major litigation arising out of events after the balance sheet date

Dividends

2.11 **Equity dividends proposed or declared after the balance sheet date should not be recognised as a liability at the balance sheet date**. Such dividends are disclosed in the notes to the financial statements.

Part D: Accounting standards

Disclosures

2.12 The following **disclosure requirements** are given **for events** which occur after the balance sheet date which do *not* require adjustment. If disclosure of events occurring after the balance sheet date is required, the following information should be provided.

(a) The nature of the event
(b) An estimate of the financial effect, or a statement that such an estimate cannot be made

Activity 11.1

State whether the following events occurring after the balance sheet date require an adjustment to the assets and liabilities of the financial statements.

(a) Purchase of an investment
(b) A change in the rate of corporate tax, applicable to the previous year
(c) An increase in pension benefits
(d) Losses due to fire
(e) A bad debt suddenly being paid
(f) The receipt of proceeds of sales or other evidence concerning the net realisable value of inventory
(g) A sudden decline in the value of property held as a long-term asset

Activity 11.2

Fabricators Ltd, an engineering company, makes up its financial statements to 31 March in each year. The financial statements for the year ended 31 March 20X1 showed a turnover of £3m and trading profit of £400,000.

Before approval of the financial statements by the board of directors on 30 June 20X1 the following events took place.

(a) The financial statements of Patchup Ltd for the year ended 28 February 20X1 were received which indicated a permanent decline in that company's financial position. Fabricators Ltd had bought shares in Patchup Ltd some years ago and this purchase was included in unquoted investments at its cost of £100,000. The financial statements received indicated that this investment was now worth only £50,000.

(b) There was a fire at the company's warehouse on 30 April 20X1 when stock to the value of £500,000 was destroyed. It transpired that the stock in the warehouse was under-insured by some 50%.

(c) It was announced on 1 June 20X1 that the company's design for tank cleaning equipment had been approved by the major oil companies and this could result in an increase in the annual turnover of some £1m with a relative effect on profits.

3 FRS 12 PROVISIONS, CONTINGENT LIABILITIES AND CONTINGENT ASSETS

3.1 As we have seen with regard to post balance sheet events, financial statements must include **all the information necessary for an understanding of the company's financial position**. Provisions, contingent liabilities and contingent assets are 'uncertainties' that must be accounted for consistently if are to achieve this understanding.

3.2 FRS 12 *Provisions, contingent liabilities and contingent assets* aims to ensure that appropriate **recognition criteria** and **measurement bases** are applied to provisions, contingent liabilities and contingent assets and that **sufficient information** is disclosed in the **notes** to the financial statements to enable users to understand their nature, timing and amount.

Provisions

3.3 You will be familiar with provisions for depreciation and doubtful debts from your earlier studies. The sorts of provisions addressed by FRS 12 are, however, rather different.

3.4 Before FRS 12, there was no accounting standard dealing with provisions. Companies wanting to show their results in the most favourable light used to make large '**one off' provisions** in years where a high level of underlying profits was generated. These provisions, often known as '**big bath**' provisions, were then available to shield expenditure in future years when perhaps the underlying profits were not as good.

3.5 In other words, **provisions were used for profit smoothing**. Profit smoothing is misleading.

> **IMPORTANT**
>
> The key aim of FRS 12 is to ensure that **provisions are made only where there are valid grounds for them**.

3.6 FRS 12 views a provision as a **liability**.

> **KEY TERMS**
>
> A **provision** is a **liability** of uncertain timing or amount.
>
> A **liability** is an obligation of an entity to transfer economic benefits as a result of past transactions or events. *(FRS 12)*

3.7 The FRS distinguishes provisions from other liabilities such as trade creditors and accruals. This is on the basis that for a provision there is **uncertainty** about the timing or amount of the future expenditure. Whilst uncertainty is clearly present in the case of certain accruals the uncertainty is generally much less than for provisions.

Recognition

3.8 FRS 12 states that a provision should be **recognised** as a liability in the financial statements when:

- An entity has a **present obligation** (legal or constructive) as a result of a past event
- It is probable that a **transfer of economic benefits** will be required to settle the obligation
- A **reliable estimate** can be made of the obligation

Meaning of obligation

3.9 It is fairly clear what a legal obligation is. However, you may not know what a **constructive obligation** is.

Part D: Accounting standards

> **KEY TERM**
>
> FRS 12 defines a **constructive obligation** as
>
> 'An obligation that derives from an entity's actions where:
>
> - By an established pattern of past practice, published policies or a sufficiently specific current statement the entity has indicated to other parties that it will accept certain responsibilities
> - As a result, the entity has created a valid expectation on the part of those other parties that it will discharge those responsibilities

---

Activity 11.3

In which of the following circumstances might a provision be recognised?

(a) On 13 December 20X9 the board of an entity decided to close down a division. The accounting date of the company is 31 December. Before 31 December 20X9 the decision was not communicated to any of those affected and no other steps were taken to implement the decision.

(b) The board agreed a detailed closure plan on 20 December 20X9 and details were given to customers and employees.

(c) A company is obliged to incur clean up costs for environmental damage (that has already been caused).

(d) A company intends to carry out future expenditure to operate in a particular way in the future.

Probable transfer of economic benefits

3.10 For the purpose of the FRS, a transfer of economic benefits is regarded as **'probable'** if the event is **more likely than not** to occur. This appears to indicate a probability of more than 50%. However, the standard makes it clear that where there is a number of similar obligations the probability should be based on considering the population as a whole, rather than one single item.

3.11 EXAMPLE: TRANSFER OF ECONOMIC BENEFITS

If a company has entered into a warranty obligation then the probability of transfer of economic benefits may well be extremely small in respect of one specific item. However, when considering the population as a whole the probability of some transfer of economic benefits is quite likely to be much higher. If there is a **greater than 50% probability** of some transfer of economic benefits then a **provision** should be made for the **expected amount**.

Measurement of provisions

> **IMPORTANT**
>
> The amount recognised as a provision should be the best estimate of the expenditure required to settle the present obligation at the balance sheet date.

3.12 The estimates will be determined by the **judgement** of the entity's management supplemented by the experience of similar transactions.

3.13 Allowance is made for **uncertainty**.

3.14 Where the effect of the **time value of money** is material, the amount of a provision should be the **present value** of the expenditure required to settle the obligation. An appropriate **discount** rate should be used.

Provisions for restructuring

3.15 One of the main purposes of FRS 12 was to target abuses of provisions for restructuring. Accordingly, FRS 12 lays down **strict criteria** to determine when such a provision can be made.

> **KEY TERM**
>
> FRS 12 defines a **restructuring** as:
>
> A programme that is planned and is controlled by management and materially changes either:
>
> - The scope of a business undertaken by an entity
> - The manner in which that business is conducted

3.16 The FRS gives the following **examples** of events that may fall under the definition of restructuring.

- The **sale or termination** of a line of business
- The **closure of business locations** in a country or region or the **relocation** of business activities from one country region to another
- **Changes in management structure**, for example, the elimination of a layer of management
- **Fundamental reorganisations** that have a material effect on the **nature and focus** of the entity's operations

3.17 The question is whether or not an entity has an obligation - legal or constructive - at the balance sheet date.

- An entity must have a **detailed formal plan** for the restructuring.
- It must have **raised a valid expectation** in those affected that it will carry out the restructuring by starting to implement that plan or announcing its main features to those affected by it

> **IMPORTANT**
>
> **A mere management decision is not normally sufficient.** Management decisions may sometimes trigger off recognition, but only if earlier events such as negotiations with employee representatives and other interested parties have been concluded subject only to management approval.

3.18 Where the restructuring involves the **sale of an operation** then FRS 12 states that no obligation arises until the entity has entered into a **binding sale agreement**. This is because until this has occurred the entity will be able to change its mind and withdraw from the sale even if its intentions have been announced publicly.

Costs to be included within a restructuring provision

3.19 The FRS states that a restructuring provision should include only the **direct expenditures** arising from the restructuring, which are those that are both:

- **Necessarily entailed** by the restructuring; and
- Not associated with the **ongoing activities** of the entity.

3.20 The following costs should specifically **not** be included within a restructuring provision.

- **Retraining** or relocating continuing staff
- **Marketing**
- **Investment in new systems** and distribution networks

Disclosure

3.21 Disclosures for provisions fall into two parts.

- Disclosure of details of the **change in carrying value** of a provision from the beginning to the end of the year
- Disclosure of the **background** to the making of the provision and the uncertainties affecting its outcome

Contingent liabilities

3.22 Now you understand provisions it will be easier to understand contingent assets and liabilities.

> **KEY TERM**
>
> FRS 12 defines a **contingent liability** as:
>
> - A possible obligation that arises from past events and whose existence will be confirmed only by the occurrence or non-occurrence of one or more uncertain future events not wholly within the entity's control; or
> - A present obligation that arises from past events but is not recognised because:
>   - It is not probable that a transfer of economic benefits will be required to settle the obligation; or
>   - The amount of the obligation cannot be measured with sufficient reliability.

3.23 As a rule of thumb, probable means more than 50% likely. **If an obligation is probable, it is not a contingent liability** - instead, a **provision is needed**.

Treatment of contingent liabilities

3.24 Contingent liabilities **should not be recognised in financial statements** but they **should be disclosed**. The required disclosures are:

- A brief description of the nature of the contingent liability

- An estimate of its financial effect
- An indication of the uncertainties that exist
- The possibility of any reimbursement

Contingent assets

KEY TERM

FRS 12 defines a **contingent asset** as:

A possible asset that arises from past events and whose existence will be confirmed by the occurrence of one or more uncertain future events not wholly within the entity's control.

3.25 **A contingent asset must not be recognised.** Only when the realisation of the related economic benefits is **virtually certain** should recognition take place. At that point, **the asset is not longer a contingent asset!**

3.26 Before trying Activity 11.5, study the flow chart, taken from FRS 12, which is a good summary of the requirements of the standard.

Exam alert

If you learn this flow chart you should be able to deal with most tasks you are likely to meet in a central assessment.

Activity 11.4

During 20X0 Smack Ltd gives a guarantee of certain borrowings of Pony Ltd, whose financial condition at that time is sound. During 20X1, the financial condition of Pony Ltd deteriorates and at 30 June 19Y0 Pony Ltd files for protection from its creditors.

What accounting treatment is required:

(a) At 31 December 20X0?
(b) At 31 December 20X1?

Section summary

3.27
- The objective of FRS 12 is to ensure that **appropriate recognition criteria** and measurement bases are applied to **provisions and contingencies** and that **sufficient information** is disclosed.

- The FRS seeks to ensure that provisions are **only recognised** when a **measurable obligation** exists. It includes detailed rules that can be used to ascertain when an obligation exists and how to measure the obligation.

- The standard attempts to **eliminate** the **'profit smoothing'** which has gone on before it was issued.

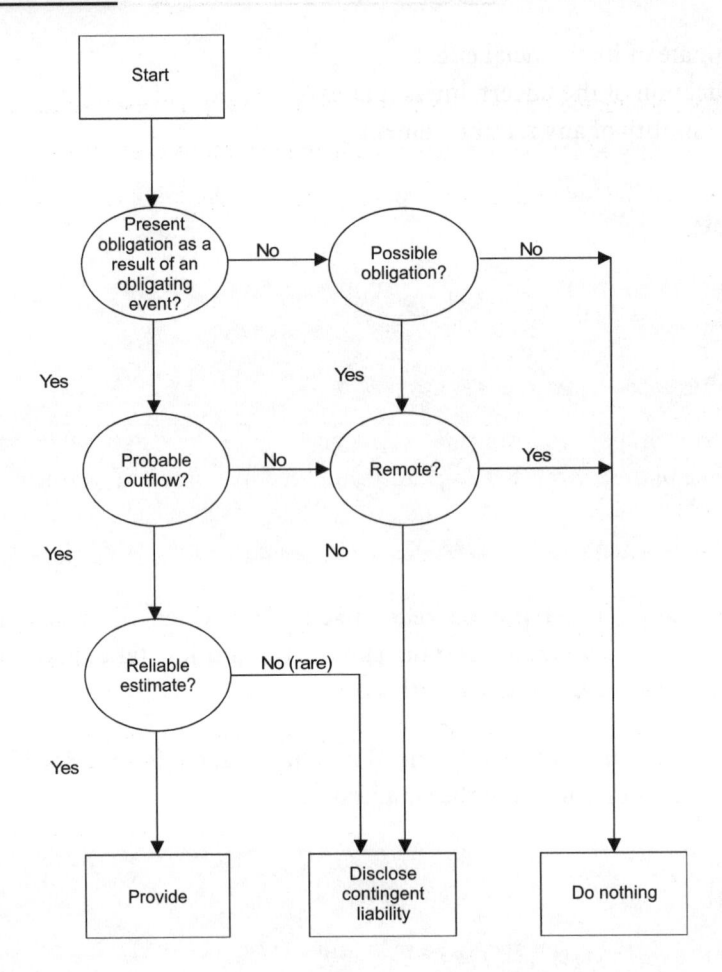

```
                    ┌─────────┐
                    │  Start  │
                    └────┬────┘
                         ↓
              ┌──────────────────┐    No    ┌──────────────┐    No
              │ Present          │─────────→│   Possible   │─────────→
              │ obligation as a  │          │  obligation? │
              │ result of an     │          └──────┬───────┘
              │ obligating event?│                 │
              └────────┬─────────┘                 │ Yes
                       │ Yes                       ↓
                       ↓                    ┌──────────────┐    Yes
              ┌──────────────┐    No        │   Remote?    │─────────→
              │  Probable    │─────────────→│              │
              │  outflow?    │              └──────┬───────┘
              └──────┬───────┘                     │ No
                     │ Yes                         │
                     ↓                             │
              ┌──────────────┐   No (rare)         │
              │  Reliable    │─────────────────────┤
              │  estimate?   │                     │
              └──────┬───────┘                     │
                     │ Yes                         │
                     ↓                             ↓                    ↓
              ┌───────────┐              ┌──────────────┐       ┌────────────┐
              │  Provide  │              │   Disclose   │       │ Do nothing │
              │           │              │  contingent  │       │            │
              │           │              │   liability  │       │            │
              └───────────┘              └──────────────┘       └────────────┘
```

Key learning points

- **FRS 21** defines *events after the balance sheet date.*

- **Events** after the balance sheet date which provide **additional evidence** of conditions existing at the balance sheet date, will cause **adjustments** to be made to the assets and liabilities in the financial statements.

- **Events** which **do not affect the situation at the balance sheet date** should **not be adjusted for**, but should be **disclosed** in the financial statements.

- Where events indicate that the **going concern concept** is no longer appropriate then the **accounts may have to be restated** on a break-up basis.

- Under FRS 12, a **provision** should be recognised
    - When an enterprise has a **present obligation**
    - It is **probable** that a **transfer of economic benefits** will be required to settle it
    - A **reliable estimate** can be made of its amount

- An entity should not recognise a contingent asset or liability, but they should be disclosed.

- You will certainly be given **practical examples** in the exam, so you must be able to apply the theory in the standard.

11: Contingencies and events after the balance sheet date

Quick quiz

1. When does an event after the balance sheet date require changes to the financial statements?
2. What treatment is required for dividends declared after the balance sheet date?
3. What disclosure is required when it is not possible to estimate the financial effect of an event not requiring adjustment?
4. How does FRS 12 define a contingent liability?
5. When should a contingent liability be recognised?

Answers to quick quiz

1. When the event assists in estimating amounts relating to conditions existing at the balance sheet date.
2. They must be disclosed by note.
3. A statement that it is not possible to estimate the amount must be made.
4. A possible obligation arising from past events whose existence will be confirmed only by the occurrence or non-occurrence of one or more uncertain future events not wholly within the entity's control; or a present obligation not recognised because it is not probable that a transfer of economic benefits will arise or the amount of the obligation cannot be measured with reasonable accuracy.
5. Never. If they are virtually certain they are recognised, but they then cease to be contingent.

Answers to activities

Answer 11.1

(b), (e) and (f) are adjusting; the others are non-adjusting.

Answer 11.2

The treatment of the events arising in the case of Fabricators Ltd would be as follows.

(a) The fall in value of the investment in Patchup Ltd has arisen over the previous year and that company's financial accounts for the year to 28 February 20X1 provide additional evidence of conditions that existed at the balance sheet date. The loss of £50,000 is material in terms of the trading profit figure and, as an adjusting event, should be reflected in the financial statements of Fabricators Ltd as an exceptional item in accordance with FRS 3.

(b) The destruction of stock by fire on 30 April (one month after the balance sheet date) must be considered to be a non-adjusting event (ie this is 'a new condition which did not exist at the balance sheet date'). Since the loss is material, being £250,000, it should be disclosed by way of a note to the accounts. The note should describe the nature of the event and an estimate of its financial effect. Non-reporting of this event would prevent users of the financial statements from reaching a proper understanding of the financial position.

(c) The approval on 1 June of the company's design for tank cleaning equipment creates a new condition which did not exist at the balance sheet date. This is, therefore, a non-adjusting event and if it is of such material significance that non-reporting would prevent a proper understanding of the financial position it should be disclosed by way of note. In this instance non-disclosure should not prevent a proper understanding of the financial position and disclosure by note may be unnecessary.

Answer 11.3

(a) No provision would be recognised as the decision has not been communicated.
(b) A provision would be made in the 20X9 financial statements.
(c) A provision for such costs is appropriate.

Part D: Accounting standards

(d) No present obligation exists and under FRS 12 no provision would be appropriate. This is because the entity could avoid the future expenditure by its future actions, maybe by changing its method of operation.

Answer 11.4

(a) *At 31 December 20X0*

There is a present obligation as a result of a past obligating event. The obligating event is the giving of the guarantee, which gives rise to a legal obligation. However, at 31 December 20X9 no transfer of economic benefits is probable in settlement of the obligation.

No provision is recognised. The guarantee is disclosed as a contingent liability unless the probability of any transfer is regarded as remote.

(b) *At 31 December 20X1*

As above, there is a present obligation as a result of a past obligating event, namely the giving of the guarantee.

At 31 December 20X1 it is probable that a transfer of economic events will be required to settle the obligation. A provision is therefore recognised for the best estimate of the obligation.

Now try Question 11 in the Exam Question Bank at the end of the Text.

Chapter 12 Intangibles and taxation

Chapter topic list

1. Goodwill
2. Research and development
3. Corporation tax
4. SSAP 5 and FRS 19
5. Taxation in company accounts
6. Disclosure requirements

The following study sessions are covered in this chapter.

		Syllabus reference
13(a)	Define current tax	2
13(b)	Account for current tax on the profits of companies (a detailed knowledge of deferred tax is not required)	2
13(c)	Draft appropriate disclosure in the published statements	2
14(a)	Define and calculate goodwill	2
14(b)	Distinguish between purchased and internally generated goodwill	2
14(c)	Explain and apply the accounting treatment for both types of goodwill	2
14(d)	Explain and apply the requirements of accounting standards for research and development	2

Part D: Accounting standards

1 GOODWILL

> **KEY TERM**
>
> If a business has **goodwill** it means that the value of the business as a going concern is greater than the value of its separate tangible assets.

1.1 Goodwill is created by good relationships between a business and its customers, for example:

   (a) By building up a reputation (by word of mouth perhaps) for high quality products or high standards of service

   (b) By responding promptly and helpfully to queries and complaints from customers

   (c) Through the personality of the staff and their attitudes to customers

1.2 The value of goodwill to a business might be extremely significant. However, **goodwill is not usually valued** in the accounts of a business at all, and we should not normally expect to find an amount for goodwill in its balance sheet.

1.3 For example, the welcoming smile of the bar staff may contribute more to a pub's profits than the fact that a new electronic cash register has recently been acquired; even so, whereas the cash register will be recorded in the accounts as a fixed asset, the value of staff would be ignored for accounting purposes.

1.4 On reflection, this omission of goodwill from the accounts of a business might be easy to understand.

   (a) The goodwill is inherent in the business but it has not been paid for, and it does not have an 'objective' value. We can guess at what such goodwill is worth, but such guesswork would be a matter of individual opinion, and not based on hard facts.

   (b) Goodwill changes from day to day. One act of bad customer relations might damage goodwill and one act of good relations might improve it. Staff with a favourable personality might retire or leave to find another job, to be replaced by staff who need time to find their feet in the job, etc. Since goodwill is continually changing in value, it cannot realistically be recorded in the accounts of the business.

Purchased goodwill

1.5 There is one exception to the general rule that goodwill has no objective valuation. This is when a business is sold. People wishing to set up in business have a choice of how to do it - they can either buy their own fixed assets and stock and set up their business from scratch, or they can buy up an existing business from a proprietor willing to sell it.

1.6 When a buyer purchases an existing business, he will have to purchase not only its fixed assets and stocks (and perhaps take over its creditors and debtors too) but also the goodwill of the business.

1.7 **EXAMPLE: GOODWILL**

For example, suppose that Tony Tycoon agrees to purchase the business of Clive Dunwell for £30,000. Clive's business has net fixed assets valued at £14,000 and net current assets of

£11,000, all of which are taken over by Tony. Tony will be paying more for the business than its tangible assets are worth, because he is purchasing the goodwill of the business too. The balance sheet of Tony's business when it begins operations (assuming that he does not change the value of the tangible fixed and current assets) will be:

TONY TYCOON
BALANCE SHEET AS AT THE START OF BUSINESS

	£
Intangible fixed asset: goodwill	5,000
Tangible fixed assets: net book value	14,000
Net current assets	11,000
Net assets	30,000
Capital	30,000

1.8 Purchased goodwill is shown in this balance sheet because it has been paid for. It has no tangible substance, and so it is an intangible fixed asset.

KEY TERM

Purchased goodwill has been defined as 'the excess of the price paid for a business over the fair market value of the individual assets and liabilities acquired'.

Activity 12.1

To make sure that you understand goodwill, try a solution to the following quick exercise.

Toad goes into business with £10,000 capital and agrees to buy Thrush's shoe-repair shop in the centre of a busy town for £6,500. Thrush's recent accounts show net assets of £3,500, which Toad values at £4,000.

Required

Prepare the balance sheet of Toad's business:

(a) Before he purchases Thrush's business
(b) After the purchase

The accounting treatment of purchased goodwill

1.9 Once purchased goodwill appears in the accounts of a business, we must decide what to do with it. Purchased goodwill is basically a premium paid for the acquisition of a business as a going concern: indeed, it is often referred to as a 'premium on acquisition'. When a purchaser agrees to pay such a premium for goodwill, he does so because he believes that the true value of the business is worth more to him than the value of its tangible assets.

1.10 One major reason why he might think so is that the business will earn good profits over the next few years, and so he will pay a premium now to get the business, in the expectation of getting his money back later. However, he pays for the goodwill at the time of purchase, and the value of the goodwill will eventually wear off.

1.11 Goodwill, it was suggested earlier, is a continually changing thing. A business cannot last forever on its past reputation; it must create new goodwill as time goes on. Even goodwill created by a favourable location might suddenly disappear - for example, a newsagent's shop by a bus stop will lose its location value if the bus route is axed by the local transport authorities.

1.12 Since goodwill wears off, and is basically unstable anyway, it is generally inadvisable to keep purchased goodwill indefinitely in the accounts of a business.

Accounting treatment of goodwill

1.13 The accounting treatment specified in FRS 10 is as follows.

(a) If the value of goodwill in the acquired business was **significant** and if it was expected to be **maintained indefinitely** and to be **readily measurable** in future the purchased goodwill would not be written down, unless an **annual impairment review** showed a diminution in value.

(b) If however the life of the goodwill within the business was expected to be **limited**, if **annual impairment reviews** would not be feasible, or if the value of the goodwill was **not significant**, the purchased goodwill would be amortised on a systematic basis.

(c) There would be a **rebuttable presumption** that the life of goodwill within a business was limited and did not exceed 20 years. The amortisation period would be restricted to 20 years unless there were valid and disclosed grounds, based on the nature of the underlying investment, for believing the life to be longer.

How is the value of purchased goodwill decided?

1.14 When a business is sold, there is likely to be some purchased goodwill in the selling price. But how is the amount of this purchased goodwill decided?

1.15 This is not really a problem for accountants, who must simply record the goodwill in the accounts of the new business. The value of the goodwill is a matter for the purchaser and seller to agree upon in fixing the purchase/sale price. However, two methods of valuation are worth mentioning here.

(a) The seller and buyer agree on a price without specifically quantifying the goodwill. The purchased goodwill will then be the difference between the price agreed and the value of the tangible assets in the books of the new business.

(b) However, the calculation of goodwill often precedes the fixing of the purchase price and becomes a central element of negotiation. There are many ways of arriving at a value for goodwill and most of them are related to the profit record of the business in question. Some of these ways are illustrated below.

1.16 EXAMPLES: METHODS OF VALUING GOODWILL

For an illustration of a few possible methods, let us suppose that a business being sold on 31.12.X3 has recently generated profits as follows:

Year ending 31.12.X1 - £4,000
Year ending 31.12.X2 - £5,000
Year ending 31.12.X3 - £7,000
Capital employed £20,000

Goodwill might be valued at:

(a) twice the final year's profit - ie 2 × £7,000 =   £14,000

or

(b) twice the average profit for the past three years

ie $2 \times \dfrac{£4,000 + £5,000 + £7,000}{3}$ £10,667

or perhaps

(c) three times the average profit for the past two years

ie $3 \times \dfrac{£5,000 + £7,000}{2} =$ £18,000

(d) Alternatively the 'super profits' approach could be used. This relates the profit to the capital employed in one of a number of ways. Let us assume that in this particular business a reasonable return on capital employed would be 10% and that a reasonable salary for the proprietor would be £4,000. For the year 20X3 the return on the proprietor's funds, in excess of the salary that he could earn elsewhere, is therefore £3,000.

We could say:

(i) the £3,000 represents a 10% return on the assets of the business; the assets must therefore be:

$\dfrac{100}{10} \times £3,000 =$ £30,000

Of the £30,000 we know that £20,000 exists in tangible form (net assets employed). Therefore the remaining £10,000 must be intangible, ie goodwill is £10,000.

In other words as well as our 10% return on tangible assets (£20,000 × 10% = £2,000) our intangible asset, goodwill, earns us a further £1,000 (£10,000 × 10%) which is the 'super profit';

(ii) we could regard the intangible asset as having limited life and purchase, say seven years 'super profits'

Goodwill would therefore be $7 \times £1,000 =$ £7,000

Many other variations are possible. A formula may be agreed between vendor and purchaser in advance or there may be much haggling to reach agreement. The goodwill element of the purchase price is of course additional to the value of tangible assets acquired.

1.17 Any attempt to quantify goodwill in financial terms is purely arbitrary. Using the above methods we have calculated goodwill as high as £18,000 and as low as £7,000. Neither of these figures is the 'correct' figure because there is no correct figure; once a basis for the calculation has been agreed (eg two years purchase of average profits for the past three years) then a figure can be arrived at, but selection of the basis is entirely subjective.

Exam alert

In practice, examination questions will always tell you the basis on which goodwill is to be calculated, and it will usually be some version of methods (a) to (c) above. The 'super profits' concept is generally considered rather old-fashioned, but it is mentioned for completeness.

1.18 No matter how goodwill is calculated within the total agreed purchase price, the goodwill shown by the purchaser in his accounts will be the difference between the purchase consideration and his own valuation of the tangible net assets acquired. If A values his

Part D: Accounting standards

tangible net assets at £40,000, goodwill is agreed at £21,000 and B agrees to pay £61,000 for the business but values the tangible net assets at only £38,000, then the goodwill in B's books will be £61,000 − £38,000 = £23,000.

2 RESEARCH AND DEVELOPMENT

2.1 Large companies may spend significant amounts of money on **research and development** (R & D) activities. Obviously, any amounts so expended must be credited to cash and debited to an account for research and development expenditure. The accounting problem is how to treat the debit balance on R & D account at the balance sheet date.

2.2 There are two possibilities.

(a) The debit balance may be classified as an **expense** and transferred to the profit and loss account. This is referred to as 'writing off' the expenditure.

(b) The debit balance may be classified as an **asset** and included in the balance sheet. This is referred to as 'capitalising' or 'carrying forward' or 'deferring' the expenditure.

2.3 The argument for writing off R & D expenditure is that it is an expense just like rates or wages and its accounting treatment should be the same.

The argument for carrying forward R & D expenditure is based on the accruals concept. If R & D activity eventually leads to new or improved products which generate revenue, the costs should be carried forward to be matched against that revenue in future accounting periods.

2.4 Like goodwill, R & D expenditure is the subject of an accounting standard, SSAP 13 *Accounting for research and development*. SSAP 13 defines research and development expenditure as falling into one or more of the following categories.

(a) **Pure research** is original research to obtain new scientific or technical knowledge or understanding. There is no clear commercial end in view and such research work does not have a practical application. Companies and other business entities might carry out this type of research in the hope that it will provide new knowledge which can subsequently be exploited.

(b) **Applied research** is original research work which also seeks to obtain new scientific or technical knowledge, but which has a specific practical aim or application (eg research on improvements in the effectiveness of toothpastes or medicines etc). Applied research may develop from 'pioneering' pure research, but many companies have full-time research teams working on applied research projects.

(c) **Development** is the use of existing scientific and technical knowledge to produce new (or substantially improved) products or systems, prior to starting commercial production operations.

How do we distinguish these categories?

2.5 The dividing line between each of these categories will often be indistinct in practice, and some expenditure might be classified as research or as development. It may be even more difficult to distinguish development costs from production costs. For example, if a prototype model of a new product is developed and then sold to a customer, the costs of the prototype will include both development and production expenditure.

12: Intangibles and taxation

2.6 SSAP 13 states that although there may be practical difficulties in isolating research costs and development costs, there is a difference of principle in the method of accounting for each type of expenditure.

(a) (i) Expenditure on pure and applied research is usually a continuing operation which is necessary to ensure a company's survival.

(ii) One accounting period does not gain more than any other from such work, and it is therefore appropriate that research costs should be written off as they are incurred (ie in the year of expenditure).

(iii) This conforms with CA 1985, which seems not to envisage the capitalisation of research expenditure in any circumstances.

(b) (i) The development of new and improved products is different, because development expenditure is incurred with a particular commercial aim in view and in the reasonable expectation of earning profits or reducing costs.

(ii) In these circumstances it is appropriate that development costs should be deferred (capitalised) and matched against the future revenues.

Exam alert
If you are in a hurry, or revising, read the SECTOR mnemonic below.

2.7 SSAP 13 attempts to restrict indiscriminate deferrals of development expenditure and states that development costs may only be deferred to future periods, when the following criteria are met.

(a) There must be a **clearly defined development project**, and the related expenditure on this project is separately identifiable.

(b) The **expected outcome** of the project must have been assessed, and there should be **reasonable certainty** that:

(i) It is **technically feasible**

(ii) It is **commercially viable**, having regard to market conditions, competition, public opinion and consumer and environmental legislation

(c) The **eventual profits** from the developed product or system should reasonably be expected to **cover the past and future development costs.**

(d) The company should have **adequate resources to complete** the development project.

If *any* of these conditions are not satisfied the development costs should be written off in the year of expenditure.

2.8 The following mnemonic may be helpful. Remember: SECTOR.

S	Separately defined project
E	Expenditure separately identifiable
C	Commercially viable
T	Technically feasible
O	Overall profit expected
R	Resources exist to complete project

Part D: Accounting standards

2.9 Where development expenditure is deferred to future periods, its **amortisation should begin with the commencement of production**, and should then be written off over the period in which the product is expected to be sold. Deferred development expenditure should be reviewed at the end of every accounting period. If the conditions which justified the deferral of the expenditure no longer apply or are considered doubtful, the deferred expenditure, to the extent that it is now considered to be irrecoverable, should be written off.

2.10 Development expenditure once written off can now be reinstated, if the uncertainties which had led to its being written off no longer apply. This was not permitted by the original SSAP 13, but has been amended because the CA 1985 does permit the reinstatement of costs previously written off.

2.11 EXAMPLES OF R & D ITEMS

Examples given by SSAP 13 (revised) of activities that would normally be **included** in R & D are:

(a) Experimental, theoretical or other work aimed at the discovery of new knowledge or the advancement of existing knowledge.

(b) Searching for applications of that knowledge.

(c) Formulation and design of possible applications for such work.

(d) Testing in search for, or evaluation of, product, service or process alternatives.

(e) Design, construction and testing of pre-production prototypes and models and development batches.

(f) Design of products, services, processes or systems involving new technology or substantially improving those already produced or installed.

(g) Construction and operation of pilot plants.

2.12 EXAMPLES OF NON R & D ITEMS

Examples of activities that would normally be **excluded** from research and development include:

(a) Testing and analysis either of equipment or product for purposes of quality or quantity control.

(b) Periodic alterations to existing products, services or processes even though these may represent some improvement.

(c) Operational research not tied to a specific research and development activity.

(d) Cost of corrective action in connection with break-downs during commercial production.

(e) Legal and administrative work in connection with patent applications, records and litigation and the sale or licensing of patents.

(f) Activity, including design and construction engineering, relating to the construction, relocation, rearrangement or start-up of facilities or equipment other than facilities or equipment whose sole use is for a particular research and development project.

(g) Market research.

Under the revised SSAP 13, a company can still defer the expenditure under the accruals concept (if it is prudent so to do) but it must be disclosed entirely separately from deferred development expenditure.

2.13 EXAMPLES OF ITEMS EXCLUDED FROM SSAP 13

The above provisions of SSAP 13 do not extend to the following cases.

(a) Expenditure on tangible fixed assets acquired or constructed to provide facilities for research and/or development activities should be capitalised and depreciated over their useful lives in the usual way. However, the depreciation may be capitalised as part of deferred development expenditure if the development work for which the assets are used meets the criteria given above.

(b) Expenditure incurred in locating mineral deposits in extractive industries is outside the scope of SSAP 13.

(c) Expenditure incurred where there is a firm contract to:

   (i) carry out development work on behalf of third parties on such terms that the related expenditure is to be fully reimbursed; or

   (ii) develop and manufacture at an agreed price which has been calculated to reimburse expenditure on development as well as on manufacture

is not to be treated as deferred development expenditure.

Any such expenditure which has not been reimbursed at the balance sheet date should be included in work in progress.

Activity 12.2

Tank Top Ltd has purchased a tank for £50,000. The purpose of the tank is to investigate the possibility of growing food under water. What would be the appropriate accounting treatment for this item as per SSAP 13?

Disclosure requirements

2.14 The Companies Act 1985 does not require disclosure of the total amount of R & D expenditure during an accounting period, but SSAP 13 (revised) requires that all large companies (defined below) should disclose this total, distinguishing between current year expenditure and amortisation of deferred development expenditure.

2.15 SSAP 13 (revised) requires the following companies to disclose R & D expenditure.

   (a) All public companies

   (b) All special category companies (ie banking and insurance companies)

   (c) All holding companies with a plc or special category company as a subsidiary

   (d) All companies who satisfy the criteria, multiplied by 10, for defining a medium-sized company

This means that, currently, a private company will be exempted if it is not itself (and does not control) a special category company and it meets two of the following criteria:

Part D: Accounting standards

- Turnover ≤ £112 million
- Total assets (*before* deduction of current or long-term liabilities) ≤ £56 million
- ≤ 2,500 employees

2.16 Where deferred development costs are included in a company's balance sheet the following information must be given in the notes to the accounts:

(a) Movements on deferred development expenditure, and the amount brought forward and carried forward at the beginning and end of the period.

(b) The accounting policy used to account for R & D expenditure should be clearly explained.

3 CORPORATION TAX

3.1 Companies are required to pay **corporation tax** on their taxable profits. The **taxable profits** of a company are essentially its net profit before dividends, adjusted for certain items where the tax treatment differs from the accounts treatment.

3.2 The rate at which companies are charged to corporation tax depends on the level of their profits. Companies with small profits currently (2003) pay corporation tax at a rate of 19%; other companies currently pay at a rate of 30%.

3.3 The amount of tax to which a company is assessed on its profit for an accounting period is called its **tax liability** for that period. In general, a company must pay its tax liability nine months after the end of the relevant accounting period.

4 SSAP 5 AND FRS 19

SSAP 5 *Accounting for value added tax*

4.1 VAT is a tax on the **supply of goods and services**. The tax authority responsible for collecting VAT is HM Customs & Excise. Tax is collected at each transfer point in the chain from prime producer to final consumer. Eventually, the consumer bears the tax in full and any tax paid earlier in the chain can be recovered by the trader who paid it.

> **Exam alert**
> You've covered VAT in detail in your earlier studies, so you are more likely to be tested on the disclosure requirements of SSAP 5 in Paper 6.

4.2 EXAMPLE: VAT

A manufacturing company, A Ltd, purchases raw materials at a cost of £1,000 plus VAT at 17½%. From the raw materials A Ltd makes finished products which it sells to a retail outlet, B Ltd, for £1,600 plus VAT. B Ltd sells the products to customers at a total price of £2,000 plus VAT. How much VAT is paid to Customs & Excise at each stage in the chain?

4.3 SOLUTION

	Value of goods sold £	VAT at 17½% £
Supplier of raw materials	1,000	175
Value added by A Ltd	600	105
Sale to B Ltd	1,600	280
Value added by B Ltd	400	70
Sales to 'consumers'	2,000	350

How is VAT collected?

4.4 Although it is the final consumer who eventually bears the full tax of £350, the sum is **collected and paid over to Customs & Excise by the traders who make up the chain.** Each trader must assume that his customer is the final consumer and must collect and pay over VAT at the appropriate rate on the full sales value of the goods sold. He is entitled to reclaim VAT paid on his own purchases (inputs) and so makes a net payment to Customs & Excise equal to the tax on value added by himself.

4.5 In the example above, the supplier of raw materials collects from A Ltd VAT of £175, all of which he pays over to Customs & Excise. When A Ltd sells goods to B Ltd VAT is charged at the rate of 17½% on £1,600 = £280. Only £105, however, is paid by A Ltd to Customs & Excise because the company is entitled to deduct VAT of £175 suffered on its own purchases. Similarly, B Ltd must charge its customers £350 in VAT but need only pay over the net amount of £70 after deducting the £280 VAT suffered on its purchase from A Ltd.

Registered and non-registered persons

4.6 Traders whose sales (outputs) are below a certain minimum need not register for VAT. Such traders neither charge VAT on their outputs nor are entitled to reclaim VAT on their inputs. They are in the same position as a final consumer.

4.7 All outputs of registered traders are either **taxable** or **exempt**. Traders carrying on exempt activities (such as banks) cannot charge VAT on their outputs and consequently cannot reclaim VAT paid on their inputs.

4.8 Taxable outputs are chargeable at one of **two rates**

(a) Zero per cent (**zero-rated items**)
(b) 17½% (**standard-rated items**)

Customs & Excise publish lists of supplies falling into each category. Persons carrying on taxable activities (even activities taxable at zero per cent) are entitled to reclaim VAT paid on their inputs.

4.9 Some traders carry on a mixture of taxable and exempt activities. Such traders need to apportion the VAT suffered on inputs and can only reclaim the proportion relating to taxable outputs.

Accounting for VAT

4.10 As a general principle the treatment of VAT in the accounts of a trader should reflect his role as a collector of the tax and **VAT should not be included in income or in expenditure whether of a capital or of a revenue nature.**

Part D: Accounting standards

4.11 Where the **trader bears the VAT** himself, as in the following cases, this should be reflected in the accounts.

(a) **Persons not registered** for VAT will suffer VAT on inputs. This will effectively increase the cost of their consumable materials and their fixed assets and must be so reflected, ie shown **inclusive of VAT.**

(b) **Registered persons** who also carry on **exempted** activities will have a residue of VAT which falls directly on them. In this situation the costs to which this residue applies will be inflated by the **irrecoverable VAT**.

(c) **Non-deductible inputs will be borne** by all traders (examples are tax on cars bought which are not for resale, entertaining expenses and provision of domestic accommodation for a company's directors).

Further points

4.12 VAT is charged on the price net of any discount and this general principle is carried to the extent that where a cash discount is offered, VAT is charged on the net amount even where the discount is not taken up.

4.13 Most VAT registered persons are obliged to record VAT when a supply is received or made (effectively when a credit sales invoice is raised or a purchase invoice recorded). This has the effect that the net VAT liability has on occasion to be paid to Customs & Excise before all output tax has been paid by customers. If a debt is subsequently written off, the VAT element may not be recovered from Customs & Excise for six months from the date of sale, even if the customer becomes insolvent.

4.14 Some small businesses can join the cash accounting scheme whereby VAT is only paid to Customs & Excise after it is received from customers. This delays recovery of input tax but improves cash flow overall, although it may involve extra record keeping. Bad debt relief is automatic under this scheme since if VAT is not paid by the customer it is not due to Customs & Excise.

Activity 12.3

Mussel Ltd is preparing accounts for the year ended 31 May 20X9. Included in its balance sheet as at 31 May 20X8 was a balance for VAT recoverable of £15,000.

Its summary profit and loss account for the year is as follows.

	£'000
Sales (all standard rated)	500
Purchases (all standard rated)	120
Gross profit	380
Expenses	280
Operating profit	100
Interest receivable	20
Profit before tax	120
Note: expenses	
Wages and salaries	200
Entertainment expenditure	10
Other (all standard rated)	70
	280

Payments of £5,000, £15,000 and £20,000 have been made in the year and a repayment of £12,000 was received. What is the balance for VAT in the balance sheet as at 31 May 20X9? Assume a 17.5% standard rate of VAT.

12: Intangibles and taxation

Requirements of SSAP 5

4.15 SSAP 5 requires the following accounting rules to be followed.

(a) **Turnover** shown in the profit and loss account should **exclude VAT** on taxable outputs. If gross turnover must be shown then the VAT in that figure must also be shown as a deduction in arriving at the turnover exclusive of VAT.

(b) **Irrecoverable VAT** allocated to fixed assets and other items separately disclosed should be **included in their cost** where material and practical.

(c) The **net amount due to (or from) Customs & Excise** should be included in the **total for creditors** (or **debtors**), and need not be separately disclosed.

4.16 Note that the CA 1985 also requires disclosure of the cost of sales figure in the published accounts. This amount should exclude VAT on taxable inputs.

FRS 19 *Deferred tax*

4.17 Accounting profits form the basis for computing **taxable profits**, on which the corporation tax liability for the year is calculated; however accounting profits and taxable profits are different. There are two reasons for the differences.

(a) **Permanent differences**. These occur when certain items of revenue or expense are excluded from the computation of taxable profits (for example, entertainment expenses are not normally allowable for tax purposes).

(b) **Originating timing differences**. These occur when items of revenue or expense are included in both accounting profits and taxable profits, but not for the same accounting period. For example, an expense which is allowable as a deduction in arriving at taxable profits for 20X7 might not be included in the financial accounts until 20X8 or later. In the long run, the total taxable profits and total accounting profits will be the same (except for permanent differences) so that:

> 'timing differences originate in one period and are capable of reversal in one or more subsequent periods.'

4.18 Deferred tax is the tax attributable to *timing differences*. **Deferred tax applies the matching concept to taxation, in an attempt to produce less distorted results**. Income recorded in a period is matched with the related tax charge, even though that income may be taxed in a different period, ie deferred tax provides for future tax liabilities.

4.19 FRS 19 identifies the main categories in which timing differences can occur.

(a) **Accelerated capital allowances.** Tax deductions for the cost of a fixed asset are accelerated or decelerated, ie received before or after the cost of the fixed asset is recognised in the profit and loss account.

(b) **Pension liabilities** are accrued in the financial statements but are allowed for tax purposes only when paid or contributed at a later date.

(c) **interest charges or development costs** are capitalised on the balance sheet but are treated as revenue expenditure and allowed as incurred for tax purposes.

(d) **Intragroup profits in stock**, unrealised at group level, are reversed on consolidation.

(e) **Revaluations.** An asset is revalued in the financial statements but the revaluation gain becomes taxable only if and when the asset is sold.

Part D: Accounting standards

(f) **Unrelieved tax losses.** A tax loss is not relieved against past or present taxable profits but can be carried forward to reduce future taxable profits.

(g) **Unremitted earnings of subsidiaries.** The unremitted earnings of subsidiary and associated undertakings and joint ventures are recognised in the group results but will be subject to further taxation only if and when remitted to the parent undertaking.

> **Exam alert**
> You will not need to calculate the deferred tax balance in the exam or have a detailed knowledge of deferred tax.

4.20 You may need to know the following for your exam.

(a) A **provision** is made for timing differences. Like a doubtful debts provision, this may be increased from year to year, any increase being charged to the profit and loss account for the year.

(b) The deferred tax account is a credit balance and comes under 'provisions for liabilities and charges' in the published balance sheet of a company.

5 TAXATION IN COMPANY ACCOUNTS

5.1 We have now looked at the 'ingredients' of taxation in company accounts. There are two aspects to be learned

(a) Taxation on profits in the profit and loss account
(b) Taxation payments due, shown as a liability in the balance sheet

Taxation in the profit and loss account

5.2 The tax on profit on ordinary activities is calculated by **aggregating**:

- **Corporation tax** on taxable profits
- **Transfers to or from deferred** taxation
- Any **under provision or overprovision** of corporation tax on profits of previous years

5.3 When corporation tax on profits is calculated for the profit and loss account, the calculation is only an estimate of what the company thinks its tax liability will be. In subsequent dealings with the Inland Revenue, a different corporation tax charge might eventually be agreed.

5.4 The difference between the estimated tax on profits for one year and the actual tax charge finally agreed for the year is made as an adjustment to taxation on profits in the following year, resulting in the disclosure of either an **underprovision** of tax or an **overprovision** of tax.

Activity 12.4

In the accounting year to 31 December 20X3, Ben Nevis Ltd made an operating profit before investment income and taxation of £110,000. Income from dividends was £15,000 (that is, without the associated tax credit).

Corporation tax on the operating profit has been estimated as £45,000.

In the previous year (20X2) corporation tax on 20X2 profits had been estimated as £38,000 but it was subsequently agreed at £40,500 with the Inland Revenue.

A transfer to the deferred taxation account of £16,000 will be made in 20X3.

Required

Calculate the tax on profits for 20X3 for disclosure in the accounts.

Taxation in the balance sheet

5.5 It should already be apparent from the previous examples that the corporation tax charge in the profit and loss account will not be the same as corporation tax liabilities in the balance sheet.

5.6 In the balance sheet, there are several items which we might expect to find.

   (a) **Income tax may be payable** in respect of (say) interest payments paid in the last accounting return period of the year, or accrued.

   (b) If no corporation tax is payable (or very little), then there might be an **income tax recoverable asset** disclosed in current assets (income tax is normally recovered by offset against the tax liability for the year).

   (c) There will usually be a **liability for mainstream corporation tax**, possibly including the amounts due in respect of previous years but not yet paid.

   (d) We may also find a **liability on the deferred taxation account**. Deferred taxation is shown under 'provisions for liabilities and charges' in the balance sheet.

6 DISCLOSURE REQUIREMENTS

6.1 The CA 1985 requires that the **'tax on profit or loss on ordinary activities' is disclosed on the face of the profit and loss account or in a note to the accounts.** In addition, the notes to the profit and loss account must state:

   (a) The **basis** on which the charge for UK corporation tax and UK income tax is computed

   (b) The **amounts** of the charge for:

      (i) UK corporation tax (showing separately the amount, if greater, of UK corporation tax before any double taxation relief)

      (ii) UK income tax

      (iii) Non-UK taxation on profits, income and capital gains

(*Note*. The same details must be given, if relevant, in respect of the 'tax on extraordinary profit or loss'.)

FRS 16

6.2 FRS 16 *Current tax* specifies how current tax should be reflected in financial statements. Current tax should be recognised in the **profit and loss account for the period,** except to the extent that it is attributable to a gain or loss that has been recognised directly in the statement of total recorded gains and losses.

6.3 Where a gain or loss has been recognised directly in the statement of total recognised gains and losses, the tax relating to that gain or loss should also be recognised directly in that statement.

Part D: Accounting standards

6.4 Dividends, interest and other amounts payable or receivable should be recognised at an amount that:

(a) **Includes withholding taxes** payable to the tax authorities wholly on behalf of the recipient

(b) **Excludes any other taxes, such as attributable tax credits**, not payable wholly on behalf of the recipient.

6.5 Subject to the above, income and expenses should be included in the pre-tax results on the basis of the **income or expenses actually receivable or payable**, without any adjustment to reflect a notional amount of tax that would have been paid or relieved in respect of the transaction if it had been taxable, or allowable for tax purposes, on a different basis.

6.6 Current tax should be measured using tax rates and laws that have been enacted or substantively enacted by the balance sheet date.

6.7 EXAMPLE: CURRENT TAX

Taxus Ltd made a profit of £1,000,000. It received a dividend of £80,000 on which there was a tax credit of £20,000. From an overseas company it received a dividend of £3,000 on which 25% withholding tax had been deducted. The corporation tax charge was £300,000.

Required

Show how this information would be presented in the financial statements in accordance with FRS 16 *Current tax*.

6.8 SOLUTION

	£
Operating profit	1,000,000
Income from fixed asset investments	
UK (note 1)	80,000
Foreign (note 2)	4,000
Profit before tax	1,084,000
Taxation (note 3)	301,000
Profit after tax	783,000

Notes

1 Excludes tax credit.

2 Includes withholding tax: £3,000 + £1,000 = £4,000. Read the question carefully - 25% had been deducted already.

3 Add back withholding tax of £1,000.

12: Intangibles and taxation

Key learning points

- If a business has **goodwill**, it means that the value of the business as a going concern is greater than the value of its separate tangible assets.
  - The valuation of goodwill is extremely subjective and fluctuates constantly.
  - For this reason, goodwill is not normally shown as an asset in the balance sheet.

- The exception to this rule is **purchased goodwill,** when someone purchases a business as a going concern. In this case the purchaser and vendor will fix an agreed price which includes an element in respect of goodwill. The way in which goodwill is then valued is not an accounting problem, but a matter of agreement between the two parties.

- **Purchased** goodwill should **normally** be **amortised** as an expense in the profit and loss account but it may be retained in the balance sheet. If it is retained in the balance sheet without amortisation, annual impairment reviews must be performed.

- Expenditure on **research** activities must always be **written off** in the period in which it is incurred.

- Expenditure on **development** activities may also be written off in the same way. But if the criteria laid down by SSAP 13 are satisfied, such expenditure *may* be **capitalised** as an intangible asset. It must then be amortised, beginning from the time when the development project is brought into commercial production.

- Companies pay **corporation tax** on their profits. Taxable profits are net profit before dividends adjusted for items where the tax treatment differs from the accounts treatment.

- Generally **VAT** is **not included** in the accounts of a trader in income and expenditure.

- You should learn how to calculate the tax charge in the profit and loss account, the mainstream corporation tax liability in the balance sheet and the presentation of both in the published accounts of companies per **FRS 16**.

Quick quiz

1. Why is it unusual to record goodwill as an asset in the accounts?
2. What is purchased goodwill?
3. What method of accounting for purchased goodwill is permitted by FRS 10?
4. How is the amount of purchased goodwill calculated?
5. What is the required accounting treatment for expenditure on research?
6. In what circumstances may development costs be recognised as an asset?
7. When can a write down of capitalised development be recognised as an asset?
8. What is the SSAP 5 requirement relating to disclosure of turnover in company accounts?
9. What are the components of the profit and loss figure for 'tax on profit on ordinary activities'?

Answers to quick quiz

1. Goodwill does not have an objective value and it fluctuates.
2. The excess of the price paid for a business over the fair market value of the individual assets and liabilities acquired.
3. Capitalise and amortise or keep in the balance sheet, subject to impairment.
4. Various methods may be used, eg twice the final year's profit, twice the average profit for the past three years or use the 'super profit' approach.
5. It is an expense in the period in which it was incurred.
6. Apply the SECTOR criteria (see paragraph 2.8)

Part D: Accounting standards

7   If the events that led to the write off cease to exist and there is persuasive evidence that the new circumstances will persist for the foreseeable future.

8   Turnover must be shown exclusive of VAT

9   Corporation tax on taxable profits *plus* transfer to or from deferred taxation *plus* any over or under provision of corporation tax on profits of previous years.

Answers to activities

Answer 12.1

(a) Toad's balance sheet before the purchase is:

	£
Cash	10,000
Proprietor's interest	10,000

(b) Thrush's valuation of the assets to be acquired is irrelevant to Toad who sees the situation thus:

	£
Consideration (cash to be paid)	6,500
Less net assets acquired (at Toad's valuation)	4,000
Difference (= goodwill)	2,500

Toad must credit his cash book with the £6,500 paid. He can only debit sundry assets with £4,000. A further debit of £2,500 is thus an accounting necessity and he must open up a goodwill account.

Toad's balance sheet immediately after the transfer would therefore be:

	£
Goodwill	2,500
Sundry assets	4,000
Cash (£10,000 - £6,500)	3,500
	10,000
Proprietor's interest	10,000

(Normally one would have more detail as to the breakdown of the sundry assets into fixed assets, current assets etc, but this is not relevant to the illustration. The main point is that the sundry assets acquired are tangible whereas the goodwill is not.)

This exercise highlights the difference between 'internally generated' goodwill, which (as in Thrush's case above) is not shown in the books and 'purchased' goodwill, which is. The purchased goodwill in this case is simply Thrush's internally generated goodwill, which has changed hands, bought by Toad at a price shown in Toad's accounts.

Answer 12.2

SSAP 13 states that expenditure on tangible fixed assets acquired or constructed to provide facilities for research and/or development activities should be capitalised and depreciated over their useful lives in the usual way. The depreciation may be capitalised as part of deferred development expenditure if the development work for which the assets are used meets the criteria given in the SSAP. However, since the tank is for pure research, this does not apply.

Answer 12.3

MUSSEL LIMITED: VAT ACCOUNT

	£		£
Balance b/d	15,000	Sales (£500,000 × 17.5%)	87,500
Purchases (£120,000 × 17.5%)	21,000	Bank	12,000
Expenses (£70,000 × 17.5%)	12,250		
Bank	40,000		
Balance c/d	11,250		
	99,500		99,500

Answer 12.4

	£
Corporation tax on profits	45,000
Deferred taxation	16,000
Underprovision of tax in previous year £(40,500 – 38,000)	2,500
Tax on profits for 20X3	63,500

Now try Question 12 in the Exam Question Bank at the end of the Text.

Part E
Interpretation of accounts

Chapter 13 Cash flow statements

Chapter topic list

1 FRS 1 *Cash flow statements*
2 Preparing a cash flow statement
3 Interpretation of cash flow statements

The following study sessions are covered in this chapter.

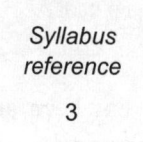

		Syllabus reference
19-21(a)	Explain the need for a cash flow statement	3
19-21(b)	Prepare a cash flow statement including relevant notes for a single company in accordance with accounting standards	3
19-21(c)	Appraise the usefulness of, and interpret the information in a cash flow statement	3

Part E: Interpretation of accounts

1 FRS 1 CASH FLOW STATEMENTS

1.1 In the long run, a profit will result in an increase in the company's cash balance but, as Keynes observed, 'in the long run we are all dead'. In the short run, the making of a profit will not necessarily result in an increased cash balance. The observation leads us to two questions:

- What is the difference between cash and profit?
- How useful are the profit and loss account and balance sheet in demonstrating whether a company has sufficient cash to finance its operations?

1.2 The importance of the distinction between cash and profit and the scant attention paid to this by the profit and loss account has resulted in the development of cash flow statements.

> **Exam alert**
> This chapter adopts a systematic approach to the preparation of cash flow statements in examinations; you should learn this method and you will then be equipped for any problems in the exam itself.

1.3 It has been argued that 'profit' does not always give a useful or meaningful picture of a company's operations. Readers of a company's financial statements might even be **misled by a reported profit figure**.

(a) Shareholders might believe that if a company makes a profit after tax, of say, £100,000 then this is the amount which it could afford to pay as a dividend. Unless the company has sufficient cash available to stay in business and also to pay a dividend, the shareholders' expectations would be wrong.

(b) Employees might believe that if a company makes profits, it can afford to pay higher wages next year. This opinion may not be correct: the ability to pay wages depends on the availability of cash.

(c) Survival of a business entity depends not so much on profits as on its ability to pay its debts when they fall due. Such payments might include 'profit and loss' items such as material purchases, wages, interest and taxation etc, but also capital payments for new fixed assets and the repayment of loan capital when this falls due (for example on the redemption of debentures).

1.4 From these examples, it may be apparent that a company's performance and prospects depend not so much on the 'profits' earned in a period, but more realistically on liquidity or **cash flows**.

1.5 The great advantage of a cash flow statement is that it is unambiguous and provides information which is additional to that provided in the rest of the accounts. It also describes the cash flows of an organisation by activity and not by balance sheet classification.

1.6 EXAMPLE: CASH FLOW STATEMENT

Baldwin Ltd commenced trading on 1 January 20X1 with a medium-term loan of £21,000 and a share issue which raised £35,000. The company purchased fixed assets for £21,000 cash, and during the year to 31 December 20X1 entered into the following transactions.

(a) Purchases from suppliers were £19,500, of which £2,550 was unpaid at the year end.

(b) Wages and salaries amounted to £10,500, of which £750 was unpaid at the year end.

(c) Interest on the loan of £2,100 was fully paid in the year and a repayment of £5,250 was made.

(d) Sales turnover was £29,400, including £900 debtors at the year end.

(e) Interest on cash deposits at the bank amounted to £75.

(f) A dividend of £4,000 was proposed as at 31 December 20X1.

You are required to prepare a historical cash flow statement for the year ended 31 December 20X1.

1.7 SOLUTION

BALDWIN LIMITED
STATEMENT OF CASH FLOWS FOR
THE YEAR ENDED 31 DECEMBER 20X1

	£	£
Operating activities		
Cash received from customers	28,500	
(£29,400 – £900)		
Cash paid to suppliers (£19,500 – £2,550)	(16,950)	
Cash paid to and on behalf of employees (£10,500 – £750)	(9,750)	
Cash flow from operating activities		1,800
Returns on investment and servicing of finance		
Interest paid	(2,100)	
Interest received	75	
		(2,025)
Capital expenditure		
Purchase of fixed assets	(21,000)	
Cash flow from investing activities		(21,000)
Financing		
Issue of shares	35,000	
Proceeds from medium-term loan	21,000	
Repayment of medium-term loan	(5,250)	
Cash flow from financing activities		50,750
Net increase in cash		29,525
Cash at 1 January 20X1		-
Cash at 31 December 20X1		29,525

Note that the dividend is only proposed and so there is no related cash flow in 20X1.

Activity 13.1

The directors of Baldwin Ltd obtain the following information in respect of projected cash flows for the year to 31 December 20X2.

(a) Fixed asset purchases for cash will be £3,000.

(b) Further expenses will be:

(i) Purchases from suppliers: £18,750 (£4,125 owed at the year end)
(ii) Wages and salaries: £11,250 (£600 owed at the year end)
(iii) Loan interest: £1,575

(c) Turnover will be £36,000 (£450 debtors at the year end).

(d) Interest on bank deposits will be £150.

(e) A further capital repayment of £5,250 will be made on the loan.

(f) A dividend of £5,000 will be proposed and last year's final dividend paid.

Part E: Interpretation of accounts

(g) Corporation tax of £2,300 will be paid in respect of 20X1.

Prepare the cash flow forecast for the year to 31 December 20X2.

Indirect method

1.8 Another way of arriving at net cash flows from operating activities is to start from operating profit and adjust for non-cash items, such as depreciation, debtors etc. This is known as the **indirect method**. A proforma calculation is given below.

> **FORMULA TO LEARN**
>
> | | £ |
> |---|---|
> | Operating profit (P&L) | X |
> | Add depreciation | X |
> | Loss (profit) on sale of fixed assets | X |
> | (Increase)/decrease in stocks | (X)/X |
> | (Increase)/decrease in debtors | (X)/X |
> | Increase/(decrease) in creditors | X/(X) |
> | Net cash flow from operating activities | X |

1.9 It is important to understand why certain items are added and others subtracted. Note the following points.

(a) Depreciation is not a cash expense, but is deducted in arriving at the profit figure in the profit and loss account. It makes sense, therefore, to eliminate it by adding it back.

(b) By the same logic, a loss on a disposal of a fixed asset (arising through underprovision of depreciation) needs to be added back and a profit deducted.

(c) An increase in stocks means less cash - you have spent cash on buying stock.

(d) An increase in debtors means debtors have not paid as much, therefore less cash.

(e) If we pay off creditors, causing the figure to decrease, again we have less cash.

1.10 It is the **indirect method** which examination questions, based around FRS 1 (see below), will probably require you to use.

FRS 1 *Cash flow statements* (revised)

1.11 FRS 1 sets out the structure of a cash flow statement and it also sets the minimum level of disclosure. Examination questions are likely to be computational, but some discussion and interpretation may be required.

In October 1996 the ASB issued a revised version of FRS 1 *Cash flow statements*. The revision of FRS 1 was part of a normal process of revision, but it also responded to various criticisms of the original FRS 1.

Objective

1.12 The FRS begins with the following statement.

> 'The objective of this FRS is to ensure that reporting entities falling within its scope:
>
> (a) report their cash generation and cash absorption for a period by highlighting the significant components of cash flow in a way that facilitates comparison of the cash flow performance of different businesses; and
>
> (b) provide information that assists in the assessment of their liquidity, solvency and financial adaptability.'

Scope

1.13 The FRS applies to all financial statements intended to give a true and fair view of the financial position and profit or loss (or income and expenditure), except those of various exempt bodies in group accounts situations or where the content of the financial statement is governed by other statutes or regulatory regimes. In addition, small entities are excluded as defined by companies legislation.

Format of the cash flow statement

1.14 An example is given of the format of a cash flow statement for a single company and this is reproduced below.

1.15 A cash flow statement should list its cash flows for the period classified under the following **standard headings**:

   (a) **Operating activities** (using either the direct or *indirect* method)
   (b) **Dividends from associates and joint ventures**.
   (c) **Returns on investments and servicing of finance**
   (d) **Taxation**
   (e) **Capital expenditure** and financial investment
   (f) **Acquisitions and disposals**
   (g) **Equity dividends paid**
   (h) **Management of liquid resources**
   (i) **Financing**

The last two headings can be shown in a single section provided a subtotal is given for each heading. Acquisitions and disposals are not on your syllabus; the heading is included here for completeness.

1.16 Individual categories of inflows and outflows under the standard headings should be disclosed separately either in the cash flow statements or in a note to it unless they are allowed to be shown net.

1.17 Each cash flow should be classified according to the substance of the transaction giving rise to it.

Links to other primary statements

1.18 Because the information given by a cash flow statement is best appreciated in the context of the information given by the other primary statements, the FRS requires **two reconciliations**, between:

   (a) **operating profit and the net cash flow from operating activities**; and
   (b) **the movement in cash in the period and the movement in net debt**.

Neither reconciliation forms part of the cash flow statement but each may be given either adjoining the statement or in a separate note.

1.19 The **movement in net debt** should identify the following components and reconcile these to the opening and closing balance sheet amount:

   (a) The cash flows of the entity
   (b) Other non-cash changes
   (c) The recognition of changes in market value and exchange rate movements

Part E: Interpretation of accounts

Definitions

1.20 The FRS includes the following important definitions (only those of direct concern to your syllabus are included here). Note particularly the definitions of cash and liquid resources.

(a) An **active market** is a market of sufficient depth to absorb the investment held without a significant effect on the price. (This definition affects the definition of liquid resources below.)

(b) **Cash** is cash in hand and deposits repayable on demand with any qualifying financial institution, less overdrafts from any qualifying financial institution repayable on demand. Deposits are repayable on demand if they can be withdrawn at any time without notice and without penalty or if a maturity or period of notice of not more than 24 hours or one working day has been agreed. Cash includes cash in hand and deposit denominated in foreign currencies.

(c) **Cash flow** is an increase or decrease in an amount of cash.

(d) **Liquid resources** are current asset investments held as readily disposable stores of value.

(e) **Net debt** is the borrowings of the reporting entity less cash and liquid resources. Where cash and liquid resources exceed the borrowings of the entity reference should be to 'net funds' rather than to 'net debt'.

(f) **Overdraft** is a borrowing facility repayable on demand that is used by drawing on a current account with a qualifying financial institution.

Classification of cash flows by standard heading

1.21 The FRS looks at each of the cash flow categories in turn.

Operating activities

1.22 Cash flows from operating activities are in general the cash effects of transactions and other events relating to operating or trading activities, normally shown in the profit and loss account in arriving at operating profit. They include cash flows in respect of operating items relating to provisions, whether or not the provision was included in operating profit.

1.23 A reconciliation between the **operating profit** reported in the profit and loss account and the **net cash flow from operating activities** should be given either adjoining the cash flow statement or as a note. The reconciliation is not part of the cash flow statement: if adjoining the cash flow statement, it should be clearly labelled and kept separate. The reconciliation should disclose separately the movements in stocks, debtors and creditors related to operating activities and other differences between cash flows and profits.

> **Exam alert**
>
> You *must* know the **reconciliation** and **format** of the cash flow statement, even if you don't know any of the other notes. When you come to revise, skip over paragraphs 1.24-1.38 and go straight to the example in paragraph 1.39.

Returns on investments and servicing of finance

1.24 These are receipts resulting from the ownership of an investment and payments to providers of finance and non-equity shareholders (eg the holders of preference shares).

1.25 Cash inflows from returns on investments and servicing of finance include:

(a) interest received, including any related tax recovered; and
(b) dividends received, net of any tax credits.

1.26 Cash outflows from returns on investments and servicing of finance include:

(a) Interest paid (even if capitalised), including any tax deducted and paid to the relevant tax authority

(b) Cash flows that are treated as finance costs (this will include issue costs on debt and non-equity share capital)

(c) The interest element of finance lease rental payments

(d) Dividends paid on non-equity shares of the entity

Taxation

1.27 These are cash flows to or from taxation authorities in respect of the reporting entity's revenue and capital profits.

Capital expenditure and financial investment

1.28 These cash flows are those related to the acquisition or disposal of any fixed asset other than one required to be classified under 'acquisitions and disposals' (discussed below), and any current asset investment not included in liquid resources (also dealt with below). If no cash flows relating to financial investment fall to be included under this heading the caption may be reduced to 'capital expenditure'.

1.29 The cash inflows here include:

(a) Receipts from sales or disposals of property, plant or equipment
(b) Receipts from the repayment of the reporting entity's loans to other entities

1.30 Cash outflows in this category include:

(a) Payments to acquire property, plant or equipment
(b) Loans made by the reporting entity.

Acquisitions and disposals

1.31 These cash flows are related to the acquisition or disposal of any trade or business, or of an investment in an entity that is either an associate, a joint venture, or a subsidiary undertaking (these group matters are beyond the scope of your syllabus).

(a) Cash inflows here include receipts from sales of trades or businesses
(b) Cash outflows here include payments to acquire trades or businesses

Equity dividends paid

1.32 The cash outflows are dividends paid on the reporting entity's equity shares, excluding any advance corporation tax.

Management of liquid resources

1.33 This section should include cash flows in respect of liquid resources as defined above. Each entity should explain what it includes as liquid resources and any changes in its policy. The cash flows in this section can be shown in a single section with those under 'financing' provided that separate subtotals for each are given.

1.34 Cash inflows include:

(a) Withdrawals from short-term deposits not qualifying as cash
(b) Inflows from disposal or redemption of any other investments held as liquid resources

1.35 Cash outflows include:

(a) Payments into short-term deposits not qualifying as cash
(b) Outflows to acquire any other investments held as liquid resources

Financing

1.36 Financing cash flows comprise receipts or repayments of principal from or to external providers of finance. The cash flows in this section can be shown in a single section with those under 'management of liquid resources' provided that separate subtotals for each are given.

1.37 Financing cash inflows include:

(a) Receipts from issuing shares or other equity instruments; and
(b) Receipts from issuing debentures, loans and from other short-term borrowings

1.38 Financing cash outflows include:

(a) Repayments of amounts borrowed (other than overdrafts)
(b) The capital element of finance lease rental payments
(c) Payments to reacquire or redeem the entity's shares
(d) Payments of expenses or commission on any issue of equity shares

1.39 EXAMPLE: SINGLE COMPANY

The following example is provided by the standard for a single company.

XYZ LIMITED
CASH FLOW STATEMENT FOR THE YEAR ENDED 31 DECEMBER 20X6

Reconciliation of operating profit to net cash inflow from operating activities

	£'000
Operating profit	6,022
Depreciation charges	899
Increase in stocks	(194)
Increase in debtors	(72)
Increase in creditors	234
Net cash inflow from operating activities	6,899

CASH FLOW STATEMENT

	£'000
Net cash inflow from operating activities	6,889
Returns on investments and servicing of finance (note 1)	2,999
Taxation	(2,922)
Capital expenditure (note 1)	(1,525)
	5,441
Equity dividends paid	(2,417)
	3,024
Management of liquid resources (note 1)	(450)
Financing (note 1)	57
Increase in cash	2,631

Reconciliation of net cash flow to movement in net debt (note 2)

	£'000	£'000
Increase in cash in the period	2,631	
Cash to repurchase debenture	149	
Cash used to increase liquid resources	450	
Change in net debt*		3,230
Net debt at 1.1.X6		(2,903)
Net funds at 31.12.X6		327

*In this example all change in net debt are cash flows.

The reconciliation of operating profit to net cash flows from operating activities can be shown in a note.

NOTES TO THE CASH FLOW STATEMENT

1 *Gross cash flows*

	£'000	£'000
Returns on investments and servicing of finance		
Interest received	3,011	
Interest paid	(12)	
		2,999
Capital expenditure		
Payments to acquire intangible fixed assets	(71)	
Payments to acquire tangible fixed assets	(1,496)	
Receipts from sales of tangible fixed assets	42	
		(1,525)
Management of liquid resources		
Purchase of treasury bills	(650)	
Sale of treasury bills	200	
		(450)
Financing		
Issue of ordinary share capital	211	
Repurchase of debenture loan	(149)	
Expenses paid in connection with share issues	(5)	
		57

Note. These gross cash flows can be shown on the face of the cash flow statement, but it may sometimes be neater to show them as a note like this.

2 *Analysis of changes in net debt*

	As at 1 Jan 20X6 £'000	Cash flows £'000	Other changes £'000	At 31 Dec 20X6 £'000
Cash in hand, at bank	42	847		889
Overdrafts	(1,784)	1,784		
		2,631		
Debt due within 1 year	(149)	149	(230)	(230)
Debt due after 1 year	(1,262)		230	(1,032)
Current asset investments	250	450		700
Total	(2,903)	3,230	–	327

Activity 13.2

Close the book for a moment and jot down the format of the cash flow statement.

2 PREPARING A CASH FLOW STATEMENT

2.1 In essence, preparing a cash flow statement is very straightforward. You should therefore simply learn the format given above and apply the steps noted in the example below. Note that the following items are treated in a way that might seem confusing, but the treatment is logical if you think in terms of **cash**.

(a) Increase in stock is treated as **negative** (in brackets). This is because it represents a cash **outflow**; cash is being spent on stock.

(b) An increase in debtors would be treated as **negative** for the same reasons; more debtors means less cash.

(c) By contrast an increase in creditors is **positive** because cash is being retained and not used to pay off creditors. There is therefore more of it.

2.2 EXAMPLE: PREPARATION OF A CASH FLOW STATEMENT

Tadman Ltd's profit and loss account for the year ended 31 December 20X2 and balance sheets at 31 December 20X1 and 31 December 20X2 were as follows.

TADMAN LIMITED
PROFIT AND LOSS ACCOUNT FOR THE YEAR ENDED 31 DECEMBER 20X2

	£'000	£'000
Sales		720
Raw materials consumed	70	
Staff costs	94	
Depreciation	118	
Loss on disposal	18	
		300
Operating profit		420
Interest payable		28
Profit before tax		392
Taxation		124
		268
Dividend		72
Profit retained for year		196
Balance brought forward		490
		686

TADMAN LIMITED
BALANCE SHEETS AS AT 31 DECEMBER

	20X2		20X1	
	£'000	£'000	£'000	£'000
Fixed assets				
Cost		1,596		1,560
Depreciation		318		224
		1,278		1,336
Current assets				
Stock	24		20	
Trade debtors	76		58	
Bank	48		56	
	148		134	

	20X2		20X1	
	£'000	£'000	£'000	£'000
Current liabilities				
Trade creditors	12		6	
Taxation	102		86	
Proposed dividend	30		24	
	144		116	
Working capital		4		18
		1,282		1,354
Long-term liabilities				
Long-term loans		200		500
		1,082		854
Share capital		360		340
Share premium		36		24
Profit and loss		686		490
		1,082		854

During the year, the company paid £90,000 for a new piece of machinery.

Task

Prepare a cash flow statement for Tadman Ltd for the year ended 31 December 20X2 in accordance with the requirements of FRS 1 (revised).

2.3 SOLUTION

Step 1. Set out the proforma cash flow statement with all the headings required by FRS 1 (revised). You should leave plenty of space. Ideally, use three or more sheets of paper, one for the main statement, one for the notes (particularly if you have a separate note for the gross cash flows) and one for your workings. It is obviously essential to know the formats very well.

Step 2. Complete the reconciliation of operating profit to net cash inflow as far as possible. When preparing the statement from balance sheets, you will usually have to calculate such items as depreciation, loss on sale of fixed assets and profit for the year (see Step 4).

Step 3. Calculate the figures for tax paid, dividends paid, purchase or sale of fixed assets, issue of shares and repayment of loans if these are not already given to you (as they may be). Note that you may not be given the tax charge in the profit loss account. You will then have to assume that the tax paid in the year is last year's year-end provision and calculate the charge as the balancing figure.

Step 4. If you are not given the profit figure, open up a working for the profit and loss account. Using the opening and closing balances, the taxation charge and dividends paid and proposed, you will be able to calculate profit for the year as the balancing figure to put in the statement.

Step 5. Complete Note 1, the gross cash flows, if asked for it. Alternatively, the information may go straight into the statement.

Step 6. You will now be able to complete the statement by slotting in the figures given or calculated.

Step 7. Complete Note 2, the analysis of changes in net debt, if asked.

Part E: Interpretation of accounts

TADMAN LIMITED
CASH FLOW STATEMENT FOR THE YEAR ENDED 31 DECEMBER 20X2

Reconciliation of operating profit to net cash inflow

	£'000
Operating profit	420
Depreciation charges	118
Loss on sale of tangible fixed assets	18
Increase in stocks	(4)
Increase in debtors	(18)
Increase in creditors	6
Net cash inflow from operating activities	540

CASH FLOW STATEMENT

	£'000	£'000
Net cash flows from operating activities		540
Returns on investment and servicing of finance		
Interest paid		(28)
Taxation		
Corporation tax paid (W1)		(108)
Capital expenditure		
Payments to acquire tangible fixed assets	(90)	
Receipts from sales of tangible fixed assets	12	
Net cash outflow from capital expenditure		(78)
		326
Equity dividends paid (72 – 30 + 24)		(66)
		260
Financing		
Issues of share capital (360 + 36 – 340 – 24)	32	
Long-term loans repaid (500 – 200)	(300)	
Net cash outflow from financing		(268)
Decrease in cash		(8)

NOTES TO THE CASH FLOW STATEMENT

Analysis of changes in net debt

	At 1 Jan 20X2 £'000	Cash flows £'000	At 31 Dec 20X2 £'000
Cash in hand, at bank	56	(8)	48
Debt due after 1 year	(500)	300	(200)
Total	(444)	292	(152)

Workings

1   Corporation tax paid

	£'000
Opening CT payable	86
Charge for year	124
Net CT payable at 31.12.X2 (102 – 10)	(102)
Paid	108

2   Fixed asset disposals

COST

	£'000		£'000
At 1.1.X2	1,560	At 31.12.X2	1,596
Purchases	90	Disposals	54
	1,650		1,650

ACCUMULATED DEPRECIATION

	£'000		£'000
At 31.1.X2	318	At 1.1.X2	224
Depreciation on disposals	24	Charge for year	118
	342		342

	£'000
NBV of disposals	30
Net loss reported	(18)
Proceeds of disposals	12

Activity 13.3

The summarised accounts of Seager plc for the year ended 31 December 20X8 are as follows.

SEAGER PLC
BALANCE SHEET AS AT 31 DECEMBER 20X8

	20X8		20X7	
	£'000	£'000	£'000	£'000
Fixed assets				
Tangible assets		628		514
Current assets				
Stocks	214		210	
Debtors	168		147	
Cash	7		-	
	389		357	
Creditors: amounts falling due within one year				
Trade creditors	136		121	
Tax payable	39		28	
Dividends payable	18		16	
Overdraft	-		14	
	193		179	
Net current assets		196		178
Total assets less current liabilities		824		692
Creditors: amounts falling due after more than one year				
10% debentures		(80)		(50)
		744		642
Capital and reserves				
Share capital (£1 ords)		250		200
Share premium account		70		60
Revaluation reserve		110		100
Profit and loss account		314		282
		744		642

SEAGER PLC
PROFIT AND LOSS ACCOUNT
FOR THE YEAR ENDED 31 DECEMBER 20X8

	£'000
Sales	600
Cost of sales	(319)
Gross profit	281
Other expenses (including depreciation of £42,000)	(194)
Profit before tax	87
Tax	(31)
Profit after tax	56
Dividends	(24)
Retained profit for the year	32

You are additionally informed that there have been no disposals of fixed assets during the year. New debentures were issued on 1 January 20X8. Wages for the year amounted to £86,000.

Part E: Interpretation of accounts

Task

Produce a cash flow statement using the direct method suitable for inclusion in the financial statements, as per FRS 1 (revised 1996).

The advantages of cash flow accounting

2.4 The advantages of cash flow accounting are as follows.

(a) Survival in business depends on the ability to generate cash. Cash flow accounting directs attention towards this critical issue.

(b) Cash flow is more comprehensive than 'profit' which is dependent on accounting conventions and concepts.

(c) Creditors (long and short-term) are more interested in an entity's ability to repay them than in its profitability. Whereas 'profits' might indicate that cash is likely to be available, cash flow accounting is more direct with its message.

(d) Cash flow reporting provides a better means of comparing the results of different companies than traditional profit reporting.

(e) Cash flow reporting satisfies the needs of all users better.

  (i) For management, it provides the sort of information on which decisions should be taken: (in management accounting, 'relevant costs' to a decision are future cash flows); traditional profit accounting does not help with decision-making.

  (ii) For shareholders and auditors, cash flow accounting can provide a satisfactory basis for stewardship accounting.

  (iii) As described previously, the information needs of creditors and employees will be better served by cash flow accounting.

(f) Cash flow forecasts are easier to prepare, as well as more useful, than profit forecasts.

(g) They can in some respects be audited more easily than accounts based on the accruals concept.

(h) The accruals concept is confusing, and cash flows are more easily understood.

(i) Cash flow accounting should be both retrospective, and also include a forecast for the future. This is of great information value to all users of accounting information.

(j) Forecasts can subsequently be monitored by the publication of variance statements which compare actual cash flows against the forecast.

Activity 13.4

Can you think of some possible disadvantages of cash flow accounting?

Activity 13.5

The balance sheet of Cat plc for the year ended 31 December 20X7, together with comparative figures for the previous year, is shown below (all figures £'000).

	20X7	20X6
Fixed assets	540	360
Less depreciation	(180)	(112)
	360	248
Current assets		
Stock	100	84
Debtors	80	66
Cash	-	22
	180	172
Current liabilities		
Trade and operating creditors	66	48
Taxation	38	34
Dividend	56	52
Bank overdraft	20	-
	(180)	(134)
Net current assets	-	38
Net assets	360	286

	20X7	20X6
Represented by		
Ordinary share capital £1 shares	50	40
Share premium	20	16
Profit and loss account	130	110
Shareholders' funds	200	166
15% debentures, repayable 2001	160	120
Capital employed	360	286

You are informed that:

(a) There were no sales of fixed assets during 20X7
(b) The company does not pay interim dividends
(c) New debentures and shares issued in 20X7 were issued on 1 January

Task

(a) Show your calculation of the operating profit of Cat plc for the year ended 31 December 20X7.

(b) Prepare a cash flow statement for the year, in accordance with FRS 1 (revised) *Cash flow statements* including the reconciliation of operating profit to net cash inflow from operating activities and Note 1 as required by the standard, ie the 'gross cash flows'.

(c) State the headings of the other reconciliation and note which you would be required to include in practice under FRS 1 (revised).

3 INTERPRETATION OF CASH FLOW STATEMENTS

3.1 FRS 1 *Cash flow statements* was introduced on the basis that it would provide better, more comprehensive and more useful information than its predecessor standard. So what kind of information does the cash flow statement, along with its notes, provide?

3.2 Some of the main areas where FRS 1 should provide information not found elsewhere in the accounts are as follows.

(a) The **relationships between profit and cash** can be seen clearly and analysed accordingly.

(b) **Management of liquid resources** is highlighted, giving a better picture of the liquidity of the company.

(c) **Financing inflows** and outflows must be **shown, rather than simply passed through reserves**.

Part E: Interpretation of accounts

3.3 It is wrong to try to assess the health or predict the death of a reporting entity solely on the basis of a single indicator. When analysing cash flow data, the **comparison should not just be between cash flows and profit, but also between cash flows over a period of time** (say three to five years).

3.4 The **behaviour** of profit and cash flows will be very different. **Profit is smoothed out** through accruals, prepayments, provisions and other accounting conventions. This does not apply to cash, so the **cash flow figures** are likely to be **'lumpy'** in comparison. You must distinguish between this 'lumpiness' and the trends which will appear over time.

3.5 The **relationship between profit and cash flows will vary constantly**. Healthy companies do not always have reported profits exceeding operating cash flows. Similarly, unhealthy companies can have operating cash flows well in excess of reported profit. The value of comparing them is in determining the extent to which earned profits are being converted into the necessary cash flows.

3.6 Profit is not as important as the extent to which a company can **convert its profits into cash on a continuing basis.** This process should be judged over a period longer than one year. The cash flows should be compared with profits over the same periods to decide how successfully the reporting entity has converted earnings into cash.

3.7 Cash flow figures should also be considered in terms of their specific relationships with each other over time. A form of **'cash flow gearing'** can be determined by comparing operating cash flows and financing flows, particularly borrowing, to establish the extent of dependence of the reporting entity on external funding.

3.8 **Other relationships** can be examined.

(a) Operating cash flows and investment flows can be related to match cash recovery from investment to investment.

(b) Investment can be compared to distribution to indicate the proportion of total cash outflow designated specifically to investor return and reinstatement.

(c) A comparison of tax outflow to operating cash flow minus investment flow will establish a 'cash basis tax rate'.

Key learning points

- Cash flow statements were made compulsory for companies because it was recognised that accounting profit is not the only indicator of a company's performance. FRS 1 *Cash flow statements* sets oft the requirements for these statements.

- Cash flow statements concentrate on the sources and uses of cash and are a useful indicator of a company's liquidity and solvency.

- You need to learn the format of the statement; setting out the format is an essential first stage in preparing the statement but it will only really sink in with more question practice.

- Remember the **step-by-step** preparation procedure and use it for all the questions you practise.

Quick quiz

1. What are the aims of a cash flow statement?
2. 'Equity dividends paid' is one of the standard headings required by FRS 1. True or false?
3. What are the two reconciliations required by FRS 1 (revised)?
4. Define cash according to FRS 1 (revised).
5. Define 'liquid resources'.
6. Cash flow information is of more use to creditors than the profit figure. Why?

Answers to quick quiz

1. (a) To ensure that reporting entities report cash generation and absorption by highlighting key, comparable components of cash flow.
   (b) To ensure such entities provide information that assists in the assessment of their liquidity, solvency and financial adaptability.
2. True
3. (a) A reconciliation of operating profit to net cash inflow from operating activities
   (b) A reconciliation of movement in cash and movement in net debt
4. Cash in hand and deposits repayable on demand with any qualifying financial institution less overdrafts from any qualifying financial institution repayable on demand
5. Current asset investments held as readily disposable stores of value.
6. While profits might point to a healthy cash flow, the cash flow statement is a more direct indicator of a company's ability to repay a debt.

Answers to activities

Answer 13.1

BALDWIN LIMITED
STATEMENT OF FORECAST CASH FLOWS FOR
THE YEAR ENDING 31 DECEMBER 20X2

	£	£
Operating activities		
Cash received from customers	36,450	
(£36,000 + £900 – £450)		
Cash paid to suppliers (£18,750 + £2,550 – £4,125)	(17,175)	
Cash paid to and on behalf of employees		
(£11,250 + £750 – £600)	(11,400)	
Net cash flow from operating activities		7,875
Returns on investments and servicing of finance		
Interest paid	(1,575)	
Interest received	150	
		(1,425)
Taxation		(2,300)
Capital expenditure		
Purchase of fixed assets		(3,000)
		1,150
Equity dividends paid		(4,000)
Financing		
Repayment of medium-term loan		(5,250)
Forecast net decrease in cash at 31 December 20X2		(8,100)
Cash as at 31 December 20X1		29,525
Forecast cash as at 31 December 20X2		21,425

Part E: Interpretation of accounts

Answer 13.3

SEAGER PLC
CASH FLOW STATEMENT
FOR THE YEAR ENDED 31 DECEMBER 20X8

	£'000	£'000
Operating activities		
Cash received from customers (W1)	579	
Cash payments to suppliers (W2)	(366)	
Cash payments to and on behalf of employees	(86)	
		127
Returns on investments and servicing of finance		
Interest paid		(8)
Taxation		
UK corporation tax paid (W5)		(20)
Capital expenditure		
Purchase of tangible fixed assets (W6)	(146)	
Net cash outflow from capital expenditure		(146)
		(47)
Equity dividends paid (W4)		(22)
Financing		
Issue of share capital	60	
Issue of debentures	30	
Net cash inflow from financing		90
Increase in cash		21

NOTES TO THE CASHFLOW STATEMENT

1   Reconciliation of operating profit to net cash inflow from operating activities

	£'000
Operating profit (87 + 8)	95
Depreciation	42
Increase in stock	(4)
Increase in debtors	(21)
Increase in creditors	15
	127

2   Reconciliation of net cash flow to movement in net debt

	£'000
Net cash inflow for the period	21
Cash received from debenture issue	(30)
Change in net debt	(9)
Net debt at 1 January 20X8	(64)
Net debt at 31 December 20X8	(73)

3   Analysis of changes in net debt

	At 1 January 20X8 £'000	Cash flows £'000	At 31 December 20X8 £'000
Cash at bank	-	7	7
Overdrafts	(14)	14	-
		21	
Debt due after 1 year	(50)	(30)	(80)
Total	(64)	(9)	(73)

13: Cash flow statements

Workings

1   *Cash received from customers*

    DEBTORS CONTROL ACCOUNT

	£'000		£'000
B/f	147	Cash received (bal)	579
Sales	600	C/f	168
	747		747

2   *Cash paid to suppliers*

    CREDITORS CONTROL ACCOUNT

	£'000		£'000
Cash paid (bal)	366	B/f	121
C/f	136	Purchases (W3)	381
	502		502

3   *Purchases*

	£'000
Cost of sales	319
Opening stock	(210)
Closing stock	214
Expenses (194 – 42 – 86 – 8 debenture interest)	58
	381

4   *Dividends*

    DIVIDENDS

	£'000		£'000
∴ Dividends paid	22	Balance b/f	16
Balance c/f	18	Dividend for year	24
	40		40

5   *Taxation*

    TAXATION

	£'000		£'000
∴ Tax paid	20	Balance b/f	28
Balance c/f	39	Charge for year	31
	59		59

6   *Purchase of fixed assets*

	£'000
Opening fixed assets	514
Less depreciation	(42)
Add revaluation (110 – 100)	10
	482
Closing fixed assets	628
Difference = additions	146

Answer 13.4

The main disadvantages of cash accounting are essentially the advantages of accruals accounting (proper matching of related items). There is also the practical problem that few businesses keep historical cash flow information in the form needed to prepare a historical cash flow statement and so extra record keeping is likely to be necessary.

Part E: Interpretation of accounts

Answer 13.5

(a) *Calculation of operating profit*

PROFIT AND LOSS ACCOUNT

	£'000		£'000
Taxation*	38	Balance at 1.1.X7	110
Dividends	56	Profit for the year (bal fig)	138
Debenture interest (160 × 15%)	24		
Balance at 31.12.X7	130		
	248		248

* Last year's year end provision

(b) CAT PLC
CASH FLOW STATEMENT
FOR THE YEAR ENDED 31 DECEMBER 20X7

Reconciliation of operating profit to net cash inflow from operating activities

	£'000
Operating profit (part (a))	138
Depreciation (180 – 112)	68
Increase in stocks	(16)
Increase in debtors	(14)
Increase in creditors	18
Net cash inflow from operating activities	194

CASH FLOW STATEMENT

	£'000
Net cash inflow from operating activities	194
Returns on investments and servicing of finance (note 1)	(24)
Taxation	(34)
Capital expenditure (note 1)	(180)
	(44)
Equity dividends paid	(52)
	(96)
Financing (note 1)	54
Decrease in cash	(42)

Note 1 – Gross cash flows

	£'000	£'000
Returns on investments and servicing of finance		
Interest paid	(24)	
		(24)
Capital expenditure		
Purchase of fixed assets (540 – 360)	(180)	
		(180)
Financing		
Issue of share capital	10	
Share premium	4	
Issue of debentures	40	
		54

(c) Attached to the cash flow statement is a reconciliation of net cash flow to movement in net debt. Note 2 to the cash flow statement is an analysis of changes in net debt.

Now try Question 13 in the Exam Question Bank at the end of the Text.

Chapter 14 Ratio analysis

Chapter topic list

1 The broad categories of ratios
2 Profitability and return on capital
3 Liquidity, gearing and working capital
4 Shareholders' investment ratios
5 Presentation of a ratio analysis report
6 Limitations of ratio and trend analysis

The following study sessions are covered in this chapter.

Syllabus reference

26-29(a) Calculate the following ratios: 4
    (i) profitability
    (ii) liquidity
    (iii) efficiency
    (iv) investor
    (v) financial

26-29(b) Analyse and interpret the ratios to give an assessment of a company's performance in comparison with: 4
    (i) a company's previous period's financial statements
    (ii) another similar company for the same period
    (iii) industry average ratios

26-29(c) Identify and discuss the limitations of ratio analysis   4

26-29(d) Prepare a financial analysis report of a company in a suitable format   4

Part E: Interpretation of accounts

1 THE BROAD CATEGORIES OF RATIOS

1.1 If you were to look at a balance sheet or P & L account, how would you decide whether the company was doing well or badly? Or whether it was financially strong or financially vulnerable? And what would you be looking at in the figures to help you to make your judgement?

1.2 Your syllabus requires you to appraise and communicate the position and prospects of a business based on given and prepared statements and ratios.

1.3 Ratio analysis involves comparing one figure against another to produce a ratio, and assessing whether the ratio indicates a weakness or strength in the company's affairs.

The broad categories of ratios

1.4 Broadly speaking, basic ratios can be grouped into five categories:

(a) Profitability and return
(b) Long-term solvency and stability
(c) Short-term solvency and liquidity
(d) Efficiency (turnover ratios)
(e) Shareholders' investment ratios

1.5 Within each heading we will identify a number of standard measures or ratios that are normally calculated and generally accepted as meaningful indicators. One must stress however that each individual business must be considered separately, and a ratio that is meaningful for a manufacturing company may be completely meaningless for a financial institution. Try not to be too mechanical when working out ratios and constantly think about what you are trying to achieve.

1.6 The key to obtaining meaningful information from ratio analysis is **comparison**. This may involve comparing ratios over time within the same business to establish whether things are improving or declining, and comparing ratios between similar businesses to see whether the company you are analysing is better or worse than average within its specific business sector.

1.7 It must be stressed that ratio analysis on its own is not sufficient for interpreting company accounts, and that there are other items of information which should be looked at, for example:

(a) Comments in the Chairman's report and directors' report
(b) The age and nature of the company's assets
(c) Current and future developments in the company's markets, at home and overseas;
(d) Any other noticeable features of the report and accounts, such as post balance sheet events, contingent liabilities, a qualified auditors' report, the company's taxation position, and so on

1.8 EXAMPLE: CALCULATING RATIOS

To illustrate the calculation of ratios, the following balance sheet and P & L account figures will be used.

BETATEC PLC PROFIT AND LOSS ACCOUNT
FOR THE YEAR ENDED 31 DECEMBER 20X8

	Notes	20X8 £	20X7 £
Turnover	1	3,095,576	1,909,051
Operating profit	1	359,501	244,229
Interest	2	17,371	19,127
Profit on ordinary activities before taxation		342,130	225,102
Taxation on ordinary activities		74,200	31,272
Profit on ordinary activities after taxation		267,930	193,830
Dividend		41,000	16,800
Retained profit for the year		226,930	177,030
Earnings per share		12.8p	9.3p

BETATEC PLC BALANCE SHEET
AS AT 31 DECEMBER 20X8

	Notes	20X8 £	20X7 £
Fixed assets			
Tangible fixed assets		802,180	656,071
Current assets			
Stocks and work in progress		64,422	86,550
Debtors	3	1,002,701	853,441
Cash at bank and in hand		1,327	68,363
		1,068,450	1,008,354
Creditors: amounts falling due within one year	4	881,731	912,456
Net current assets		186,719	95,898
Total assets less current liabilities		988,899	751,969
Creditors: amounts falling due after more than one year			
10% first mortgage debenture stock 20Y4/20Y9		(100,000)	(100,000)
Provision for liabilities and charges		(20,000)	(10,000)
		868,899	641,969
Capital and reserves			
Called up share capital	5	210,000	210,000
Share premium account		48,178	48,178
Profit and loss account		610,721	383,791
		868,899	641,969

NOTES TO THE ACCOUNTS

			20X8 £	20X7 £
1	Turnover and profit			
	(i)	Turnover	3,095,576	1,909,051
		Cost of sales	2,402,609	1,441,950
		Gross profit	692,967	467,101
		Administration expenses	333,466	222,872
		Operating profit	359,501	244,229
	(ii)	Operating profit is stated after charging:		
		Depreciation	151,107	120,147
		Auditors' remuneration	6,500	5,000
		Leasing charges	47,636	46,336
		Directors' emoluments	94,945	66,675

Part E: Interpretation of accounts

		20X8 £	20X7 £
2	*Interest*		
	Payable on bank overdrafts and other loans	8,115	11,909
	Payable on debenture stock	10,000	10,000
		18,115	21,909
	Receivable on short-term deposits	744	2,782
	Net payable	17,371	19,127
3	*Debtors*		
	Amounts falling due within one year		
	Trade debtors	884,559	760,252
	Prepayments and accrued income	89,822	45,729
	Advance corporation tax recoverable	7,200	-
		981,581	805,981
	Amounts falling due after more than one year		
	Advance corporation tax recoverable	9,000	7,200
	Trade debtors	12,120	40,260
		21,120	47,460
	Total debtors	1,002,701	853,441
4	*Creditors: amounts falling due within one year*		
	Trade creditors	627,018	545,340
	Accruals and deferred income	81,279	280,464
	Corporation tax	108,000	37,200
	Other taxes and social security costs	44,434	32,652
	Dividend	21,000	16,800
		881,731	912,456
5	*Called up share capital*		
	Authorised ordinary shares of 10p each	1,000,000	1,000,000
	Issued and fully paid ordinary shares of 10p each	210,000	210,00

2 PROFITABILITY AND RETURN ON CAPITAL

2.1 In our example, the company made a profit in both 20X8 and 20X7, and there was an increase in profit on ordinary activities between one year and the next:

(a) of 52% before taxation;
(b) of 39% after taxation.

2.2 Profit on ordinary activities *before* taxation is generally thought to be a better figure to use than profit after taxation, because there might be unusual variations in the tax charge from year to year which would not affect the underlying profitability of the company's operations.

2.3 Another profit figure that should be calculated is PBIT, profit before interest and tax. This is the amount of profit which the company earned before having to pay interest to the providers of loan capital. By providers of loan capital, we usually mean longer-term loan capital, such as debentures and medium-term bank loans, which will be shown in the balance sheet as 'creditors: amounts falling due after more than one year'.

2.4 Profit before interest and tax is therefore:

(a) The profit on ordinary activities before taxation
(b) Interest charges on long-term loan capital

Published accounts do not always give sufficient detail on interest payable to determine how much is interest on long-term finance. We will assume in our example that the whole of the interest payable (£18,115, note 2) relates to long-term finance.

2.5 PBIT in our example is therefore:

	20X8 £	20X7 £
Profit on ordinary activities before tax	342,130	225,102
Interest payable	18,115	21,909
PBIT	360,245	247,011

This shows a 46% growth between 20X7 and 20X8.

Return on capital employed (ROCE)

2.6 It is impossible to assess profits or profit growth properly without relating them to the amount of funds (capital) that were employed in making the profits. The most important profitability ratio is therefore return on capital employed (ROCE), which states the profit as a percentage of the amount of capital employed.

FORMULA TO LEARN

$$\text{ROCE} = \frac{\text{Profit on ordinary activities before interest and taxation}}{\text{Capital employed}}$$

2.7 Capital employed = Shareholders' funds plus 'creditors: amounts falling due after more than one year' plus any long-term provision for liabilities and charges (*or* total assets less current liabilities).

The underlying principle is that we must compare like with like, and so if capital means share capital and reserves plus long-term liabilities and debt capital, profit must mean the profit earned by all this capital together. This is PBIT, since interest is the return for loan capital.

2.8 EXAMPLE: ROCE

In our example, capital employed = 20X8 868,899 + 100,000 + 20,000 = £988,899
20X7 641,969 + 100,000 + 10,000 = £751,969

These total figures are the total assets less current liabilities figures for 20X8 and 20X7 in the balance sheet.

	20X8	20X7
ROCE =	$\frac{360,245}{988,899}$	$\frac{247,011}{751,969}$
=	36.4%	32.8%

2.9 What does a company's ROCE tell us? What should we be looking for? There are three comparisons that can be made.

(a) The change in ROCE from one year to the next can be examined. In this example, there has been an increase in ROCE by about 10% or 11% from its 20X7 level.

(b) The ROCE being earned by other companies, if this information is available, can be compared with the ROCE of this company. Here the information is not available.

Part E: Interpretation of accounts

(c) A comparison of the ROCE with current market borrowing rates may be made.

(i) What would be the cost of extra borrowing to the company if it needed more loans, and is it earning a ROCE that suggests it could make profits to make such borrowing worthwhile?

(ii) Is the company making a ROCE which suggests that it is getting value for money from its current borrowing?

(iii) Companies are in a risk business and commercial borrowing rates are a good independent yardstick against which company performance can be judged.

2.10 In this example, if we suppose that current market interest rates, say, for medium-term borrowing from banks, is around 10%, then the company's actual ROCE of 36% in 20X8 would not seem low. On the contrary, it might seem high.

2.11 However, it is easier to spot a low ROCE than a high one, because there is always a chance that the company's fixed assets, especially property, are undervalued in its balance sheet, and so the capital employed figure might be unrealistically low. If the company had earned a ROCE, not of 36%, but of, say only 6%, then its return would have been below current borrowing rates and so disappointingly low.

Exam alert

There are different ways of calculating ROCE, and the examiner will give you credit for them. If he tells you how to calculate it you should, of course, follow his instructions.

Return on shareholders' capital (ROSC)

2.12 Another measure of profitability and return is the return on shareholders' capital (ROSC):

FORMULA TO LEARN

$$\text{ROSC} = \frac{\text{Profit on ordinary activities before tax}}{\text{Share capital and reserves}}$$

2.13 It is intended to focus on the return being made by the company for the benefit of its shareholders, and in our example, the figures are:

$$\begin{array}{cc} 20X8 & 20X7 \\ \dfrac{342{,}130}{868{,}899} = 39.4\% & \dfrac{225{,}102}{641{,}969} = 35.1\% \end{array}$$

These figures show an improvement between 20X7 and 20X8, and a return which is clearly in excess of current borrowing rates.

2.14 ROSC is not a widely-used ratio, however, because there are more useful ratios that give an indication of the return to shareholders, such as earnings per share, dividend per share, dividend yield and earnings yield, which are described later.

Analysing profitability and return in more detail: the secondary ratios

2.15 We often sub-analyse ROCE, to find out more about why the ROCE is high or low, or better or worse than last year. There are two factors that contribute towards a return on capital employed, both related to sales turnover.

(a) **Profit margin.** A company might make a high or low profit margin on its sales. For example, a company that makes a profit of 25p per £1 of sales is making a bigger return on its turnover than another company making a profit of only 10p per £1 of sales.

(b) **Asset turnover.** Asset turnover is a measure of how well the assets of a business are being used to generate sales. For example, if two companies each have capital employed of £100,000 and Company A makes sales of £400,000 per annum whereas Company B makes sales of only £200,000 per annum, Company A is making a higher turnover from the same amount of assets (twice as much asset turnover as Company B) and this will help A to make a higher return on capital employed than B. Asset turnover is expressed as 'x times' so that assets generate x times their value in annual turnover. Here, Company A's asset turnover is 4 times and B's is 2 times.

2.16 Profit margin and asset turnover together explain the ROCE and if the ROCE is the primary profitability ratio, these other two are the secondary ratios. The relationship between the three ratios can be shown mathematically.

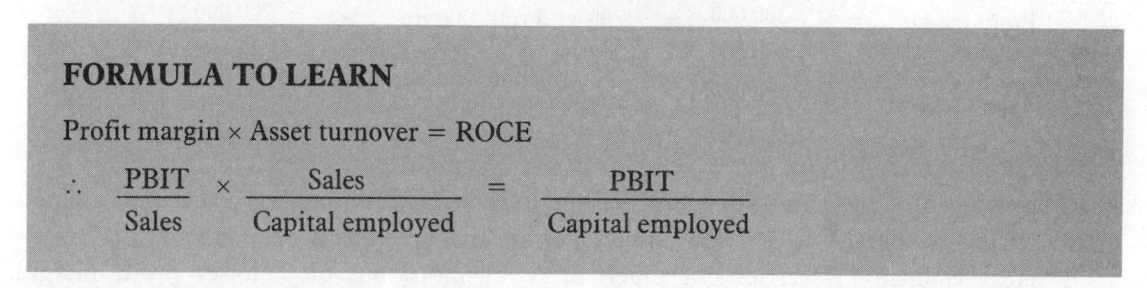

FORMULA TO LEARN

Profit margin × Asset turnover = ROCE

$$\therefore \frac{PBIT}{Sales} \times \frac{Sales}{Capital\ employed} = \frac{PBIT}{Capital\ employed}$$

2.17 In our example:

		Profit margin		Asset turnover		ROCE
(a)	20X8	360,245 / 3,095,576	×	3,095,576 / 988,899	=	360,245 / 988,899
		11.64%	×	3.13 times	=	36.4%
(b)	20X7	247,011 / 1,909,051	×	1,909,051 / 751,969	=	247,011 / 751,969
		12.94%	×	2.54 times	=	32.8%

2.18 In this example, the company's improvement in ROCE between 20X7 and 20X8 is attributable to a higher asset turnover. Indeed the profit margin has fallen a little, but the higher asset turnover has more than compensated for this.

2.19 It is also worth commenting on the change in sales turnover from one year to the next. You may already have noticed that Betatec plc achieved sales growth of over 60% from £1.9 million to £3.1 million between 20X7 and 20X8. This is very strong growth, and this is certainly one of the most significant items in the P & L account and balance sheet.

Part E: Interpretation of accounts

A warning about comments on profit margin and asset turnover

2.20 It might be tempting to think that a high profit margin is good, and a low asset turnover means sluggish trading. In broad terms, this is so. But there is a trade-off between profit margin and asset turnover, and you cannot look at one without allowing for the other.

(a) A high profit margin means a high profit per £1 of sales, but if this also means that sales prices are high, there is a strong possibility that sales turnover will be depressed, and so asset turnover lower.

(b) A high asset turnover means that the company is generating a lot of sales, but to do this it might have to keep its prices down and so accept a low profit margin per £1 of sales.

2.21 Consider the following.

Company A		Company B	
Sales	£1,000,000	Sales	£4,000,000
Capital employed	£1,000,000	Capital employed	£1,000,000
PBIT	£200,000	PBIT	£200,000

These figures would give the following ratios.

$$\text{ROCE} = \frac{200,000}{1,000,000} = 20\% \qquad \text{ROCE} = \frac{200,000}{1,000,000} = 20\%$$

$$\text{Profit margin} = \frac{200,000}{1,000,000} = 20\% \qquad \text{Profit margin} = \frac{200,000}{4,000,000} = 5\%$$

$$\text{Asset turnover} = \frac{1,000,000}{1,000,000} = 1 \qquad \text{Asset turnover} = \frac{4,000,000}{1,000,000} = 4$$

2.22 The companies have the same ROCE, but it is arrived at in a very different fashion. Company A operates with a low asset turnover and a comparatively high profit margin whereas company B carries out much more business, but on a lower profit margin. Company A could be operating at the luxury end of the market, whilst company B is operating at the popular end of the market (Fortnum and Masons v Sainsbury's).

Activity 14.1

Which one of the following formulae correctly expresses the relationship between return on capital employed (ROCE), profit margin (PM) and asset turnover (AT)?

A $PM = \dfrac{AT}{ROCE}$

B $ROCE = \dfrac{PM}{AT}$

C $AT = PM \times ROCE$

D $PM = \dfrac{ROCE}{AT}$

Gross profit margin, net profit margin and profit analysis

2.23 Depending on the format of the P & L account, you may be able to calculate the gross profit margin as well as the net profit margin. Looking at the two together can be quite informative.

2.24 For example, suppose that a company has the following summarised profit and loss accounts for two consecutive years.

	Year 1 £	Year 2 £
Turnover	70,000	100,000
Cost of sales	42,000	55,000
Gross profit	28,000	45,000
Expenses	21,000	35,000
Net profit	7,000	10,000

Although the net profit margin is the same for both years at 10%, the gross profit margin is not.

In year 1 it is: $\dfrac{28,000}{70,000} = 40\%$

and in year 2 it is: $\dfrac{45,000}{100,000} = 45\%$

The improved gross profit margin has not led to an improvement in the net profit margin. This is because expenses as a percentage of sales have risen from 30% in year 1 to 35% in year 2.

3 LIQUIDITY, GEARING AND WORKING CAPITAL

Long-term solvency: debt and gearing ratios

3.1 Debt ratios are concerned with how much the company owes in relation to its size, whether it is getting into heavier debt or improving its situation, and whether its debt burden seems heavy or light.

(a) When a company is heavily in debt banks and other potential lenders may be unwilling to advance further funds.

(b) When a company is earning only a modest profit before interest and tax, and has a heavy debt burden, there will be very little profit left over for shareholders after the interest charges have been paid. And so if interest rates were to go up (on bank overdrafts and so on) or the company were to borrow even more, it might soon be incurring interest charges in excess of PBIT. This might eventually lead to the liquidation of the company.

These are two big reasons why companies should keep their debt burden under control. There are four ratios that are particularly worth looking at, the **debt** ratio, **gearing** ratio, **interest cover** and **cash flow** ratio.

Debt ratio

> **KEY TERM**
>
> The **debt ratio** is the ratio of a company's total debts to its total assets.

3.2 (a) Assets consist of fixed assets at their balance sheet value, plus current assets.

(b) Debts consist of all creditors, whether amounts falling due within one year or after more than one year.

You can ignore long-term provisions and liabilities, such as deferred taxation.

Part E: Interpretation of accounts

3.3 There is no absolute guide to the maximum safe debt ratio, but as a very general guide, you might regard 50% as a safe limit to debt. In practice, many companies operate successfully with a higher debt ratio than this, but 50% is nonetheless a helpful benchmark. In addition, if the debt ratio is over 50% and getting worse, the company's debt position will be worth looking at more carefully.

3.4 In the case of Betatec plc the debt ratio is as follows.

	20X8	*20X7*
Total debts	(881,731 + 100,000)	(912,456 + 100,000)
Total assets	(802,180 + 1,068,450)	(656,071 + 1,008,354)
	= 52%	= 61%

3.5 In this case, the debt ratio is quite high, mainly because of the large amount of current liabilities. However, the debt ratio has fallen from 61% to 52% between 20X7 and 20X8, and so the company appears to be improving its debt position.

Gearing ratio

3.6 Capital gearing is concerned with a company's **long-term capital structure**. We can think of a company as consisting of fixed assets and net current assets (ie working capital, which is current assets minus current liabilities). These assets must be financed by long-term capital of the company, which is one of two things.

(a) share capital and reserves (shareholders' funds) which can be divided into:

  (i) Ordinary shares plus reserves
  (ii) Preference shares

(b) Long-term debt capital: 'creditors: amounts falling due after more than one year'

3.7 Preference share capital is not debt. It would certainly not be included as debt in the debt ratio. However, like loan capital, preference share capital has a prior claim over profits before interest and tax, ahead of ordinary shareholders. Preference dividends must be paid out of profits before ordinary shareholders are entitled to an ordinary dividend, and so we refer to preference share capital and loan capital as prior charge capital.

3.8 The **capital gearing ratio** is a measure of the proportion of a company's capital that is prior charge capital. It is measured as follows:

> **FORMULA TO LEARN**
>
> $$\text{Capital gearing ratio} = \frac{\text{prior charge capital}}{\text{total capital}}$$

(a) **Prior charge capital** is capital carrying a right to a fixed return. It will include preference shares and debentures.

(b) **Total capital** is ordinary share capital and reserves plus prior charge capital plus any long-term liabilities or provisions. In group accounts we would also include minority interests. It is easier to identify the same figure for total capital as total assets less current liabilities, which you will find given to you in the balance sheet.

3.9 As with the debt ratio, there is no absolute limit to what a gearing ratio ought to be. A company with a gearing ratio of more than 50% is said to be high-geared (whereas low gearing means a gearing ratio of less than 50%). Many companies are high geared, but if a high geared company is becoming increasingly high geared, it is likely to have difficulty in the future when it wants to borrow even more, unless it can also boost its shareholders' capital, either with retained profits or by a new share issue.

3.10 A similar ratio to the gearing ratio is the **debt/equity ratio**, which is calculated as follows.

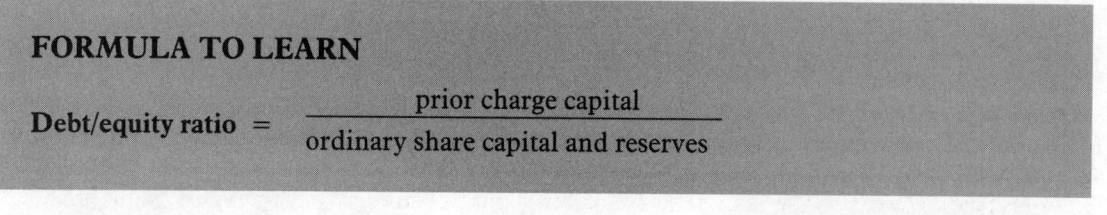

> **FORMULA TO LEARN**
>
> $$\text{Debt/equity ratio} = \frac{\text{prior charge capital}}{\text{ordinary share capital and reserves}}$$

This gives us the same sort of information as the gearing ratio, and a ratio of 100% or more would indicate high gearing.

3.11 In the example of Betatec plc, we find that the company, although having a high debt ratio because of its current liabilities, has a low gearing ratio. It has no preference share capital and its only long-term debt is the 10% debenture stock.

	20X8	20X7
Gearing ratio	$\frac{100{,}000}{988{,}899}$	$\frac{100{,}000}{751{,}969}$
	= 10%	= 13%
Debt/equity ratio	$\frac{100{,}000}{868{,}899}$	$\frac{100{,}000}{641{,}969}$
	= 12%	= 16%

The implications of high or low gearing

3.12 We mentioned earlier that gearing is, amongst other things, an attempt to quantify the degree of risk involved in holding equity shares in a company, risk both in terms of the company's ability to remain in business and in terms of expected ordinary dividends from the company. The problem with a high geared company is that by definition there is a lot of debt. Debt generally carries a fixed rate of interest (or fixed rate of dividend if in the form of preference shares), hence there is a given (and large) amount to be paid out from profits to holders of debt before arriving at a residue available for distribution to the holders of equity. The riskiness will perhaps become clearer with the aid of an example.

	Company A £'000	Company B £'000	Company C £'000
Ordinary share capital	600	400	300
Profit and loss account	200	200	200
Revaluation reserve	100	100	100
	900	700	600
6% preference shares	-	-	100
10% loan stock	100	300	300
Capital employed	1,000	1,000	1,000
Gearing ratio	10%	30%	40%

Part E: Interpretation of accounts

3.13 Now suppose that each company makes a profit before interest and tax of £50,000, and the rate of corporation tax is 30%. Amounts available for distribution to equity shareholders will be as follows:

	Company A £'000	Company B £'000	Company C £'000
Profit before interest and tax	50	50	50
Interest	10	30	30
Profit before tax	40	20	20
Taxation at 30%	12	6	6
Profit after tax	28	14	14
Preference dividend	-	-	6
Available for ordinary shareholders	28	14	8

3.14 If in the subsequent year profit before interest and tax falls to £40,000, the amounts available to ordinary shareholders will become:

	Company A £'000	Company B £'000	Company C £'000
Profit before interest and tax	40	40	40
Interest	10	30	30
Profit before tax	30	10	10
Taxation at 30%	9	3	3
Profit after tax	21	7	7
Preference dividend	-	-	6
Available for ordinary shareholders	21	7	1

Note the following.

Gearing ratio	10%	30%	40%
Change in PBIT	– 20%	– 20%	– 20%
Change in profit available for ordinary shareholders	– 25%	– 50%	– 87.5%

3.15 The more highly geared the company, the greater the risk that little (if anything) will be available to distribute by way of dividend to the ordinary shareholders.

(a) The example clearly displays this fact in so far as the more highly geared the company, the greater the percentage change in profit available for ordinary shareholders for any given percentage change in profit before interest and tax.

(b) The relationship similarly holds when profits increase, and if PBIT had risen by 20% rather than fallen, you would find that once again the largest percentage change in profit available for ordinary shareholders (this means an increase) will be for the highly geared company.

(c) This means that there will be greater volatility of amounts available for ordinary shareholders, and presumably therefore greater volatility in dividends paid to those shareholders, where a company is highly geared. That is the risk: you may do extremely well or extremely badly without a particularly large movement in the PBIT of the company.

3.16 The risk of a company's ability to remain in business was referred to earlier. Gearing is relevant to this. A high geared company has a large amount of interest to pay annually (assuming that the debt is external borrowing rather than preference shares). If those borrowings are 'secured' in any way (and debentures in particular are secured), then the holders of the debt are perfectly entitled to force the company to realise assets to pay their interest if funds are not available from other sources. Clearly the more highly geared a company the more likely this is to occur when and if profits fall. **Higher gearing may mean higher returns, but also higher risk.**

Interest cover

3.17 The interest cover ratio shows whether a company is earning enough profits before interest and tax to pay its interest costs comfortably, or whether its interest costs are high in relation to the size of its profits, so that a fall in PBIT would then have a significant effect on profits available for ordinary shareholders.

> **FORMULA TO LEARN**
>
> $$\text{Interest cover} = \frac{\text{profit before interest and tax}}{\text{interest charges}}$$

3.18 An interest cover of 2 times or less would be low, and should really exceed 3 times before the company's interest costs are to be considered within acceptable limits.

3.19 Returning first to the example of Companies A, B and C, the interest cover was as follows.

		Company A	Company B	Company C
(a)	When PBIT was £50,000 =	50,000 / 10,000 = 5 times	50,000 / 30,000 = 1.67 times	50,000 / 30,000 = 1.67 times
(b)	When PBIT was £40,000 =	40,000 / 10,000 = 4 times	40,000 / 30,000 = 1.33 times	40,000 / 30,000 = 1.33 times

Note. Although preference share capital is included as prior charge capital for the gearing ratio, it is usual to exclude preference dividends from 'interest' charges. We also look at all interest payments, even interest charges on short-term debt, and so interest cover and gearing do not quite look at the same thing.

3.20 Both B and C have a low interest cover, which is a warning to ordinary shareholders that their profits are highly vulnerable, in percentage terms, to even small changes in PBIT.

Activity 14.2

Returning to the example of Betatec plc in Paragraph 1.8, what is the company's interest cover?

Cash flow ratio

> **KEY TERM**
>
> The **cash flow ratio** is the ratio of a company's net cash inflow to its total debts.

3.21 (a) Net cash inflow is the amount of cash which the company has coming into the business from its operations. A suitable figure for net cash inflow can be obtained from the cash flow statement.

Part E: Interpretation of accounts

(b) Total debts are short-term and long-term creditors, together with provisions for liabilities and charges. A distinction can be made between debts payable within one year and other debts and provisions.

3.22 Obviously, a company needs to be earning enough cash from operations to be able to meet its foreseeable debts and future commitments, and the cash flow ratio, and changes in the cash flow ratio from one year to the next, provide a useful indicator of a company's cash position.

Short-term solvency and liquidity

3.23 **Profitability** is of course an important aspect of a company's performance and debt or gearing is another. Neither, however, addresses directly the key issue of **liquidity**.

> **KEY TERM**
>
> **Liquidity** is the amount of cash a company can put its hands on quickly to settle its debts (and possibly to meet other unforeseen demands for cash payments too).

3.24 Liquid funds consist of:

(a) Cash

(b) Short-term investments for which there is a ready market

(c) Fixed-term deposits with a bank or building society, for example, a six month high-interest deposit with a bank

(d) Trade debtors (because they will pay what they owe within a reasonably short period of time)

(e) Bills of exchange receivable (because like ordinary trade debtors, these represent amounts of cash due to be received within a relatively short period of time)

3.25 In summary, **liquid assets** are current asset items that will or could soon be **converted into cash, and cash itself**. Two common definitions of liquid assets are:

(a) All current assets without exception
(b) All current assets with the exception of stocks

3.26 A company can obtain liquid assets from sources other than sales, such as the issue of shares for cash, a new loan or the sale of fixed assets. But a company cannot rely on these at all times, and in general, obtaining liquid funds depends on making sales and profits. Even so, profits do not always lead to increases in liquidity. This is mainly because funds generated from trading may be immediately invested in fixed assets or paid out as dividends. You should refer back to the chapter on cash flow statements to examine this issue.

3.27 The reason why a company needs liquid assets is so that it can meet its debts when they fall due. Payments are continually made for operating expenses and other costs, and so there is a cash cycle from trading activities of cash coming in from sales and cash going out for expenses. This is illustrated by the diagram overleaf.

The cash cycle

3.28 To help you to understand liquidity ratios, it is useful to begin with a brief explanation of the cash cycle. The cash cycle describes the flow of cash out of a business and back into it again as a result of normal trading operations.

3.29 Cash goes out to pay for supplies, wages and salaries and other expenses, although payments can be delayed by taking some credit. A business might hold stock for a while and then sell it. Cash will come back into the business from the sales, although customers might delay payment by themselves taking some credit.

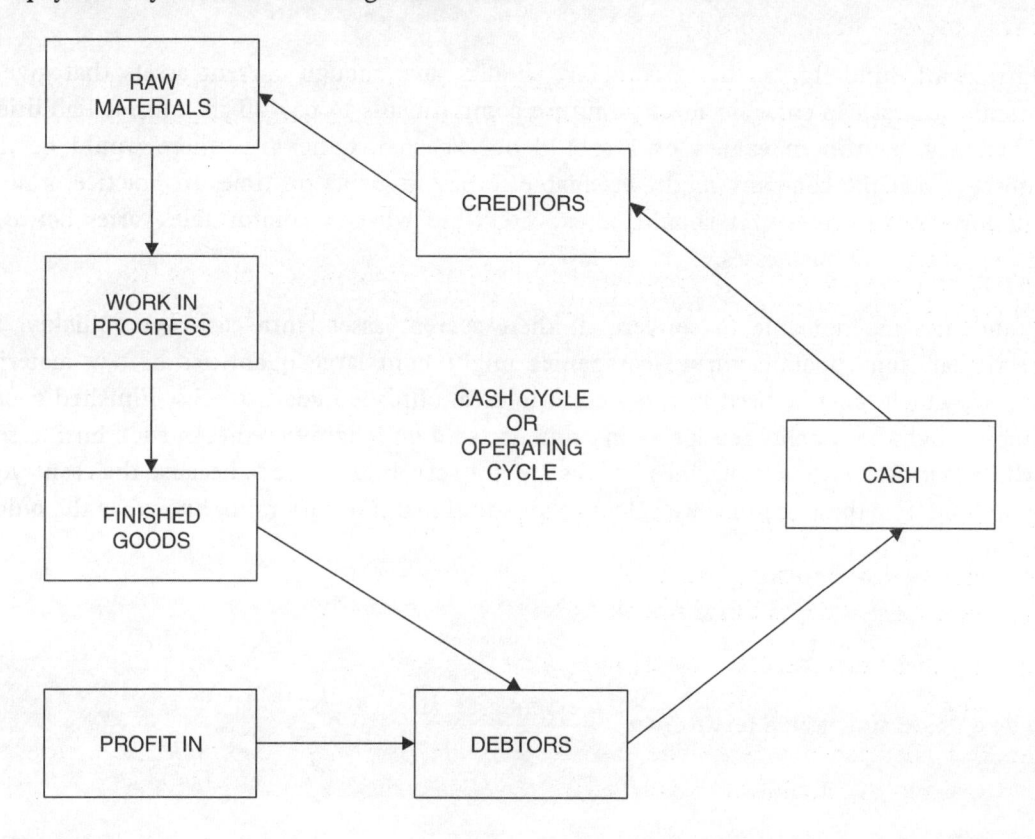

```
      RAW
    MATERIALS  ←──────────────┐
        │                     │
        ↓                CREDITORS
     WORK IN                  ↑
    PROGRESS                  │
        │        CASH CYCLE   │
        ↓           OR        │
     FINISHED   OPERATING   CASH
      GOODS       CYCLE       ↑
        │                     │
        ↓                     │
    PROFIT IN ──→ DEBTORS ────┘
```

3.30 The main points about the cash cycle are as follows.

(a) The timing of cash flows in and out of a business does not coincide with the time when sales and costs of sales occur. Cash flows out can be postponed by taking credit. Cash flows in can be delayed by having debtors.

(b) The time between making a purchase and making a sale also affects cash flows. If stocks are held for a long time, the delay between the cash payment for stocks and cash receipts from selling them will also be a long one.

(c) Holding stocks and having debtors can therefore be seen as two reasons why cash receipts are delayed. Another way of saying this is that if a company invests in working capital, its cash position will show a corresponding decrease.

(d) Similarly, taking credit from creditors can be seen as a reason why cash payments are delayed. The company's liquidity position will worsen when it has to pay the creditors, unless it can get more cash in from sales and debtors in the meantime.

3.31 The liquidity ratios and working capital turnover ratios are used to test a company's liquidity, length of cash cycle, and investment in working capital.

Part E: Interpretation of accounts

Liquidity ratios: current ratio and quick ratio

3.32 The 'standard' test of liquidity is the **current ratio**. It can be obtained from the balance sheet, and is calculated as follows.

> **FORMULA TO LEARN**
>
> Current ratio = $\dfrac{\text{current assets}}{\text{current liabilities}}$

The idea behind this is that a company should have enough current assets that give a promise of 'cash to come' to meet its future commitments to pay off its current liabilities. Obviously, a **ratio in excess of 1** should be expected. Otherwise, there would be the prospect that the company might be unable to pay its debts on time. In practice, a ratio comfortably in excess of 1 should be expected, but what is 'comfortable' varies between different types of businesses.

3.33 Companies are not able to convert all their current assets into cash very quickly. In particular, some manufacturing companies might hold large quantities of raw material stocks, which must be used in production to create finished goods stocks. Finished goods stocks might be warehoused for a long time, or sold on lengthy credit. In such businesses, where stock turnover is slow, most stocks are not very 'liquid' assets, because the cash cycle is so long. For these reasons, we calculate an additional liquidity ratio, known as the **quick ratio** or **acid test** ratio.

> **FORMULA TO LEARN**
>
> The **quick ratio**, or **acid test ratio** is: $\dfrac{\text{current assets less stocks}}{\text{current liabilities}}$

3.34 This ratio should ideally be at least 1 for companies with a slow stock turnover. For companies with a fast stock turnover, a quick ratio can be comfortably less than 1 without suggesting that the company should be in cash flow trouble.

3.35 Both the current ratio and the quick ratio offer an indication of the company's liquidity position, but the absolute figures should not be interpreted too literally. It is often theorised that an acceptable current ratio is 1.5 and an acceptable quick ratio is 0.8, but these should only be used as a guide.

Case example

Different businesses operate in very different ways. Budgens (the supermarket group) for example had (as at 30 April 1993) a current ratio of 0.52 and a quick ratio of 0.17. Budgens has low debtors (people do not buy groceries on credit), low cash (good cash management), medium stocks (high stocks but quick turnover, particularly in view of perishability) and very high creditors (Budgens buys its supplies of groceries on credit).

Compare the Budgens ratios with the Tomkins group which had a current ratio of 1.44 and a quick ratio of 1.03 (as at 1 May 1993). Tomkins is a manufacturing and retail organisation and operates with liquidity ratios closer to the standard. At 25 September 1993, Tate & Lyle's figures gave a current ratio of 1.18 and a quick ratio of 0.80.

3.36 What is important is the **trend** of these ratios. From this, one can easily ascertain whether liquidity is improving or deteriorating. If Budgens has traded for the last 10 years (very successfully) with current ratios of 0.52 and quick ratios of 0.17 then it should be supposed that the company can continue in business with those levels of liquidity. If in the following year the current ratio were to fall to 0.38 and the quick ratio to 0.09, then further investigation into the liquidity situation would be appropriate. It is the relative position that is far more important than the absolute figures.

3.37 Don't forget the other side of the coin either. A current ratio and a quick ratio can get bigger than they need to be. A company that has large volumes of stocks and debtors might be over-investing in working capital, and so tying up more funds in the business than it needs to. This would suggest poor management of debtors (credit) or stocks by the company.

Efficiency ratios: control of debtors and stock

3.38 A rough measure of the average length of time it takes for a company's debtors to pay what they owe is the 'debtor days' ratio, or **average debtors' payment period**.

> **FORMULA TO LEARN**
>
> $$\text{Debtors payment period} = \frac{\text{trade debtors}}{\text{sales}} \times 365 \text{ days}$$

3.39 The estimated average **debtors' payment period** is calculated as follows.

3.40 The figure for sales should be taken as the turnover figure in the P & L account. The trade debtors are not the total figure for debtors in the balance sheet, which includes prepayments and non-trade debtors. The trade debtors figure will be itemised in an analysis of the debtors total, in a note to the accounts.

3.41 The estimate of debtor days is only approximate.

(a) The balance sheet value of debtors might be abnormally high or low compared with the 'normal' level the company usually has.

(b) Turnover in the P & L account is exclusive of VAT, but debtors in the balance sheet are inclusive of VAT. We are not strictly comparing like with like. (Some companies show turnover inclusive of VAT as well as turnover exclusive of VAT, and the 'inclusive' figure should be used in these cases.)

3.42 Sales are usually made on 'normal credit terms' of payment within 30 days. Debtor days significantly in excess of this might be representative of poor management of funds of a business. However, some companies must allow generous credit terms to win customers. Exporting companies in particular may have to carry large amounts of debtors, and so their average collection period might be well in excess of 30 days.

3.43 The trend of the collection period (debtor days) over time is probably the best guide. If debtor days are increasing year on year, this is indicative of a poorly managed credit control function (and potentially therefore a poorly managed company).

Part E: Interpretation of accounts

3.44 EXAMPLES: DEBTOR DAYS

Using the same examples as before, the debtor days of those companies were as follows.

Company	Date	Trade debtors / turnover	Debtor days (×365)	Previous year	Debtor days (×365)
Budgens	30.4.93	£5,016K / £284,986K =	6.4 days	£3,977K / £290,668K =	5.0 days
Tomkins	1.5.93	£458.3m / £2,059.5m =	81.2 days	£272.4m / £1,274.2m =	78.0 days
Tate & Lyle	25.9.93	£304.4m / £3,817.3m =	29.3 days	£287.0m / £3,366.3m =	31.1 days

3.45 The differences in debtor days reflect the differences between the types of business. Budgen's has hardly any trade debtors at all, whereas the manufacturing companies have far more. The debtor days are fairly constant from the previous year for all three companies.

Stock turnover period

3.46 Another ratio worth calculating is the **stock turnover period**, or **stock days**. This is another estimated figure, obtainable from published accounts, which indicates the average number of days that items of stock are held for. As with the average debt collection period, however, it is only an approximate estimated figure, but one which should be reliable enough for comparing changes year on year.

> **FORMULA TO LEARN**
>
> The number of **stock days** is calculated as:
>
> $$\frac{\text{Stock}}{\text{Cost of sales}} \times 365$$

3.47 The reciprocal of the fraction:

$$\frac{\text{cost of sales}}{\text{stock}}$$

is termed the stock turnover, and is another measure of how vigorously a business is trading. A lengthening stock turnover period from one year to the next indicates:

(a) a slowdown in trading; or

(b) a build-up in stock levels, perhaps suggesting that the investment in stocks is becoming excessive.

3.48 Presumably if we add together the stock days and the debtor days, this should give us an indication of how soon stock is convertible into cash. Both debtor days and stock days therefore give us a further indication of the company's liquidity.

3.49 EXAMPLES: STOCK TURNOVER

Returning once more to our first example, the estimated stock turnover periods for Budgens were as follows.

14: Ratio analysis

Company	Date	$\dfrac{\text{Stock}}{\text{Cost of sales}}$	Stock turnover period (days × 365)	Previous year	
Budgens	30.4.92	$\dfrac{£15,554\text{K}}{£254,571\text{K}}$	22.3 days	$\dfrac{£14,094\text{K}}{£261,368\text{K}}$ × 365 =	19.7 days

3.50 The figures for cost of sales were not shown in the accounts of either Tate & Lyle or Tomkins

---

Activity 14.3

Butthead Ltd buys raw materials on six weeks credit, holds them in store for three weeks and then issues them to the production department. The production process takes two weeks on average, and finished goods are held in store for an average of four weeks before being sold. Debtors take five weeks credit on average.

Calculate the length of the cash cycle.

Activity 14.4

During a year a business sold stock which had cost £60,000. The stock held at the beginning of the year was £6,000 and at the end of the year £10,000.

What was the annual rate of stock turnover?

Activity 14.5

Calculate liquidity and working capital ratios from the accounts of the BET Group, a business which provides service support (cleaning etc) to customers worldwide.

	1997	1996
Turnover	2,176.2	2,344.8
Cost of sales	1,659.0	1,731.5
Gross profit	517.2	613.3
Current assets		
Stocks	42.7	78.0
Debtors (note 1)	378.9	431.4
Short-term deposits and cash	205.2	145.0
	626.8	654.4
Creditors: amounts falling due within one year		
Loans and overdrafts	32.4	81.1
Corporation taxes	67.8	76.7
Dividend	11.7	17.2
Creditors (note 2)	487.2	467.2
	599.1	642.2
Net current assets	27.7	12.2
Notes		
1 Trade debtors	295.2	335.5
2 Trade creditors	190.8	188.1

3.51 BET Group is a service company and hence it would be expected to have very low stock and a very short stock turnover period. The similarity of debtors' and creditors' turnover periods means that the group is passing on most of the delay in receiving payment to its suppliers.

3.52 Creditors' turnover is ideally calculated by the formula:

Part E: Interpretation of accounts

$$\frac{\text{Trade creditors}}{\text{Purchases}} \times 365$$

However, it is rare to find purchases disclosed in published accounts and so cost of sales serves as an approximation. The creditors' turnover ratio often helps to assess a company's liquidity; an increase in creditor days is often a sign of lack of long-term finance or poor management of current assets, resulting in the use of extended credit from suppliers, increased bank overdraft and so on.

3.53 BET's current ratio is a little lower than average but its quick ratio is better than average and very little less than the current ratio. This suggests that stock levels are strictly controlled, which is reinforced by the low stock turnover period. It would seem that working capital is tightly managed, to avoid the poor liquidity which could be caused by a high debtors' turnover period and comparatively high creditors.

4 SHAREHOLDERS' INVESTMENT RATIOS

4.1 These are the ratios which help equity shareholders and other investors to assess the value and quality of an investment in the ordinary shares of a company. They are:

(a) Earnings per share
(b) Dividend per share
(c) Dividend cover
(d) P/E ratio
(e) Dividend yield
(f) Earnings yield

4.2 The value of an investment in ordinary shares in a listed company is its market value, and so investment ratios must have regard not only to information in the company's published accounts, but also to the current price, and the fourth, fifth and sixth ratios all involve using the share price.

Earnings per share

4.3 It is possible to calculate the return on each ordinary share in the year. This is the earnings per share (EPS). Earnings are profits after tax, preference dividends and 'extraordinary items' (separately disclosed, large and very unusual items), which can either be paid out as a dividend to ordinary shareholders or retained in the business. You should note that earnings per share was discussed in Chapter 9 in connection with FRS 3 *Reporting financial performance*.

4.4 **EXAMPLE: EARNINGS PER SHARE**

Suppose that Rovers Ltd reports the following figures:

PROFIT AND LOSS ACCOUNT FOR 20X4 (EXTRACT)

	£
Profit before interest and tax	120,000
Interest	(20,000)
Profit before tax	100,000
Taxation	(40,000)
Profit after tax	60,000
Preference dividend	(1,000)
Profit available for ordinary shareholders (= earnings)	59,000
Ordinary dividend	(49,000)
Retained profits	10,000

The company has 80,000 ordinary shares and 20,000 preference shares.

Calculate earnings per share for Rovers Ltd in 20X4.

4.5 SOLUTION

EPS is $\dfrac{£59,000}{80,000} = 73.75$ pence

4.6 In practice there are usually further complications in calculating the EPS, but fortunately these are outside your syllabus.

Dividend per share and dividend cover

4.7 The **dividend per share** in pence is self-explanatory, and clearly an item of some interest to shareholders.

4.8 **Dividend cover** is calculated as follows.

> **FORMULA TO LEARN**
>
> **Dividend cover** = $\dfrac{\text{Earnings per share}}{\text{Net dividend per (ordinary) share}}$

4.9 It shows the proportion of profit on ordinary activities for the year that is available for distribution to shareholders has been paid (or proposed) and what proportion will be retained in the business to finance future growth. A dividend cover of 2 times would indicate that the company had paid 50% of its distributable profits as dividends, and retained 50% in the business to help to finance future operations. Retained profits are an important source of funds for most companies, and so the dividend cover can in some cases be quite high.

4.10 A significant change in the dividend cover from one year to the next would be worth looking at closely. For example, if a company's dividend cover were to fall sharply between one year and the next, it could be that its profits had fallen, but the directors wished to pay at least the same amount of dividends as in the previous year, so as to keep shareholder expectations satisfied.

Part E: Interpretation of accounts

P/E ratio

> **KEY TERM**
>
> The **P/E ratio** is the ratio of a company's current share price to the earnings per share.

4.11 A high **P/E ratio** indicates strong shareholder confidence in the company and its future, eg in profit growth, and a lower P/E ratio indicates lower confidence.

4.12 The P/E ratio of one company can be compared with the P/E ratios of:

(a) other companies in the same business sector
(b) other companies generally

Dividend yield

4.13 **Dividend yield** is the return a shareholder is currently expecting on the shares of a company. It is calculated as follows.

> **FORMULA TO LEARN**
>
> $$\text{Dividend yield} = \frac{\text{Dividend on the share for the year}}{\text{Current market value of the share (ex div)}} \times 100\%$$

4.14 Shareholders look for both dividend yield and capital growth. Obviously, dividend yield is therefore an important aspect of a share's performance.

Activity 14.6

In the year to 31 December 1998, BPP Holdings plc declared an interim ordinary dividend of 5.75p per share and a final ordinary dividend of 11.5p per share. Assuming an ex div share price of 500 pence, what is the dividend yield?

Earnings yield

4.15 Earnings yield is a performance indicator that is not given the same publicity as EPS, P/E ratio, dividend cover and dividend yield.

> **KEY TERM**
>
> **Earnings yield** is measured as the earnings per share, grossed up, as a percentage of the current share price. It therefore, indicates what the dividend yield could be if the company paid out all its profits as dividend and retained nothing in the business.

4.16 It attempts to improve the comparison between investments in different companies by overcoming the problem that companies have differing dividend covers. Some companies retain a bigger proportion of their profits than others, and so the dividend yield between companies can vary for this reason. Earnings yield overcomes the problem of comparison by assuming that all earnings are paid out as dividends.

> **FORMULA TO LEARN**
>
> Earnings yield = dividend yield × dividend cover.

Activity 14.7

	Company P		Company Q	
	£m	£m	£m	£m
Profit on ordinary activities after tax		41.1		5.6
Dividends				
Preference	0.5		-	
Ordinary	20.6		5.4	
		21.1		5.4
Retained profits		20.0		0.2

	Company P	Company Q
Number of ordinary shares	200m	50m
Market price per share	285p	154p

Compare the dividend yield, dividend cover and earnings yield of the two companies.

5 PRESENTATION OF A RATIO ANALYSIS REPORT

5.1 Examination questions on ratio analysis may try to simulate a real life situation. A set of accounts could be presented and you may be asked to prepare a report on them, addressed to a specific interested party, such as a bank. You should begin your report with a heading showing who it is from, the name of the addressee, the subject of the report and a suitable date.

5.2 A good approach is often to head up a 'schedule of ratios and statistics' which will form an appendix to the main report. Calculate the ratios in a logical sequence, dealing in turn with operating and profitability ratios, use of assets (eg turnover periods for stocks and debtors), liquidity and gearing.

5.3 As you calculate the ratios you are likely to be struck by significant fluctuations and trends. These will form the basis of your comments in the body of the report. The report should begin with some introductory comments, setting out the scope of your analysis and mentioning that detailed figures have been included in an appendix. You should then go on to present your analysis under any categories called for by the question (eg separate sections for management, shareholders and creditors, or separate sections for profitability and liquidity).

5.4 Finally, look out for opportunities to suggest remedial action where trends appear to be unfavourable. Questions sometimes require you specifically to set out your advice and recommendations.

Part E: Interpretation of accounts

> **Exam alert**
>
> You may be asked to prepare a report on ratios which have already been calculated. Alternatively you may be given a full set of accounts and asked to calculate, evaluate and comment on the ratios.

Planning your answers

5.5 This is as good a place as any to stress the importance of planning your answers. This is particularly important for 'wordy' questions. While you may feel like breathing a sigh of relief after all that number crunching, you should not be tempted to 'waffle'. The best way to avoid going off the point is to prepare an answer plan. This has the advantage of making you think before you write and structure your answer logically.

5.6 The following approach may be adopted when preparing an answer plan.

(a) Read the question requirements.

(b) Skim through the question to see roughly what it is about.

(c) Read through the question carefully, underlining any key words.

(d) Set out the headings for the main parts of your answer. Leave space to insert points within the headings.

(e) Jot down points to make within the main sections, underlining points on which you wish to expand.

(f) Write your full answer.

5.7 You should allow yourself the full time allocation for written answers, that is 1.8 minutes per mark. If, however, you run out of time, a clear answer plan with points in note form will earn you more marks than an introductory paragraph written out in full.

Activity 14.8

Waxen Wayne plc is a well-established company. Its board of directors is committed to a programme of expansion, commencing in 20X1. Unfortunately, there are unlikely to be enough retained profits to finance the expansion, and so it will be necessary to raise new capital from outside sources. The amount of finance which the board of directors wishes to raise is £2,000,000. There are three possible courses for raising the money, and each is thought to be practicable.

(a) *Scheme 1:* to issue £2,000,000 10% debenture stock 20X7 - 20X9 redeemable at par;

(b) *Scheme 2:* to issue 2,000,000 14% redeemable preference shares of £1 each, redeemable at par;

(c) *Scheme 3:* to issue 800,000 ordinary shares of £1 each at a premium of £1.50 per share. It would be hoped to pay an annual dividend of 12% of the nominal share value, which is the rate currently paid to existing ordinary shareholders.

Extracts from the current balance sheet of Waxen Wayne plc are as follows.

	£
Ordinary share capital (£1 shares fully paid)	10,000,000
General reserve	4,000,000
Profit and loss account	2,000,000
8% debentures	12,000,000

It is estimated that without the proposed expansion, the company's profit before interest and tax would remain static at about £3,710,000 for at least five more years.

The proposed expansion would be expected to earn an additional annual profit before interest and tax of £400,000 and would increase the total sales turnover of the company to £80 million per annum.

Corporation tax is payable at the rate of 40% on profits after interest and before tax.

'Earnings per share' is defined as the profits after tax and preference dividend, and extraordinary items, divided by the number of ordinary shares issued and ranking for dividend. The EPS for the current year is 16.5 pence, calculated as follows:

	£
Profit before interest and tax	3,710,000
Interest (8% of £12,000,000)	960,000
Profit before tax	2,750,000
Corporation tax (40%)	1,100,000
Profit after tax	1,650,000
Preference dividend	0
Earnings for ordinary shareholders	1,650,000
Number of ordinary shares	10,000,000
Earnings per share (EPS)	16.5p

Required

(a) Why might a company wish to issue redeemable debentures or preference shares? (3 marks)

(b) When would the debenture stock in scheme 1 be redeemed? (2 marks)

(c) The intention is to pay dividends of 12% on nominal value to ordinary shareholders. What would this imply for the new shareholders subscribing for the 800,000 new shares? (3 marks)

(d) What would be the earnings per share:

    (i) if scheme 1 were adopted;
    (ii) if scheme 2 were adopted;
    (iii) if scheme 3 were adopted? (3 marks)

(e) What would be the gearing ratio of the company after one full year:

    (i) if scheme 1 were adopted;
    (ii) if scheme 2 were adopted;
    (iii) if scheme 3 were adopted? (3 marks)

(f) Calculate the ROCE for each scheme, in two different ways, taking capital employed at the end of one full year of operations as your measure of capital employed. (3 marks)

(g) Analyse one of your ROCE calculations between profitability and asset turnover. (3 marks)

Activity 14.9

The financial statements of Efficient Ltd for the year 20X3 contain the following information:

On 31 December 20X3

Ratio of current assets to current liabilities	1.75 to 1
Liquidity ratio - total of debtors and bank balances to current liabilities	1.25 to 1
Net current assets	£37,500
Issued capital in ordinary shares	£50,000
Fixed assets - percentage of shareholders' equity and reserves	60%
Average age of outstanding debts (based on a year of 52 weeks)	7 weeks

For the year 20X3

Net profit - percentage of issued share capital	15%
Annual rate of turnover of stock (based on cost on 31 December 20X3)	4.16 times
Gross profit - percentage of turnover	20%

On 31 December 20X3, there were:

(a) no current assets other than stock, debtors and bank balances;
(b) no liabilities other than shareholders' funds and current liabilities;
(c) no assets or debit balances other than fixed and current assets.

Part E: Interpretation of accounts

You are required to reconstruct in as much detail as possible:

(a) the balance sheet as on 31 December 20X3; and (10 marks)
(b) the trading and profit and loss accounts for the year 20X3. (10 marks)

Ignore taxation.

---

6 LIMITATIONS OF RATIO AND TREND ANALYSIS

6.1 Ratio analysis is not foolproof. There are many problems in trying to identify trends and make comparisons. Below are just a few.

- **Information problems**
  - The base information is often out of date, so timeliness of information leads to problems of interpretation
  - Historical cost information may not be the most appropriate information for the decision for which the analysis is being undertaken
  - Information in published accounts is generally summarised information and detailed information may be needed
  - Analysis of accounting information only identifies symptoms not causes and thus is of limited use

- **Comparison problems: inter-temporal**
  - Effects of price changes make comparisons difficult unless adjustments are made
  - Impacts of changes in technology on the price of assets, the likely return and the future markets
  - Impacts of a changing environment on the results reflected in the accounting information
  - Potential effects of changes in accounting policies on the reported results
  - Problems associated with establishing a normal base year to compare other years with

- **Comparison problems: inter-firm**
  - Selection of industry norms and the usefulness of norms based on averages
  - Different firms having different financial and business risk profiles and the impact on analysis
  - Different firms using different accounting policies
  - Impacts of the size of the business and its comparators on risk, structure and returns
  - Impacts of different environments on results, eg different countries or home-based versus multinational firms

14: Ratio analysis

Key learning points

- This lengthy chapter has gone into quite a lot of detail about basic **ratio analysis**. The ratios you should be able to calculate and/or comment on are as follows.

  o **Profitability ratios**
    - return on capital employed
    - net profit as a percentage of sales
    - asset turnover ratio
    - gross profit as a percentage of sales

  o **Debt and gearing ratios**
    - debt ratio
    - gearing ratio
    - interest cover
    - cash flow ratio

  o **Liquidity and working capital ratios**
    - current ratio
    - quick ratio (acid test ratio)
    - debtor days (average debt collection period)
    - average stock turnover period

  o **Ordinary shareholders' investment ratios**
    - earnings per share
    - dividend cover
    - P/E ratio
    - dividend yield
    - earnings yield

- With the exception of the last three ratios, where the share's market price is required, all of these ratios can be calculated from information in a company's **published accounts**.

- Ratios provide information through comparison:

  o **trends** in a company's ratios from one year to the next, indicating an improving or worsening position;

  o in some cases, against a **'norm'** or 'standard';

  o in some cases, against the **ratios of other companies**, although differences between one company and another should often be expected.

- Ratio analysis is not foolproof. There are several **problems** inherent in making comparisons over time and between organisations.

Quick quiz

1. Apart from ratio analysis, what other information might be helpful in interpreting a company's accounts?
2. What is the usual formula for ROCE?
3. ROCE can be calculated as the product of two other ratios. What are they?
4. Define the 'debt ratio'.
5. Give two formulae for calculating gearing.
6. In a period when profits are fluctuating, what effect does a company's level of gearing have on the profits available for ordinary shareholders?
7. What is a company's cash flow ratio?
8. What are the formulae for:
   (a) the current ratio?
   (b) the quick ratio?
   (c) the debtors payment period?
   (d) the stock turnover period?
9. What is the relationship between the dividend yield and the earnings yield?

Part E: Interpretation of accounts

Answers to quick quiz

1. (a) Comments in the Chairman's report and directors' report.
   (b) The age and nature of the company's assets.
   (c) Current and future developments in the company's markets.
   (d) Post balance sheet events, contingencies, qualified audit report and so on.

2. $$\frac{\text{Profit on ordinary activities before interest and tax}}{\text{Capital employed}}$$

3. Asset turnover and profit margin.

4. The ratio of a company's total debts to its total assets.

5. (a) Capital gearing ratio $= \dfrac{\text{Prior charge capital}}{\text{Total capital}}$

   (b) Debt/equity ratio $= \dfrac{\text{Prior charge capital}}{\text{Ordinary share capital and reserves}}$

6. The more highly geared a company, the greater the percentage change in profit available for ordinary shareholders for any given percentage change in profit before interest and tax.

7. The ratio of a company's net cash inflow to its total debts

8. (a) $\dfrac{\text{Current assets}}{\text{Current liabilities}}$

   (b) $\dfrac{\text{Current assets less stock}}{\text{Current liabilities}}$

   (c) $\dfrac{\text{Trade debtors}}{\text{Sales}} \times 365$

   (d) $\dfrac{\text{Stock}}{\text{Cost of sales}} \times 365$

9. Earnings yield = dividend yield × dividend cover

Answers to activities

Answer 14.1

ROCE $= \dfrac{\text{Profit}}{\text{Capital employed}}$

PM $= \dfrac{\text{Profit}}{\text{Sales}}$

AT $= \dfrac{\text{Sales}}{\text{Capital employed}}$

It follows that ROCE = PM × AT, which can be re-arranged to the form given in option D.

Answer 14.2

Interest payments should be taken gross, from the note to the accounts, and not net of interest receipts as shown in the P & L account.

	20X8	20X7
PBIT	360,245	247,011
Interest payable	18,115	21,909
	= 20 times	= 11 times

Betatec plc has more than sufficient interest cover. In view of the company's low gearing, this is not too surprising and so we finally obtain a picture of Betatec plc as a company that does not seem to have a debt problem, in spite of its high (although declining) debt ratio.

Answer 14.3

The cash cycle is the length of time between paying for raw materials and receiving cash from the sale of finished goods. In this case Butthead Ltd stores raw materials for three weeks, spends two weeks producing finished goods, four weeks storing the goods before sale and five weeks collecting the money from debtors: a total of 14 weeks. However, six weeks of this period is effectively financed by the company's creditors so that the length of the cash cycle is eight weeks.

Answer 14.4

$$\text{Stock turnover} = \frac{\text{Cost of goods sold}}{\text{Average stock}} = \frac{£60,000}{£8,000}$$

$$= 7.5 \text{ times}$$

Answer 14.5

	1997		1996	
Current ratio	$\frac{626.8}{599.1}$ =	1.05	$\frac{654.4}{642.2}$ =	1.02
Quick ratio	$\frac{584.1}{599.1}$ =	0.97	$\frac{576.4}{642.2}$ =	0.90
Debtors' payment period	$\frac{295.2}{2,176.2} \times 365$	= 49.5 days	$\frac{335.5}{2,344.8} \times 365$	= 52.2 days
Stock turnover period	$\frac{42.7}{1,659.0} \times 365$	= 9.4 days	$\frac{78.0}{1,731.5} \times 365$	= 16.4 days
	1997		1996	
Creditors' turnover period	$\frac{190.8}{1,659.0} \times 365$	= 42.0 days	$\frac{188.1}{1,731.5} \times 365$	= 40.0 days

Answer 14.6

The net dividend per share is (5.75 + 11.5) = 17.25 pence

$$\frac{17.25}{500} \times 100 = 3.45\%$$

Answer 14.7

	Company P £m	Company Q £m
Profit on ordinary activities after tax	41.1	5.6
Preference dividend	0.5	0
Earnings	40.6	5.6
Number of shares	200m	50m
EPS	20.3p	11.2p
Ordinary dividend per share	10.3p	10.8p
Dividend cover	$\frac{20.3}{10.3}$ = 1.97 times	$\frac{11.2}{10.8}$ = 1.04 times

Part E: Interpretation of accounts

	Company P	Company Q
Dividend yield	$\frac{10.3}{285} \times 100\%$	$\frac{10.8}{154} \times 100\%$
	= 3.6%	= 7%
Earnings yield	$\frac{20.3p}{285} \times 100\%$	$\frac{11.2}{154} \times 100\%$
	= 7.1%	= 7.3%

The dividend yield of Company Q is much higher, but the dividend cover of Company P is greater. (The dividend cover of Q is only just greater than 1 and it is only because of the extraordinary item in the P & L account that Company Q has managed to pay its dividend out of profits made in the year.)

Answer 14.8

(a) A company might wish to issue redeemable debentures and preference shares:

   (i) in order to ensure that the higher gearing will not be for the long term;

   (ii) in the hope that interest rates will come down in the future, so that when the debentures or preference shares are redeemed, new debentures or shares can be issued to replace them, but at a lower interest rate/dividend yield;

   (iii) redeemable items give greater flexibility for choosing a suitable capital structure.

(b) The debentures would become redeemable from 20X7, at the option of the company, but by 20X9 at the very latest. The company could redeem the debentures piecemeal from 20X7, all at once from 20X7 or not until all at once in 20X9.

(c) If shareholders receive a dividend at the 'coupon rate' of 12% or 12 pence per £1 share, then new shareholders who have paid a premium of £1.50 to buy each share would have an annual dividend on their investment of:

$$\frac{12p}{£1 + £1.50} \times 100\% = 4.8\%$$

(d)

	Scheme 1 £	Scheme 2 £	Scheme 3 £
Profit before interest and tax:			
Current operations	3,710,000	3,710,000	3,710,000
New scheme	400,000	400,000	400,000
	4,110,000	4,110,000	4,110,000
Interest			
8% debentures	(960,000)	(960,000)	(960,000)
10% debentures (10% × £2m)	(200,000)	-	-
Profit before tax	2,950,000	3,150,000	3,150,000
Corporation tax (40%)	(1,180,000)	(1,260,000)	(1,260,000)
Profit after tax	1,770,000	1,890,000	1,890,000
Preference dividend (14% of £2m)	-	(280,000)	-
Earnings for ordinary shareholders	1,770,000	1,610,000	1,890,000
Ordinary dividend (12p per share):			
10,000,000 shares	(1,200,000)	(1,200,000)	-
10,800,000 shares	-	-	(1,296,000)
Retained profits	570,000	410,000	594,000
Earnings per share	£1,770,000	£1,610,000	£1,890,000
	10,000,000	10,000,000	10,800,000
	17.7p	16.1p	17.5p

(*Note 1.* Scheme 1 provides a higher earnings per share because profits are boosted by the fact that corporation tax is charged on profits after interest. In other words interest is an 'allowable' expense for company tax purposes.)

14: Ratio analysis

(e)
	Scheme 1 £	Scheme 2 £	Scheme 3 £
8% debentures	12,000,000	12,000,000	12,000,000
10% debentures	2,000,000	-	-
Preference shares	-	2,000,000	-
Prior charge capital	14,000,000	14,000,000	12,000,000
Ordinary share capital	10,000,000	10,000,000	10,800,000
Share premium (800,000 × £1.5)			1,200,000
General reserve	4,000,000	4,000,000	4,000,000
P & L account b/f	2,000,000	2,000,000	2,000,000
Extra retained profit after one year	570,000	410,000	594,000
Total capital after one year	30,570,000	30,410,000	30,594,000
Gearing	14,000,000 / 30,570,000	14,000,000 / 30,410,000	12,000,000 / 30,594,000
	45.8%	46.0%	39.2%

(f) ROCE

(i) as PBIT / Total long-term capital

	Scheme 1	Scheme 2	Scheme 3
	4,110,000 / 30,570,000	4,110,000 / 30,410,000	4,110,000 / 30,594,000
	13.4%	13.5%	13.4%

(ii) as Earnings / Equity capital and reserves

	Scheme 1	Scheme 2	Scheme 3
	1,770,000 / 16,570,000	1,610,000 / 16,410,000	1,890,000 / 18,594,000
	10.7%	9.8%	10.2%

(g) Taking the ROCE in (f) (i)

(i) PBIT/sales

	Scheme 1	Scheme 2	Scheme 3
	4,110,000 / 80,000,000	same	same
	5.1%	5.1%	5.1%

(ii) Sales/capital employed

	Scheme 1	Scheme 2	Scheme 3
	80,000,000 / 30,570,000	80,000,000 / 30,410,000	80,000,000 / 30,594,000
	2.62 times	2.63 times	2.61 times

Answer 14.9

(a) BALANCE SHEET AS AT 31 DECEMBER 20X3

	£	£
Fixed assets		56,250
Current assets		
Stock	25,000	
Debtors	17,500	
Bank balances	45,000	
	87,500	
Less current liabilities	50,000	
Net current assets		37,500
		93,750
Capital and reserves		
Issued share capital		50,000
Unappropriated profits:		
Balance at 1 January 20X3	36,250	
Net profit for year	7,500	
		43,750
		93,750

Part E: Interpretation of accounts

(b) TRADING AND PROFIT AND LOSS ACCOUNT
FOR THE YEAR ENDED 31 DECEMBER 20X3:

	£
Sales	130,000
Cost of sales	104,000
Gross profit	26,000
Overheads	18,500
Net profit	7,500

Workings

1. $$\frac{\text{Current assets}}{\text{Current liabilities}} = \frac{1.75}{1}$$

   $$\therefore \frac{\text{Current assets - current liabilities (ie net current assets)}}{\text{Current liabilities}}$$

   $$= \frac{1.75 - 1}{1}$$

   $$= \frac{0.75}{1}$$

   $$\therefore \text{Current liabilities} = \frac{1}{0.75} \times \text{net current assets}$$

   $$= \frac{1}{0.75} \times £37,500$$

   $$= £50,000$$

   $\therefore$ Current assets $= 1.75 \times £50,000 = $ £87,500

		£
2	Debtors and bank balances are 125% of current liabilities = 125% of £50,000	62,500
3	Stock is therefore £87,500 - £62,500	25,000
4	If stock is £25,000, then turnover at cost is 4.16 × £25,000	104,000
	Gross profit = 25% on cost (= 20% on turnover)	26,000
	Sales	130,000
5	Net profit is 15% of share capital	7,500
	$\therefore$ Overheads are £26,000 - £7,500	18,500
6	Debtors are 7/52 × turnover = 7/52 × £130,000	17,500
7	Bank balances constitute balance of current assets ie £87,500 - (£25,000 + £17,500)	45,000
8	Fixed assets are 60% of shareholders' equity Shareholders' equity = total net assets Net current assets = £37,500 and must be 40% of total net assets	
	$\therefore$ Fixed assets = 60/40 × £37,500	56,250

Now try Question 14 in the Exam Question Bank at the end of the Text.

Part F
Simple consolidated accounts

Chapter 15 Introduction to group accounts

Chapter topic list

1 Groups and consolidation: an overview
2 Definitions
3 Exclusion of subsidiary undertakings from group accounts
4 Exemption from the requirement to prepare group accounts

The following study sessions are covered in this chapter.

Syllabus reference

23-25(a) Describe and be able to identify the general characteristics of a parent company, investment, subsidiary and associated undertaking — 5

23-25(b) Describe the concept of a group and the objective of consolidated financial statements — 5

23-25(b) Describe the circumstances and reasoning for subsidiaries to be excluded from consolidated financial statements — 5

Part F: Simple consolidated accounts

1 GROUPS AND CONSOLIDATION: AN OVERVIEW

1.1 You will probably know that many large companies actually consist of several companies controlled by one central or administrative company. Together, these companies are called a **group**.

How does a group arise?

1.2 The central company, called a **parent**, generally owns most or all of the shares in the other companies, which are called **subsidiaries**.

1.3 The parent company usually **controls** the subsidiary by owning most of the shares, but share ownership is not always the same as control, which can arise in other ways.

1.4 Businesses may operate as a group for all sorts of practical reasons. If you were going out for a pizza, you might go to Pizza Hut; if you wanted some fried chicken you might go to KFC. Both sound more appetising than 'Tricon', the parent company of these subsidiaries.

1.5 However, from the legal point of view, the **results of a group must be presented as a whole**. In other words, they need to be **consolidated**. Consolidation will be defined more formally later in the chapter. Basically, it means **presenting the results of a group of companies as if they were a single company**.

What does consolidation involve?

1.6 Before moving on to the formal definitions, think about what consolidation involves.

> **BASIC PRINCIPLES**
> - Consolidation means **adding together**.
> - Consolidation means **cancellation of like items** internal to the group.
> - Consolidate as if you **owned everything** then **show** the **extent to which you do not own everything**.

1.7 What does this mean? Consider the following example.

1.8 EXAMPLE TO SHOW BASIC PRINCIPLES

There are two companies, Pleasant Ltd and Sweet Ltd. Pleasant owns 80% of the shares in Sweet. Pleasant has a head office building worth £100,000. Sweet has a factory worth £80,000. Remember that consolidation means presenting the results of two companies as if they were one.

Adding together

You add together the values of the head office building and the factory to get an asset, land and buildings, in the group accounts of £100,000 + £80,000 = £180,000. So far so good; this is what you would expect consolidation to mean.

1.9 EXAMPLE CONTINUED

Suppose Pleasant has debtors of £40,000 and Sweet has debtors of £30,000. Included in the debtors of Pleasant is £5,000 owed by Sweet. Remember again that consolidation means presenting the results of the two companies as if they were one.

Do we then simply add together £40,000 and £30,000 to arrive at the figure for consolidated debtors? We cannot simply do this, because £5,000 of the debtors is owed within the group. This amount is irrelevant when we consider what the group as a whole is owed.

Suppose further that Pleasant has creditors of £50,000 and Sweet has creditors of £45,000. We already know that £5,000 of Sweet's creditors is a balance owed to Pleasant. If we just added the figures together, we would not reflect fairly the amount the group owes to the outside world. The outside world does not care what these companies owe to each other - that is an internal matter for the group.

Cancellation of like items

To arrive at a fair picture we eliminate both the debtor of £5,000 in Pleasant's books and the creditor of £5,000 in Sweet's books. Only then do we consolidate by adding together.

Consolidated debtors   = £40,000 + £30,000 − £5,000
                       = £65,000

Consolidated creditors = £50,000 + £45,000 − £5,000
                       = £90,000

1.10 EXAMPLE CONTINUED

So far we have established that consolidation means adding together any items that are not eliminated as internal to the group. Going back to the example, however, we see that Pleasant only owns 80% of Sweet. Should we not then add Pleasant's assets and liabilities to 80% of Sweet's?

Consolidate as if you owned everything

The answer is no. Pleasant **controls** Sweet, its subsidiary. The directors of Pleasant can visit **all** of Sweet's factory, if they wish, not just 80% of it. So the figure for consolidated land and buildings is £100,000 plus £80,000 as stated above.

Show the extent to which you do not own everything

However, if we just add the figures together, we are not telling the whole story. There may well be one or more shareholders who own the remaining 20% of the shares in Sweet Ltd. These shareholders cannot visit 20% of the factory or tell 20% of the workforce what to do, but they do have an **interest** in 20% of the net assets of Sweet. The answer is to show this **minority interest** separately in the bottom half of the consolidated balance sheet.

1.11 Summary

- Consolidation means adding together (uncancelled items).
- Consolidation means cancellation of like items internal to the group.
- Consolidate as if you owned everything then show the extent to which you do not.

Part F: Simple consolidated accounts

> **IMPORTANT**
> Keep these basic principles in mind as you work through the detailed techniques of group accounts.

2 DEFINITIONS

2.1 Now you know what a group is in general terms and what consolidation means in principle, you are ready to learn some more formal definitions.

> **Exam alert**
> These definitions have come up in exams, so you need to know them.

Parent and subsidiary undertakings: definition

2.2 Group accounts are governed by FRS 2 *Accounting for subsidiary undertakings*. FRS 2 states that an undertaking is the **parent undertaking** of another undertaking (**a subsidiary undertaking**) if any of the following apply.

> **PARENT UNDERTAKING**
> (a) It holds a **majority of the voting rights** in the undertaking.
> (b) It is a **member** of the undertaking and has the right to **appoint or remove directors** holding a majority of the voting rights at meetings of the board on all, or substantially all, matters.
> (c) It has the right to exercise a **dominant influence** over the undertaking:
>   (i) by virtue of provisions contained in the undertaking's memorandum or articles; or
>   (ii) by virtue of a control contract (in writing, authorised by the memorandum or articles of the controlled undertaking, permitted by law).
> (d) It is a member of the undertaking and controls alone, under an agreement with other shareholders or members, a majority of the voting rights in the undertaking.
> (e) It has a **participating interest** in the undertaking and:
>   (i) it actually exercises a dominant influence over the undertaking; or
>   (ii) it and the undertaking are managed on a unified basis.
> (f) A parent undertaking is also treated as the parent undertaking of the subsidiary undertakings of its subsidiary undertakings (a sub-subsidiary).

Other definitions

2.3 The above definition is extremely important and you may be asked to apply it to a given situation in an exam. It depends in turn, however, on the definition of various terms which are included in Paragraph 2.2.

15: Introduction to group accounts

Participating interest

2.4 FRS 2 states that a **participating** interest is an interest held by an undertaking in the shares of another undertaking which it holds on a **long-term basis** for the purpose of securing a contribution to its activities by the exercise of control or influence arising from or related to that interest.

(a) A holding of **20% or more** of the shares of an undertaking is **presumed** to be a participating interest unless the contrary is shown.

(b) An interest in shares includes an interest which is convertible into an interest in shares, and includes an option to acquire shares or any interest which is convertible into shares.

(c) An interest held on behalf of an undertaking shall be treated as held by that undertaking (ie all group holdings must be aggregated to determine if a subsidiary exists).

2.5 A 'participating interest', like an investment in a 'subsidiary undertaking', **need not be in a company**, because an 'undertaking' means one of three things.

(a) A body corporate

(b) A partnership

(c) An unincorporated association carrying on a trade or business, with or without a view to profit

Dominant influence

> **KEY TERM**
>
> **Dominant influence** is influence that can be exercised to achieve the operating and financial policies desired by the holder of the influence, notwithstanding the rights or influence of any other party.
>
> *(FRS 2)*

2.6 The standard then distinguishes between the two different situations involving dominant influence.

(a) In the context of Paragraph 2.2(c) above, **the right to exercise a dominant influence** means that the holder has a right to give directions regarding the operating and financial policies of another undertaking with which its directors are obliged to comply, whether or not they are for the benefit of that undertaking.

(b) **The actual exercise of dominant influence** means that the operating and financial policies of the undertaking influenced are set in accordance with the wishes of the holder of the influence and for the holder's benefit whether or not those wishes are explicit. The actual exercise of dominant influence is identified by its effect in practice rather than by the way in which it is exercised.

2.7 There are four other important definitions.

Part F: Simple consolidated accounts

> (a) **Control** is the ability of an undertaking to direct the financial and operating policies of another undertaking with a view to gaining economic benefits from its activities.
>
> (b) An **interest held on a long-term basis** is an interest which is held other than exclusively with a view to subsequent resale.
>
> (c) An **interest held exclusively with a view to subsequent resale** is either:
>
>   (i) an interest for which a purchaser has been identified or is being sought, and which is reasonably expected to be disposed of within approximately one year of its date of acquisition; or
>
>   (ii) an interest that was acquired as a result of the enforcement of a security, unless the interest has become part of the continuing activities of the group or the holder acts as if it intends the interest to become so.
>
> (d) **Managed on a unified basis:** two or more undertakings are managed on a unified basis if the whole of the operations of the undertakings are integrated and they are managed as a single unit. Unified management does not arise solely because one undertaking manages another.

Other definitions from the standard will be introduced where relevant over the next few chapters.

The requirement to consolidate

2.8 FRS 2 requires a parent undertaking to prepare consolidated financial statements for its group unless it uses one of the exemptions available in the standard (see Section 4).

> **KEY TERM**
>
> **Consolidation** is defined as: 'The process of adjusting and combining financial information from the individual financial statements of a parent undertaking and its subsidiary undertaking to prepare consolidated financial statements that present financial information for the group as a single economic entity.'
>
> **Consolidated accounts** are one form of group accounts which combines the information contained in the separate accounts of a holding company and its subsidiaries as if they were the accounts of a single entity.

2.9 In simple terms a set of consolidated accounts is prepared by **adding together** the assets and liabilities of the holding company and each subsidiary.

(a) The **whole** of the assets and liabilities of each company are included, even though some subsidiaries may be only partly owned.

(b) The 'capital and reserves' side of the balance sheet will indicate how much of the net assets are attributable to the group and how much to outside investors in partly owned subsidiaries. These **outside investors** are known as **minority interests**.

2.10 Most parent companies present their own individual accounts and their group accounts in a single **package**. The package typically comprises:

(a) **Parent company balance sheet,** which will include 'investments in subsidiary undertakings' as an asset

(b) **Consolidated balance sheet**

(c) **Consolidated profit and loss account**

(d) **Consolidated cash flow statement**

It is not necessary to publish a parent company profit and loss account (s 230 CA 1985), provided the consolidated profit and loss account contains a note stating the profit or loss for the financial year dealt with in the accounts of the parent company and the fact that the statutory exemption is being relied on.

> **Exam alert**
>
> The status of an investment has been tested in an exam.

3 EXCLUSION OF SUBSIDIARY UNDERTAKINGS FROM GROUP ACCOUNTS

3.1 S 229 CA 1985 (as amended by the CA 1989) provides that a **subsidiary may be omitted** from the consolidated accounts of a group in **any** of these cases.

(a) In the opinion of the directors, its inclusion 'is **not material** for the purpose of giving a true and fair view; but two or more undertakings may be excluded only if they are not material taken together'.

(b) There are **severe long-term restrictions** in exercising the parent company's rights.

(c) The holding is **exclusively for resale**.

(d) The information cannot be obtained 'without **disproportionate expense** or undue delay'.

3.2 If in the opinion of the directors, a subsidiary undertaking's consolidation is undesirable because the **business of the holding company and subsidiary are so different that they cannot reasonably be treated as a single undertaking, then that undertaking** *must* **be excluded.**

> This .... does not apply merely because some of the undertakings are industrial, some commercial and some provide services, or because they carry on industrial or commercial activities involving different products or provide different services.

3.3 FRS 2 states that a **subsidiary must be excluded** from consolidation in some cases.

(a) Severe long-term restrictions are **substantially hindering the exercise** of the **parent's rights** over the subsidiary's assets or management.

(b) The group's interest in the subsidiary undertaking is held **exclusively with a view to subsequent resale** *and* the subsidiary has **not been consolidated previously**.

(c) The subsidiary undertaking's **activities are so different** from those of other undertakings to be included in the consolidation that its inclusion would be incompatible with the obligation to give a true and fair view.

The FRS requires the circumstances in which subsidiary undertakings are to be excluded from consolidation to be interpreted **strictly**.

Part F: Simple consolidated accounts

3.4 Where a subsidiary is excluded from group accounts, FRS 2 lays down **supplementary provisions** on the disclosures and accounting treatment required.

4 EXEMPTION FROM THE REQUIREMENT TO PREPARE GROUP ACCOUNTS

4.1 The CA 1989 introduced a completely new provision **exempting some groups** from preparing consolidated accounts. There are two grounds.

(a) **Smaller groups** can claim exemptions on grounds of size (see below).

(b) **Parent companies** (*except* for listed companies) **whose immediate parent is established in an EU member country** need not prepare consolidated accounts. The accounts must give the name and country of incorporation of the parent and state the fact of the exemption. In addition, a copy of the audited consolidated accounts of the parent must be filed with the UK company's accounts. Minority shareholders can, however, require that consolidated accounts are prepared.

FRS 2 adds that exemption may be gained if all of the parent's subsidiary undertakings gain exemption under s 229 CA 1985 (see Paragraph 2.1).

4.2 The **exemption** from preparing consolidated accounts is **not available** to:

- Public companies
- Banking and insurance companies
- Authorised persons under the Financial Services Act 1986
- Companies belonging to a group containing a member of the above

4.3 Any two of the following **size criteria** for small and medium-sized groups must be met.

	Small	Medium-sized
Aggregate turnover	≤ £2.8 million net/ £3.36 million gross	≤ £11.2 million net/ £13.44 million gross
Aggregate gross assets	≤ £1.4 million net/ £1.68 million gross	≤ £5.6 million net/ £6.72 million gross
Aggregate number of employees (average monthly)	≤ 50	≤ 250

4.4 The aggregates can be calculated either before (gross) or after (net) consolidation adjustments for intra-group sales, unrealised profit on stock and so on (see following chapters). The qualifying conditions must be met in the **present and previous financial year**.

4.5 When the exemption is claimed, but the auditors believe that the company is not entitled to it, then they must state in their report that the company is in their opinion not entitled to the exemption and this report must be attached to the individual accounts of the company (ie no report is required when the company *is* entitled to the exemption).

Activity 15.1

Apple Ltd owns 60% of Pear Ltd. Apple has creditors of £120,000. Pear has creditors of £90,000 of which £10,000 is owed to Apple. Apple has debtors of £60,000 and Pear has debtors of £40,000. Apple has fixed assets of £80,000 and Pear has fixed assets of £50,000.

(a) Consolidated fixed assets is calculated as

	£
Apple	80,000
Pear 60% × £50,000	30,000
	110,000

True or false? Explain your answer.

(b) Calculate

(i) Consolidated debtors
(ii) Consolidated creditors

Key learning points

- This chapter has explained the concept of a group and introduced several important principles and definitions.
- Consolidation means presenting the results, assets and liabilities of a group of companies as if they were one company.
- Consolidation means adding together non-cancelled items.
- Intra-group items should be cancelled.
- Consolidate as if you owned everything, and then show the extent to which you do not.
- The principal regulations governing the preparation of group accounts have been explained. Many of these are hard to understand and you should re-read this chapter after you have completed your study of this section of the text.

Quick quiz

1 Company A holds 45% of the shares of Company B. Company B cannot, therefore, be a subsidiary of Company A. True or false?

2 Company A holds 25% of the shares of Company B. Does it therefore hold a participating interest?

3 What is dominant influence?

4 A group's interest in a subsidiary undertaking is held exclusively with a view to resale. The subsidiary has not been consolidated previously. Consolidation of the subsidiary is therefore optional. True or false?

5 What are the grounds on which some groups may be exempted from preparing consolidated accounts?

Answers to quick quiz

1 False. There are five other criteria (see Paragraph 2.2) which determine whether or not Company B is a subsidiary of Company A.

2 Company A will be presumed to hold a participating interest unless the contrary is shown.

3 The influence that can be exercised to achieve the operating and financial policies desired by the holder of the influence notwithstanding the rights or influences of any other party (FRS 2).

4 False. The subsidiary *must* be excluded from consolidation (FRS 2).

5 (a) Smaller groups may claim exemption on grounds of size.

(b) Parent companies (other than listed companies) whose immediate parent is established in an EU member country need not prepare consolidated accounts.

Part F: Simple consolidated accounts

Answers to activities

Answer 15.1

(a) False. The correct calculation is

	£
Apple	80,000
Pear	50,000
	130,000

Pear is a subsidiary of Apple, who controls **all** its fixed assets not just 60%. The 40% minority interest is accounted for separately.

(b) (i) *Consolidated debtors*

	£
Apple	60,000
Less inter-company	(10,000)
	50,000
Pear	40,000
Consolidated	90,000

(ii) *Consolidated creditors*

	£	£
Apple		120,000
Pear	90,000	
Less inter-company	(10,000)	
		80,000
		200,000

Now try Question 15 in the Exam Question Bank at the end of the Text.

Chapter 16 The consolidated balance sheet

Chapter topic list

1 Cancellation and part cancellation
2 Minority interests
3 Dividends payable by a subsidiary
4 Goodwill arising on consolidation
5 A technique of consolidation
6 Inter-company trading
7 Summary: consolidated balance sheet

The following study sessions are covered in this chapter.

		Syllabus reference
22-25(d)	Prepare a consolidated profit and loss account and balance sheet for a simple group including adjustments for pre- and post-acquisition profits, minority interests and consolidated goodwill	5
22-25(e)	Explain why intra-group transactions should be eliminated on consolidation	5
22-25(f)	Account for the effects (in the profit and loss account and balance sheet) of intra-group trading and other transactions including:	5
	(i) Unrealised profits in stock and fixed assets	
	(ii) Intra-group loans and interest and other intra-group charges	

Part F: Simple consolidated accounts

1 CANCELLATION AND PART CANCELLATION

> **Exam alert**
> The Study Guide for this paper refers to **simple consolidations** and **simple groups.**

1.1 As indicated in Chapter 15, the preparation of a consolidated balance sheet, in a very simple form, consists of two procedures.

(a) Take the individual accounts of the holding company and each subsidiary and **cancel out items** which appear as an asset in one company and a liability in another.

(b) **Add together all the uncancelled assets** and liabilities throughout the group.

1.2 **Items requiring cancellation** may include the following.

(a) There may be **inter-company trading** within the group. For example, S Ltd may sell goods to H Ltd. H Ltd would then be a debtor in the accounts of S Ltd, while S Ltd would be a creditor in the accounts of H Ltd. You covered this briefly in Chapter 15.

(b) The asset **'shares in subsidiary companies'** which appears in the parent company's accounts will be matched with the liability 'share capital' in the subsidiaries' accounts.

1.3 This second item requires explanation. A shareholder in a parent company, looking at the parent company's accounts, will see an asset 'investment in subsidiary' shown at cost. However, a shareholder in a parent company is also a shareholder in the group. Showing the investment at cost does not give a true picture of the assets and liabilities which the parent company controls. This is achieved by consolidating, ie cancelling like items and adding together uncancelled items.

1.4 So what is the item in the subsidiary's account that corresponds to the figure 'investment in subsidiary' in the accounts of the parent company? The answer is the subsidiary has issued share capital which the parent has purchased.

1.5 EXAMPLE: CANCELLATION

Parent Ltd has just bought 100% of the shares of Subsidiary Ltd. Below are the balance sheets of both companies just before consolidation.

PARENT LIMITED BALANCE SHEET	£'000	SUBSIDIARY LIMITED BALANCE SHEET	£'000
Assets			
Investment in subsidiary*	50	Debtors	20
Debtors	30	Cash	30
	80		50
Share capital	80	Share capital*	50
	80		50

* Cancelling items

The consolidated balance sheet will appear as follows.

PARENT AND SUBSIDIARY
CONSOLIDATED BALANCE SHEET

	£'000
Debtors (30 + 20)	50
Cash	30
	80
Share capital**	80
	80

**Note. This is the parent company's share capital only. The subsidiary's has been cancelled.

1.6 EXAMPLE: CANCELLATION WITH INTERCOMPANY TRADING

P Ltd regularly sells goods to its one subsidiary company, S Ltd. The balance sheets of the two companies on 31 December 20X6 are given below.

P LIMITED
BALANCE SHEET AS AT 31 DECEMBER 20X6

	£	£	£
Fixed assets			
Tangible assets			35,000
40,000 £1 shares in S Ltd at cost			40,000
			75,000
Current assets			
Stocks		16,000	
Debtors: S Ltd	2,000		
Other	6,000		
		8,000	
Cash at bank		1,000	
		25,000	
Current liabilities			
Creditors		14,000	
			11,000
			86,000
Capital and reserves			
70,000 £1 ordinary shares			70,000
Reserves			16,000
			86,000

S LIMITED
BALANCE SHEET AS AT 31 DECEMBER 20X6

	£	£	£
Fixed assets			
Tangible assets			45,000
Current assets			
Stocks		12,000	
Debtors		9,000	
		21,000	
Current liabilities			
Bank overdraft		3,000	
Creditors: P Ltd	2,000		
Other	2,000		
		4,000	
		7,000	
			14,000
			59,000

Part F: Simple consolidated accounts

	£	£	£
Capital and reserves			
40,000 £1 ordinary shares			40,000
Reserves			19,000
			59,000

Prepare the consolidated balance sheet of P Ltd.

1.7 SOLUTION

The cancelling items are:

(a) P Ltd's asset 'investment in shares of S Ltd' (£40,000) cancels with S Ltd's liability 'share capital' (£40,000);

(b) P Ltd's asset 'debtors: S Ltd' (£2,000) cancels with S Ltd's liability 'creditors: P Ltd' (£2,000).

The remaining assets and liabilities are added together to produce the following consolidated balance sheet.

P LIMITED
CONSOLIDATED BALANCE SHEET AS AT 31 DECEMBER 20X6

	£	£
Fixed assets		
Tangible assets		80,000
Current assets		
Stocks	28,000	
Debtors	15,000	
Cash at bank	1,000	
	44,000	
Current liabilities		
Bank overdraft	3,000	
Creditors	16,000	
	19,000	
		25,000
		105,000
Capital and reserves		
70,000 £1 ordinary shares		70,000
Reserves		35,000
		105,000

Notes on the example

1.8 (a) P Ltd's bank balance is not netted off with S Ltd's bank overdraft. To offset one against the other would be less informative and would conflict with the statutory principle that assets and liabilities should not be netted off.

(b) The share capital in the consolidated balance sheet is the share capital of the parent company alone. This must *always* be the case, no matter how complex the consolidation, because the share capital of subsidiary companies must *always* be a wholly cancelling item.

Part cancellation

1.9 An item may appear in the balance sheets of a parent company and its subsidiary, but not at the same amounts.

(a) The parent company may have acquired **shares in the subsidiary** at a price **greater or less than their nominal value**. The asset will appear in the parent company's accounts at cost, while the liability will appear in the subsidiary's accounts at nominal value. This raises the issue of **goodwill**, which is dealt with later in this chapter.

(b) Even if the parent company acquired shares at nominal value, it **may not** have **acquired all the shares of the subsidiary** (so the subsidiary may be only partly owned). This raises the issue of **minority interests**, which you touched on in Chapter 14 and which are also dealt with later in this chapter.

2 MINORITY INTERESTS

2.1 Let's recap on the general principles covered in the previous chapter.

- Consolidation means adding together of uncancelled items.
- Consolidation means adding together of like items.
- Consolidate as if you owned everything and then show the extent to which you do not.

It is this third concept of minority interest with which we are now concerned.

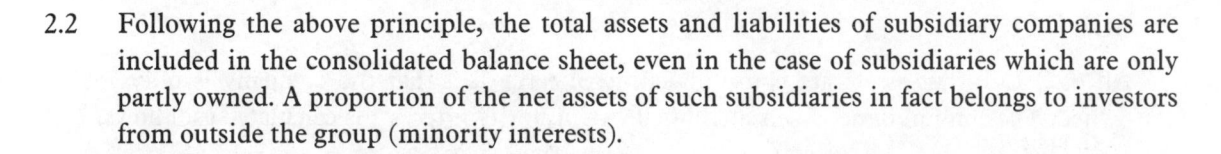

2.2 Following the above principle, the total assets and liabilities of subsidiary companies are included in the consolidated balance sheet, even in the case of subsidiaries which are only partly owned. A proportion of the net assets of such subsidiaries in fact belongs to investors from outside the group (minority interests).

KEY TERM

FRS 2 defines **minority interest** in a subsidiary undertaking as the 'interest in a subsidiary undertaking included in the consolidation that is attributable to the shares held by or on behalf of persons other than the parent undertaking and its subsidiary undertakings'.

In the consolidated balance sheet it is necessary to distinguish this proportion from those assets attributable to the group and financed by shareholders' funds.

2.3 The net assets of a company are financed by share capital and reserves. The consolidation procedure for dealing with partly owned subsidiaries is to **calculate the proportion of ordinary shares and reserves attributable to minority interests**.

2.4 EXAMPLE: MINORITY INTERESTS

P Ltd has owned 75% of the share capital of S Ltd since the date of S Ltd's incorporation. Their latest balance sheets are given below.

Part F: Simple consolidated accounts

P LIMITED
BALANCE SHEET

	£
Fixed assets	
Tangible assets	50,000
30,000 £1 ordinary shares in S Ltd at cost	30,000
	80,000
Net current assets	25,000
	105,000
Capital and reserves	
80,000 £1 ordinary shares	80,000
Reserves	25,000
	105,000

S LIMITED
BALANCE SHEET

	£
Tangible fixed assets	35,000
Net current assets	15,000
	50,000
Capital and reserves	
40,000 £1 ordinary shares	40,000
Reserves	10,000
	50,000

Prepare the consolidated balance sheet.

2.5 **SOLUTION**

All of S Ltd's net assets are consolidated despite the fact that the company is only 75% owned. The amount of net assets attributable to minority interests is calculated as follows.

	£
Minority share of share capital (25% × £40,000)	10,000
Minority share of reserves (25% × £10,000)	2,500
	12,500

Of S Ltd's share capital of £40,000, £10,000 is included in the figure for minority interest, while £30,000 is cancelled with P Ltd's asset 'investment in S Ltd'.

The consolidated balance sheet can now be prepared.

P GROUP
CONSOLIDATED BALANCE SHEET

	£
Tangible fixed assets	85,000
Net current assets	40,000
	125,000
Share capital	80,000
Reserves £(25,000 + (75% × 10,000))	32,500
Shareholders' funds	112,500
Minority interest	12,500
	125,000

2.6 In this example we have shown minority interest on the 'capital and reserves' side of the balance sheet to illustrate how some of S Ltd's net assets are financed by shareholders' funds, while some are financed by outside investors. You may see minority interest as a deduction from the other side of the balance sheet. The second half of the balance sheet will then consist entirely of shareholders' funds.

2.7 In more complicated examples the following technique is recommended for dealing with minority interests.

Step 1. Cancel common items in the draft balance sheets. If there is a minority interest, the subsidiary company's share capital will be a partly cancelled item. Ascertain the proportion of ordinary shares held by the minority.

Step 2. Produce a working for the minority interest. Add in the amounts of ordinary share capital calculated in step 1: this completes the cancellation of the subsidiary's share capital.

Add also the minority's share of reserves in the subsidiary company.

Step 3. Produce a separate working for each reserve (capital, revenue etc) found in the subsidiary company's balance sheet. The initial balances on these accounts will be taken straight from the draft balance sheets of the parent and subsidiary company.

Step 4. The closing balances in these workings can be entered directly onto the consolidated balance sheet.

Activity 16.1

Set out below are the draft balance sheets of P Ltd and its subsidiary S Ltd. You are required to prepare the consolidated balance sheet.

P LIMITED

	£
Fixed assets	
Tangible assets	31,000
Investment in S Ltd	
12,000 £1 ordinary shares at cost	12,000
	43,000
Net current assets	11,000
	54,000
Capital and reserves	
Ordinary shares of £1 each	40,000
Reserves	14,000
	54,000

S LIMITED

	£
Tangible fixed assets	25,000
Net current assets	5,000
	30,000
Capital and reserves	
Ordinary shares of £1 each	20,000
Reserves	10,000
	30,000

3 DIVIDENDS PAYABLE BY A SUBSIDIARY

3.1 When a subsidiary company pays a dividend during the year the accounting treatment is not difficult. Suppose S Ltd, a 60% subsidiary of H Ltd, pays a dividend of £1,000 on the last day of its accounting period. Its total reserves before paying the dividend stood at £5,000.

(a) £400 of the dividend is paid to minority shareholders. The cash leaves the group and will not appear anywhere in the consolidated balance sheet.

(b) The holding company receives £600 of the dividend, debiting cash and crediting profit and loss account.

(c) The remaining balance of reserves in S Ltd's balance sheet (£4,000) will be consolidated in the normal way. The group's share (60% × £4,000 = £2,400) will be included in group reserves in the balance sheet; the minority share (40% × £4,000 = £1,600) is credited to the minority interest account.

3.2 More care is needed when dealing with **proposed dividends** not yet paid by a subsidiary. The first step must be to ensure that the draft accounts of both subsidiary and parent company are up-to-date and reflect the proposed dividend.

> **Exam alert**
>
> A question may state that both companies have accrued for the proposed dividend; alternatively you may be presented with draft balance sheets in which one or other company, or possibly both companies, have omitted to make the necessary entries.

3.3 If neither company has accrued for the proposed dividend you will need to make appropriate adjustments to the draft balance sheets.

(a) If the subsidiary has not yet accrued for the proposed dividend, the adjustment is:

DEBIT   Revenue reserves
CREDIT   Dividends payable

with the full amount of the dividend payable in the subsidiary's books, whether it is due to the parent company or to minority shareholders.

(b) If the parent company has not yet accrued for its share of the proposed dividend, the adjustment is:

DEBIT   Debtors (dividend receivable)
CREDIT   Revenue reserves

with the *parent company's share* of the dividend receivable in the parent's books.

3.4 On consolidation, the **dividend payable** in S Ltd's accounts will **cancel with the dividend receivable** in H Ltd's accounts. If S Ltd is a wholly owned subsidiary, there will be complete cancellation; if S Ltd is only partly owned, there will be only part cancellation. The uncancelled portion will be the amount of dividend payable to minority shareholders and this will appear in the consolidated balance sheet as a current liability.

3.5 When preparing the workings for reserves and minority interest, the relevant reserves figures for both companies are the figures *after* adjusting for the proposed dividend.

3.6 **EXAMPLE: DIVIDENDS**

Set out below are the draft balance sheets of Hug Ltd and its subsidiary Bug Ltd. Hug Ltd has not yet taken account of the dividend proposed by Bug Ltd.

You are required to prepare the consolidated balance sheet.

HUG LIMITED

	£	£
Fixed assets		
Tangible assets		1,350
Investment in Bug Ltd: 1,500 shares at cost		1,500
		2,850
Current assets	700	
Current liabilities		
Creditors	400	
		300
		3,150

	£
Capital and reserves	
Ordinary shares of £1 each	1,000
Revenue reserves	2,150
	3,150

BUG LIMITED

	£	£
Tangible fixed assets		2,500
Current assets	900	
Current liabilities		
Creditors	200	
Proposed dividend	200	
		500
		3,000

Capital and reserves	
Ordinary shares of £1 each	2,000
Revenue reserves	1,000
	3,000

3.7 SOLUTION

The first step is to bring Hug Ltd's balance sheet up to date by accruing for its share of the dividend receivable from Bug Ltd. Hug Ltd owns 75% (1,500/2,000) of the shares in Bug Ltd. Its share of the proposed dividend is therefore 75% × £200 = £150. Hug Ltd's draft balance sheet should be adjusted as follows.

DEBIT	Debtors: dividend receivable	£150	
CREDIT	Revenue reserves		£150

3.8 Next deal with cancellation. There are two part-cancelling items, the shares of Bug Ltd and the dividend receivable/payable.

3.9 The workings may now be produced. Notice how the relevant reserves figures are the figures after adjusting for the proposed dividend. Because Bug Ltd's accounts are up-to-date, and reflect the proposed figure, the correct reserves figure (£1,000) can be taken straight from the draft balance sheet. In the case of Hug Ltd, it is the adjusted reserves figure (£2,150 + £150 = £2,300) which is used.

Workings

1   *Minority interests*

	£
Share capital (25% × 2,000)	500
Revenue reserves (25% × 1,000)	250
	750

Part F: Simple consolidated accounts

2 *Revenue reserves*

	£
Hug Ltd (as adjusted)	2,300
Share of Bug Ltd's revenue reserves (1,000 × 75%)	750
	3,050

HUG GROUP
CONSOLIDATED BALANCE SHEET

	£	£
Tangible fixed assets		3,850
Current assets	1,600	
Current liabilities		
Creditors	600	
Minority proposed dividend	50	
		950
		4,800
Capital and reserves		
Ordinary shares of £1 each		1,000
Revenue reserves		3,050
Shareholders' funds		4,050
Minority interests		750
		4,800

4 GOODWILL ARISING ON CONSOLIDATION

4.1 In the examples we have looked at so far the cost of shares acquired by the parent company has always been equal to the nominal value of those shares. This is seldom the case in practice and we must now consider some more complicated examples. To begin with, **we will examine the entries made by the parent company in its own balance sheet when it acquires shares.**

4.2 When a company P Ltd wishes to **purchase shares** in a company S Ltd it must pay the previous owners of those shares. The most obvious form of payment would be in **cash**. Suppose P Ltd purchases all 40,000 £1 shares in S Ltd and pays £60,000 cash to the previous shareholders in consideration. The entries in P Ltd's books would be:

DEBIT	Investment in S Ltd at cost	£60,000	
CREDIT	Bank		£60,000

4.3 However, the previous shareholders might be prepared to accept some other form of consideration. For example, they might accept an agreed number of **shares** in P Ltd. P Ltd would then issue new shares in the agreed number and allot them to the former shareholders of S Ltd. This kind of deal might be attractive to P Ltd since it avoids the need for a heavy cash outlay. The former shareholders of S Ltd would retain an indirect interest in that company's profitability via their new holding in its parent company.

4.4 Continuing the example, suppose the shareholders of S Ltd agreed to accept one £1 ordinary share in P Ltd for every two £1 ordinary shares in S Ltd. P Ltd would then need to issue and allot 20,000 new £1 shares. How would this transaction be recorded in the books of P Ltd?

4.5 The simplest method would be as follows.

DEBIT	Investment in S Ltd	£20,000	
CREDIT	Share capital		£20,000

However, if the 40,000 £1 shares acquired in S Ltd are thought to have a value of £60,000 this would be misleading. The former shareholders of S Ltd have presumably agreed to accept 20,000 shares in P Ltd because they consider each of those shares to have a value of £3. This view of the matter suggests the following method of recording the transaction in P Ltd's books.

DEBIT	Investment in S Ltd	£60,000	
CREDIT	Share capital		£20,000
	Share premium account		£40,000

The second method is the one which the Companies Act 1985 requires should normally be used in preparing consolidated accounts.

4.6 The amount which P Ltd records in its books as the cost of its investment in S Ltd may be more or less than the book value of the assets it acquires. Suppose that S Ltd in the previous example has nil reserves, so that its share capital of £40,000 is balanced by net assets with a book value of £40,000. For simplicity, assume that the book value of S Ltd's assets is the same as their market or fair value.

4.7 Now when the directors of P Ltd agree to pay £60,000 for a 100% investment in S Ltd they must believe that, in addition to its tangible assets of £40,000, S Ltd must also have intangible assets worth £20,000. This amount of £20,000 paid over and above the value of the tangible assets acquired is called **goodwill arising on consolidation** (sometimes **premium on acquisition**).

4.8 Following the normal cancellation procedure the £40,000 share capital in S Ltd's balance sheet could be cancelled against £40,000 of the 'investment in S Limited' in the balance sheet of P Ltd. This would leave a £20,000 debit uncancelled in the parent company's accounts and this £20,000 would appear in the consolidated balance sheet under the caption 'Intangible fixed assets. Goodwill arising on consolidation' (although see below for FRS 10's requirements on this type of goodwill).

Goodwill and pre-acquisition profits

4.9 Up to now we have assumed that S Ltd had nil reserves when its shares were purchased by P Ltd. Assuming instead that S Ltd had earned profits of £8,000 in the period before acquisition, its balance sheet just before the purchase would look as follows.

	£
Net tangible assets	48,000
Share capital	40,000
Reserves	8,000
	48,000

4.10 If P Ltd now purchases all the shares in S Ltd it will acquire net tangible assets worth £48,000 at a cost of £60,000. Clearly in this case S Ltd's intangible assets (goodwill) are being valued at £12,000. It should be apparent that any **reserves** earned by the subsidiary **prior to its acquisition** by the parent company must be **incorporated in the cancellation** process so as to arrive at a figure for goodwill arising on consolidation. In other words, not only S Ltd's share capital, but also its pre-acquisition reserves, must be cancelled against the asset 'investment in S Ltd' in the accounts of the parent company. The uncancelled balance of £12,000 appears in the consolidated balance sheet.

4.11 The consequence of this is that **any pre-acquisition reserves of a subsidiary company are not aggregated with the parent company's reserves** in the consolidated balance sheet. The

Part F: Simple consolidated accounts

figure of consolidated reserves comprises the reserves of the parent company plus the post-acquisition reserves only of subsidiary companies. The post-acquisition reserves are simply reserves now less reserves at acquisition.

> **POINT TO NOTE**
>
> If you're confused by this, think of it another way, from the point of view of group reserves. Only the profits earned by the group should be consolidated. Profits earned by the subsidiary before it became part of the group are not group profits; they reflect what the parent company is getting for its money on acquisition.

4.12 EXAMPLE: GOODWILL AND PRE-ACQUISITION PROFITS

Sing Ltd acquired the ordinary shares of Wing Ltd on 31 March when the draft balance sheets of each company were as follows.

SING LIMITED
BALANCE SHEET AS AT 31 MARCH

	£
Fixed assets	
Investment in 50,000 shares of Wing Ltd at cost	80,000
Net current assets	40,000
	120,000
Capital and reserves	
Ordinary shares	75,000
Revenue reserves	45,000
	120,000

WING LIMITED
BALANCE SHEET AS AT 31 MARCH

	£
Net current assets	60,000
Share capital and reserves	
50,000 ordinary shares of £1 each	50,000
Revenue reserves	10,000
	60,000

Prepare the consolidated balance sheet as at 31 March.

4.13 SOLUTION

The technique to adopt here is to produce a new working: 'Goodwill'. A proforma working is set out below.

Goodwill

	£	£
Cost of investment		X
Share of net assets acquired as represented by:		
Ordinary share capital	X	
Share premium	X	
Reserves on acquisition	X	
Group share	%	(X)
Goodwill		X

4.14 Applying this to our example the working will look like this.

	£	£
Cost of investment		80,000
Share of net assets acquired as represented by:		
Ordinary share capital	50,000	
Revenue reserves on acquisition	10,000	
	60,000	
Group share 100%		60,000
Goodwill		20,000

SING LIMITED
CONSOLIDATED BALANCE SHEET AS AT 31 MARCH

	£
Fixed assets	
Goodwill arising on consolidation	20,000
Net current assets	100,000
	120,000
Capital and reserves	
Ordinary shares	75,000
Revenue reserves	45,000
	120,000

Revaluation reserves

4.15 The assets of the subsidiary may be worth more than their book value. They may therefore be **revalued** on acquisition. You have met the idea of revaluations before in connection with companies and partnerships.

4.16 The assets need to be consolidated at their **fair value**. There will be a revaluation reserve representing the difference between fair and book value. This is consolidated in the same manner as a revenue reserve. The goodwill calculation will appear as follows.

Goodwill	£	£
Cost of investment		X
Share of net assets acquired as represented by		
Ordinary share capital	X	
Reserves on acquisition	X	
Revaluation reserve*	X	
	X	
Group share (%)		(X)
Goodwill		X

*Fair value of revalued assets less book value

FRS 10 *Goodwill and intangible assets*

4.17 Goodwill arising on consolidation is one form of **purchased goodwill** and is therefore governed by FRS 10. As explained in Chapter 12, goodwill should be **capitalised in the balance sheet** and should normally be **amortised over its useful economic life.**

4.18 The **consolidation adjustment** required each year is then as follows.

    DEBIT   Consolidated profit and loss account
    CREDIT   Provision for amortisation of goodwill

Part F: Simple consolidated accounts

The **unamortised portion** will be included in the consolidated balance sheet under **fixed assets**.

4.19 The standard contains a presumption that the useful life of the goodwill is less than 20 years. The presumption may be rebutted. If it is greater than 20 years, goodwill must still be amortised. If it is indefinite, goodwill should not be amortised, but a full impairment review should be performed each year. (Impairment means that the recoverable amount of an asset has fallen below the carrying amount.) An impairment review should, in any case, be performed at the end of the first full year after acquisition. The impairment review should be performed in accordance with FRS 11 *Impairment of fixed assets and goodwill*.

4.20 Goodwill arising on consolidation is the difference between the cost of an acquisition and the value of the subsidiary's net assets acquired. This difference can be **negative**: the aggregate of the fair values of the separate net assets acquired may exceed what the holding company paid for them. This 'negative goodwill', also sometimes called 'discount arising on consolidation' is required by FRS 10 to be shown as a **negative asset** in the 'assets' section of the balance sheet just below any positive goodwill. It should be released to the profit and loss account in line with the depreciation or sale of non-monetary assets acquired. (Non-monetary assets normally consist of fixed assets and stocks.)

5 A TECHNIQUE OF CONSOLIDATION

5.1 We have now looked at the topics of cancellation, minority interests and goodwill arising on consolidation. It is time to set out an approach to be used in tackling consolidated balance sheets. The approach we recommend consists of five stages.

Stage 1. Update the draft balance sheets of subsidiaries and parent company to take account of any proposed dividends not yet accrued for.

Stage 2. Agree inter-company current accounts by adjusting for items in transit.

Stage 3. Cancel items common to both balance sheets.

Stage 4. Produce working for minority interests as shown in Paragraph 2.5.

Stage 5. Produce a goodwill working as shown in Paragraph 4.13 above. Then produce a working for capital and revenue reserves, making sure to deduct from revenue reserves any pre-acquisition profits.

5.2 You should now attempt to apply this technique to the following Activity.

Activity 16.2

You have been asked to assist in the preparation of the consolidated accounts of the Thomas group. Set out below are the balance sheets of Thomas Ltd and James Ltd for the year ended 30 September 20X6.

BALANCE SHEET AS AT 30 SEPTEMBER 20X6

	Thomas Ltd £'000	James Ltd £'000
Fixed assets	13,022	3,410
Investment in James Ltd	3,760	-
Current assets		
Stocks	6,682	2,020
Debtors	5,526	852
Cash	273	58
	12,481	2,930
Current liabilities		
Trade creditors	3,987	507
Taxation	834	173
	4,821	680
Net current assets	7,660	2,250
Total assets less current liabilities	24,442	5,660
Long-term loan	8,000	1,500
	16,442	4,160
Capital and reserves		
Called up share capital	5,000	1,000
Share premium	2,500	400
Profit and loss account	8,942	2,760
	16,442	4,160

You have been given the following further information.

(a) The share capital of both Thomas Ltd and James Ltd consists of ordinary shares of £1 each. There have been no changes to the balances during the year.

(b) Thomas Ltd acquired 800,000 shares in James Ltd on 30 September 20X5 at a cost of £3,760,000.

(c) At 30 September 20X5 the balance on the profit and loss account of James Ltd was £2,000,000.

(d) The fair value of the fixed assets of James Ltd at 30 September 20X5 was £3,910,000. The revaluation has not been reflected in the books of James Ltd.

(e) Goodwill arising on consolidation is considered to have an indefinite life and is to remain in the balance sheet.

Required

Prepare a consolidated balance sheet for Thomas Ltd and its subsidiary undertaking as at 30 September 20X6.

6 INTER-COMPANY TRADING

6.1 We have already come across cases where one company in a group engages in trading with another group company. Any debtor/creditor balances outstanding between the companies are cancelled on consolidation. No further problem arises if all such intra-group transactions are undertaken at cost, without any mark-up for profit.

6.2 However, each company in a group is a separate trading entity and may wish to treat other group companies in the same way as any other customer. In this case, a company (say A Ltd) may buy goods at one price and sell them at a higher price to another group company (B Ltd). The accounts of A Ltd will quite properly include the profit earned on sales to B Ltd; and similarly B Ltd's balance sheet will include stocks at their cost to B Ltd at the amount at which they were purchased from A Ltd.

6.3 This gives rise to two problems.

(a) Although A Ltd makes a profit as soon as it sells goods to B Ltd, the group does not make a sale or achieve a profit until an outside customer buys the goods from B Ltd.

Part F: Simple consolidated accounts

(b) Any purchases from A Ltd which remain unsold by B Ltd at the year end will be included in B Ltd's stock. Their balance sheet value will be their cost to B Ltd, which is not the same as their cost to the group.

6.4 The objective of consolidated accounts is to present the financial position of several connected companies as that of a single entity, the group. This means that **in a consolidated balance sheet the only profits recognised should be those earned by the group** in providing goods or services to outsiders; and similarly, stock in the consolidated balance sheet should be valued at cost to the group.

6.5 Suppose that a holding company H Ltd buys goods for £1,600 and sells them to a wholly owned subsidiary S Ltd for £2,000. The goods are in S Ltd's stock at the year end and appear in S Ltd's balance sheet at £2,000. In this case, H Ltd will record a profit of £400 in its individual accounts, but from the group's point of view the figures are:

Cost	£1,600
External sales	nil
Closing stock at cost	£1,600
Profit/loss	nil

6.6 If we add together the figures for retained reserves and stock in the individual balance sheets of H Ltd and S Ltd the resulting figures for consolidated reserves and consolidated stock will each be overstated by £400. **A consolidation adjustment** is therefore necessary as follows.

DEBIT   Group reserves
CREDIT Group stock (balance sheet)

with the amount of **profit unrealised** by the group.

Activity 16.3

P Ltd acquired all the shares in S Ltd when the reserves of S Ltd stood at £10,000. Draft balance sheets for each company are as follows.

	P Ltd		S Ltd	
	£	£	£	£
Fixed assets				
Tangible assets		80,000		40,000
Investment in S Ltd at cost		46,000		
		126,000		
Current assets	40,000		30,000	
Current liabilities	21,000		18,000	
		19,000		12,000
		145,000		52,000
Capital and reserves				
Ordinary shares of £1 each		100,000		30,000
Reserves		45,000		22,000
		145,000		52,000

During the year S Ltd sold goods to P Ltd for £50,000, the profit to S Ltd being 20% of selling price. At the balance sheet date, £15,000 of these goods remained unsold in the stocks of P Ltd. At the same date, P Ltd owed S Ltd £12,000 for goods bought and this debt is included in the creditors of P Ltd and the debtors of S Ltd.

Required

Prepare a draft consolidated balance sheet for P Ltd. Assume that the goodwill has an indefinite useful economic life.

7 SUMMARY: CONSOLIDATED BALANCE SHEET

Purpose	To show the net assets which H controls and the ownership of those assets.
Net assets	Always 100% H plus 100% S providing H holds a majority of voting rights.
Share capital	H only.
Reason	Simply reporting to the holding company's shareholders in another form.
Reserves	100% H plus group share of post-acquisition retained reserves of S less consolidation adjustments.
Reason	To show the extent to which the group actually owns net assets included in the top half of the balance sheet.
Minority interest	MI share of S's consolidated net assets.
Reason	To show the extent to which other parties own net assets that are under the control of the holding company.

Key learning points

- This chapter has covered the mechanics of preparing simple **consolidated balance sheets**. In particular, procedures have been described for dealing with
    - Cancellation
    - Calculation of minority interests
    - Calculation of goodwill arising on consolidation
- A five-stage drill has been described and exemplified in a comprehensive example.
- The stages are as follows.
    - Update the draft balance sheets to take account of proposed dividends not accrued for
    - Agree intercompany current accounts by adjusting for items in transit
    - Cancel items common to both balance sheets
    - Minority interests
    - Goodwill
- We have examined the consolidation adjustments necessary when group companies **trade with each other**.
    - Any profit arising on intra-group transactions must be eliminated from the group accounts unless and until it is realised by a sale outside the group.

Quick quiz

1. What are the components making up the figure of minority interest in a consolidated balance sheet?
2. What adjustment is necessary before consolidation in cases where a holding company has not accrued for dividends receivable from a subsidiary?
3. What is 'goodwill arising on consolidation'?
4. How should 'negative goodwill' be disclosed in the consolidated balance sheet?
5. What is the basic principle of consolidation that determines the accounting treatment of inter-company trading?

Part F: Simple consolidated accounts

Answers to quick quiz

1. Interest in a subsidiary undertaking included in the consolidation that is attributable to the shares held by or on behalf of persons other than the parent undertaking and its subsidiary undertakings. (In practice, minority interest consists of the minority's share of the subsidiary's share capital and reserves.)

2. DEBIT   Debtors (dividend receivable)
   CREDIT   Revenue reserves

3. The amount paid over and above the fair value of the net assets acquired.

4. It should appear as a credit in the balance sheet just below positive goodwill.

5. The only profits recognised should be those earned by the group.

Answers to activities

Answer 16.1

The partly cancelling item is P Ltd's investment in S Ltd, ie ordinary shares. Minorities have an interest in 40% (8,000/20,000) of S Ltd's equity, including reserves.

You should now produce workings for minority interests and reserves as follows.

Workings

1   *Minority interests*

	£
Ordinary share capital: 40% of 20,000	8,000
Reserves: 40% of 10,000	4,000
	12,000

2   *Reserves*

	£
P Ltd	14,000
Share of S Ltd's reserves (60% × 10,000)	6,000
	20,000

The results of the workings are now used to construct the consolidated balance sheet (CBS).

P GROUP
CONSOLIDATED BALANCE SHEET

	£
Tangible fixed assets (31,000 + 25,000)	56,000
Net current assets (11,000 + 5,000)	16,000
	72,000
Capital and reserves	
Ordinary shares of £1 each	40,000
Reserves	20,000
Shareholders' funds	60,000
Minority interests	12,000
	72,000

Notes

(a) S Ltd is a subsidiary of P Ltd because P Ltd owns 60% of its equity capital.

(b) As always, the share capital in the consolidated balance sheet is that of the parent company alone. The share capital in S Ltd's balance sheet was partly cancelled against the investment shown in P Ltd's balance sheet, while the uncancelled portion was credited to minority interest.

(c) The figure for minority interest comprises the interest of outside investors in the share capital and reserves of the subsidiary.

Answer 16.2

THOMAS LIMITED
CONSOLIDATED BALANCE SHEET AS AT 30 SEPTEMBER 20X6

	£'000	£'000
Fixed assets		
Intangible: goodwill		640
Tangible		16,932
Current assets		
Stocks	8,702	
Debtors	6,378	
Cash	331	
	15,411	
Current liabilities		
Trade creditors	4,494	
Taxation	1,007	
	5,501	
Net current assets		9,910
Total assets less current liabilities		27,482
Long-term loan		9,500
		17,982
Capital and reserves		
Called up share capital		5,000
Share premium		2,500
Profit and loss account		9,550
		17,050
Minority interest		932
		17,982

Workings

1 Group structure

$$\frac{800,000}{1,000,000}$$

Thomas Ltd
|
80%
|
James Ltd

2 Goodwill

	£'000	£'000
Cost of investment		3,760
Net assets acquired		
Share capital	1,000	
Share premium	400	
Revaluation reserve (3,910 – 3,410)	500	
Profit and loss account	2,000	
	3,900	
Group share × 80%		3,120
Goodwill		640

3 Minority interest

	£'000
Net assets at 30 September 20X6	
Share capital	1,000
Share premium	400
Revaluation reserve	500
Profit and loss account	2,760
	4,660

Minority interest = £4,660,000 × 20% = £932,000.

Part F: Simple consolidated accounts

4   *Profit and loss account*

	£'000
Thomas Ltd	8,942
James Ltd 80% × (2,760 – 2,000)	608
	9,550

Answer 16.3

1   *Goodwill*

	£	£
Cost of investment		46,000
Share of net assets acquired as represented by		
Share capital	30,000	
Reserves	10,000	
	40,000	
Group share (100%)		40,000
Goodwill		6,000

2   *Reserves*

	£
P Ltd	45,000
Share of S Ltd's post acquisition reserves	
£(22,000 – 10,000)	12,000
	57,000
Stock: unrealised profit (20% × £15,000)	3,000
Group reserves	54,000

P LIMITED
CONSOLIDATED BALANCE SHEET

	£	£
Intangible fixed asset: goodwill		6,000
Tangible fixed assets		120,000
Current assets (W1)	55,000	
Current liabilities (W2)	27,000	
		28,000
		154,000
Capital and reserves		
Ordinary shares of £1 each		100,000
Reserves		54,000
		154,000

Workings

1   *Current assets*

	£	£
In P Ltd's balance sheet		40,000
In S Ltd's balance sheet	30,000	
Less S Ltd's current account with P Ltd cancelled	12,000	
		18,000
		58,000
Less unrealised profit excluded from stock valuation		3,000
		55,000

2   *Current liabilities*

	£
In P Ltd's balance sheet	21,000
Less P Ltd's current account with S Ltd cancelled	12,000
	9,000
In S Ltd's balance sheet	18,000
	27,000

Now try Question 16 in the Exam Question Bank at the end of the Text.

Chapter 17 The consolidated profit and loss account

Chapter topic list

1 Introduction
2 Inter-company trading
3 Inter-company dividends
4 Pre-acquisition profits
5 Disclosure requirements
6 Summary: consolidated P&L
7 Associates

The following study sessions are covered in this chapter.

		Syllabus reference
22-25(d)	Prepare a consolidated profit and loss account and balance sheet for a simple group including adjustments for pre- and post-acquisition profits, minority interests and consolidated goodwill	5
22-25(e)	Explain why intra-group transactions should be eliminated on consolidation	5
22-25(f)	Account for the effects (in the profit and loss account and balance sheet) of intra-group trading and other transactions including:	5
	(i) Unrealised profits in stock and fixed assets	
	(ii) Intra-group loans and interest and other intra-group charges	

Part F: Simple consolidated accounts

1 INTRODUCTION

1.1 As always, the source of the consolidated statement is the individual accounts of the separate companies in the group. It is customary in practice to prepare a working paper (known as a **consolidation schedule**) on which the individual profit and loss accounts are set out side by side and totalled to form the basis of the consolidated profit and loss account.

> **Exam alert**
>
> In an examination it is very much quicker not to do this. Use workings to show the calculation of complex figures such as the minority interest and show the derivation of others on the face of the profit and loss account, as shown in our examples.

1.2 CONSOLIDATED PROFIT AND LOSS ACCOUNT: SIMPLE EXAMPLE

P Ltd acquired 75% of the ordinary shares of S Ltd on that company's incorporation in 20X3. The summarised profit and loss accounts of the two companies for the year ending 31 December 20X6 are set out below.

	H Ltd £	S Ltd £
Turnover	75,000	38,000
Cost of sales	30,000	20,000
Gross profit	45,000	18,000
Administrative expenses	14,000	8,000
Profit before taxation	31,000	10,000
Taxation	10,000	2,000
Retained profit for the year	21,000	8,000
Retained profits brought forward	87,000	17,000
Retained profits carried forward	108,000	25,000

Required

Prepare the consolidated profit and loss account.

1.3 SOLUTION

P LIMITED
CONSOLIDATED PROFIT AND LOSS ACCOUNT
FOR THE YEAR ENDED 31 DECEMBER 20X6

	£
Turnover (75 + 38)	113,000
Cost of sales (30 + 20)	50,000
Gross profit	63,000
Administrative expenses (14 + 8)	22,000
Profit before taxation	41,000
Taxation (10 + 2)	12,000
Profit after taxation	29,000
Minority interest (25% × £8,000)	2,000
Group retained profit for the year	27,000
Retained profits brought forward (group share only: 87 + (17 × 75%))	99,750
Retained profits carried forward	126,750

1.4 Notice how the minority interest is dealt with.

(a) Down to the line '**profit after taxation**' the **whole** of S Ltd's results is included without reference to group share or minority share. A **one-line adjustment** is then inserted to deduct the minority's share of S Ltd's profit after taxation.

(b) The minority's share (£4,250) of S Ltd's retained profits brought forward is excluded. This means that the carried forward figure of £126,750 is the figure which would appear in the balance sheet for group retained reserves.

1.5 This last point may be clearer if we revert to our balance sheet technique and construct the working for group reserves.

Group reserves

	£
P Ltd	108,000
Share of S Ltd's PARR (75% × £25,000)	18,750
	126,750

The minority share of S Ltd's reserves comprises the minority interest in the £17,000 profits brought forward plus the minority interest (£2,000) in £8,000 retained profits for the year. (*Note.* PARR = Post acquisition retained reserves.)

1.6 Notice that a consolidated profit and loss account links up with a consolidated balance sheet exactly as in the case of an individual company's accounts: the figure of retained profits carried forward at the bottom of the profit and loss account appears as the figure for retained profits in the balance sheet.

1.7 We will now look at the complications introduced by **inter-company trading**, **inter-company dividends** and **pre-acquisition profits** in the subsidiary.

2 INTER-COMPANY TRADING

2.1 Like the consolidated balance sheet, the consolidated profit and loss account should deal with the results of the group as those of a single entity. When one company in a group sells goods to another an identical amount is added to the turnover of the first company and to the cost of sales of the second. Yet as far as the entity's dealings with outsiders are concerned no sale has taken place.

> The consolidated figures for turnover and cost of sales should represent sales to, and purchases from, outsiders. An adjustment is therefore necessary to reduce the turnover and cost of sales figures by the value of inter-company sales during the year.

2.2 We have also seen in an earlier chapter that any unrealised profits on inter-company trading should be excluded from the figure of group profits. This will occur whenever goods sold at a profit within the group remain in the stock of the purchasing company at the year end. The best way to deal with this is to **calculate the unrealised profit** on **unsold stocks at the year end and reduce consolidated gross profit by this amount**. Cost of sales will be the balancing figure

2.3 EXAMPLE: INTER-COMPANY TRADING

Suppose in our earlier example that S Ltd had recorded sales of £5,000 to P Ltd during 20X6. S Ltd had purchased these goods from outside suppliers at a cost of £3,000. One half of the goods remained in P Ltd's stock at 31 December 20X6.

2.4 SOLUTION

The consolidated profit and loss account for the year ended 31 December 20X6 would now be as follows.

	Group £
Turnover (75 + 38 – 5)	108,000
Cost of sales (balancing figure)	46,000
Gross profit (45 + 18 – 1*)	62,000
Administrative expenses	(22,000)
Profit before taxation	40,000
Taxation	(12,000)
	28,000
Minority interest (25% × (£8,000 – £1,000*))	1,750
Group retained profit for the year	26,250
Retained profits brought forward	99,750
Retained profits carried forward	126,000

*Provision for unrealised profit: ½ × (£5,000 – £3,000)

A provision will be made for the unrealised profit against the stock figure in the consolidated balance sheet, as explained in Chapter 16.

3 INTER-COMPANY DIVIDENDS

3.1 In our example so far we have assumed that S Ltd retains all of its after-tax profit. It may be, however, that S Ltd distributes some of its profits as dividends. As before, the minority interest in the subsidiary's profit should be calculated immediately after the figure of after-tax profit. For this purpose, no account need be taken of how much of the minority interest is to be distributed by S Ltd as dividend.

3.2 A complication may arise if the subsidiary has **preference shares** and wishes to pay a **preference dividend** as well as an ordinary dividend. In such a case great care is needed in calculating the minority interest in S Ltd's after-tax profit.

3.3 EXAMPLE: INTER-COMPANY DIVIDENDS

Sam Ltd's capital consists of 10,000 6% £1 preference shares and 10,000 £1 ordinary shares. On 1 January 20X3, the date of Sam Ltd's incorporation, Ham Ltd acquired 3,000 of the preference shares and 7,500 of the ordinary shares. The profit and loss accounts of the two companies for the year ended 31 December 20X6 are set out below.

	Ham Ltd £	Sam Ltd £
Turnover	200,000	98,000
Cost of sales	90,000	40,000
Gross profit	110,000	58,000
Administrative expenses	35,000	19,000
Profit before tax	75,000	39,000
Taxation	23,000	18,000
Profit after tax	52,000	21,000
Dividends proposed: preference	-	600
ordinary	14,000	2,000
Retained profit for the year	38,000	18,400
Retained profits brought forward	79,000	23,000
	117,000	41,400

Ham Ltd has not yet accounted for its share of the dividends receivable from Sam Ltd.

Prepare Ham Ltd's consolidated profit and loss account.

3.4 SOLUTION

To calculate the minority interest in Sam Ltd's after-tax profit it is necessary to remember that the first £600 of such profits goes to pay the preference dividend. The balance of after-tax profits belongs to the equity shareholders. The calculation is as follows.

	Total £		Minority share £
Profits earned for preference shareholders	600	(70%)	420
Balance earned for equity shareholders	20,400	(25%)	5,100
Total profits after tax	21,000		5,520

It is irrelevant how much of this is distributed to the minority as dividends: the whole £5,520 must be deducted in arriving at the figure for group profit. The dividends receivable by Ham Ltd, calculated below would cancel with the dividends payable by Sam Ltd to its holding company.

	£
Preference dividend (30% × £600)	180
Ordinary dividend (75% × £2,000)	1,500
	1,680

3.5 HAM LIMITED
CONSOLIDATED PROFIT AND LOSS ACCOUNT
FOR THE YEAR ENDED 31 DECEMBER 20X5

	Group £
Turnover (200 + 98)	298,000
Cost of sales (90 + 40)	130,000
Gross profit	168,000
Administrative expenses (35 + 19)	54,000
Profit before tax	114,000
Taxation (23 + 18)	41,000
Profit after tax	73,000
Minority interest (as above)	5,520
Group profit for the year	67,480
Dividend proposed (parent company only)	14,000
Retained profit for the year	53,480
Retained profits brought forward (group share only: 79 + (23 × 75%))	96,250
Retained profits carried forward	149,730

4 PRE-ACQUISITION PROFITS

4.1 As explained above, the figure for retained profits at the bottom of the consolidated profit and loss account must be the same as the figure for retained profits in the consolidated balance sheet. We have seen in previous chapters that retained profits in the consolidated balance sheet comprise:

(a) The **whole of the parent company's** retained profits

(b) A **proportion of the subsidiary company's** retained profits. The proportion is the **group's share of post-acquisition retained profits** in the subsidiary. From the total retained profits of the subsidiary we must therefore **exclude** both the **minority's share** of total retained profits and the **group's share of pre-acquisition** retained profits

4.2 A **similar procedure is necessary in the consolidated profit and loss account** if it is to link up with the consolidated balance sheet. Previous examples have shown how the minority share of profits is excluded in the profit and loss account: their share of profits for

Part F: Simple consolidated accounts

the year is deducted from profit after tax; while the figure for profits brought forward in the consolidation schedule includes only the group's proportion of the subsidiary's profits.

4.3 In the same way, when considering examples which include pre-acquisition profits in a subsidiary, the figure for profits brought forward should include only the group's share of the post-acquisition retained profits. If the subsidiary is acquired *during* the accounting year, it is therefore necessary to apportion its profit for the year between pre-acquisition and post-acquisition elements. There are two approaches which may be used for this in the consolidated profit and loss account: the whole-year method and the part-year method.

4.4 With the **whole-year method,** the whole of the subsidiary's turnover, cost of sales and so on is included and a deduction is then made lower down to exclude the profit accruing prior to acquisition.

4.5 With the **part-year method, the entire profit and loss account of the subsidiary is split between pre-acquisition and post-acquisition proportions**. Only the post-acquisition figures are included in the profit and loss account. **This method is more usual** than the whole-year method and is the one which is used here.

Activity 17.1

P Ltd acquired 60% of the equity of S Ltd on 1 April 20X5. The profit and loss accounts of the two companies for the year ended 31 December 20X5 are set out below.

	P Ltd £	S Ltd £	S Ltd ($^9/_{12}$) £
Turnover	170,000	80,000	60,000
Cost of sales	65,000	36,000	27,000
Gross profit	105,000	44,000	33,000
Administrative expenses	43,000	12,000	9,000
Profit before tax	62,000	32,000	24,000
Taxation	23,000	8,000	6,000
Profit after tax	39,000	24,000	18,000
Dividends (paid 31 December)	12,000	6,000	
Retained profit for the year	27,000	18,000	
Retained profits brought forward	81,000	40,000	
Retained profits carried forward	108,000	58,000	

P Ltd has not yet accounted for the dividends received from S Ltd.

Prepare the consolidated profit and loss account.

5 DISCLOSURE REQUIREMENTS

5.1 S 230 CA 1985 allows a parent company to dispense with the need to publish its own individual profit and loss account.

(a) Companies taking advantage of this dispensation are obliged to state in their consolidated profit and loss account how much of the group's profit for the financial year is dealt with in the parent company's own profit and loss account.

(b) For internal purposes, of course, it will still be necessary to prepare the parent company's profit and loss account and the profit or loss shown there is the figure to be shown in the note to the group accounts.

(c) This is a point which has been clarified by the CA 1989. In the example above, P Ltd should disclose its own profit after adjustment for its share of the S Ltd dividend (from post-acquisition profits - remember that the pre-acquisition element should be credited to the cost of P's investment in S Ltd).

Activity 17.2

The following information relates to the Warren group of companies for the year to 30 April 20X7.

	Warren plc £'000	Anna Ltd £'000	Egg Ltd £'000
Turnover	1,100	500	130
Cost of sales	630	300	70
Gross profit	470	200	60
Administrative expenses	105	150	20
Dividend from Anna Ltd	24	-	-
Dividend from Egg Ltd	6	-	-
Profit before tax	395	50	40
Taxation	65	10	20
Profit after tax	330	40	20
Interim dividend	50	10	-
Proposed dividend	150	20	10
Retained profit for the year	130	10	10
Retained profits brought forward	460	106	30
Retained profits carried forward	590	116	40

Additional information

(a) The issued share capital of the group was as follows.

　　Warren plc　: 5,000,000 ordinary shares of £1 each.
　　Anna Ltd　　: 1,000,000 ordinary shares of £1 each.
　　Egg Ltd　　 : 400,000 ordinary shares of £1 each.

(b) Warren plc purchased 80% of the issued share capital of Anna Ltd in 20X0. At that time, the retained profits of Anna amounted to £56,000.

(c) Warren plc purchased 60% of the issued share capital of Egg Ltd in 20X4. At that time, the retained profits of Egg amounted to £20,000.

(d) Warren plc recognises dividends proposed by other group companies in its profit and loss account.

Task

Insofar as the information permits, prepare the Warren group of companies' consolidated profit and loss account for the year to 30 April 20X7 in accordance with the Companies Act 1985 and related statements of accounting practice.

Note. Notes to the profit and loss account are not required but you should append a statement showing the make up of the 'retained profits carried forward', and your workings should be submitted.

Part F: Simple consolidated accounts

6 SUMMARY: CONSOLIDATED P&L

6.1 The table below summaries the main points about the consolidated profit and loss account.

Summary: consolidated P & L account

Purpose	To show the results of the group for an accounting period as if it were a single entity.
Turnover to profit after tax Reason	100% P + 100% S (excluding dividend receivable from subsidiary and adjustments for inter-company transactions). To show the results of the group which were controlled by the holding company.
Inter-company sales Unrealised profit on inter-company sales	Strip out inter-company activity from both turnover and cost sales. (a) *Goods sold by P Ltd*. Increase cost of sales by unrealised profit. (b) *Goods sold by S Ltd*. Increase cost of sales by full amount of unrealised profit and decrease minority interest by their share of unrealised profit.
Depreciation	If the value of S Ltd's fixed assets have been subjected to a fair value uplift then any additional depreciation must be charged in the consolidated profit and loss account. The minority interest will need to be adjusted for their share.
Transfer of fixed assets	Expenses must be increased by any profit on the transfer and reduced by any additional depreciation arising from the increased carrying value of the asset.

Minority interests
 	
Reason
	S's profit after tax (PAT) X
	Less: * unrealised profit (X)
	             * profit on disposal of fixed assets (X)
	             additional depreciation following FV uplift (X)
	Add: ** additional depreciation following
	             disposal of fixed assets X
	                                                                                    X
	            MI% X
	
	* Only applicable if sales of goods and fixed assets made by subsidiary.
	
	** Only applicable if sale of fixed assets made by holding company.
	
	To show the extent to which profits generated through P's control are in fact owned by other parties.

Dividends Reason	P's only. S's dividend is due (a) to P; and (b) to MI. P has taken in its share by including the results of S in the consolidated P & L a/c. The MI have taken their share by being given a proportion of S's PAT. Remember: PAT = dividends + retained profit.
Retained reserves	As per the balance sheet calculations.

7 ASSOCIATES

7.1 Certain substantial investments are known as 'associated undertakings' for the purpose of consolidated accounts. These are holdings too significant to be treated simply as trade investments but not qualifying as investments in subsidiaries. To cater for this situation a form of accounting known as **equity accounting** has developed. FRS 9 *Associates and joint ventures* requires that X Ltd should adopt equity accounting principles if its investment in Y Ltd is such that Y Ltd has the status of an **associated company**.

> **KEY TERM**
>
> An **associate** is a long term investment where the investor holds a 'participating interest' and exercises 'significant influence'.

7.2 A **participating interest** is deemed to be a shareholding of over 20%. This holding, however, must be one held for the purpose of contributing to the associate's activities in order to generate financial benefits for the investor. The exercise of significant influence means that the investor is actively involved in influencing the associate's strategic decisions - the holding company should influence decisions such as changes in the associate's products, markets, direction and general activities. The investor's percentage holding on its own is not enough to give associate status.

> **Exam alert**
>
> Your syllabus and Study Guide state that only an **overview** of the distinction between an associate and a subsidiary is required.

Equity accounting

7.3 (a) The investor should **include its associates** in its consolidated financial statements using the **equity method.**

(b) In the investor's consolidated profit and loss account the **investor's share** of its **associates' operating** results should be included immediately after group operating results.

(c) **From the level of profit before tax,** the **investor's share of the relevant amounts for associates** should be included within the amounts for the group.

(d) In the consolidated statement of total recognised gains and losses the **investor's** share of the **total recognised gains and losses** of its associates should be included, shown separately under each heading, if material.

(e) In the **balance sheet** the **investor's share** of the **net assets of its associate** should be **included and separately disclosed**.

(f) The **cash flow statement** should include the **cash flows between the investor and its associates.**

(g) **Goodwill** arising on the investor's acquisition of its associates, less any amortisation or write-down, should be **included** in the carrying amount for the associates but should be **disclosed separately.**

Part F: Simple consolidated accounts

(h) In the **profit and loss account** the amortisation or write-down of such goodwill should be **separately disclosed as part of the investor's share of its associates' results**.

The investor's own financial statements

7.4 In the investor's own financial statements associates should be treated as fixed asset investments, at cost less any amounts written off, or at a valuation.

Activity 17.3

Socket Ltd has 100,000 ordinary shares of £1 each. On 1 January 20X3, Power plc acquired 45,000 of these shares. In addition, Power plc is able to appoint four out of the five directors of Socket Ltd, thus exercising control over their activities.

How should Socket Ltd be treated in the consolidated accounts of Power plc?

Key learning points

- This chapter has explained how to prepare a **consolidated profit and loss account** by combining the profit and loss accounts of each group company.
- **Adjustments** must be made:
    - to reduce turnover by the amount of any **intra-group trading**, and to deduct from consolidated gross profit any unrealised profit on stocks thus acquired which are held at the year end. Cost of sales will be the balancing figure;
    - to reduce stock values by the amount of any **unrealised profit** on intra-group trading;
    - to calculate the **minority interest** in subsidiary companies' results for the year;
    - to account for **intra-group dividends**;
    - to **eliminate pre-acquisition** profits.
- FRS 9 and CA 85 require that, in consolidated accounts, investments in **associated companies** should be accounted or using **equity accounting**.

Quick quiz

1. Describe the preparation of a consolidated profit and loss account in its simplest form.
2. At what stage in the consolidated profit and loss account does the figure for minority interests appear?
3. What adjustments are made to the consolidated profit and loss account in respect of inter-company trading?
4. What dispensation is granted to a parent company by s 230 CA 1985?
5. Describe the make-up of the figure for directors' emoluments in a consolidated profit and loss account.
6. A shareholding of 25% is always a participating interest. *True or false?*

Answers to quick quiz

1. The individual profit and loss accounts are totalled and certain adjustments made.
2. After 'profit after tax'.

3   An adjustment is made to reduce the turnover and cost of sales figures by the value of inter-company sales during the year. Thus the consolidated figures for turnover and cost of sales should represent sales to and purchases from outsiders.

4   A parent company may dispense with the need to publish its own profit and loss account.

5   The figure should represent the emoluments of parent company directors only.

6   False. Significant influence must be exercised.

Answers to activities

Answer 17.1

The shares in S Ltd were acquired three months into the year. Only the post-acquisition proportion (9/12ths) of S Ltd's P & L account is included in the consolidated profit and loss account. This is shown above for convenience.

P LIMITED CONSOLIDATED PROFIT AND LOSS ACCOUNT
FOR THE YEAR ENDED 31 DECEMBER 20X5

	£
Turnover (170 + 60)	230,000
Cost of sales (65 + 27)	92,000
Gross profit	138,000
Administrative expenses (43 + 9)	52,000
Profit before tax	86,000
Taxation (23 + 6)	29,000
Profit after tax	57,000
Minority interest (40% × £18,000)	7,200
Group profit for the year	49,800
Dividends (P Ltd only)	12,000
Retained profit for the year	37,800
Retained profits brought forward*	81,000
Retained profits carried forward	118,800

* All of S Ltd's profits brought forward are pre-acquisition.

Answer 17.2

You are not asked for notes, but you should know that Warren would have to state in the notes that it had taken advantage of the provisions of s 230 CA and was not publishing its own profit and loss account. It would then show its own profit for the year, which the Act now states clearly should be the profit shown in its own books (in this case, including dividends received and receivable from Anna and Egg). Warren's profit for the financial year is £330,000, as shown in the question. An analysis of reserves would also be given as a note to the balance sheet, showing movements on both company and consolidated reserves.

CONSOLIDATED PROFIT AND LOSS ACCOUNT
FOR THE YEAR TO 30 APRIL 20X7

	£'000
Turnover (1,100 + 500 + 130)	1,730
Cost of sales (630 + 300 + 70)	1,000
Gross profit	730
Administrative expenses (105 + 150 + 20)	275
Profit on ordinary activities before taxation	455
Tax on profit on ordinary activities (65 + 10 + 20)	95
Profit on ordinary activities after taxation	360
Minority interests (W1)	16
Profit for the financial year	344
Dividends paid and proposed (parent only)	200
Retained profit for the year	144
Retained profit brought forward 1 May 20X6 (W2)	506
Retained profit carried forward 30 April 20X7	650

Part F: Simple consolidated accounts

Workings

1 Minority interests

		£
In Anna (20% × profit after tax)		8,000
In Egg (40% × profit after tax)		8,000
		16,000

2 Retained profits brought forward

	£
Warren plc	460,000
Group share of post-acquisition retained profits brought forward	
Anna 80% × £(106,000 - 56,000)	40,000
Egg 60% × £(30,000 - 20,000)	60,000
	506,000

Answer 17.3

Plug plc holds **less than 50%** of the ordinary shares of Socket Ltd. Nevertheless, Socket Ltd is a **subsidiary** of Plug plc because its status is determined by a number of factors other than percentage of shares held. The key point is **control** rather than share ownership.

The requirement for Socket Ltd to be treated as a subsidiary is determined by the Companies Act 1985 as amended by the Companies Act 1989 and by FRS 2 *Accounting for subsidiary undertakings*. FRS 2 states that an undertaking is the parent of another undertaking (a subsidiary undertaking) if any of the following apply.

(a) It holds a majority of the voting rights.

(b) It is a member of the undertaking and has the right to appoint or remove directors holding the majority of the voting rights at meetings of the board on all or all substantial matters.

(c) It has a right to exercise a dominant influence over the undertaking by virtue of a contract or provisions in the memorandum and articles.

(d) It has the right to control alone, under an agreement with other shareholders, a majority of the voting rights.

(e) It has a participating interest and actually exercises a dominant influence over operating and financial policies or it and the undertakings are managed on a unified basis.

Socket Ltd falls to be treated as a **subsidiary** on the grounds that Plug plc is able to appoint four out of the five directors (criterion (ii)). Assuming that the other criteria do not apply, if Plug plc did not have such a power, consolidation would not be appropriate because Socket Ltd would not be a subsidiary.

Exam question bank

Exam question bank

1 ACCOUNTING STATEMENTS *18 mins*

It has been suggested that published accounting statements should attempt to be relevant, understandable, reliable, complete, objective, timely and comparable.

Required

(a) Explain briefly in your own words, the meaning of these terms as applied to accounting. (8 marks)

(b) Are there any difficulties in applying all of them at the same time? (2 marks)

(10 marks)

2 FIXED ASSETS AND STOCKS *36 mins*

1   What is the purpose of charging depreciation in accounts?

   A   To allocate the cost less residual value of a fixed asset over the accounting periods expected to benefit from its use

   B   To ensure that funds are available for the eventual replacement of the asset

   C   To reduce the cost of the asset in the balance sheet to its estimated market value

   D   To comply with the prudence concept

2   Your firm bought a machine for £5,000 on 1 January 20X1, which had an expected useful life of four years and an expected residual value of £1,000; the asset was to be depreciated on the straight-line basis. On 31 December 20X3, the machine was sold for £1,600.

   The amount to be entered in the 20X3 profit and loss account for profit or loss on disposal, is

   A   profit of £600
   B   loss of £600
   C   profit of £350
   D   loss of £400

3   A fixed asset register showed a net book value of £67,460. A fixed asset costing £15,000 had been sold for £4,000, making a loss on disposal of £1,250. No entries had been made in the fixed asset register for this disposal.

   The balance on the fixed asset register is

   A   £42,710
   B   £51,210
   C   £53,710
   D   £62,210

4   An organisation's fixed asset register shows a net book value of £125,600. The fixed asset account in the nominal ledger shows a net book value of £135,600. The difference could be due to a disposed asset not having been deducted from the nominal ledger.

   A   With disposal proceeds of £15,000 and a profit on disposal of £5,000
   B   With disposal proceeds of £15,000 and a net book value of £5,000
   C   With disposal proceeds of £15,000 and a loss on disposal of £5,000
   D   With disposal proceeds of £5,000 and a net book value of £5,000

5   Recording the purchase of computer stationery by debiting the computer equipment at cost account would result in

    A   an overstatement of profit and an overstatement of fixed assets
    B   an understatement of profit and an overstatement of fixed assets
    C   an overstatement of profit and an understatement of fixed assets
    D   an understatement of profit and an understatement of fixed assets

6   In times of rising prices, the FIFO method of stock valuation, when compared to the average cost method of stock valuation, will usually produce

    A   a higher profit and a lower closing stock value
    B   a higher profit and a higher closing stock value
    C   a lower profit and a lower closing stock value
    D   a lower profit and a higher closing stock value

7   Following the preparation of the profit and loss account, it is discovered that accrued expenses of £1,000 have been ignored and that closing stock has been overvalued by £1,300. This will have resulted in

    A   an overstatement of net profit of £300
    B   an understatement of net profit of £300
    C   an overstatement of net profit of £2,300
    D   an understatement of net profit of £2,300

8   Stock is valued using FIFO. Opening stock was 10 units at £2 each. Purchases were 30 units at £3 each, then issues of 12 units were made, followed by issues of 8 units.

    What is closing stock valued at?

    A   £50
    B   £58
    C   £60
    D   £70

9   An organisation's stock at 1 July is 15 units @ £3.00 each. The following movements occur:

    - 3 July 20X6   5 units sold at £3.30 each
    - 8 July 20X6   10 units bought at £3.50 each
    - 12 July 20X6   8 units sold at £4.00 each

    Closing stock at 31 July, using the FIFO method of stock valuation would be

    A   £31.50
    B   £36.00
    C   £39.00
    D   £41.00

10 Your organisation uses the weighted average cost method of valuing stocks. During August 20X1, the following stock details were recorded:

Opening balance	30 units valued at £2 each
5 August	purchase of 50 units at £2.40 each
10 August	issue of 40 units
18 August	purchase of 60 units at £2.50 each
23 August	issue of 25 units

    The value of the balance at 31 August 20X1 was

A　£172.50
　　　B　£176.25
　　　C　£180.00
　　　D　£187.50

(20 marks)

3　TURNER　　　　　　　　　　　　　　　　　　　　　　　　　　　　*18 mins*

The bookkeeping system of Turner Ltd is not computerised, and at 30 September 20X8 the bookkeeper was unable to balance the accounts.

The trial balance totals were:

Debit　　　　　　　　　£1,796,100
Credit　　　　　　　　　£1,852,817

He nevertheless proceeded to prepare draft financial statements inserting the difference as a balancing figure in the balance sheet. The draft profit and loss account showed a profit of £141,280 for the year ended 30 September 20X8.

He then opened a suspense account for the difference and began to check through the accounting records to find the difference. He found the following errors and omissions:

(a) £8,980, the total of the sales returns book for September 20X8, had been credited to purchases returns account.

(b) £9,600 paid for an item of plant purchased on 1 April 20X8 had been debited to plant repairs account. The company depreciates its plant at 20% per annum on the straight-line basis, with proportional depreciation in the year of purchase.

(c) The cash discount totals for the month of September 20X8, had not been posted to the discount accounts in the nominal ledger. The figures were:

　　Discount allowed　　　　£836
　　Discount received　　　　£919

(d) £580 insurance prepaid at 30 September 20X7 had not been brought down as an opening balance.

(e) The balance of £38,260 on the telephone expense account had been omitted from the trial balance.

(f) A car held as a fixed asset had been sold during the year for £4,800. The proceeds of sale were entered in the cash book but had been credited to sales account in the nominal ledger. The original cost of the car £12,000, and the accumulated depreciation to date £8,000, were included in the motor vehicle account and the accumulated depreciation account. The company depreciates motor vehicles at 25% per annum on the straight-line basis with proportionate depreciation in the year of purchase but none in the year of sale.

Required

Open a suspense account for the difference between the trial balance totals. Prepare the journal entries necessary to correct the errors and eliminate the balance on the suspense account. Narratives are not required.

(10 marks)

Exam question bank

4 ACCOUNTING STANDARDS AND MATERIALITY *18 mins*

Your finance director is proposing that certain Statements of Standard Accounting Practice or Financial Reporting Standards should not be applied in the published accounts. Some of the items are material and some are immaterial.

Required

(a) Explain what is meant by an 'immaterial item'. (6 marks)

(b) Explain what action is required by the directors if they decide to depart from the requirements of a SSAP or FRS. (4 marks)

(10 marks)

5 BESS, CHARLES AND GEORGE *22 mins*

Bess, Charles and George are in partnership together. They operate a retail jewellery business. They are considering dissolving the partnership next year. They have asked you to assist in the preparation of the year end financial statements of their business. The trial balance as at 31 March 20X1 is set out on the following page.

Further information

(a) The stock at the close of business on 31 March 20X1 was valued at cost at £143,936.

(b) The partners are entitled to the following salaries per annum.

Bess	£30,000
Charles	£25,000
George	£17,000

(c) Interest on capital is to be paid to the partners at a rate of 5% on the balance at the end of the year on the capital accounts. No interest is to be paid on the current accounts.

(d) The profit sharing ratios in the partnership are:

Bess	5/12
Charles	4/12
George	3/12

Required

(a) Draft a profit and loss account for the year ended 31 March 20X1. (9 marks)

(b) Prepare an appropriation account for the partnership for the year ended 31 March 20X1. (3 marks)

(12 marks)

BESS, CHARLES AND GEORGE
TRIAL BALANCE AS AT 31 MARCH 20X1

	Debit £	Credit £
Motor expenses	3,769	
Drawings: Bess	46,000	
Charles	42,000	
George	38,000	
Capital account: Bess		60,000
Charles		40,000
George		20,000
Sales		568,092
Returns outwards		7,004
Carriage inwards	872	
Trade creditors		9,904
Returns inwards	8,271	
Purchases	302,117	
Carriage outwards	617	
Salespersons' commission	6,659	
Rent, rates and insurance	32,522	
Current account: Bess		4,670
Charles		5,600
George		3,750
Stock as at 1 April 20X0	127,535	
Motor vehicles at cost	37,412	
Office equipment at cost	2,363	
Fixtures and fittings at cost	8,575	
Staff wages and National Insurance contribution	48,317	
Lighting and heating	3,240	
Postage and stationery	705	
Accumulated depreciation: motor vehicles		18,651
office equipment		1,285
fixtures and fittings		3,754
Depreciation charge: motor vehicles	4,765	
office equipment	236	
fixtures and fittings	1,613	
Telephone	2,926	
Sundries	868	
Cash at bank	23,980	
Cash in hand	228	
Accruals		880
	743,590	743,590

6 ERNIE

22 mins

Ernie is a building contractor, doing repair work for local householders. His wife keeps some accounting records but not on a double-entry basis.

The assets and liabilities of the business at 30 June 20X7 were as follows:

		£
Assets		
Plant and equipment: cost		12,600
depreciation to date		5,800
Motor vehicle: cost		9,000
depreciation to date		6,500
Stock of materials		14,160
Debtors		9,490
Rent of premises paid in advance to 30 September 20X7		750
Insurance paid in advance to 31 December 20X7		700

Exam question bank

	£
Bank balance	1,860
Cash in hand	230
Liabilities	
Creditors for supplies	3,460
Telephone bill owing	210
Electricity owing	180

His cash and bank transactions for the year from 1 July 20X7 to 30 June 20X8 are as follows.

Cash and Bank summary

Receipts	Cash £	Bank £	Payments	Cash £	Bank £
Opening balances	230	1,860	Suppliers		83,990
Receipts from customers	52,640	150,880	Rent of premises		3,600
Loan received		10,000	Insurance (to 31.12.X8)		1,600
Proceeds of sale of vehicle held at beginning of year		3,000	Purchase of plant and equipment		8,400
Cash paid into bank		24,040	Purchase of new vehicle		12,800
Cash withdrawn from bank	48,260		Telephone		860
Closing balance		2,100	Electricity		890
			Wages of repair staff	68,200	
			Miscellaneous expenses		1,280
			Drawings by Ernie for personal use	8,000	29,800
			Refund to customer		400
			Cash paid into bank	24,040	
			Cash withdrawn from bank		48,260
			Closing balance	890	
	101,130	191,880		101,130	191,880

The following further information is available:

(a) Plant and equipment is to be depreciated at 25% per annum on the reducing balance with a full year's charge in the year of purchase.

(b) The new motor vehicle was purchased on 1 January 20X8. Ernie's depreciation policy is to charge depreciation at 25% per annum on the straight-line basis, with a proportionate charge in the year of purchase but none in the year of sale.

(c) The rent of the premises was increased by 20% from 1 October 20X7.

(d) The loan of £10,000 was obtained from Ernie's brother on 1 April 20X8. It carries interest at 10% per annum, payable on 30 September and 31 March.

(e) At 30 June 20X8, Ernie owed the following amounts.

	£
Suppliers	4,090
Telephone	240
Electricity	220
Miscellaneous expenses	490

(f) At 30 June 20X8, amounts due from customers totalled £10,860. Of this amount, Ernie considered that debts totalling £1,280 were bad and should be written off.

(g) Stock of materials at 30 June was £12,170.

(h) Ernie agreed to pay his wife £5,000 for her assistance with his office work during the year. This amount was actually paid in August 20X8.

Required

Prepare Ernie's trading and profit and loss account for the year ended 30 June 20X8.

(12 marks)

7 ATOK *43 mins*

Atok Ltd compiles its financial statements to 30 June annually. At 30 June 20X9, the company's trial balance was as follows:

	£'000	£'000
Sales revenue		14,800
Purchases	8,280	
Stock at 1 July 20X8	1,390	
Distribution costs	1,080	
Administration expenses	1,460	
Land at valuation	10,500	
Building: cost	8,000	
Accumulated depreciation at 1 July 20X8		2,130
Plant and equipment: cost	12,800	
Accumulated depreciation at 1 July 20X8		2,480
Trade debtors and creditors	4,120	2,240
Cash at bank	160	
Ordinary shares of 50p each: as at 1 July 20X8		10,000
issued during year		4,000
Share premium account: as at 1 July 20X8		2,000
arising on shares issued during year		2,000
Revaluation reserve as at 1 July 20X8		3,000
Profit and loss account		3,140
10% debentures (redeemable 20Y8) (issued 1 April 20X9 with interest payable 31 March and 30 September each year)		2,000
	47,790	47,790

The following matters remain to be adjusted for in preparing the financial statements for the year ended 30 June 20X9:

(a) Stock at 30 June 20X9 amounted to £1,560,000 at cost. A review of stock items revealed the need for some adjustments for two stock lines:

  (i) Items which had cost £80,000 and which would normally sell for £120,000 were found to have deteriorated. Remedial work costing £20,000 would be needed to enable the items to be sold for £90,000.

  (ii) Some items sent to customers on sale or return terms had been omitted from stock and included as sales in June 20X9. The cost of these items was £16,000 and they were included in sales at £24,000. In July 20X9 the items were returned in good condition by the customers.

(b) Depreciation is to be provided as follows:

  Buildings   2% per year on cost
  Plant and equipment 20% per year on cost

  80% of the depreciation is to be charged in cost of sales, and 10% each in distribution costs and administrative expenses.

(c) The land is to be revalued to £12,000,000. No charge was required to the value of the buildings.

Exam question bank

(d) Accruals and prepayments were:

	Accruals £'000	Prepayments £'000
Distribution costs	190	120
Administrative expenses	70	60

(e) A dividend of 2 ½ pence per share is proposed. All shares in issue at 30 June 20X9 qualify for this dividend.

Required

(a) Prepare the company's profit and loss account for the year ended 30 June 20X9 and balance sheet as at that date for publication, complying as far as possible with the provisions of the Companies Acts and accounting standards. **(20 marks)**

(b) Prepare a statement detailing all reserve movements during the year. Other notes to the financial statements are *not* required. **(4 marks)**

> **Tutor's note.** This question and the next two are longer than the questions you will meet in the exam. However, these questions are well worth doing in order to practice all the techniques you will need to deal with any company accounts questions in the exam.

(24 marks)

8 STANDARD SETTERS *18 mins*

The existing procedures for setting accounting standards in the UK were established in 1990.

Required

Explain the roles of the following in relation to accounting standards.

(a) Financial Reporting Council (FRC)
(b) Accounting Standards Board (ASB)
(c) Financial Reporting Review Panel (FRRP)
(d) Urgent Issues Task Force (UITF)

(10 marks)

9 TOPAZ *18 mins*

Topaz Ltd makes up its accounts regularly to 31 December each year. The company has operated for some years with four divisions A, B, C and D, but on 30 June 20X6 Division B was sold for £8m, realising a profit of £2.5m. During 20X6 there was a fundamental reorganisation of Division C, the costs of which were £1.8m.

The trial balance of the company at 31 December 20X6 included the following balances.

	Division B		Divisions A, C and D Combined	
	Dr £m	Cr £m	Dr £m	Cr £m
Sales		13		68
Costs of sales	8		41	
Distribution costs (including a bad debt of £1.9m - Division D)	1		6	
Administrative expenses	2		4	
Profit on sale of Division B		2.5		
Reorganisation costs				

	Division B		Divisions A, C and D Combined	
	Dr £m	Cr £m	Dr £m	Cr £m
Division C			1.8	
Interest on £10m 10% debenture stock issued in 20X0			1	
Taxation			4.8	
Interim dividend paid			2	
Revaluation reserve				10

A final dividend of £4m is proposed.

The balance on the revaluation reserve relates to the company's freehold property and arose as follows.

	£m
Balance at 1.1.X6	6
Revaluation during 20X6	4
Balance at 31.12.X6 per trial balance	10

Required

(a) Prepare the profit and loss account of Topaz Ltd for the year ended 31 December 20X6, complying as far as possible with the provisions of the Companies Act 1985 and FRS 3 Reporting Financial Performance. (10 marks)

(b) Using the information in the previous question, prepare the statement of total recognised gains and losses for Topaz Ltd for the year as required by FRS 3. (4 marks)

(c) Explain why the changes to the profit and loss account introduced by FRS 3 improve the quality of information available to users of the financial statements. (6 marks)

(20 marks)

10 HISTORICAL COST ACCOUNTING *18 mins*

(a) List and briefly explain *three* ways in which the use of historical cost accounting may cause financial statements to be misleading. (7 marks)

(b) List *three* advantages of historical cost accounting. (3 marks)

(10 marks)

11 GERMAINE *18 mins*

Germaine Ltd prepared its draft financial statements for the year ended 31 March 20X9 shortly after the balance sheet date. They showed a profit of £980,000. After they were prepared and before the directors formally approved them, the following events took place:

(a) A customer commenced an action against the company to recover £120,000 of losses incurred as a result of Germaine's alleged supply of faulty components in February 20X9. Germaine Ltd intends to defend the case vigorously. The company's legal advisers consider it has a 70% chance of successfully defending the action. If the customer's action is successful, damages and costs are expected to amount to £180,000. If Germaine successfully defends the action, non-recoverable legal costs of £30,000 will be incurred. (6 marks)

(b) A trade debtor, for whose full balance specific provision had been made at 31 March 20X9, paid the account of £84,000 in full. (4 marks)

Exam question bank

Required

Advise the directors of Germaine Ltd as to the correct accounting treatment of these items, giving your reasons. If you consider that the financial statements require adjustment, draft journal entries with narratives to give effect to the adjustment. If you consider that a note to the financial statements is required, draft a suitable disclosure note.

(10 marks)

12 RUBENS
18 mins

Rubens plc is a company in the pharmaceuticals industry which spends heavily on research and development each year. The company's policy is to capitalise development expenditure meeting the conditions of SSAP 13 *Accounting for research and development* and to amortise it over five years on the straight-line basis beginning when sales revenue is first generated from the developed product. Amortisation is apportioned on a time basis in the first year of amortisation.

The company's finance director has asked you to compute the amounts for research and development to be included in the financial statements for the year ended 30 September 20X8 in accordance with the company's accounting policy. The company's profit is expected to be about £8m.

The company's ledger accounts for development expenditure and research expenditure, before amortisation and other adjustments for the year ended 30 September 20X8, showed the following details.

Development expenditure

Project	Balance at 30.9.X7	Expenditure year ended 30.9.X8	Balance at 30.9.X8
	£'000	£'000	£'000
A	600		
B	2,400		
C	3,600	400	4,000
D	1,200	300	1,500
E		800	800
F		400	400

Notes on the projects

A   Project A was completed in 20X5 at a total cost of £1,000,000 and is being amortised in accordance with the company's policy.

B   Project B was completed in June 20X7. Sales revenue began on 1 November 20X7.

C   Project C is not yet complete and development is proceeding. It continues to meet the criteria for capitalisation in SSAP 13.

D   Project D was abandoned during the year ended 30 September 20X8 when a competitor launched a superior product.

E   Project E is a new development project commenced in 20X7/X8. It meets the criteria for capitalisation in SSAP 13.

F   Project F was commenced and completed during 20X7/X8. Sales revenue is expected to begin in 20X9.

Research expenditure

The balance on the research expenditure account was £1,800,000, representing payments made during the year ended 30 September 20X8.

Required

(a) State the criteria which must be met under SSAP 13 *Accounting for research and development* if development expenditure is to be capitalised. (5 marks)

(b) Compute the amounts to be included in the profit and loss account for research and development expenditure and in the balance sheet for deferred development expenditure, and state the heading under which they should be included or disclosed. (5 marks)

(10 marks)

13 JANE *36 mins*

The balance sheets of Jane Ltd at 31 December 20X7 and 20X8 were as follows

	Reference to notes	Year ended 31 December 20X7 £'000	Year ended 31 December 20X8 £'000
Fixed assets			
Tangible assets	1	730	1,100
Investment at cost	2	100	50
		830	1,150
Current assets			
Stock		80	110
Debtors		110	180
Cash at bank		20	30
		210	320
Creditors: amounts falling due within one year			
Trade creditors		(70)	(80)
Bank overdraft		(40)	(130)
Proposed dividend	3	(30)	(40)
		(140)	(250)
Net current assets		70	70
Total assets less current liabilities		900	1,220
Creditors: amounts falling after more that one year			
10% Debentures	4	(100)	(150)
		800	1,070
Capital and reserves			
Called-up share capital	5	300	380
Share premium		200	300
Revaluation reserve	6	100	200
Profit and loss account		200	190
		800	1,070

Notes

1 *Tangible assets*

During the year tangible assets with a net book value of £80,000 were sold for £60,000. The depreciation charge for the year on all tangible assets held at the end of the year was £100,000.

2 *Investments*

Investments which cost £50,000 were sold during the year for £40,000.

3 *Proposed dividends*

The proposed dividends are on the company's ordinary share capital. No interim dividends were paid.

4 10% Debentures

£50,000 of 10% debentures were issued on 1 January 20X8. All interest to 31 December has been paid.

5 Called up share capital

The company's called up share capital at 31 December 20X7 consisted of 300,000 ordinary shares at £1 each. Another 80,000 shares were issued during the year at a price of £2.25 per share.

6 Revaluation reserve

The freehold land and buildings were revalued upwards by £100,000 during the year.

Required

Prepare the company's cash flow statement for the year ended 31 December 20X8 complying with FRS 1 (revised) Cash flow statements. The reconciliation of the cash flow to movement in net debt is not required. Ignore taxation. **(20 marks)**

14 ARH *18 mins*

ARH plc has the following results for the last two years of trading.

ARH PLC
TRADING AND PROFIT AND LOSS ACCOUNT FOR THE YEAR ENDED

	31.12.X4 £'000	31.12.X5 £'000
Sales	14,400	17,000
Less cost of sales	11,800	12,600
Gross profit	2,600	4,400
Less expenses	1,200	2,000
Net profit for the year	1,400	2,400
Dividends proposed	520	780
Retained profit for the year	880	1,620

ARH PLC
BALANCE SHEET

	31 December 20X4 £'000	31 December 20X4 £'000	31 December 20X5 £'000	31 December 20X5 £'000
Fixed assts		2,500		4,000
Current assets				
Stocks	1,300		2,000	
Debtors	2,000		1,600	
Bank balances	2,400		820	
	5,700		4,420	
Less current liabilities				
Creditors	1,500		2,700	
Net current assets		4,200		1,720
		6,700		5,720
Less long term liabilities				
10% debentures		2,600		-
		4,100		5,720
Financed by:				
2.4 million ordinary shares of £1 each		2,400		2,400
Revaluation reserves		500		500
Retained profits		1,200		2,820
		4,100		5,720

Exam question bank

Required

(a) Calculate *three* profitability ratios for *each* year. (3 marks)

(b) Compare the profitability of the second year with the decrease in bank balances *and* discuss possible reasons for this decrease. Include liquidity ratios of your choice to illustrate your comparison. (7 marks)

(10 marks)

15 BASIC CONSOLIDATED FINANCIAL STATEMENTS *18 mins*

1 Castor plc acquires 75% of the share capital of Pollux Ltd on 1 December 20X9. The consideration given is £1 million in cash and 300,000 £1 ordinary shares of Castor plc. The market value of each of Castor plc's shares on 1 December is 300 pence. On 1 December, the fair value of Pollux Ltd's net tangible assets is £1,000,000. What is the amount of goodwill on acquisition to be dealt with in Castor plc's consolidated accounts?

A £300,000
B £550,000
C £900,000
D £1,150,000

2 Holder plc acquired 150,000 £1 ordinary shares in Sub plc on 1 July 20X6 at a cost of £300,000. Sub plc's reserves at 1 July 20X6 were £36,000, and its issued ordinary share capital was £200,000.

At 30 June 20X9, Sub plc's reserves were £16,000. The amount of goodwill arising on consolidation is

A £64,000
B £84,000
C £123,000
D £138,000

3 Wolf plc acquired 80,000 £1 ordinary shares in Fox plc on 1 April 20W7 at a cost of £77,000. Fox plc's reserves at that date were £50,000 and its issued ordinary share capital was £100,000.

At 31 March 20X7 Fox plc's reserves were £40,000. The amount of the negative goodwill arising on consolidation is

A £35,000
B £43,000
C £63,000
D £73,000

4 Witham Ltd is the sole subsidiary of Aveley plc. Witham Ltd's balance sheet at 31 December 20X9 can be summarised as

	£'000	£'000
Total assets less current liabilities		310
Debentures		100
Capital and reserves		
Ordinary shares	50	
Preference shares	100	
Profit and loss account	60	210
		310

Aveley plc held the following proportions of the securities of Witham Ltd:

385

Debentures 50%
Ordinary shares 60%
Preference shares 40%

What is the minority interest in Aveley plc's consolidated balance sheet as on 31 December 20X9?

A £ 44,000
B £ 84,000
C £104,000
D £154,000

(10 marks)

16 MORE CONSOLIDATED ACCOUNTS *18 mins*

1   The following information relates to Daviot Ltd and Tey Ltd.

	Daviot Ltd £	Tey Ltd £
Share capital at 1 January and 31 December 20X7 (ordinary shares)	200,000	150,000
Profit and loss account at 1 January 20X7	450,000	250,000
Profit for the year ended 31 December 20X7	40,000	20,000

On 1 January 20X7 Daviot Ltd purchased 90% of the ordinary share capital of Tey Ltd for £400,000. Goodwill arising on consolidation is to be amortised over 4 years from the date of acquisition.

What are consolidated reserves at 31 December 20X7? (2 marks)

2   Alpha Ltd acquired 80% of the share capital of Beta Ltd on 1 January 20X1. The consideration given was £500,000. On 1 January the fair value of Beta Ltd's net tangible assets is £450,000. What is the amount of goodwill to be entered in the consolidated accounts? (2 marks)

3   Gemini plc acquired 100,000 £1 ordinary shares in Taurus Ltd on 1 June 20X1 at a cost of £250,000. Taurus Ltd's reserves at 1 June 20X1 were £25,000 and its issued ordinary share capital was £125,000.

At 1 June 20X4, Taurus Ltd's reserves were £5,000. The goodwill on consolidation is
(2 marks)

4   Goose Ltd acquired 75% of Gander Ltd's issued share capital on 1 August 20X1 for a cost of £75,000. Gander Ltd's reserves at that date were £50,000 and its issued share capital was £100,000. Calculate the goodwill on consolidation. (2 marks)

5   Dragon plc owns the following proportions of shares in Monkey Ltd.

Ordinary shares 60%
Preference shares 40%
Debentures 50%

Monkey Ltd's balance sheet at 30 September 20X2 is:

	£'000	£'000
Net assets less current liabilities		250
Debentures		50
Capital and reserves		
Ordinary shares	100	
Preference shares	50	
Profit and loss account	50	200
		250

What is the minority interest in the consolidated balance sheet of Dragon plc at 30 September 20X2. (2 marks)

(10 marks)

17 EVON
18 mins

On 1 April 20X5, Evon Ltd acquired 75% of the ordinary share capital of Orset Ltd for £180,000. At that date the balance sheet of Orset Ltd was as follows:

	£
Sundry net assets	160,000
Share capital	100,000
100,000 Ordinary shares of £1 each	
Profit and loss account	60,000
	160,000

At 31 March 20X8, the balance sheets of the two companies were as follows:

	Evon Ltd £	Orset Ltd £
Sundry net assets	560,000	230,000
Investment in Orset	180,000	
	740,000	230,000
Share capital		
Shares of £1 each	500,000	100,000
Profit and loss account	240,000	130,000
	740,000	230,000

Goodwill arising on consolidation is to be amortised over five years.

Required

Prepare the consolidated balance sheet of Evon Ltd and its subsidiary as at 31 March 20X8.

(10 marks)

Exam answer bank

1 ACCOUNTING STATEMENTS

> **Tutor's hints.** In answering this question take care not to be repetitive. A good answer plan is needed before you start.

(a) **Relevant**

Published financial statements are directed to a number of different user groups: employees; the government; shareholders or owners of an enterprise; bankers; suppliers and customers; investment analysts. All of these user groups have different information needs, all of which must be satisfied in part by the information presented in published financial statements. **Relevance** in this context means that the **information** contained **serves the needs of users**.

There is great debate as to how relevant published financial statements in fact are, especially to investors. The use of historical costs is sometimes felt to obscure the real operating performance of an enterprise. Many users also want more information from financial statements than is currently provided.

Understandable

Many users are not accounting professionals. This is an especially important issue when shareholders are private individuals rather than large investment institutions with teams of analysts. Given that the purpose of financial statements is to **convey information** to shareholders, if that information is impossible to understand, then it is of little use. **Graphs, diagrams,** and **summary information** can be used to make the often technical content of published accounts easier to understand.

Reliable

Reliability means that the information presented in a set of financial statements **can be relied on** to be an accurate description of the transactions of the enterprise as recorded in the accounting records and show a true and fair view. This means that users should have **confidence** that the information is **correct**, and that there are **no material errors** in the accounts.

Complete

A set of published financial statements is in essence a report on the activities of the enterprise over a particular period, and a description of its assets, liabilities at the end of it. Therefore, completeness is important. **All material transactions or circumstances** should be recorded so that the user gets a **full picture** of an enterprise's position and performance. There has been much debate as to whether the exclusion of 'special purpose transactions' or 'off balance sheet finance', by which enterprises hide major transactions or liabilities from published accounts, should be permitted. This has led to the issue of a number of Financial Reporting Standards to deal with the perceived abuse.

Objective

As far as is reasonably possible, the information presented in published financial statements **should not be distorted** by the wishes of those preparing it. There is always a temptation to overstate profits and performance. It is the task of the auditors to ensure that these statements are **objective**.

Timely

Financial statements should be produced in such a timescale that the information it contains is **still relevant** to users. Those who make investment decisions value **timeliness**, as it allows them to make decisions on **recent information**. Another feature of the timing of financial reports is the regularity with which they are produced. Producing financial statements every year, covering the same twelve months, enables the time periods to be compared.

Comparable

Comparability has two aspects. Firstly, it means that accounts produced by an enterprise for one accounting period should be **readily comparable** with the accounts for the previous accounting period. This requirement affects accounting policies. If the basis for measuring, say, profit, is different, then comparing two successive profit figures does not give a meaningful appreciation of any improvement or decline in operating performance. **Inflation** produces problems of comparability, as the value of money, the unit of measurement, is declining in successive accounting periods. Secondly, the financial statements of different enterprises in the same industry **should be comparable**: one might be operating more efficiently than another.

(b) These matters can come into conflict in a number of ways.

The effort required to make a set of accounts **absolutely complete** may result in **extra time** being spent to prepare them, thus reducing their timeliness.

Objectivity might conflict with **understandability**: the transactions of a business enterprise are often complex, especially, for example, with the reporting of taxation. Objectively speaking, the enterprise is complex, and therefore its financial statements may also be complex. Making matters easy to understand may introduce subjectivity or oversimplification.

Objectivity might also be in conflict with **comparability**. No two enterprises are exactly the same, and comparisons drawn may be unjust, especially if different accounting policies are used.

2 FIXED ASSETS AND STOCKS

1 A   It is **never** B as funds are not set aside; nor C, this is revaluation.

2 D   (£5,000 – £1,000)/4 = £1,000 depreciation per annum ∴ NBV = £2,000.

3 D
		£
Balance b/d		67,460
Less NBV of fixed asset sold		
15,000 – (15,000 – (4,000 + 1,250))		5,250
		62,210

4 A   If disposal proceeds were £15,000 and profit on disposal is £5,000, then net book value must be £10,000, the difference between the fixed asset register figure and the fixed asset account in the nominal ledger.

5 A   Costs are understated, so profit is overstated. Revenue expenditure is recorded as capital, so fixed assets are overstated.

6 B   FIFO will leave the latest (and highest priced) goods as closing stock. So this reduces cost of sales and increases profit, as well as closing stock value.

7 C   Cost of sales is £1,300 understated and expenses £1,000 understated.

8 C   Closing stock = 20 units @ £3 each = £60

9 D   2 @ £3.00 + 10 @ £3.50 = £41.00

10 C

	Units	Unit cost £	Total £	Average £
Opening stock	30	2	60	
5 August purchase	50	2.40	120	
	80		180	2.25
10 August issue	(40)	2.25	(90)	
	40		90	
18 August purchase	60	2.50	150	
	100		240	2.40
23 August issue	(25)	2.40	(60)	
	75		180	

3 TURNER

> **Tutor's hints.** This is a straightforward question. If you have gone wrong then revise your double entry as this is an important skill not only for this exam but also for Paper 2.5 and Paper 3.6.
>
> When problems arise it is generally with the double entry. Remember to post the figures on the correct side of the suspense account and to apply the company's deprecation policy correctly.

SUSPENSE ACCOUNT

	£		£
Difference (1,852,817 – 1,796,100)	56,717	Sales return (a)	8,980
Discounts received (c)	919	Purchase return (a)	8,980
		Discount allowed (c)	836
		Insurance (d)	580
		Telephone (e)	38,260
	57,636		57,636

Journals

				£	£
(a)	DEBIT	Sales returns account		8,980	
	CREDIT	Suspense account			8,980
	DEBIT	Purchases returns account		8,980	
	CREDIT	Suspense account			8,980
(b)	DEBIT	Fixed assets: plant and machinery		9,600	
	CREDIT	plant repairs			9,600
	DEBIT	Depreciation expense (9,600 × 20% × 6/12)		960	
	CREDIT	Depreciation (accumulated)			960
(c)	DEBIT	Discount allowed		836	
	CREDIT	Suspense account			836
	DEBIT	Suspense account		919	
	CREDIT	Discount received			919
(d)	DEBIT	Insurance expense		580	
	CREDIT	Suspense account			580
(e)	DEBIT	Telephone expense		38,260	
	CREDIT	Suspense account			38,260

			£	£
(f)	DEBIT	Disposals account	12,000	
	CREDIT	Fixed asset cost		12,000
	DEBIT	Depreciation (accumulated)	8,000	
	CREDIT	Disposals account		8,000
	DEBIT	Sales	4,800	
	CREDIT	Disposals account		4,800
	DEBIT	Disposals account	800	
	CREDIT	Profits on disposal		800
	DEBIT	Depreciation (accumulated)	3,000	
	CREDIT	Depreciation (12,000 × 25%)		3,000

4 ACCOUNTING STANDARDS AND MATERIALITY

> **Tutor's hints.** The basic description of materiality in the context of accounting standards and financial statements is in the *Explanatory foreword* to the accounting standards. Without knowing this, you should still be able to produce a reasonable answer using some common sense. Issues relating to part (b) are topical at the moment. You should know all the (very straightforward) rules relating to compliance with the Standards.

(a) An '**immaterial item**' is one which is not significant enough to effect evaluations or decisions relating to the financial statements.

The judgement as to whether an item is material or immaterial is subjective. **Materiality** may be considered in the context of individual items within the financial statements or the statements as a whole. The nature of the item has to be considered, to decide whether to judge it in relative or absolute terms.

Materiality may depend upon context in the following ways.

(i) If the treatment of the item reverses a trend or turns a profit into a loss or affects the solvency ratios in the balance sheet, then materiality must be judged in a narrower context.

(ii) If the profits are unusually low, or there is a loss, then materiality should be judged against the more normal trading pattern.

(iii) A relatively small item should not be assumed to be immaterial, as in the context the user may have expected the figure to be substantially larger.

(iv) Items should not be offset until their materiality has been considered separately; the net effect may be immaterial, but it may not give a true and fair view to disclose only the net effect. The same possibility may arise when a larger number of small items are aggregated.

(v) If an item must be disclosed by statute, then materiality takes on a different meaning. An example is directors' emoluments.

(b) The directors may only justify departure from the accounting standards if compliance would have meant that **the financial statements did not show a true and fair view**. The circumstances in which this would arise would be very rare.

The departure from the accounting standards might require a **prior year adjustment** if it constituted a change in accounting policy. The previous year's financial statements would have to be adjusted accordingly.

The directors are obliged to disclose all details of the **material departures** from the accounting standards in the notes to the financial statements, showing the numerical effect where possible. Under the Companies Act 1985 (as amended by CA 1989) the Secretary of State has the power to force a company to amend 'defective' accounts, such as those which, unjustifiably, do not comply with the accounting standards. The Financial Reporting Review Panel also plays a role by dealing with companies in breach of accounting standards, with the legal backing of CA1989.

5 BESS, CHARLES AND GEORGE

> **Tutor's hints**. This is a straightforward question requiring preparation of the partnership profit and loss account and appropriation account. Remember to take salaries and interest on capital before allocating the balance in the PSR.

(a) BESS, CHARLES AND GEORGE
PROFIT AND LOSS ACCOUNT FOR THE YEAR ENDED 31 MARCH 20X1

	£	£
Sales (W1)		559,821
Cost of sales (W2)		279,584
Gross profit		280,237
Less expenses		
Salesperson's commission	6,659	
Carriage outwards	617	
Rent, rates and insurance	32,522	
Motor expenses	3,769	
Wages and NIC	48,317	
Lighting and heating	3,240	
Postage and stationery	705	
Depreciation charge (4,765 + 236 + 1,613)	6,614	
Telephone	2,926	
Sundries	868	
		106,237
Net profit		174,000

Workings

1 Sales

	£
Per trial balance	568,092
Less returns inwards	8,271
	559,821

2 Cost of sales

	£
Opening stock	127,535
Purchases	302,117
	429,652
Carriage inwards	872
Returns outwards	(7,004)
	423,520
Less closing stock	(143,936)
	279,584

(b) BESS, CHARLES AND GEORGE
APPROPRIATION ACCOUNT FOR THE YEAR ENDED 31 MARCH 20X1

	£	£
Net profit		174,000
Partners' salaries		
Bess	30,000	
Charles	25,000	
George	17,000	
		(72,000)
Interest on capital		
Bess: 5% × 60,000	3,000	
Charles: 5% × 40,000	2,000	
George: 5% × 20,000	1,000	
		(6,000)
		96,000
Balance of profits shared		
Bess: 5/12	40,000	
Charles: 4/12	32,000	
George: 3/12	24,000	
		96,000

6 ERNIE

> **Tutor's hint.** Ernie is a builder therefore the repair staff are part of the direct costs and should be taken as part of the cost of sales. Note that if there are prepayments/accruals brought forward then there are likely to be some to carry forward.
>
> Do not waste time producing T accounts when workings on the face of the accounts will suffice. Make sure you know how to calculate the sales and purchases figures.
>
> *Prizewinner's points.* The adjustment for rent was quite tricky. If you got this and completed the question in the time, well done.

ERNIE
TRADING, PROFIT AND LOSS ACCOUNT
FOR THE YEAR ENDED 30 JUNE 20X8

	£	£
Sales (W1)		204,490
Cost of sales		
Opening stock	14,160	
Purchases (W2)	84,620	
	98,780	
Closing stock	(12,170)	
		(86,610)
Wages: repair staff		(68,200)
Gross profit		49,680
Expenses		
Rent (W3)	3,450	
Insurance (700 + 1,600 /2)	1,500	
Electricity (890 – 180 + 220)	930	
Telephone (860 – 210 + 240)	890	
Wages: wife	5,000	
Depreciation (W4)	5,400	
Loan interest (1,000 × 3/12)	250	
Bad debts	1,280	
Profit on sale of vehicle (W4)	(500)	
Miscellaneous (1,280 + 490)	1,770	
		(19,970)
Net profit		29,710

Workings

1 *Sales*

	£
Balance b/f	(9,490)
Receipts	203,520
Refund	(400)
Debtors c/f	10,860
	204,490

2 *Purchases*

	£
Balance b/f	(3,460)
Payments	83,990
Creditors c/f	4,090
	84,620

3 *Rent*

Three months rent is £750

$$750 \times \frac{12 \text{ months}}{3 \text{ months}} = £3,000$$

	£
20% increase: £3,000 × 1.2 =	3,600
less three months paid in advance £3,600 × 3/12	(900)
Add prepayment b/f	750
	3,450

4 *Depreciation*

Plant and machinery	£
Cost (12,600 + 8,400)	21,000
Depreciation b/f	(5,800)
NBV	15,200
Depreciation expense at 25%	(3,800)
	11,400

Motor vehicle	£
Addition	12,800
Depreciation (12,800 × 25% × 6/12)	(1,600)
	11,200
Total depreciation (3,800 + 1,600)	5,400

Motor vehicle disposal	£
Proceeds	3,000
NBV (9,000 – 6,500)	2,500
Profit on disposal	500

7 ATOK

> **Tutor's hint.** This question was fairly straightforward. Candidates should note that they can still earn full marks even if they present workings alongside the figures in the financial statements they produce. Problem areas in this question were:
> - Stock adjustment
> - Accruals and prepayments in the balance sheet (ie the expense heading contained the accruals but the balance sheet did not)
> - Calculation of the dividend
> - The statement of reserve movements (which was omitted altogether in many cases)
>
> In the exam you would be asked for either the profit and loss account or the balance sheet, not both, in a question this complex.

(a) ATOK LIMITED
PROFIT AND LOSS ACCOUNT FOR THE YEAR ENDED 30 JUNE 20X9

	£'000
Sales revenue (14,800 – 24) (W1)	14,776
Cost of sales (W1)	(10,280)
Gross profit	4,496
Distribution costs (1,080+272+190 – 120)	(1,422)
Administration expenses (1,460+272+70 – 60)	(1,742)
Operating profit	1,332
Interest payable (2,000 × 10% × 3/12)	(50)
Profit for the financial year	1,282
Dividend: proposed (28,000 @ 2 ½ pence)	(700)
Retained profit for the year	582

ATOK LIMITED
BALANCE SHEET AS AT 30 JUNE 20X9

	£'000	£'000
Fixed assets		
Land and buildings (12,000+8,000 – 2,130 – 160)		17,710
Plant and equipment (12,800 – 2,480 – 2,560)		7,760
		25,470
Current assets		
Stock (W1)	1,566	
Debtors (4,120+120+60 – 24)	4,276	
Cash at bank	160	
	6,002	
Liabilities: due within one year		
Creditors	(2,240)	
Accruals (190+70+50+700)	(1,010)	
	(3,250)	
Net current assets		2,752
Total assets less current liabilities		28,222
Liabilities: due after one year		
10% debentures 20Y8		(2,000)
		26,222
Capital and reserves		
Called up share capital		14,000
Share premium account		4,000
Revaluation reserve (3,000+1,500)		4,500
Profit and loss account (3,140+582)		3,722
		26,222

(b) Movements on reserves for the year ended 30 June 20X9

	Share Premium Account £'000	Revaluation Reserve £'000	Profit and Loss Account £'000	Total £'000
As at 1 July 20X8	2,000	3,000	3,140	8,140
Premium on new issue of shares	2,000			2,000
Retained profit for the year			582	582
Surplus on revaluation		1,500		1,500
As at 30 June 20X9	4,000	4,500	3,722	12,222

Workings

1 Cost of sales

	£'000
Opening stock	1,390
Purchases	8,280
	9,670
Closing stocks ((1,560 + 16 – 10) see below)	(1,566)
	8,104
Depreciation	2,176
Cost of sales	10,280

Stock adjustments

(i) Lower of cost (£80,000) and NRV (£90,000 – £20,000) = £70,000. Therefore £10,000 (80,000 – 70,000) adjustment.

(ii) Stock understated by £16,000

Sales overstated by £24,000

2 *Depreciation*

	£'000
Buildings (8,000 @ 2%)	160
Plant (12,800 @ 20%)	2,560
	2,720

80% to cost of sales: 2,176. 10% to distribution and 10% to administration: 272

Tutor's hint. Remember that land is not depreciated.

8 STANDARD SETTERS

Tutor's hint. Written questions are as much a part of this examination as computational ones, so it is important that you practise them. This is part of an old examination question under the previous syllabus. At that time, the examiner commented that few candidates answered this question. Of those, few answered it well.

(a) The Financial Reporting Council (FRC) is a body **independent** of the **accounting profession**. It was set up to oversee and guide the standard setting process. It does this by **issuing guidance** to the ASB and also by being responsible for the funding of the whole process. The FRC receives funds from the City, the government and the accountancy profession.

(b) The Accounting Standards Board (ASB) is responsible for the **issue of new standards**. The new standards take the form of Financial Reporting Standards (FRSs). The overall aim is to guide preparation of financial statements in order to make them **comparable, consistent and user friendly**.

(c) The Financial Reporting Review Panel (FRRP) is chaired by a barrister. It is concerned with **any material departures** from accounting standards by large companies. When the FRRP becomes involved in investigating a departure it is usually resolved through **discussion** with the company. If discussion does not resolve the situation then the FRRP can resort to **legal action** to force an amendment to the accounts and subsequent **distribution** of the revised financial statements to all interested parties.

(d) The Urgent Issues Task Force (UITF) tackles **urgent matters** not covered by existing standards. It acts in an emergency to **issue advice** where the normal standard-setting process is **not practicable**.

9 TOPAZ

> **Tutor's hints.** You must remember to show Division B's results separated, as a discontinued operation. The bad debt in division D is material and needs disclosure in a note.

(a) TOPAZ LIMITED
PROFIT AND LOSS ACCOUNT
FOR THE YEAR ENDED 31 DECEMBER 20X6

	Continuing operations £m	Discontinued operation £m	Total £m
Sales	68	13	81
Cost of sales	(41)	(8)	(49)
Gross profit	27	5	32
Distribution costs (note 1)	(6)	(1)	(7)
Administrative expenses	(4)	(2)	(6)
Operating profit	17	2	19
Profit on sales of discontinued operations		2.5	2.5
Costs of fundamental reorganisation	(1.8)		(1.8)
Profit on ordinary activities before interest	15.2	4.5	19.7
Interest payable			(1)
Profit on ordinary activities before taxation			18.7
Taxation			(4.8)
Profit on ordinary activities after taxation			13.9
Dividends			
Interim paid			(2.0)
Final proposed			(4.0)
Retained profit for the financial year			7.9

Note 1 Distribution costs include a bad debt of £1.9m which arose on the continuing operations.

(b) TOPAZ LIMITED
STATEMENT OF TOTAL RECOGNISED GAINS AND LOSSES

	£m
Profit for the financial year	13.9
Unrealised surplus on revaluation of properties	4.0
Total gains recognised since last annual report	17.9

(c) FRS 3 requires an analysis of the profit and loss account as far as the figure of profit on ordinary activities before interest into three elements.

   (i)   Continuing operations
   (ii)   New acquisitions
   (iii)   Discontinued operations

This extra disclosure assists users in a number of ways.

Comparisons

Before FRS 3, it was difficult to make comparisons between one year and another because there was no information about the turnover and profit drawn from activities that ceased during the years and new activities that did not exist last year. FRS 3 addressed this problem.

Manipulation

FRS 3 put an end to the manipulation of the profit and loss account by means of exceptional and extraordinary items by clearly defining each category and prescribing the necessary accounting treatment for each item. This makes it easier for users to interpret the information and to make comparisons year-on-year and against other companies.

Forecasting

FRS 3 means that better forecasts may be prepared, since continuing operations are clearly identified.

10 HISTORICAL COST ACCOUNTING

> **Tutor's hint.** Remember to read the requirement. In (a) you need to 'list and briefly explain' while in (b) you only need a list.

(a) Three ways in which the use of historical cost accounting may lead to misleading financial statements are:

  (i) Fixed assets are shown at their net book value. Some fixed assets (especially land and building) are likely to appreciate in value and so the balance sheet value has no relation to the market value.

  (ii) Depreciation is based on original cost. This means that the true value in use to the business may not be charged through the profit and loss account.

  (iii) If prices rise whilst stocks are held, then a holding gain over inflates the profits of the business.

(b) Three advantages of historical cost accounting are:

  (i) The historical cost is an objective and documented amount.

  (ii) The absence of subjective judgement makes historical cost accounting simple and cheap to implement.

  (iii) Users and prepares of the accounts understand the concept so the financial statements are user friendly.

11 GERMAINE

> **Tutor's hint.** You need to be able to apply the knowledge displayed in question 51.

(a) The supply of components was within the accounting period, so these events have a bearing on events within the year. The amounts are also material.

The £30,000 will be incurred anyway so this figure must be recorded in the financial statements.

As the successful outcome is 70% likely, it is possible that damages and costs could be incurred so the contingent liability should be disclosed by way of a note.

DEBIT	Profit and loss account	£30,000	
CREDIT	Legal costs provision		£30,000

Provision for legal costs relating to customers legal action.

Note to accounts

A customer has commenced legal action against Germaine Limited for the supply of allegedly faulty components. Germaine Limited is confident that it will successfully contend this legal action. A provision for legal costs has been made in this year's financial statements (£30,000). If the case goes in the customer's favour costs and damages will amount to £180,000.

(b) This event relates to items existing at the balance sheet date and should be adjusted in full.

DEBIT	Bad debt provision	£84,000	
CREDIT	Profit and loss account		£84,000

Reversal of bad debt provision following receipt of payments from debtor.

12 RUBENS

> **Tutor's hint.** Remember to learn SECTOR if you had difficulties recalling the six criteria. However, if you use the mnemonic remember what it stands for. In part (b), you need to be able to apply the criteria for (a).

(a) (i) **S**eparately defined project
    (ii) **E**xpenditure separately identified
    (iii) **C**ommercially viable
    (iv) **T**echnically feasible
    (v) **O**verall profit expected
    (vi) **R**esources exist to complete the project

(b) PROFIT AND LOSS ACCOUNT

	£'000
Research and development (W1)	3,940

BALANCE SHEET
Intangible assets

	£'000
Development costs (W2)	7,560

Workings

1 *Profit and loss*

	£'000
Project A: amortisation (£1m/5)	200
Project B: amortisation (£2,400/5 × 11/12)	440
Project D: write off	1,500
Research expenditure	1,800
	3,940

2 *Balance sheet*

	£'000
Project A (600 – 200)	400
Project B (2,400 – 440)	1,960
Project C	4,000
Project E	800
Project F	400
	7,560

13 JANE

> **Tutor's hint.** Make sure that you understand the workings and how all the figures are calculated. Pay particular attention to the calculation of operating profit.

JANE LIMITED
CASH FLOW STATEMENT FOR THE
YEAR ENDED 31 DECEMBER 20X8

Reconciliation for operating profit to net cash flow from operating activities

	£'000	£'000
Operating profit (W1)		45
Depreciation		100
Loss on sale of fixed asset		20
Loss on sale of investments		10
Stock		(30)
Debtors		(70)
Creditors		10
Net cash inflow from operating activities		85

Cash flow statement

	£'000	£'000
Net cash inflow from operating activities		85
Returns on investment and servicing of finance		(15)
Capital expenditure and financial investment		
Purchase of tangible fixed assets (W2)	(450)	
Proceeds from sale of tangible fixed assets	60	
Proceeds from sale of investments	40	
		(350)
Equity dividends paid		(30)
Financing		
Share issue	180	
Debenture issue	50	
		230
Net cash outflow		(80)

Workings

1 Operating profit

	£'000
Retained loss for the year (200 – 190)	(10)
Proposed dividend	40
Interest paid (150 @ 10%)	15
	45

2 Fixed assets: purchases

	£'000
Opening balance	(730)
Disposal	80
Depreciation for the year	100
Closing balance	1,100
Revaluation in year	(100)
Fixed assets purchased	450

Note. You can quickly check that the net cash outflow is correct by:

	20X7	20X8	Movement
	£'000	£'000	£'000
Cash at bank	20	30	10
Overdraft	(40)	(130)	(90)
Total	(20)	(100)	(80)

Exam answer bank

14 ARH

> **Tutor's hint.** This question required an understanding of the difference between profit and cash flow, as well as the ability to calculate ratios and interpret them.

(a)

		20X4	20X5
Gross profit %	$= \dfrac{\text{Gross profit}}{\text{Sales}} \times 100\%$	$\dfrac{2{,}600}{14{,}400} = 18\%$	$\dfrac{4{,}400}{17{,}000} = 26\%$
Net profit %	$= \dfrac{\text{Net profit}}{\text{Sales}} \times 100\%$	$\dfrac{1{,}400}{14{,}400} = 10\%$	$\dfrac{2{,}400}{17{,}000} = 14\%$

Return on capital employed

$$= \dfrac{\text{Profit}}{\text{Capital employed}} \qquad \dfrac{1{,}400}{6{,}700} = 21\% \qquad \dfrac{2{,}400}{5{,}720} = 42\%$$

(Total assets less current liabilities)

(b) The profitability for 20X5 as demonstrated by the above ratios is much improved on 20X4. Gross profit is up 8% and return on capital employed has doubled. However, net profit has only increased by 4% indicating that administrative costs must be increasing out of proportion to the increase in sales, particularly given the fact that debenture interest costs are no longer included.

However, despite this improved profitability the bank balances have reduced.

Liquidity ratios

	20X4	20X5
Current ratio		
$\dfrac{\text{Current assets}}{\text{Current liabilities}}$	$\dfrac{5{,}700}{1{,}500} = 3.8$	$\dfrac{4{,}420}{2{,}700} = 1.6$
Quick ratio		
$\dfrac{\text{Current assets less stock}}{\text{Current liabilities}}$	$\dfrac{5{,}700 - 1{,}300}{1{,}500} = 2.9$	$\dfrac{4{,}420 - 2{,}000}{2{,}700} = 0.9$

Liquidity ratios demonstrate a marked reduction in liquidity from 20X4 to 20X5. This is highlighted by the quick ratio which has fallen from nearly 3 in 20X4 to less than 1 in 20X5.

The **reasons for** this **decrease may be as follows**.

(i) **A fall in the bank balance** due to repayment of the 10% debenture.

(ii) **An increase in creditors**. This may be due to the increases in stock holdings and expenses and the company taking longer to pay because of liquidity problems.

(iii) **A fall in debtors** despite an increase in sales, indicating a more rigorous collection policy, again to maximise liquidity.

(iv) **Acquisitions of fixed assets**, funded from operating activities.

Overall, the liquidity of ARH is of concern. The decrease in the bank balances is generally down to a change in investments, the debenture being an example of this as well as the increase in fixed assets. As cash if the lifeblood of a company it would be useful to see a cashflow in order to see the *quality* of the profits ARH has earned.

Exam answer bank

15 BASIC CONSOLIDATED FINANCIAL STATEMENTS

1   D

	£'000
Consideration (at fair value)	1,900
Net assets acquired	750
	1,150

2   C

	£'000
Cost	300
Net assets acquired	
75% × (£200,000 + 36,000)	177
	123

The reduction in net assets since acquisition is not relevant for the purposes of determining goodwill.

3   B

	£
Cost	77,000
Net assets acquired	
80% × £150,000	(120,000)
Negative goodwill	(43,000)

4   C

	£
Preference shares	60,000
Ordinary shares (50 + 60) × 40%	44,000
	104,000

The minority interest never includes any amount in respect of debentures. The debentures held outside the group will be shown as a separate liability.

16 MORE CONSOLIDATED ACCOUNTS

1   £498,000

	£
Daviot Ltd (450,000 + 40,000)	490,000
Tey Ltd (90% × 20,000)	18,000
Amortisation of goodwill (40 ÷ 4)	(10,000)
	498,000

Goodwill	
Cost of investment	400,000
Less group share of net asset acquired (90% ×) (150,00 – 250,000)	(360,000)
Goodwill on purchase	40,000

2   £50,000

	£'000
Consideration	500
Fair value of net assets acquired	450
Goodwill	50

3   £130,000

	£'000
Cost	250
Net assets acquired (80% × (£125,000 + £25,000))	120
Goodwill	130

Notes

1   Acquired 100,000 out of 125,000 issued shares, so Gemini owns 80% of Taurus.

Exam answer bank

2 The reduction in reserves since acquisition is not relevant in determining goodwill.

4 £(37,500) negative goodwill

	£
Cost	75,000
Net assets acquired	
(75% × (£100,000 + £50,000))	112,500
Negative goodwill	(37,500)

5 £90,000

Minority interest includes only the shares, not the debentures. Any debentures held outside the group are shown as a separate liability. Therefore the minority interest is as follows:

	£'000
Preference shares (60% × £50,000)	30
Ordinary shares (40% × (£100,000 + £50,000))	60
	90

17 EVON

> **Tutor's hint.** This is a straightforward question, but you must understand consolidated accounts. Work through the answer carefully and make sure you understand the entries.

EVON LIMITED GROUP
BALANCE SHEET AS AT 31 MARCH 20X8

	£'000	£'000
Goodwill (W1)	60,000	
Less depreciation (W1)	36,000	
		24,000
Sundry net assets (£560,000 + £230,000)		790,000
		814,000
Share capital		
500,000 shares of £1 each		500,000
Profit and loss account (W3)		256,500
		756,500
Minority interest (W2)		57,500
		814,000

Workings

1 Goodwill

	£'000	£'000
Cost		180
Share capital	100	
Pre-acquisition profits	60	
	160	
75% thereof:		120
Goodwill		60
Depreciation (3/5 × £60,000)		36

2 Minority interest

	£'000
Share capital (25% × £100,000)	25.0
Profit and loss account (25% × £130,000)	32.5
	57.5

3   *Profit and loss account*

	£'000
Evon	240.0
Orset (75% × £130,000)	97.5
	337.5
Less: Orset pre-acquisition profits (75% × £60,000)	(45.0)
Goodwill written off (W1)	(36.0)
	256.5

Index

Index

Note: **Key Terms** and their references are given in **bold**.

Accounting information, 4
Accounting policies, 88
Accounting standards and choice, 203
Accounting standards, 196, 373, 376
Accounting standards Board, 214
Accruals, 12
Accruals and prepayments, 128, 138
Accruals concept, 12, 82
Acid test ratio, 310
Adjusting events, 242
Alternative accounting rules, 37
Alternative accounting, 37
Analysis of cash flow statements, 289
Appropriation of net profits, 102
ASB, 214
Asset turnover, 301
Assets, 11, 233
Associate, 367
Authorised (or nominal) capital, 167
Average cost, 50

Bad debts, 58, 130
Balance sheet, 11, 199, 235, 380
Bonus issues, 179

CA 1985, 267, 367
CA 1989, 336
Called-up capital, 167
Capital, 9, 13
Capital account, 101
Capital expenditure, 20
Capital gearing ratio, 304
Capital income, 20
Capital transactions, 21
Capitalisation of finance costs, 40
Cash book, 128, 135
Cash cycle, 309
Cash flow ratio, 307
Cash flow statement, 235
Chairman's report, 296
Change in accounting policy, 217
Class of fixed assets, 47
Companies Act 1985, 37, 171
Conceptual framework, 229, 230
Consistency concept, 84
Consolidated accounts, 334
Consolidation, 334
Constructive obligation, 246
Contingent asset, 249
Contingent liability, 248

Continuing operations, 208
Control, 334
Cost, 39
Credit sales and debtors, 128
Creditors' turnover, 313
Current account, 101
Current cost accounting (CCA), 228
Current purchasing power (CPP), 228
Current ratio, 310

Debenture loans, 174
Debt ratio, 303
Debt/equity ratio, 305
Debtor days ratio, 311
Debtor days, 312
Debtors payment period, 311
Depreciation, 41
Derecognition, 233
Directly attributable finance costs, 40
Directors' report, 296
Discontinued operations, 208, 212
Disposal of fixed assets, 32, 33, 34
Dissolution of a partnership, 113
Dividend cover, 315
Dividend per share and dividend cover, 315
Dividend yield, 316
Dividends, 168, 243
Dividends payable by a subsidiary, 345
Dominant influence, 333
Drawings account, 101
Drawings, 98, 128, 139

Earnings per share (EPS), 209, **216**, 314, 315
Earnings yield, 316
Efficiency ratios, 311
Elements of financial statements, 231, 233
Entity concept, 6
Equity accounting, 367
Errors, 375
Estimation technique, 88
Events after the balance sheet date, 242
Exceptional items, 209, 210
Exemption of subsidiary undertakings from
    preparing group account, 336
Extraordinary items, 209, 210, **211**

FIFO (first in, first out), 50
Financial adaptability, 231
Financial statements, 11
Fixed assets valuation: alternative
    accounting rules, 37

Index

Fixed assets, 36
Fixed assets: disclosure, 38
Framework on the preparation and presentation of financial stat, 229
FRS 1 Cash flow statements, 278, 289, 384
FRS 2 Accounting for subsidiary undertakings, 335
FRS 3 Reporting financial performance, 42, 208, 209, 381
FRS 9 Associates and joint ventures, 367
FRS 10 Goodwill and intangible assets, 351
FRS 11 Impairment of fixed assets and goodwill, 43
FRS 12 Provisions, contingent liabilities and contingent assets, 39, 244
FRS 14 Earnings per share, 216
FRS 15 Tangible fixed assets, 37, 39, 41
FRS 16 Current tax, 267
FRS 18 Accounting policies, 80
FRS 19 Deferred tax, 265
FRS 21 Events after the balance sheet date, 241, 242
Fundamental errors, 217
Fungible assets, 91

Gains, 233
Garner v Murray, 117
Gearing ratio, 304
Generally accepted accounting practice (GAAP), 202
Going concern concept, 80, 242
Goods destroyed, 133
Goods stolen, 133
Goodwill, 108, 254, 257
  and pre-acquisition profits, 349
  arising on consolidation, 348
Gross profit margin, 302

Historical cost, 87
Historical cost accounting, 226, 381
HM Customs & Excise, 262

Implications of high or low gearing, 305
Income and expenditure account, 12
Incomplete records, 128, 140
Indirect method, 278
Initial recognition, 233
Insolvency of a partner, 117
Intangible fixed asset, 36, 173, 200, 255
Inter-company trading, 361
Interest cover, 307
Interest held on a long-term basis, 334
Investments, 36, 173

Issued capital, 167

Journal entries, 375

Liability, 5, 11, **233, 245**
LIFO (last in, first out), 50
Limited companies, 6, 100, 164, 171, 197
Limited company accounts, 171
Limited liability, 164, 165
Liquidity, 303, **308**, 310
Loans by partners, 102
Long-term solvency, 303

Machine hour method, 43
Market value of shares, 171
Materiality, 376
Materiality concept, 85
Measurement in financial statements, 231, 234
Medium-sized company, 202
Methods of calculating depreciation, 42, 43
Minority interest, 343, 360
Multiple choice questions, 373, 385

Net book value (NBV), 41
Net profit margin, 302
Net realisable value (NRV), 48
New acquisitions, 208
Nominal value, 175
Non-adjusting events, 243
Notes to the accounts, 199

Objective of financial statements, 231
Objectivity, 87
Opening balance sheet, 128
Operating profit, 199
Ordinary activities, 210
Ordinary shares, 170
Organisational structure, 15
Ownership interest, 233

P/E ratio, 316
Paid-up capital, 167
Parent undertaking, 332
Participating interest, 333
Partnership, 98
Partnership accounts, 97
Partnership Act 1890, 98
Partnership agreement, 98
Partnership from two or more sole traders, 111
PBIT (profit before interest and tax), 298
Pre-acquisition profits, 363

412

Preference shares, 169
Presentation of financial information, 231, 235
Primary profitability ratio, 301
Primary statement, 214
Prior period adjustments, 217
Private companies, 165
Profit, 4, 10
Profit analysis, 302
Profit and loss account, 11, 198, 235, 380
Profit before interest and tax, 298
Profit margin, 301
Profit smoothing, 245
Profitability, 298
Profit-sharing ratio, 98
Provision, 179, 245
Provision for depreciation, 29
Provision for doubtful debts, 59
Prudence concept, 83
Public companies, 165
Published accounts, 197
Purchased goodwill, 254, **255**, 256
Purchases and trade creditors, 128
Purchases, stocks and the cost of sales, 128

Qualitative characteristics of financial information, 231, 232
Quick ratio, 310

Ratio analysis, 296
Ratios, 385
Realised profits, 213, 214
Recognition in financial statements, 231, 233
Reconciliation of movements in shareholders' funds, 214
Reducing balance method (depreciation), 23, 25, 43
Replacement cost, 50
Reporting entity, 231
Research and development, 258
Reserve, 176, **179**, 201
Reserve movements, 380
Restructuring, 247
Return on capital employed (ROCE), 299
Return on shareholders' capital (ROSC), 300
Revaluation account, 111
Revaluation reserve, 38, 46
Revaluations, 45
Revenue expenditure, 20
Revenue income, 20
Rights issues, 180
ROCE, 299

ROSC, 300

Secondary ratios, 301
Separate valuation principle, 85
Share capital, 175
Share premium account, 177, **178**
Short-term solvency, 308
Small and medium-sized groups, 336
Small company, 201
Solomons report, 230
SSAP 9 Stocks and long-term contracts, 49
SSAP 13 Accounting for research and development, 258, 382
Standard cost, 50
Standard setters, 380
Standard setting process, 195, 207
Statement of Principles for Financial Reporting, 84, 230, 231
Statement of total recognised gains and losses, 209, **213**, 235, 381
Statutory accounts, 197
Statutory books, 166
Stock days, 312
Stock destroyed, 134
Stock Exchange, 202
Stock turnover period, 312
Stock valuation, 48
Stolen goods or goods destroyed, 128, 132
Straight line method (depareciation), 23, 24, 43
Subsequent expenditure, 40
Subsequent remeasurement, 233
Subsidiary undertaking, 332
Substance over form, 88
Sum of digits method, 23, 43
Suspense account, 375

Tangible fixed assets, 36, 173
Taxation, 174, 266
Trading and profit and loss account, 379
Two column cash book, 136
Two sole traders becoming a partnership, 112

Unlimited liability, 164
Unrealised profits, 213
Urgent Issues Task Force (UITF), 196
Users of accounting information, 7
Users of financial statements, 232

Valuation of fixed assets, 37
VAT, 262

CAT Paper 6 – Drafting Financial Statements (6/04)

REVIEW FORM & FREE PRIZE DRAW

All original review forms from the entire BPP range, completed with genuine comments, will be entered into one of two draws on 31 January 2005 and 31 July 2005. The names on the first four forms picked out on each occasion will be sent a cheque for £50.

Name: _____   Address: _____

How have you used this Interactive Text?
(Tick one box only)
☐ Home study (book only)
☐ On a course: college _____
☐ With 'correspondence' package
☐ Other _____

Why did you decide to purchase this Interactive Text? *(Tick one box only)*
☐ Have used BPP Texts in the past
☐ Recommendation by friend/colleague
☐ Recommendation by a lecturer at college
☐ Saw advertising
☐ Other _____

Which BPP products have you used?
☑ Text ☐ Kit ☐ i-Pass ☐ i-Learn

During the past six months do you recall seeing/receiving any of the following?
(Tick as many boxes as are relevant)
☐ Our advertisement in *ACCA Student Accountant*
☐ Other advertisement _____
☐ Our brochure with a letter through the post
☐ Our website www.bpp.com

Which (if any) aspects of our advertising do you find useful?
(Tick as many boxes as are relevant)
☐ Prices and publication dates of new editions
☐ Information on Interactive Text content
☐ Facility to order books off-the-page
☐ None of the above

Your ratings, comments and suggestions would be appreciated on the following areas

	Very useful	Useful	Not useful
Introductory section (How to use this Interactive Text)	☐	☐	☐
Key terms	☐	☐	☐
Examples	☐	☐	☐
Activities and answers	☐	☐	☐
Key learning points	☐	☐	☐
Quick quizzes	☐	☐	☐
Exam alerts	☐	☐	☐
Question Bank	☐	☐	☐
Answer Bank	☐	☐	☐
List of key terms and index	☐	☐	☐
Structure and presentation	☐	☐	☐
Icons	☐	☐	☐

	Excellent	Good	Adequate	Poor
Overall opinion of this Interactive Text	☐	☐	☐	☐

Do you intend to continue using BPP products?   ☐ Yes   ☐ No

Please note any further comments and suggestions/errors on the reverse of this page. The BPP author of this edition can be emailed at katyhibbert@bpp.com

Please return this form to: Mary Maclean, CAT Range Manager, BPP Professional Education, FREEPOST, London, W12 8BR

CAT Paper 6 – Drafting Financial Statements (6/04)

REVIEW FORM & FREE PRIZE DRAW (continued)
Please note any further comments and suggestions/errors below

FREE PRIZE DRAW RULES

1. Closing date for 31 January 2005 draw is 31 December 2004. Closing date for 31 July 2005 draw is 30 June 2005.

2. No purchase necessary. Entry forms are available upon request from BPP Professional Education. No more than one entry per title, per person. Draw restricted to persons aged 16 and over.

3. Winners will be notified by post and receive their cheques not later than 6 weeks after the relevant draw date.

4. The decision of the promoter in all matters is final and binding. No correspondence will be entered into.

See overleaf for information on other
BPP products and how to order

CAT Order

To BPP Professional Education, Aldine Place, London W12 8AW
Tel: 020 8740 2211 Fax: 020 8740 1184
email: publishing@bpp.com website: www.bpp.com
Order online www.bpp.com

Mr/Mrs/Ms (Full name) _____
Daytime delivery address _____
Postcode _____
Daytime Tel _____ Email _____
Date of exam (month/year) _____

Occasionally we may wish to email you relevant offers and information about courses and products. Please tick to opt into this service. ☐

		6/04 Texts	1/04 Kits	1/04 i-Learn CD	1/04 i-Pass CD	Virtual Campus enrolment
INTRODUCTORY						
Paper 1	Recording Financial Transactions	£17.95 ☐	£9.95 ☐	£29.95 ☐	£19.95 ☐	£80 ☐
Paper 2	Information for Management Control	£17.95 ☐	£9.95 ☐	£29.95 ☐	£19.95 ☐	£80 ☐
INTERMEDIATE						
Paper 3	Maintaining Financial Records	£17.95 ☐	£9.95 ☐	£30.95 ☐	£19.95 ☐	£80 ☐
Paper 4	Accounting for Costs	£17.95 ☐	£9.95 ☐	£30.95 ☐	£19.95 ☐	£80 ☐
ADVANCED CORE						
Paper 5	Managing People and Systems	£17.95 ☐	£9.95 ☐	£30.95 ☐	£21.95 ☐	£80 ☐
Paper 6	Drafting Financial Statements	£17.95 ☐	£9.95 ☐	£30.95 ☐	£21.95 ☐	£80 ☐
Paper 7	Planning, Control & Performance Management	£17.95 ☐	£9.95 ☐	£30.95 ☐	£21.95 ☐	£80 ☐
ADVANCED OPTION						
Paper 8	Implementing Audit Procedures	£17.95 ☐ (12/04 exam)	£9.95 ☐	£30.95 ☐	£21.95 ☐	£80 ☐
Paper 8	Implementing Audit Procedures	£17.95 ☐ (6/05 exam)	£9.95 ☐ (2/04)	£30.95 ☐	£21.95 ☐	£80 ☐
Paper 9	Preparing Taxation Computations (FA2004)	£17.95 ☐ (10/04)	£9.95 ☐	£30.95 ☐	£21.95 ☐	£80 ☐
Paper 10	Managing Finances	£17.95 ☐	£9.95 ☐			
INTERNATIONAL STREAM						
Paper 1	Recording Financial Transactions	£17.95 ☐	£9.95 ☐			
Paper 3	Maintaining Financial Records	£17.95 ☐	£9.95 ☐			
Paper 6	Drafting Financial Statements	£17.95 ☐	£9.95 ☐			
Paper 8	Implementing Audit Procedures	£17.95 ☐	£9.95 ☐			

SUBTOTAL £ _____

POSTAGE & PACKING

Study Texts
	First	Each extra	Online
UK	£5.00	£2.00	£ ___
Europe*	£6.00	£4.00	£ ___
Rest of world	£20.00	£10.00	£ ___

Kits
	First	Each extra	Online
UK	£5.00	£2.00	£ ___
Europe*	£6.00	£4.00	£ ___
Rest of world	£20.00	£10.00	£ ___

CDs
	First	Each extra	Online
UK	£2.00	£1.00	£ ___
Europe*	£3.00	£2.00	£ ___
Rest of world	£8.00	£8.00	£ ___

Grand Total (incl. Postage) £ _____

I enclose a cheque for
(Cheques to BPP Professional Education)
Or charge to Visa/Mastercard/Switch

Card Number _____
Expiry date _____ Start Date _____
Issue Number (Switch Only) _____
Signature _____

Register via our website, www.bpp.com/virtualcampus/cat and pay on-line

We aim to deliver to all UK addresses inside 5 working days; a signature will be required. Orders to all EU addresses should be delivered within 6 working days. All other orders to overseas addresses should be delivered within 8 working days. * Europe includes the Republic of Ireland and the Channel Islands.